WHO'S AFRAID
OF *LEONARD* WOOLF?

A CASE FOR THE SANITY OF VIRGINIA WOOLF

IRENE COATES

ALSO BY IRENE COATES

BOOKS

Poems of Change Fortune Press
Claudia's War Black Lightning Press
Don't Panic – Paint!! Black Lightning Press
Claudia's India Women's Redress Press
The Seed Bearers: Role of the Female in Biology and Genetics Pentland Press

PLAYS

The Wideawakes – Royal Shakespeare Company, Aldwych Theatre, London 1965
This Space is Mine – Hampstead Theatre Club, London 1969
Self Service – Edinburgh Festival, 1980; Traverse Theatre, Edinburgh 1980;
Cafe Theatre, Charing X Road, London; Now Theatre Group, NSW Australia 1983
Thieves – Abbey Theatre Club, Paddington, London 1981
Three Short Plays – London 1980; Now Theatre Group NSW 1982
Sweet Fanny Adams – National Playwrights Conference (reading), Canberra, 1983

WHO'S AFRAID
OF *LEONARD* WOOLF?

A CASE FOR THE SANITY OF VIRGINIA WOOLF

IRENE COATES

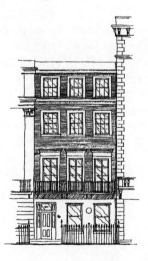

Published by
Soho Press Inc.
853 Broadway
New York, NY 10003

Library of Congress Cataloging-in-Publication Data

Coates, Irene, 1925–
Who's afraid of Leonard Woolf? : a case for the sanity of Virginia Woolf /
Irene Coates.
p.   cm.
"First published in Australia by Brandl & Schlesinger Pty Ltd in 1998"—T.p. verso.
Includes bibliographical references and index.
ISBN I-56947-222-X (alk. paper)
1. Woolf, Virginia, 1882–1941—Psychology.   2. Novelists, English—20th century—Biography.   3. Political scientists—Great Britain—Biography.   4. Suicide victims—Great Britain—Biography.   5. Married people—Great Britain—Biography.
6. Woolf, Virginia, 1882–1941—Marriage.   7. Suicide—Psychological aspects.
8. Woolf, Leonard, 1880–1969.   I. Title.

PR6045.O72 Z5785   2000
823'.912—dc21
[B]   00-034529

First U.S. Edition, 2000

10   9   8   7   6   5   4   3   2   1

With thanks
to Sophia Coates, Rudi Field, Hilary Gregory,
Jan Wood, Larry Reardon
each for different, positive reasons

ACKNOWLEDGEMENTS

I wish to acknowledge the willing hard work of Veronica Sumegi and Andras Berkes of Brandl & Schlesinger, Rose Bay, Sydney, Australia, in bringing out the first edition of this book.

It would not be possible to write any book requiring research without the assistance of libraries, especially when many source books are out of print. I am grateful to the enlightened inter-library loan scheme in New South Wales, and particularly to Chris Collins in my local Blackheath branch.

I am grateful to Varuna Writers' Centre, Katoomba, Australia, for holding a Seminar in 1991, to mark the fiftieth anniversary of Virginia Woolf's death, and to the Leura Adult Literary Discussion Group for listening to me on a number of occasions.

CONTENTS

LIST OF ILLUSTRATIONS

Virginia Stephen had beauty, wit, charm and a determination to become a major writer when she married Leonard Woolf in 1912. She had a problematic childhood, sexually molested by her elder half-brothers and saddened by the deaths of some of her closest relatives, including her mother when she was thirteen. She did not go to school, picking up an education in the library of her father Sir Leslie Stephen where she gained a clear perception of patriarchy.

Leonard's father died when he was eleven. His mother raised nine children on her own in a suburban house in Putney; Leonard was the third child. He renounced his Jewish faith when he went up to Trinity College Cambridge in the early years of the twentieth century, where he was known as a brilliant classical scholar and became a member of the exclusive secret society, the Apostles. Virginia's brother Thoby brought some of his Cambridge friends, including Leonard, down to London to meet his sisters Vanessa and Virginia, who had moved into their own house in Bloomsbury after the death of their father. Leonard did less well than expected in his final examinations and entered the Colonial Service, spending seven years in Ceylon (now Sri Lanka). Marriage to Virginia enabled him to return to England and become a key member of the Bloomsbury Group.

Soon after their marriage Virginia suffered two major nervous breakdowns. She found a way of escaping into an altered state of consciousness within which she discovered a deeper level of creativity: indeed, an enriched sanity. Leonard, however, believed she was mad. He denied her children and took control over her money and the publication of her books, all of which came out under the imprint of the Hogarth Press which they set up jointly.

Finding out more about Leonard means we can understand the work of Virginia Woolf a great deal better, as well as the circumstances of her life and death.

Irene Coates, September 1998

PROLOGUE

'Oh, no! They're going to pull it down!'

My daughter had a copy of that day's *Guardian* open and was staring at a page-long article. We were sitting in a cafe in the delightful town of Lewes, Sussex, set among the chalk downs south of London. It was summer, 1993. The sun was shining outside and I was feeling happy. I had come over from Australia to visit the various homes lived in by Virginia and Leonard Woolf. We had already explored Monk's House in the village of Rodmell, beautifully cared for and furnished with many of the original items of furniture and paintings on the wall that had been collected by Virginia. On the morrow we were to go to Charleston a few miles away, once the home of Virginia's sister Vanessa Bell.

'Pull what down, Sophia?'

'Asheham House! To make way for a concrete dump!'

Sophia turned a tragic face towards me, the newspaper trembling in her hand. I didn't know she cared. Actually, I was surprised Asheham House still existed. In the early nineteen thirties Virginia had watched some grey sheds being built beside her beloved Asheham House on the other side of the River Ouse from the garden of Monk's House. She did her best to imagine them as Greek temples but felt agonized and helpless.

Asheham had been Virginia's essential escape from London, both before and during the first world war. She had discovered it nestling under a sweeping down that she likened to a breaking wave and she and Vanessa had taken a lease on it in 1911. After Leonard had returned on leave from Ceylon and proposed to her, Virginia wrote the letter from Asheham House that made him decide to stay in England. He certainly took a gamble, as she told him: "I feel angry sometimes at the strength of your desire. Possibly, your being a Jew comes in also at this point. You seem so foreign. And then I am fearfully unstable. I pass from hot to cold in an instant, without any reason... I don't know what the future will bring." [1]

'The Woolfs spent the first night of their disastrous honeymoon there,' I said.

I had a mental image of Asheham House from photographs and paintings done by Vanessa and Carrington, standing isolated at the end of its own driveway, a pocket-sized regency mansion with an eighteenth century facade.

'Members of the Bloomsbury Group would be invited for the weekend. They would sit and talk endlessly, either inside or on the terrace–'

'Why doesn't somebody save it?'

'George Bernard Shaw used it as the original for his play 'Heartbreak House,' I added. 'He wrote to Virginia and told her so–'

'Irene!'

I dragged myself back to the cafe in Lewes. How great to share the world I was exploring with my daughter.

'We could at least go and see it! I've got a car, remember?'

'Yes, we could do that.'

I almost didn't want to. Asheham was so much part of Virginia Woolf's story. Even when she was depressed, ill and trying to regain her balance, being there 'had its holiness'. What would it look like now, desolate and abandoned under the down that cut off the morning sun and often made the rooms cold and damp? It was more than fifty years since she had died; we lived in a different age on the brink of another century, another millennium.

We paid for our tea. Sophia drove us the few miles to a small lay-by beside the busy road. There was a padlocked gate with a notice saying 'Private Property', trespassers will be prosecuted.

' "Whenever you see a board up with 'Trespassers will be prosecuted', trespass at once",' I muttered, quoting from Virginia's last lecture, *The Leaning Tower*. 'She was handing on her father's advice, encouraging us, in our turn, to write,' I said. I went on quoting: ' "Literature is no one's private ground... Let us trespass freely and fearlessly and find our own way for ourselves" '

Suddenly I had to be there. I scrambled through the barbed wire. The driveway stretched ahead into darkness, through a tunnel of tall trees the sun behind me making a pattern of gold, barred with the dark shadows of branches. The trees had not been there in Virginia's time. I saw a flash of white at the end of the path, where the house must be. Then I heard men's voices ahead. Would I be stopped in my tracks? Even arrested by atavistic concrete owners defending their territory? Were there guard dogs? 'Trespass at once...' I walked on and met two young men coming from the house. They stopped and looked at me. To explain my presence, I said:

'I am writing a book about Virginia Woolf.'

There was a pause.

'What is it about?' asked one of the young men.

'Her death doesn't add up.'

'So long as you don't attack Leonard,' he said. And then: 'You can get in round the side, there's a board loose.' They continued on their way down the drive.

What was that extraordinary thing he said? So long as you don't attack Leonard? I wished I had asked him what he meant. At least those two young men were not watchdogs for the concrete company; indeed, they were trespassers too, looking more relaxed and assured than I felt.

Here was Sophia, having decided to join me. Together we stood in front of the facade that was so familiar to me, though now battered and boarded up. We went round to the small terrace at the back. Mentally I peopled it with members of the Bloomsbury Group. There was Lytton Strachey in the largest chair, draped long and thin, apparently in a state of abstraction. In contrast Clive Bell was pink and paunchy, managing to combine a well-to-do rural family background of huntin', shootin' and fishin' with endless talk about literature, beauty and women. He was aware of everyone around him. Saxon Sydney-Turner sat still as a rock, as though he would never speak again. Desmond MacCarthy leant forward wanting to talk; but Virginia was speaking. Her musical voice seemed disembodied as she launched into one of her flights of imagination, seeming to hold the others in a trance. Leonard Woolf sat slightly apart from the rest of the group, one of his arms trembling so that his hand knocked audibly on his chair. His eyes, dark and intense, were fixed on his wife. He said in a tone of suppressed impatience: 'Virginia, there's a cold wind. You had better go indoors.'

There was silence. Clive Bell, embarrassed, shifted uneasily. Everyone waited. Virginia stood wrapped in her vision, as though it was an effort to return to the company around her. Should she walk up to the top of the down with long strides, like her father, and feel the sea breeze on her face, that reminded her of Cornwall, of Talland House, of her childhood? Instead, as an act of free will, she turned and ran lightly into the house, aiming a kiss at her beloved elder sister Vanessa who was standing near the doorway. From the house the chuckling sound of her laugh came to the silent group outside. At once, they all started talking their usual mixture of philosophy based on the work of G.E. Moore, and gossip.

They were so real, so alive. I shook myself. Now all I saw were broken paving stones and a tangle of weeds. Sophia was pulling a loose board away from a side window. I looked into a small room whose walls were covered in a revolting kitchen wallpaper. The house had been divided by later inhabitants; I didn't want to see the travesty perpetrated within. We wandered away and saw the mounting pile of concrete waste that would soon engulf a vital piece of Bloomsbury Group history.

'Asheham came up for sale in the nineteen-twenties and Virginia wanted to buy it,' I said. 'She had enough money.'

'Then why didn't she?'

I paused, knowing Leonard had not allowed her to do so. 'He preferred Monk's House,' I said, 'partly because of the name, though no monks had really lived there. The rooms were too small for Virginia. She often wanted to escape.'

We turned and walked back down the drive into the staring yellow eye of the setting sun, as she must so often have walked.

The next day I met the same young man in the shop at Charleston, home of Clive and Vanessa Bell and their three children Julian, Quentin and Angelica. Both house and garden had been wonderfully restored and were full of tourists shepherded through the rooms in groups, ending up having tea and cake at the back. What a difference! Apparently all the available money had been spent on Charleston and Monk's House, while Asheham (this is how Virginia spelt it, Leonard preferred Asham) had been left to its fate. I approached the young man.

'Why don't you want me to attack Leonard?' I asked

'Some people have an axe to grind,' he said.

To my surprise, he began criticizing several books that have approached the life of Virginia Woolf taking a different perspective from that of the majority of commentators beginning with Quentin Bell's authorized biography, as though no other view would be acceptable. *The Unknown Virginia Woolf* by Roger Poole came under fire, and so did Louise DeSalvo's *Virginia Woolf: The Impact of Childhood Sexual Abuse on Her Life and Work*. I thought of asking him if he had read *Who Killed Virginia Woolf?* a psychobiography by Alma Halbert Bond, since he didn't mention that, when Sophia gave me my ticket and we were guided in through the low arched doorway, where we fell under the seductive spell of Charleston. I knew that neither Monk's House nor Charleston had been Virginia Woolf's true spiritual abode: it was, is and always will be Asheham House.

Fresh insights need to be brought to bear on the biography of this major writer, on the way she perceived the world around her and the circumstances of her life, if Virginia Woolf is to be part of the experience of future generations and not remain encapsulated in her own times.

Leonard Woolf needs to be revealed in his own right, as the person who emerges from his considerable quantity of published work including his two novels, his political books, his autobiography and his letters; and as Virginia's husband. There is no full biography. Duncan Wilson, in his *Leonard Woolf: A Political Biography* (1978), expressly disclaims having written a personal account of the man. *A Marriage of True Minds: An Intimate Portrait of Leonard and Virginia Woolf* is useful because one of the authors, Ian Parsons, husband of Leonard's later companion Trekkie, knew him; but this book does not delve deeply, concluding that: "it was a happy marriage for Leonard. It could have been happier than it was; not if Leonard had married someone else, but if Virginia had been other than she was." [2]

That is one sort of truth: the truth that sees a relationship from the male point of view and expects the woman to adapt to him. There is another sort of truth, the truth of discovering what it is like to be a woman living with her husband in a patriarchal society. Virginia Woolf was a pioneer in this exploration, helped by her periods of so-called madness from which she brought back insights that have inspired her greatest books. I believe the Woolfs had a far more interesting, complex and dynamic relationship than has been admitted by the orthodox view – expressed clearly by Quentin Bell's wife Anne Olivier Bell, who has done such excellent work editing Virginia's diaries. In one of her prefaces Anne Bell speaks of: 'the reckless mythology recently propounded, wherein Leonard and Virginia are depicted as mutually inimical – a theory which would be laughable were it not apparently taken seriously – these diaries should serve to convince the unprejudiced reader that, despite minor differences and disagreements which it would be surprising not to find between two such exceptional characters, her marriage was the bedrock of Virginia's life: a truly fortunate, prosperous, and happy alliance.' [3]

Here is more defended territory. The growl of the guard dog. But if I trespass I am in good company with Virginia and her father:

"Let us trespass freely and fearlessly and find our own way for ourselves. It is thus that English literature will survive this war and cross the gulf – if commoners like ourselves make that country our own country, if we teach ourselves how to read and write, how to preserve and how to create." [4]

How to preserve and how to create, I thought. Yes, and also how to reveal. Why *did* Virginia Woolf kill herself that March day in 1941? What was it like for her, living with Leonard? What sort of person was he? Lack of an adequate portrait, aside from the view he himself sought to present in his autobiography, was one of my motives for writing *Who's Afraid of Leonard Woolf?* but it is also part of the difficulty of doing so. The texture, the warp and woof of the Woolfs' marriage as they lived it every day, is not obvious. The image of Leonard the 'good man', even of Leonard the 'saint' as he looks after his ailing genius of a wife, runs through all of the official literature. And we realise that Virginia herself at the end of her life helped to create that impression. She wrote in the first of her suicide notes to Leonard:

"What I want to say is that I owe all the happiness of my life to you. You have been entirely patient with me and incredibly good. I want to say that – everybody knows it." [5]

Is this the only story that can be told and retold? or is there, like one of those strange pictures that deceive the eye, a different truth to be discovered?

Throughout her life Virginia tried to understand more and more about maleness, her first rude lessons being taught her in a practical way by her older half-brothers, George and Gerald Duckworth, who interfered with her although she remained a virgin. She also witnessed the alternate towering rages and abject self-pity that her father, Sir Leslie Stephen, inflicted on his family. His death in 1904 was a necessary precondition for her writing. Freed from her father's influence, she could describe her discoveries in feminist books and articles that are sensitive, humorous and hardhitting. Virginia saw patriarchal society in general, and wars in particular, as expressions of maleness. By objectifying these as male, she became aware of the other truth, the female perspective, which she embodied in the invented character of Judith, Shakespeare's sister who is reborn in each generation; the creative woman with a female-male brain whose lowly position in a patriarchal society stunts the artistic flowering of which she is capable.

Leonard could be relaxed and charming when in a secure and unchallenged position, for instance when he interviewed an aspiring author at the Hogarth Press; or when a new trainee manager came to take the place of his predecessor and was being taught the ropes: but those early days didn't last and one after another trainee managers came and went. He was notoriously stingy with money, a trait that intensified as he grew older; and he easily became irritable, he would tremble all over and refuse to consider any other view than his own. He was certainly a very difficult man to work for, whether at the Press or in his attitude towards the domestic servants at home, especially if he took a dislike to someone as he detested Mabel Haskins, the cook who came to replace Nelly Boxall in 1934. Virginia was at first thankful to have her 'treasure', the trained servant going about her duties quietly and methodically enabling her to get on with her work; until Leonard began bullying and humiliating Mabel, that interesting person with her broken-down shoes and quietly watchful eye.

If Leonard was so difficult to work for, was he also very difficult to live with? Virginia recorded at least some such scenes in her diary, when he lost patience and his sudden words to her were devastating. Self-assured (male) biographers might have difficulty comprehending the effect on Virginia as she struggled to cope with them. On one occasion it took her over a year to recover. Such episodes would have left some permanent damage as, painstakingly, she had to restore the tranquility she needed in order to write.

In his autobiography, written twenty years and more after her death, Leonard does not admit to causing any such incidents. Instead, he misquotes from her diary description of one event in an attempt to prove that Virginia was on the brink of madness all the time and that her so-called madness was directly related to finishing a book. His insistence that his view was the only correct one, and his refusal to accept responsibility, were very much part of Leonard's character. Belatedly, he seemed to recognise this when he wrote a note on the day of Virginia's death which was found crumpled among his effects after his own death twenty-six years later. On the afternoon of 28th March, 1941, Leonard knew that she had drowned herself, although her body was not found until three weeks later. His note ends: 'I know that it is the last page & yet I turn it over. There is no limit to one's stupidity & selfishness'. [6]

I do not excuse this remark as a minor expression of regret in a moment of loss and grief, as Lyndall Gordon does in her otherwise excellent book *Virginia Woolf: A Writer's Life* (1984). I believe that his writing those words under those circumstances: 'there is no limit to one's stupidity & selfishness', was a rare instance of Leonard recognising another side

to his character, albeit to himself and when it was too late to help
Virginia. I first read this note of Leonard's sitting under the blue dome of
the British Library when it was still part of the British Museum, as
Virginia had often sat, reading the library copy of *A Marriage of True Minds*
where it makes an early appearance. It was one of those revelations that
for me makes research so exciting. The silent readers around me absorbed
in their own explorations, the blue dome itself, all whirled around those
words. Why had he written them, especially at such a moment?

Leonard insisted that he never felt guilt, even when in 1913 he left the
box of Veronal open by Virginia's bed and she took an overdose that
would have proved fatal if her friend Ka Cox had not come in and found
her in a coma. He not only never admitted to feeling either guilt or
remorse; he almost never accepted that he was wrong or apologised.

When he was up at Trinity College, Cambridge, in company with
Lytton Strachey and other members of what would become the
Bloomsbury Group, Leonard Woolf dreamt of replacing class-ridden,
capitalist Britain with an idealised version of Athens in ancient Greece at
the time of Pericles: in the eyes of those young men this was the greatest
civilisation that had ever existed. He was a member of the Apostles, a
secret Cambridge society whose members believed they were destined to
take wings and become highly successful 'angels'. But he also continued
to take pride in his Semitic ancestry, although he had renounced his
Jewish faith when he went up to Cambridge, seeing himself as Job, sto-
ically enduring everything that befell him when he tried to out-argue
God. Leonard spoke of his own 'secret and sinuous psychology': this was
the hidden aspect of his personality, like the undertow of a wave, that
Virginia apparently never fully comprehended or recognised when it
affected herself. His vision was very different from hers; looking back to
an idealised past civilisation from his particular vantage point, he saw 'barbarism' all about him in a modern world he despised.

Virginia, on the other hand, felt herself to be part of the English literary tradition that began with Chaucer and centred on Shakespeare; she
was intent on entering the twentieth century with the new stream-of-
consciousness writers who were grappling with the changes forced on
society during and after the first world war as they looked towards the
future.

Virginia Woolf discovered much about the characteristics of her own
female brain at a time when even less was known about this organ than it

is today. She also realised that female and male brains are different and largely incompatible. In *A Room of One's Own*, a book that began as two lectures she gave to women's colleges in 1928, she wrote:

"One has a profound, if irrational, instinct in favour of the theory that the union of man and woman makes for the greatest satisfaction, the most complete happiness. But the... satisfaction it gave me made me also ask whether there are two sexes in the mind corresponding to the two sexes in the body, and whether they also require to be united in order to get complete satisfaction and happiness? ...so that in each of us two powers preside, one male, one female; and in the man's brain the man predominates over the woman, and in the woman's brain the woman predominates over the man... Coleridge perhaps meant this when he said that a great mind is androgynous... He meant, perhaps, that the androgynous mind is resonant and porous; that it transmits emotion without impediment; that it is naturally creative, incandescent and undivided." [7]

The view Virginia gives here underlies the efforts she made throughout her marriage to find a unity with, or at least a mutual understanding of, male brains in general and Leonard's in particular. However, it is precisely this unity that Leonard resisted. He identified with the 'hard' grandfather's side of his family and not with his 'soft' grandmother's and did not attempt to unify these two opposed images in himself, nor did he identify with his mother. He wrote:

"I was very much my father's and very little my mother's son, and there were many sides of my character and mind which were unsympathetic to my mother; I had no patience with her invincible, optimistic sentimentality, and my unsentimentality, which seemed to her hardness and harshness, distressed her... though she would never have admitted it even to herself, I was, I think, her least-loved child." [8]

The difference between the Woolfs' attitudes was intensified by the fact that Virginia did not go to school at all, staying at home where she had a limited amount of private tuition as well as the run of her father's library, whereas Leonard worked long and hard, even obsessively, through his school years to reach the pinnacle of the male-oriented educational system at Cambridge. This, together with the seven years he spent as a civil servant in Ceylon (Sri Lanka) before marrying Virginia Stephen, served to reinforce their sexual, social and ethnic differences even further.

If Virginia strove for reconciliation between her own vision as a writer with a female-male brain, and that of Leonard – if she wanted to achieve a 'marriage of opposites' between them, as I think she did – then she was doomed to disappointment. Instead of converging, their visions diverged through the nineteen thirties until, by 1938, a dangerous chasm had developed that she expressed in the almost unbearable tension between the central characters in *Between the Acts*. In this novel-drama each of her protagonists is presented in a younger and an older version. Old Bartholomew looks at his opposite, the elderly Lucy Swithin, as he puts their difference into words: 'She was thinking, he supposed, God is peace. God is love. For she belonged to the unifiers; he to the separatists.' [9]

Virginia, as she desperately attempted to be the unifier, came at last to acknowledge that there was an unbridgeable difference between herself and Leonard.

Writing this book I wanted to find out whether, or to what extent, Virginia's suicide was the end-game of a conflict between the Woolfs' two visions. Despite Anne Bell's disclaimer, I have come to believe that the Woolfs were inimical.

When we look carefully at Leonard's own agenda for living and include this in the picture we realise how important it was for him to believe that his wife was insane since this confirmed him in a sense of his own sanity and maleness. This raises a more general question: could a greater understanding of the ways the female and male brains function help to reconcile us to our differences and improve the human condition?

It is time to pull off the Private Property – Trespassers will be prosecuted notices, and cut through the barbed wire; to tear down the wallpaper of later generations and remove the partitions within, as we rediscover the Woolf relationship.

Irene Coates, January 2000

PART ONE

ABOARD THE SEE-SAW

VIRGINIA STEPHEN IN 1903

Chapter One

VIRGINIA'S NEED FOR SUPPORT

'Hold yourself straight, my little Goat.'

These were her mother's last words to the thirteen-year-old Virginia Stephen before she died of rheumatic fever at the age of forty-nine, having borne three children to her first husband Herbert Duckworth and then, after his death and a lengthy period of grief, a further four children to Leslie Stephen: writer, biographer and a most demanding husband and father. Altogether there were eight children in their large London house since Leslie, too, had been previously married and was a widower with one daughter, Laura.

Virginia was the second to youngest child of the entire brood. She did not hold herself straight. All her life, she needed someone to support her: someone with an extraordinary capacity for loyalty and concern for her welfare, who would be rewarded by the quality of her mind – sensitive, bright, original. There was also a mordant side to her personality, to which was given various animal names: during her childhood she was Goat, and from this Billy; later, she called her other self a number of different names, such as the apes, Mandrill, and, with her friend Vita Sackville-West, Potto.

Virginia began to perceive her world over a hundred years ago, at the end of the nineteenth century. That time may seem distant to us, who have entered the twenty-first. Yet her work continues to live, her books are in print and she is surrounded by an ever-growing penumbra of commentators. We need to perform an act of imagination to realise that Virginia had to fight hard for her very survival in that large family home where she was born at Number 22 Hyde Park Gate, Kensington. London, on 25 January, 1882.

My daughter and I went and stood outside this solid, tall house which is in a cul de sac. As we mentally placed the Stephen family and their seven live-in servants behind the windows, from basement to attic, one of the windows opened and a scroll of paper dropped to the pavement: it was a photostat copy of an article by Richard Brunner on some of the famous who had lived in Hyde Park Gate, including Sir Leslie Stephen of No. 22, 'the preeminent 19th-century man of English letters. His two

JULIA STEPHEN

SIR LESLIE STEPHEN

22 HYDE PARK GATE
LONDON

TALLAND HOUSE
ST IVES, CORNWALL

daughters, Virginia and Vanessa (better known as Virginia Woolf, the novelist, and Vanessa Bell, the painter) were born here.' After a brief wave to the now-shut window we drove away, Sophia both impressed and amused at this evidence of living history.

In that great London house the four younger children, Vanessa, Thoby, Virginia and Adrian, formed a separate group from their older half-brothers and sisters. Within this group Virginia tried to keep up with her elder sister Vanessa and brother Thoby, while distancing herself from Adrian, the baby of the family. During their years in the nursery Vanessa and Thoby found a way of infuriating Virginia. In his authorised biography of Virginia, Quentin Bell says:

"There was some technique for making her turn 'purple with rage'. What it was we do not know, but Thoby and Vanessa knew and there were terrible occasions when she did turn a colour which her sister described as 'the most lovely flaming red'. It would be interesting to know how this was done, still more interesting to know whether, as Vanessa surmised, these paroxysms were not wholly painful to Virginia herself." [1]

Here we get a glimpse of Vanessa and Thoby tormenting their younger sister. We don't know what they did to upset her so profoundly but we can be sure that they were repulsing her need to be close to them. We should not assume that this rejection was anything but extremely painful to Virginia who, being younger and weaker, must have done all she could to minimise the damage so that they would once more accept her. If Vanessa remembered these occasions as not being 'wholly painful' to her sister, then we can assume that she herself was ambivalent. Indeed, it was probably Vanessa's game, perhaps played to keep control when she feared Thoby was getting too close to Virginia. We can guess this because a similar game was played after Vanessa married Clive Bell, with Clive taking the place of Thoby.

Virginia needed to relate closely to her sister, given that her beautiful mother Julia was a busy and mostly distant figure who escaped as often as she could from the overheated family atmosphere by taking up charitable work, visiting the poor and sick. When she did turn her attention to her children it was her youngest child, Adrian, to whom she gave most of her affection.

Unable to rely on her mother, Virginia turned to Vanessa for support in a house where their father set the emotional tone, alternating between bouts of maudlin self-pity and the rages of a frustrated tyrant. Such scenes were extremely upsetting to his young daughter who could only watch, shocked, and wait for them to end. She had no other world to enter, since she never went to school, spending her time at home where she received occasional tuition and had the run of her father's library: here, early in life she decided to become a writer.

As a child, Virginia was the live wire behind a home newspaper, the *Hyde Park Gate News*, written mainly by herself but contributed to by all the younger Stephens. She would recount the doings of the Stephen family, changing their names but retaining factual details so that each person was identifiable, while the story was entertaining. In a state of suppressed excitement, she would place the newly-written newspaper near her mother, and wait. When Julia gave it a casual look and said 'rather good, I think,' she made her youngest daughter's day. From her early years, Virginia told stories in the evening, listened to by both Vanessa and Thoby.

By the time Virginia became aware, her father's first daughter Laura was in trouble. Laura's mother, Minnie, was the younger daughter of the novelist Thackeray. Minnie had had a sheltered upbringing protected by her sister Annie, and she could not cope with being Leslie Stephen's wife. Neither could Minnie's daughter, Laura, cope with her father. Through some dramatic episodes of breakdown and Leslie's misguided efforts to teach her through strict discipline, Laura deteriorated. She had to dress and attend for tea every day, where the whole family was assembled, until she was removed first to her own quarters and then to a mental home where, in seclusion, she outlived Virginia and most of her half-siblings.

The children's only escape from the hot-house atmosphere of the big London house was during the long summer months, when the entire family migrated to Talland House, at St. Ives in Cornwall. Here they played in the garden, within sight of the lighthouse, and explored the beach. Throughout her life, the sound and rhythm of the waves along the shore were ever-present to Virginia and return again and again in her writing. Yet as soon as Julia died in 1896, Leslie gave up Talland House, the one place that could have helped Virginia who was so overwhelmed by the burden of adult grief, her father's in particular, that she herself could not grieve for the loss of her mother. The shock was such that she became numb in a household that expressed its grief extravagantly, her father weeping and wailing surrounded by numerous mainly female relations dressed from head to foot in black. Suddenly her life was changed, she was, literally, living a nightmare.

Standing at a window after that last scene with Julia, ignored and isolated, she watched the doctor walk away down the street with a sense of desolation. Utterly oppressed by a grief that she could not herself feel, Virginia had her first mental breakdown. For years she was obsessed by her beautiful mother's face and form, her presence, and was only relieved of this burden after writing *To the Lighthouse*, in which both her parents were brought back to life.

The list of female casualties lengthened. After Julia's death Virginia's elder half-sister, Stella, aged twenty-six, took over the management of the household. Stella had always lived in the shadow of her mother and seemed like a pale reflection of Julia. However, she was being passionately wooed by the ardent Jack Hills and soon there was the excitement of their marriage. But Stella returned from their honeymoon exhausted and ill. She died in 1897, only two years after her mother's death. Whereupon Vanessa and Virginia tried to cope with Jack's inordinate grief, a major ingredient of which was the sexual deprivation he suffered from the loss of his partner. There was a very close link between sex and death that burnt into Virginia's being.

The existence of the deranged Laura could not be ignored; nor could the message she represented, that another in that family could go the same way. Yet so far from having a personal fear of madness, Virginia could write to Emma Vaughan, her 'dearest Toad', in 1901, when she was nineteen:

"This world of human beings grows too complicated, my only wonder is that we don't fill more madhouses: the insane view of life has much to be said for it – perhaps its the sane one after all: and *we* the sad sober respectable citizens really rave every moment of our lives and deserve to be shut up perpetually. My spring melancholy is developing in these hot days into summer madness." [2]

After Stella's death Vanessa, the next oldest woman in the house, aged sixteen, had to take on the burden of managing the household although she had decided to be a painter and wanted to continue her studies at Art School. Vanessa proved to be a tower of strength, coping with their father's tantrums by using the most effective of all weapons – silence and stillness. She not only ran the house but got onto her bicycle and took art lessons as often as she could. This was the time that the two sisters formed a close conspiracy to continue their work at all costs, even though their world seemed to be tumbling about their ears.

The young Vanessa and Virginia were now the only two surviving women in a family of five males. It was a dangerous imbalance between the sexes. This was particularly so given the characters of the three older men: Leslie himself, in many ways the Victorian patriarch, continuing to indulge in extravagant paroxysms of grief for the loss of his wife; and George and Gerald Duckworth, Julia's two eldest sons.

Some of the complications of Virginia's early life were caused by George and Gerald. At this time George, the elder, was trying to make his mark in conventional society. To help him, he insisted on one or the other of his half-sisters accompanying him when he paid formal visits and attended dinners and dances; they must be dressed suitably, behave becomingly and be a credit to him. From his point of view, those two young, beautiful women were a social asset and he thought he was doing the right thing by trying to 'bring them out'. But neither Vanessa nor Virginia had any desire, or aptitude, for making their way in conventional society. They were already committed, Vanessa to art and Virginia to writing. They caused him much embarrassment when they refused to dress correctly, refused to dance, and finally refused to accompany him. George, all his life, remained a snob and eventually married a titled lady; but not before he had managed to damage Virginia by molesting her.

The activities of George and Gerald in relation to the two girls are well documented. Louise DeSalvo has researched this aspect of Virginia's life in *Virginia Woolf: The Impact of Childhood Sexual Abuse on her Life and Work* (1989). Virginia herself discussed it later in her life in *Moments of Being*; and there are also contemporary accounts in letters between the two sisters. In 1911, Virginia wrote to Vanessa about an intimate conversation she held with Janet Case, with whom she had studied Greek. Janet Case was a spinster who visited Virginia in her first rented house in Firle, Sussex. Sitting demurely with a piece of embroidery in her hand, Virginia writes of her:

"She is a woman of great magnanimity... She sat stitching... and listened to a magnificent tirade which I delivered upon life in general. She has a calm interest in copulation... and this led us to the revelation of all Georges malefactions. To my surprise she has always had an intense dislike of him; and used to say 'Whew – you nasty creature', when he came in and began fondling me over my Greek. When I got to the bedroom scenes, she dropped her lace, and gasped like a benevolent gudgeon. By bedtime she said she was feeling quite sick, and did go to the W.C., which, needless to say, had no water in it." [3]

When Virginia was about six, her younger half-brother Gerald sat her on a ledge and explored her genitals. This was apparently the only time he molested her. Virginia was surprised at the depth of shame she felt and attributes her dislike of her own body to this event.

That there was sexual abuse as we understand the term now, there can be no doubt, although occasionally one meets a commentator such as Peter Alexander, in *Leonard and Virginia Woolf: A Literary Partnership*, who is at some pains to condone George's behaviour, preferring to see any damage that might have been done as being due to Virginia's sensitivity:

"George Duckworth... fourteen years older than she, was a deeply affectionate young man who expressed his fondness for his sister and half-sisters in rather extravagant endearments and embraces, both in private and in public. He had the habit of kissing and caressing Virginia as she sat at her lessons... and he would also kiss her at night before she went to bed... A good many, perhaps most, children have sexual experiences and come to no harm from them; but Virginia was not one of these... No one seems to have reproached him or even spoken to him of his behaviour until Virginia's physician, Dr Savage, warned him to be careful during Virginia's second spell of madness in 1904... George Duckworth was by no means the monster of Virginia's imagination." [4]

Leonard Woolf, in his autobiography, ignored the possibility that Virginia had been damaged by her half-brothers. He offered Virginia's first novel *The Voyage Out* to Gerald Duckworth for publication and went out of his way to praise George without, apparently, a hint of irony: 'He was an extremely kind man and, I think, very fond of Vanessa and Virginia.' [5]; although he does describe him as a snob.

Thus two men – Leonard Woolf in the 1960's and Peter Alexander in the 1990's – have taken it upon themselves to condone the impact of George's sexual intrusions on his defenceless young half-sister. Neither of them considered Virginia's reference to 'bedroom scenes' that she discussed with Janet Case making her feel sick. That is their truth, the patriarchal truth, which essentially assumes that a man's freedom of action is more important than a woman's reactions. But Virginia knew herself to have been abused; she was shocked and frightened and her body shamed at the invasion of her private space. The younger of the two brothers, Gerald, was the first perpetrator, followed by George after their mother's death. This is her truth and it needs to be recognised as such. She never forgot the harm they did to her and wrote about it until the end of her life.

George 'comforted' her during the years when Leslie Stephen was dying downstairs. He not only interrupted her lessons and fondled her. He entered her room at night, kissed, cuddled, and (presumably) worked himself up sexually while she felt utterly powerless. This type of abuse within a family would have been allowable by Victorian standards, so long as the girl's virginity remained intact, an essential requirement for marriage. Virginia said she lost her virginity on her honeymoon. The seven live-in maids provided alternatives for the sex-starved young men, apart from whatever liaisons they formed outside the home.

The question of whether George also visited the room of Virginia's elder sister Vanessa at night, during this time, has not been so amply discussed. Vanessa certainly had a very different approach to sex. Before world war one she wrote gloriously indiscreet letters to other members of the Bloomsbury Group in which sex was a frequent topic for discussion; she certainly had an open-minded, not to say Bohemian approach towards sexual activity. In 1912, when Virginia's honeymoon had gone horribly wrong, Vanessa wrote to her husband Clive Bell with frank bewilderment:

"Apparently [Virginia] still gets no pleasure at all from the act, which I think is curious. They [Leonard and Virginia] were very anxious to know when I first had an orgasm. I couldn't remember. Do you? But no doubt I sympathised with such things if I didn't have them from the time I was 2." [6]

To judge from the sisters' contrasting attitudes to sex, I suspect that if George did enter Vanessa's room at night (and why wouldn't he?), she would have welcomed him with open arms. Vanessa's problem in later life was that she couldn't get enough of it. The man who became her working companion and, after some persuasion, fathered her youngest child Angelica, was the artist Duncan Grant, who was gay.

Vanessa managed to escape from the close family environment for hours each day when she was accepted into the Royal Academy Schools, where she learned her craft as a painter. But Virginia, who envied her sister this freedom, was more or less imprisoned in the big, tall house in the cul de sac of Hyde Park Gate. She stayed upstairs in her room that was divided, with her bed and clothes cupboard on one side; and, on the other, her tall desk at which she stood up to write, and her books; she conscientiously set herself to learn the difficult skill of composition. There were to be no half-measures, she must learn to use words selectively so that they were able to bear the wealth of feeling within her; she must find the sentence that was right for her – and it was different from the type of sentence used by men. These words, these sentences of hers must take on the shape of her own brain, her female brain. This is the task she set herself, as she was to recount later in *A Room of One's Own*. Only at tea time did the family gather round the table in the living room, often receiving older relatives or family friends. A certain 'tea-table manner' was necessary to carry off these visits, when conversation had to be made even in the most trying of circumstances. Being the hostess was a social skill that Virginia learnt thoroughly, as did Vanessa.

The third death in that claustrophobic family was that of Sir Leslie Stephen who died of cancer aged seventy-two, in February 1904 after a long illness. During those years Virginia saw a great deal of her father and in doing so gained an understanding of his character which was in some ways like her own; she learned to have some sympathy for him despite his temperamental outbursts. He had edited, and written large parts of, a Dictionary of National Biography, and was engaged in a series, English Men of Letters. He also left his unpublished Mausoleum Book, in which he recounted his life, for the sake of his children. She knew him from the books in his library, well stocked with the work of English writers from the age of Chaucer, both suitable and unsuitable for the eyes of a young woman; also the major French authors. Virginia devoured these books with much greater depth of attention than most casual readers, for she was training herself to be one of them, a descendant of the English literary tradition in her own generation. Later, she said that if her father had not died when he did, she would never have written.

Among the many changes that took place in 1904, during that same year of her father's death, Virginia's first piece of writing was published. It was an unsigned review in the *Guardian*, and she was paid for it. Virginia from the first valued the money she earned from her work: it gave her an objective yardstick with which to measure her achievements and she needed this, as she had no school record with which to monitor her progress. And so began her most productive writing career.

After their father's funeral the four younger Stephens, together with Gerald Duckworth, went first to Manorbier on the Pembroke coast and then to Venice where they were joined by Violet Dickinson, a very tall, thin woman who had been Virginia's chief correspondent during Sir Leslie's illness and remained a true all-weather supporter until 1912. On their return through Paris Virginia met Clive Bell, one of Thoby's University friends, and realised the conversations she had with him were what she really enjoyed. She was distrustful of men and Clive with his urbane manner and country background was the friend she needed. But much as he enjoyed talking with Virginia, he began wooing Vanessa.

On their return to England, Virginia suffered her second nervous breakdown. She stayed with Violet Dickinson and was looked after by three nurses. For the first time, she heard horrible voices. In her ravings, she distrusted Vanessa and made a token gesture at committing suicide by jumping out of a low window; she was not hurt. Fortunately Violet proved to be a loyal, trustworthy and benign support.

Only during an episode of so-called madness, which was heralded by bad headaches, tension and insomnia, could her pent-up rage break through the cheerful 'tea-table manner' with which she normally related to other people. Mental breakdown was her method of freeing herself from other people's attitudes and regaining her intimate connection with the present moment, which was essential for her writing: then, she was in touch with her vision, with her inner sense of truth, exalted, the words coming to her as though from another source.

We should ask ourselves whether Virginia was justified in distrusting her sister. This episode, three months after her father's death, may be a later version of the 'game' Vanessa and Thoby played on her in the nursery, which was capable of reducing her to impotent fury: a game in which Vanessa distanced herself from Virginia and used Thoby as an emotional buffer, getting him on her side. If so, this is the second recorded instance. There is a third such episode in 1910 when Virginia once more distrusted her sister and Clive Bell, having married Vanessa, became the emotional buffer. Did Virginia's pleasure in meeting and talking with Clive, when she met him in Paris, arouse Vanessa's jealousy?

I am arguing that an important factor in Virginia's mental instability was an underlying tension between Vanessa and herself. Virginia always maintained that she loved Vanessa more than Vanessa loved her, and this may have been true. Vanessa liked to keep her sister in her orbit, so long as she did not get too close. This co-dependence which could reduce Virginia to mental breakdown when the game was played against her and she, feeling entirely innocent, was rejected, was never resolved by either of them. Hence, neither was able to break away. And Virginia was unable to form satisfying relationships with anyone else.

Virginia's love for Vanessa was the love of the younger for the older, of the almost supernaturally sensitive and aware for the strong, of the vine for the tree. Her breakdown in 1904 may have been not only her desperate reaction to her father's death, although she undoubtedly missed him and felt the loss of his support, but to Vanessa's rejection as she once again tried to cling to her, in the life-long battle between the two sisters. Each time Virginia was doomed to lose, but in the losing she rediscovered new-born within her, her creativity, her song.

If we accept that there was a down-side to the close relationship between these two sisters, then we will recognise a repeating pattern when Leonard Woolf enters the equation. With the publication of a selection of Vanessa's letters in 1993, we have a much clearer idea of their relationship. It is surprising how early the pattern was set. Many of the themes that run through Virginia's life are present well before her marriage, to the extent that we can see Leonard taking over many aspects of Vanessa's attitude towards her sister.

On her recovery Virginia went to stay with her aunt in Cambridge. Sir Leslie Stephen's sister, Caroline Emelia Stephen, was a Quaker and was often called 'the Nun'. The Nun sympathised with Virginia and provided the very environment she needed to complete her convalescence.

Whilst Virginia was away Vanessa, Thoby and Adrian moved house. This signalled complete change in life-style for the four younger Stephens. They simply had to escape from the gloomy No. 22 Hyde Park Gate, haunted by memories of death and grieving. The stalwart Vanessa, assisted by Thoby, rented a house in Bloomsbury, an area of London located behind the British Museum which was at that time unfashionable and therefore cheaper. To make this fundamental break with the past was a brave and remarkable decision on Vanessa's part. By doing so, the four siblings were able to shrug off the Victorian age, the deaths of both parents and generations of relatives. With no elders to make the rules, they were able to begin a different life. And they moved not only into a new house but a new century.

Vanessa, the young artist, celebrated by painting all the rooms white, so that pictures could be hung on them, and installed a minimum amount of furniture. She was once again firmly in control and she blossomed. Restored to health, Virginia left Cambridge and joined Vanessa and Adrian to live at No. 46 Gordon Square, Bloomsbury.

As an undergraduate at Cambridge, Thoby spent the term up at University and the holidays with his siblings. He was in the habit of telling Virginia highly-coloured stories about his friends, so that she had a fanciful idea of them before she met them. Among these were the tall, thin eccentric Lytton Strachey, the pink and rather tubby Clive Bell, John Maynard Keynes (later, the economist), and the silent Sydney Saxon-Turner. He invited them to their new London house, where they soon held regular meetings on Thursday evenings – and thus began what became known as the Bloomsbury Group. Although Leonard Woolf was part of the circle of young men at Cambridge, he was not apparently one of those invited by Thoby to meet his sisters in London.

What do we make of Virginia's early years? It dangerously lacked any possibility for her to build up a self-image, by which she could have seen herself through others' eyes. She, as it were, lacked a layer of skin. She had a negative attitude to mirrors all her life and hated anyone looking at her. She was afraid of her body and of all bodily sensations including, during her breakdowns, eating; and was always morbidly self-conscious about her clothes. Buying clothes, especially underwear, was a major ordeal. That she was beautiful to look at, slim and ethereal with abundant hair and large eyes, did not help her. She thought she was unattractive. Her times of pleasure were perceived as escapes, her first and most satisfying being the annual exodus of the Stephen family from London to Talland House in Cornwall. There were also escapes when the 'cotton-wool' of everyday existence was torn asunder by a flash of extreme clarity, a shock of realisation, a flood of light, of awareness, which resulted in an intense experience of the present moment. Virginia, lacking a sense of the security of continued existence – the deaths of her parents and Stella had seen to that – relied on her intuition and the presence of Vanessa, with whom she felt an almost mystical sense of closeness. In her last diary entry she wrote 'if only we could infuse souls.' But they never could. Vanessa would not permit that and perhaps it was essential for her own well-being that she had the strength to resist.

We hear too little about Virginia's physical health. She was weaned at three months to make way for her younger brother Adrian – he had his own severe problems after Julia died. When she was six years old, all four of them fell ill with whooping cough from which her brothers and sister recovered unscathed, but not Virginia: afterwards she was noticeably thinner and more shadowy than the others. This may have left her with a permanently damaged heart; in any case a heart murmur was diagnosed years later, and she became exhausted easily. Thus, over-tiredness was one trigger for her headaches and instability. With few reserves of energy, she did not have the stamina to fight back directly; instead, she absorbed and forgave.

In the same year as that attack of whooping-cough, her half-brother Gerald interfered with her, his explorations accompanied by the sound of laughter ringing in her ears. These two events must have combined to induce in her a feeling of helplessness and panic, to which she would fall victim whenever she was under particular strain and felt she was at risk of losing autonomy. Although she could make cutting, even malicious, remarks Virginia never learnt to play power games; she may not have consciously realised when they were being played against her, until accumulated rage was released during a breakdown. Concentrating on her writing, the lambent and ever more accurate vision that she was able to transmit to paper enabled her not only to survive but to emerge triumphant. But, as she often felt, she was balancing on a narrow pavement with a dangerous drop on either side.

Together the stronger and more judgmental Vanessa, and Virginia with her far greater quicksilver imagination, challenged the patriarchal world which had to be conquered through their arts. But their turbulent upbringing left deeper scars on Virginia. She was younger and had to fight harder for survival.

By January 1905, when she was just twenty-three, Virginia's nerve doctor Dr. Savage, on the whole a sensible and kindly man despite his name, pronounced her cured and she accepted a part-time job teaching English Literature at Morley College in the East end of London, an evening institute for working people. She was also writing her recollections of her father for a *Life* of Sir Leslie Stephen and contributed articles and reviews to magazines, experiencing the mixed fortunes of any aspiring author.

It seemed that Virginia Stephen, the intelligent and gifted writer, was well and truly on her way. It also seemed, in that age brought up on the

Greek classics, to be an excellent plan, in the summer of 1906, for Virginia, Vanessa and Violet Dickinson to go to Greece, where they met Thoby and Adrian. Together they visited a number of cities, including Athens. However the entire party, with the exception of Virginia, fell ill. Vanessa apparently had appendicitis, while Violet Dickinson, Thoby and Adrian went down with typhoid.

On their return, Virginia had the responsibility of running a house full of sick people. Her correspondence with Violet Dickinson, who was critically ill in her own home, was aimed at helping her friend recover; and she sent the latest bulletins to friends and relatives. During that month of illness at 46 Gordon Square, Clive Bell became a frequent visitor. He read to the invalids and his visits were increasingly welcome to Vanessa, who had previously rejected his proposal of marriage.

Their doctor was slow to diagnose Thoby's life-threatening illness. Vanessa and Adrian recovered, but Thoby died. We can understand what may have contributed to his death from a letter written by Vanessa to Duncan Grant, who was about to visit Greece in 1910:

"When I think how everybody refrained from giving us advice before we set out for the East [in 1906] because they thought somebody else would do so, I make bold to be superfluous and officious. I thought last night that the word diarrhea would shock Philip [Morrell] too much... but what I wanted to say was that if you do get it, as everyone does, don't at once stop it with chlorodyne, as Thoby and Adrian did, but take castor oil and rest and feed on sloppy foods. Also take a supply of Bromo [toilet paper]. Don't wash your teeth in ordinary water, but get some mineral water. It doesn't really cost much and it's quite as bad to wash your teeth in plain water as to drink it." [7]

So Thoby and Adrian took chlorodyne, which prevented the body evacuating and thus put a greater strain on it. Adrian survived, but Thoby did not. That is evidently the reality. If Thoby had not died, Virginia's achievement in being the mainstay of the family would have been recognised and would no doubt have led to a different perception of her abilities which would have helped give her the necessary confidence to 'stand up straight', as an independent woman and writer.

For nearly a month after her brother's death Virginia continued to write affectionate letters to Violet, pretending that he was still alive, for fear the news would make her friend worse. Virginia's preoccupation with keeping Violet Dickinson cheerful probably helped her cope with

Thoby's death. This time she did not suffer a nervous breakdown. Part of the explanation may be found in the words she wrote to Violet when she did feel able to tell her: 'You are part of all that is best and happiest in our lives... I know you loved him, and he loved you... I can feel happy about him; he was so brave and strong, and his life was perfect.' [8]

Soon the news of Thoby's death spread to other members of the Bloomsbury Group. Lytton Strachey wrote to Leonard Woolf who, on leaving Cambridge, had had to take a job in the Colonial Service; he was an administrator in Ceylon (now Sri Lanka), then part of the British Empire, where he worked very hard while, according to himself, leading a 'degraded' life, on occasion getting drunk, hiring prostitutes and then falling into a depression on the rebound.

Before he left England Leonard had hardly met the Stephen sisters. When they attended a May Ball at Trinity College, he saw them as a radiant vision in long white dresses, carrying parasols. At once, he decided that he was in love with Vanessa. Just before leaving the country, he had been to dinner with Thoby but Vanessa was not there and Virginia remained silent; nevertheless, he took his vision of those two sisters of the admired Thoby Stephen, whom they called the Goth because of his handsome physique, to Ceylon with him.

Lytton and Leonard corresponded regularly, Lytton's letters being Leonard's main link with Britain. Their letters were sexually explicit, partly because Lytton believed that total sexual freedom was a means of blowing away the cobwebs of the Victorian age. That autumn of 1906, Lytton and Leonard were deep in correspondence about the sexual preferences of their Cambridge friends, most of whom were homosexual. Leonard wrote, having torn up Lytton's previous letter through fear of its falling into the wrong hands, and then proceeded to describe what was in it:

"Pure fright, it is not safe to keep, once opened, for a week in this place. It was a description of the intrigues ending in Keynes. It made me feel a little sick, as I see it did you... The Congolese contagion seems to spread in Cambridge not but what these young fellows are all humbugs. He [Thoby] stands, doesn't he?" [9]

Clive Bell and Leonard were exceptions. Leonard saw Thoby as an 'anchor' in a sea of sodomy, as his letters make clear. Lytton wrote to him: 'I can only hope that you may know the dreadful thing that has happened, from other letters or papers, for I feel that to break it to you is almost beyond my force. You must be prepared for something terrible.

You will never see the Goth again. He died yesterday.' To which Leonard replied:

"I have just got your letter. I knew nothing before. The last I had heard was from [Saxon Sydney-] Turner that he had seen him & he was recovering. I am overwhelmed, crushed... It was only a week or two ago that I wrote to you what we had so often written & said, that he was an anchor. He was above everyone in his nobility. God! what an accursed thing life is, great stretches of dull insensibility & then these unbearable bitternesses. If I could only see you & talk to you!" [10]

A few days later he wrote to Saxon Sydney-Turner: 'What can we say? Life can be no blacker than it is now.' But for Leonard, almost immediately, it did get a great deal blacker as he heard that, only two days after Thoby's death, Vanessa had agreed to marry Clive Bell, whom he despised: 'I seem to see & hear the Goth all day. It is appalling to think that it is only death that makes it altogether clear what he was to us... And Bell? & Vanessa? I am too weary to mind the mockery of it all.'

Virginia did not correspond directly with Leonard but, through Lytton, she offered him one of Thoby's books; he accepted a volume of John Milton's poems.

Vanessa's hasty acceptance of Clive Bell's offer of marriage drew an agonised response from Virginia to Violet: 'I shall want all my sweetness to gild Nessa's happiness. It does seem strange and intolerable sometimes. When I think of father and Thoby and then see that funny little creature twitching his pink skin and jerking out his little spasm of laughter I wonder what odd freak there is in Nessa's eyesight. But I dont say this, and I wont say it, except to you.' [11]

She wrote this from Hampshire, where she and Adrian spent Christmas: it snowed with a picture postcard perfection. This freedom to get away from horror was very important to Virginia. 'I have to tune myself into a good temper with something musical, and I run to a book as a child to its mother.' By early January 1907, she was able to tell Violet of seeing Vanessa and Clive together at his family's large country house, Cleeve House in Wiltshire: 'I feel very calm and domestic. Clive certainly is an interesting person, and I really feel happier, and get some glimpse of what Nessa means by marrying him. She is as happy as anyone can be; and more like herself than she was. She seems to have taken her bearings, and to see her life ahead of her in her own clear and reasonable way.' [12]

The day before their wedding she wrote congratulating Vanessa: 'We the undersigned Apes and a Wombat [herself and her dog] wish to make known to you our great grief and joy at the news that you intend to marry... [Clive] is better than all other apes because he can both talk and marry you: from which we are debarred.' [13] Thus Virginia accepted their marriage, while Vanessa once more felt secure behind her new emotional buffer.

Clive and Vanessa Bell remained at 46 Gordon Square, while Virginia and Adrian moved to 29 Fitzroy Square, also in Bloomsbury. The Thursday evenings were continued there.

Thoby was the first of the four family dead to reappear in Virginia's books, as Jacob in *Jacob's Room* (1922), her third novel. He also appeared as Percival in *The Waves*. In both novels he is silent, a catalyst for the other characters.

From October 1907 Virginia worked on her first novel, to be called *The Voyage Out*. She stayed with friends, then went on her own to Manorbier on the Pembrokeshire coast, where the Stephens had gone after her father's death. There, she renewed her love of the sea which is 'a miracle – more congenial to me than any human being,' as she wrote to Clive Bell. She was in constant touch with both Vanessa and her new brother-in-law, either by letter or living near them.

The three of them were repeating the pattern she and Vanessa had had with Thoby, although Clive was no Thoby. Pink and stocky, soon to be balding, he was despised by those who thought he was not nearly good enough for the statuesque Vanessa. But Virginia got over her initial distaste and the shock of their precipitate marriage, when he took a real and kindly interest in her writing; he read whatever she showed to him and offered her his views with no trace of condescension and a good deal of helpful comment, which she much appreciated. Later, Virginia wrote that she should have married Clive and Vanessa should have married Leonard. As is often the case, they teamed up with unlike partners.

All went well with this odd threesome until another character entered their world: Julian Bell, Vanessa's first child. Unfortunately, while Vanessa was entirely devoted to motherhood both Clive and Virginia were repelled by the crying baby and felt left out by Vanessa. As though in self-defence, they drew closer to each other and Virginia flirted with Clive; this she afterwards regretted; but she also felt a sense of insecurity, of being the odd one out, while at the same time envying Vanessa's mother-hood. In May 1908, she wrote to Clive:

"Ness has all that I should like to have, and you, besides your own charms and exquisite fine sweetness (which I always appreciate somehow) have her. Thus I seem often to be only an erratic external force, capable of shocks, but without any lodging in your lives. But the main point of all this is that we are very fond of each other; and I expect we shall make out a compromise in time." [14].

Virginia describes to Clive Bell the way she sees herself at this time: 'I am (to be candid) bored by general conversation, and usually very much excited by what I am thinking myself.' Then adds in self-mockery: 'I bid fair to become a prophetess, with only one worshipper.' She explains a so-called 'maniacal' letter she sent to her friend Emma Vaughan, by say-ing that she is trying out a style of writing; and adds 'I keep calm and vir-tuous here by the sea shore.' [15] It is a mistake, therefore, to use this letter as a sign of madness, as some commentators have suggested.

Whilst she was alone at Manorbier, Virginia was certainly not feeling suicidal; she was annoyed when a path by the edge of a cliff nearly took her over, as she writes to Vanessa:

"I walked along the Cliff yesterday, and found myself slipping on a little ridge just at the edge of a red fissure. I did not remember that they came so near the edge of the path; I have no wish to perish. I can imagine sticking out ones arms on the way down, and feeling them tear, and finally whirling over, and cracking ones head. I think I should feel as though I saw a china vase fall from a table; a useless thing to happen – and without any reason or good in it. But numbers of people do fall over." [16]

Vanessa admired Virginia's writing ability to the point of awe, especial-ly now that Virginia had embarked on her first novel, for which she made suggestions on the names of the characters. Here is already the theme of genius in a letter she wrote from Cleeve House, where Clive's parents wanted her to spend a considerable amount of time so that they could see their grandson, but where Vanessa was not happy:

"I purr all down my back when I get such gems of imagery thrown at my feet and reflect how envied I shall be of the world some day when it learns on what terms I was with that great genius, the creator of Valentine Ambrose and his wife Helen... will none of my suggestions do?" [17] In this same letter Vanessa looks ahead to when Virginia, too, would be married:

"Can't you imagine us in 20 years' time, you and I two celebrated ladies, with our families about us, yours very odd and small and you with a growing reputation for your works, I with nothing but my capacities as a hostess and my husband's value to live upon? Your husband will probably be dead, I think, for you won't have boiled his milk with enough care, but you will be quite happy and enjoy sparring with your clever and cranky daughter. I'm afraid she'll be more beautiful than mine, who I know will take after the Bells."

Vanessa, it will be noted, did not see any problem with Virginia becoming a mother. This was the daughter Virginia always wanted; she gave Clarissa Dalloway one, Elizabeth, in *Mrs. Dalloway*.

The theme of their petting is also here. This, years later, was to be called 'Virginia's rights' that she claimed on her visits to Charleston, the Bell's house in Sussex, to the annoyance of both Vanessa and Vanessa's third and last child, Angelica. And here, too, is the theme of men as different from women, with their love of shooting. Vanessa writes from Glencarron Lodge, in Scotland, where Clive and his relatives hunted:

"... we went for a short walk, during which Clive killed three rabbits. Oh Billy! poor little furry beasts. It surpasses my imagination entirely, this wish to kill – does it yours? Of course another animal with fur such as a monkey would feel for them, but I don't understand why anyone gets any pleasure from killing them... They have all gone off to shoot or to fish and I am left to spend my morning alone...

"There is an atmosphere of undiluted male here. How you would hate it! If only you were here we should now light a fire and sit over it talking the whole morning, with our skirts up to our trousers. You would say "Now what shall we talk about?" and I if I were tactful would say "Our past," and then we should begin to discuss all our marvelous past and George's delinquencies, etc., and so come to our present and then on to your future and whether and whom you would marry, and then at last to the one great subject. "Now what do you really think of your brains, Billy?" I should say with such genuine interest that you'd have to tell me and we should probably reach the most exalted spheres. Why aren't you here?" [18]

Through close talk and intimacy the sisters could, after discussing 'our marvelous past and George's delinquencies' reach 'exalted spheres'. This escalation from bestiality to vision was never achieved between Virginia and Leonard: he had a sense of personal destiny, while his feet were planted all too firmly on the ground, as she was to write in March 1941 only a fortnight before her death: 'of course I'm not a politician, and so take one leap to the desirable lands. L's view would be, I think, that ones got to plod along the road, indeed to make it, before one gets there. But Lord! what a relief to have a vision!' [19]

As a couple, Clive and Vanessa were not always either kind or gentle. In June 1910, when Virginia had joined the Women's Suffrage Movement and was actively writing out envelopes to help the cause, she wrote to Saxon Sydney-Turner: 'Mr Lefevre... alluded to the death of his prolific wife, which happened in sad circumstances which I shall explain one day. At this, Nessa and Clive suddenly lost their tempers and showed their intolerant brutality in such a way that the old man was led out by his daughter... in tears.' [20]

Virginia's relationship with Clive began to feel like a threat to Vanessa, while she was left alone with young Julian. The almost too-affectionate relationship between these sisters where Virginia was 'my Billy' to Vanessa and Vanessa was 'Beloved' or 'Dolphin' to Virginia, changes from 1909 onwards. Tension between them increases, and this is due to Vanessa. She became anxious to find a husband for Virginia. Her first choice was Lytton Strachey. Apparently Vanessa did not realise he was homosexual and only admitted it to herself after a dream she had, in which she saw him with a number of boys in separate cubicles. Lytton proposed marriage to Virginia in February 1909 and then withdrew his offer twenty minutes later, to their mutual relief. They remained friends.

In April 1909, Vanessa wrote to Virginia from Cleeve House:

"Like all Stephens... my sense of proportion gets lost in solitude... I feel like a dolphin stranded high and dry, lashing about to find some water... I don't even see Clive much – hardly ever alone – now that I have Julian, so it is unrelieved family. What a mercy it will be to get away." [21]

In this same month Virginia's aunt, the Nun, died, leaving Virginia a fortune of 2,500 pounds. Only 100 pounds each were left to Vanessa and Adrian. From then on, Virginia's finances were always more healthy than her sister's, but this disparity cannot have helped their relationship.

In May Hilton Young rather half-heartedly proposed to Virginia who refused him, saying as an excuse that she could marry no-one but Lytton Strachey. [22]

Virginia was living with her younger brother; but Adrian was depressed and morose, he blamed her for some of his own childhood problems. They went to concerts and operas almost every evening and in August they journeyed to Bayreuth to attend the opera in company with Saxon Sydney-Turner, who was wrapped in his usual silence. The trip was not a success and it is clear that Virginia was over-taxing her strength.

Early in 1910, Virginia took part in what has become known as 'the Dreadnought Affair', with Adrian. A group of young men, with Virginia disguised as a man, dressed up as the Emperor of Abyssinia and his retinue, and were invited to look over H.M.S *Dreadnought* at Weymouth. They were treated with all the dignity to which such august visitors were entitled. Afterwards, they gave the game away; there could have been serious repercussions but good sense prevailed. This episode reinforced Virginia's contempt for male pomposity.

Increasingly during this period there are signs that Vanessa's sense of proportion had deserted her as she saw her sister enjoying the freedom she lacked. Without any evidence, she feared that Virginia was having a lesbian relationship with Lady Ottoline Morrell, a dark, dramatic-looking woman who held off-beat parties and did a great deal of informal entertaining; members of the Bloomsbury Group called her 'Ott' and used to enjoy her hospitality – but Vanessa was wrong, Lady Ottoline was straight. In June Vanessa wrote quite suddenly to Dr Savage, without consulting Virginia or suggesting she should see him, telling the doctor her sister was suffering from headaches and numbness. Whereupon Dr. Savage recommended a stay at a nursing home run by Jean Thomas in Twickenham. Only after arranging this did Vanessa write to Virginia: 'Savage... had come to the conclusion he had tried half-measures long enough... and thought it was too risky to go on with them any longer and that you would never get quite well unless you had a rest cure.' He 'thinks you ought to have what he calls slightly modified treatment for a month... He said he supposed that on some days you felt quite well and on others bad again.' [23] And to Clive she wrote: 'I am only anxious that the Goat shouldn't think that I have in any way tried to make Savage suggest a rest cure, of which I do see all the disadvantages very clearly.' [24] One of the disadvantages was that news of her incarceration would damage Virginia's marital prospects.

Virginia did her best to cope with what seems to be an unnecessary move on Vanessa's part, for which she blames her sister. Just before going into the nursing home she wrote to her: 'I fear you abuse me a good deal in private, and it is very galling to think of it... as I never abuse you, I feel it rather hard; and possibly I ought to consider a scheme for the future.' But she also says: 'Of course, I adore you!' [25]

While Virginia was in the nursing home, Vanessa continued to attack her. She had heard from Clive, who visited the nursing home, that Virginia was 'seducing the household of that hitherto respectable Miss Thomas,' and suspects: 'that your own lusts are increasing at the same time... Perhaps you find massage inductive to lust. I can imagine it might be.' [26] She then puts the boot in:

"Really, what with your cultivation of Sapphism with a Swede at Twickenham and Lytton's of Sodomism with Swedes in Sweden [he went there for a ten-week cure], which apparently is the breeding ground of vice, you will be a fine couple worthy of each other when you both come out."

This side of Vanessa's character is not often pointed out. She is writing in the same judgmental tone of voice that she used in her final letter to Virginia in 1941. Yet she was far less restrained in her life-style than Virginia.

In the nursing home Virginia is at last able to express the rage she had been suppressing. She writes to Vanessa as: 'Beloved, or rather, Dark Devil':

"I gather that some great conspiracy is going on behind my back. What a mercy we cant have at each other! or we should quarrel till midnight... [Miss Thomas] wont read me or quote your letters. But I gather you want me to stay on here. Savage wanted me to stay in bed more or less this week... But I really dont think I can stand much more of this... They are always wondering what God is up to. The religious mind is quite amazing... However, what I mean is that I shall soon have to jump out of a window. My God! What a mercy to be done with it!... Anyhow, I will abide by Savage... I have been out in the garden for 2 hours; and feel quite normal. I feel my brains, like a pear, to see if its ripe; it will be exquisite by September... Give Clive my love. His visits are the brightest spots. He must come again. I will be very reasonable.' [27]

Evidently Vanessa had felt herself increasingly to be losing control; and, as the elder sister, this was an intolerable situation. She remedied it by having Virginia incarcerated. She was expecting her second child whom she thought would be a girl to be called Clarissa (another boy was born in

August 1910, later named Quentin) and no doubt she blamed Virginia's influence on the increasing distance between herself and Clive. But Clive was a man who liked the good life and could not cope with babies; he was also a womaniser, so that their marriage as an exclusive relationship was in any case most unlikely to have lasted long. Clive and Vanessa grew more distant, although he often stayed with her and Vanessa learnt greater tolerance. She met her need for the company of others by sharing a studio with Duncan Grant. Together, they painted many of the pictures that are so characteristic of the post-impressionist visual art of the Bloomsbury Group.

However, Vanessa had now become extremely anxious to shift the burden of her responsibility for her sister onto someone else as soon as possible. A husband was essential, perhaps partly to deter Virginia from becoming a lesbian. The imminent home-coming of Leonard Woolf could not have been more welcome to her, although she knew very little about him. Indeed, Virginia's word 'conspiracy' about what was going on behind her back was not so far from the truth.

Virginia decided to live more independently of her sister. After going on holiday to Cornwall with Jean Thomas, she found herself a house in Firle, Sussex, where she could invite her friends. Despite the fact that it was a red-brick, semi-detached and rather ugly building, she named it Little Talland House to remind herself of their childhood holiday home in Cornwall. In her new house Virginia not only gave Janet Case a full account of George's molestation of her, she also renewed her friendship with Violet Dickinson. However, she was not happy with her unmarried state. She was in London in June 1911. After a dramatic thunder storm, she wrote to Vanessa:

"Did you feel horribly depressed? I did. I could not write, and all the devils came out – black hairy ones. To be 29 and unmarried – to be a failure – childless – insane too, no writer. I went off to the Museum to try and subdue them." [28]

Virginia knew that Lytton had been exchanging correspondence with Leonard Woolf and when she heard that this strange, intense, trembling man, a friend of her beloved brother Thoby, had made an indirect proposal from Ceylon she was, to say the least of it, intrigued.

Whatever one thinks of the impending union between Virginia and Leonard, those of us who treasure her writing can not seriously wish that things had been different without considering that, if she had lived a more independent life, her work would not have been as we know it. But neither should we assume that her marriage to Leonard was as beneficial for her as many commentators would like us to believe.

Retaining her individual sense of herself was essential to Virginia's well-being and for her creativity. Her limited sympathy with people not of her class or race can probably be traced to a need to define her world, her friends and her audience. In this sense she was an elitist and remained one all her life. She grew up with the sense that her father and his Victorian friends were 'giants', something she expressed in her second novel. Speaking for Katharine Hilbery, she says:

"from hearing constant talk of great men and their works, her earliest conceptions of the world included an august circle of beings to whom she gave the names of Shakespeare, Milton, Wordsworth, Shelley, and so on, who were, for some reason, much more nearly akin to the Hilberys [that is, Stephens], than to other people. They made a kind of boundary to her vision of life, and played a considerable part in determining her scale of good and bad in her own small affairs." [29]

Virginia's vision was that she would one day sit amongst the elite race of literary giants, writing in a contemporary idiom that she herself helped to form, and be acknowledged. In *A Room of One's Own* she created a sister to Shakespeare – Judith, who reappears in generation after generation, and struggles to make her voice heard. I think this is how she saw herself, the Judith who lived between world war one and world war two. And who among us is to say that she did not achieve her vision?

In cosmic terms, Vanessa was the earth and Virginia the brilliant moon circling about her with periods of absence and darkness. Thanks to their father's death, and later Thoby's, in this female-centred universe there was no male sun glaring overhead, whether as patriarch or as god. No wonder generations of women come to celebrate the lives of Virginia and Vanessa and relive their existence through their writings and painting.

By 1911 these two women, Vanessa aged thirty two and Virginia twenty nine, are consciously separated from the patriarchal male world. They are looking at life from their own individual female points of view. Neither of them suffers from the 'dark bar of the 'I' – that is, from the alienated and alienating male egocentricity that drives a man to attempt to make the world in his image. On the contrary, Virginia's wit and laughter and Vanessa's outrageous behaviour in public and private, as well as in her letters, puncture such pomposity. But there was also tension between the two sisters, as Vanessa both attracted and repelled Virginia: she wanted her to be in her orbit, but not to get in too close. In this sense, Vanessa was and remained the dominant elder sister.

The circumstances of those early years meant that Virginia retained a childish sense of magic, of mystery. She was able to enter a visionary world. When she was under pressure this visionary world took over, leaving her very vulnerable to other people's assumption that she was 'insane', or 'mad'. Leonard may well have adopted this way of interpreting Virginia's behaviour from Vanessa, whose deeper emotions had been to some extent frozen as a result of her silent battles with her father and who tried to keep her life and the life of those around her on an even keel through a permissiveness, especially towards her children, that evokes the earth-mother.

Interestingly, Virginia thought that Vanessa's artistic potential was limited by her refusal to enter any states that she did not think were 'reasonable'. The only time she went over the edge was when she was told of the death in Spain of her elder son Julian in 1938. Then, she was literally prostrated with grief. Virginia was one of the few people who could help her.

Entering that dangerous, visionary world is an important part of Virginia's writing. She has often said that after an episode where she 'submerges', the material for her next novel comes to her. One is reminded of *Hamlet* – a play she must have read many times – with its equivocal exploration of the borderland between sanity and insanity, and the use Hamlet makes of it to uncover the truth about his father's murder. The difference is that Shakespeare himself is not accused of having been mad. Women in the early years of the twentieth century were far more at risk of having this simplistic and disempowering label applied to them; and maybe we still are.

Leonard Woolf's early and complete acceptance that Virginia had to be treated as somebody who was somewhat mad all the time, with bouts of overt insanity, locked her into a life that proved to be a forcing house for her writing but turned Leonard into her life-long and, when he failed her, fatal support. By over-protection he denied her the possibility of the personal development that would have given her independence and taken her beyond the need for such a dangerous prop. That she made great efforts to grow beyond this dependent state is to be found in her work, while she admired other women who managed to live their own lives, such as Vita Sackville-West and Dame Ethel Smyth.

Virginia did indeed struggle to live as an autonomous human being. However, Vanessa's distancing herself and her incarceration in Miss Thomas's nursing home shortly before Leonard returned from Ceylon was an important turning point which made it less likely that the 'little Goat', despite her mother's last words to her, would ever be able to hold herself straight. This did not stop her exercising an independence of mind that fascinated and sometimes outraged her contemporaries, and continues to communicate to us through the years with an ever more vibrant voice.

ASHEHAM HOUSE, LEWES, SUSSEX

Chapter Two

LEONARD TELLS HIS STORY

Leonard Woolf was born on 25 November, 1880. He was eighty years old before he began to tell his story. The five volumes of his autobiography were published during the 1960's, more than twenty years after Virginia's death. The first volume, *Sowing,* recounts his early life from 1880 to 1904 taking him from his family background through his years at school and University. *Growing,* 1904 to 1911, describes his career as a member of the Colonial Service in Ceylon (now Sri Lanka. I shall use the old-fashioned name as that is how it was known in Leonard's day). This second volume ends with his sailing for England to begin a year's leave.

There was a two-year gap between the publication of the first two volumes of Leonard's autobiography and the third, *Beginning again,* 1911 to 1918, which was published in 1964 and dedicated to Trekkie Parsons. In this volume Leonard gives his account of the early years of the Woolfs' marriage, including the most devastating breakdowns that Virginia was to suffer and her slow recovery at Richmond, where she began to write her diary. During these years that span the first world war, Leonard published two novels, *The Village in the Jungle* and *The Wise Virgins* – both appearing before Virginia's first novel, *The Voyage Out,* was published in 1915. In this book there is a description of the setting up of The Hogarth Press, which they owned and ran jointly.

The fourth volume, *Downhill All the Way* (1919 to 1939), describes from Leonard's point of view the twenty years between the end of the first world war and the beginning of the second. Virginia became established as a major modern writer during these years, producing most of her novels, stories, essays and criticism as well as providing her own contemporary record in her diary and *Letters.* While Leonard wrote political books, including the first two volumes of *After the Deluge,* as well as an (unperformed) play, *The Hotel.* He edited magazines and sat on several committees in an unpaid capacity, while also managing The Hogarth Press.

In 1969, the year of his death, the final volume of his autobiography, *The Journey not the Arrival Matters* (1939 to 1969), made its appearance. In this, Leonard gives his account of Virginia's death, together with thoughts about his own work and his later life with Trekkie Parsons.

LEONARD IN HAMBANTOTA
DECEMBER, 1908

Apart from some contemporary references in letters and Virginia's diary, and Leonard's story as he told it through these five autobiographical volumes, there is a surprising lack of any sustained account of the man from later commentators. He makes some rather fugitive appearances as Virginia's Woolf's husband in many books written by scholars, in which she is the focus of attention. There are a few books which try to include both Leonard and Virginia, such as *A Marriage of True Minds* (1977) by George Spater and Ian Parsons, dedicated to Ian Parsons' wife Trekkie, and the more recent *Leonard and Virginia Woolf: A Literary Partnership* (1992) by Peter F. Alexander. Both these authors have obviously found considerable difficulty in presenting Leonard as anything like a rounded or convincing character. We need to wonder what there was about him that made this so hard a task. It is important that we gain a greater knowledge of Leonard Woolf's attitudes and character if we wish to understand more about Virginia's life and work, while Leonard provides an interesting study in his own right.

Duncan Wilson in *Leonard Woolf, A Political Biography* (published by The Hogarth Press in 1978), makes a major disclaimer: 'I should draw attention to the limitations implicit in the title of this work. It is not a complete biography of Leonard Woolf, but only an account of his political activities.' His Preface ends:

"Finally, I owe a very great debt of gratitude to Ian and Trekkie Parsons. They cannot avoid some responsibility for what follows, in that they commissioned the book, but of course it, and perhaps the last chapter in particular, reflects my own views and not necessarily theirs." [1]

According to Peter F. Alexander in his *Leonard and Virginia Woolf*, Trekkie stayed with Leonard at Monk's House for the first time in January 1942, less than a year after Virginia's death. After that, she divided her time between Leonard and her husband Ian Parsons, in a triangular relationship. She denied that her liaison with Leonard was sexual, despite receiving passionate love letters and several unsuccessful proposals of marriage from him.

Wilson sums Leonard up as being, not a systematic philosopher but a 'sharp, free-ranging, bright eyed fox'. [2] In this we can recognise a major characteristic that is reflected in Virginia's pet name for Leonard, she called him Mongoose.

John Lehmann gives considerable insights on the difficulties of working with Leonard in his *Virginia Woolf* (1975), and *Thrown to the Woolves*

MARIE WOOLF, WHO LIVED TO BE 91   SIDNEY WOOLF, Q.C.

LEONARD AS A SCHOOLBOY

(1978). He worked as trainee manager at the Hogarth Press for eighteen months from January 1931 and later bought out Virginia's share of the Press to become a partner.

Alma Halbert Bond's *Who Killed Virginia Woolf? A Psychobiography* (1989) sums up Leonard's character by saying he was 'all super-ego', a compulsion neurotic: 'Apparently he legislated the actions of Virginia into his neurotic system as consistently as if they were his own. Ostensibly, this was done to ensure her health and productivity'. [3] In Bond's book the trappings of 'psychobiography' tend to remove the personal motives, the element of free will, from both Virginia and Leonard: they seem to be observed as specimens under the microscope. However, Bond is the only person to my knowledge who has said unequivocally: 'I believe that Leonard actually was unfaithful to Virginia, and that in the last years of her life formed an important alliance with another woman.' Bond saw Virginia's death, in 1941, in terms of deprivation of the pleasure principle:

"Virginia Woolf's last few years, with their deprivation of all that gave life meaning, document a dizzying descent into death... At the end every pleasure that bound her to earth was cut off, until only the return to the inanimate remained." [4]

I shall be referring again to these books. Suffice it for the moment to recognise that Wilson did not set out to write a complete biography of Leonard Woolf and that, so far, none exists.

There is a brief description of Leonard by Frederick Spotts in his Preface to *Letters of Leonard Woolf*, (1989), in which 600 letters are collected. A large number of Leonard's letters have been omitted from this selection, among them most of those dealing with the running of The Hogarth Press; four out of five of the letters he wrote during his years as an undergraduate at Trinity College, Cambridge, and over half from Ceylon. All but one (an 'insubstantial and largely illegible postcard') of his letters to Virginia are included. The *Letters* are not numbered and are arranged according to subject so that it is difficult to consult this book, however, they do give an invaluable insight into Leonard's mind at the time he wrote them; these, together with his second novel *The Wise Virgins*, enable us to gain an insight into his contemporary attitudes, that is missing from his account of his life which was begun over twenty years after Virginia's death. Although Leonard said that he never changed from the age of ten, certainly his angle of vision is very different when he writes at the time from when he looked back at his life in old age, with hindsight. And we must remember that Virginia was living with the man who wrote the letters and the novel. Spotts says:

"Leonard Woolf had a life whose scope and variety of accomplishments were equaled by few other Englishmen of the century... he exercised a significant intellectual and cultural influence in the interwar period and beyond... he was a leading proponent of democratic socialism... His marriage to a literary genius and his close friendship with many other eminent writers placed him at the center of the most remarkable intellectual coterie of our time." [5]

It is easy to make this type of impressive generalisation about Leonard, but the reality is not so simple. He himself recognised that his years of attending committees and writing political books had very little influence on the course of events:

"Looking back at the age of eighty-eight... I see clearly that I achieved practically nothing. The world today and the history of the human anthill during the last fifty-seven years would be exactly the same as it is if I had played pingpong instead of sitting on committees and writing books and memoranda." [6]

Spotts goes on to quote part of a letter written by Leonard to Lord Annan in 1967 in which he criticises in general terms the publication of letters and diaries, since these had been written at the time by their authors without due thought for their long-term effects, particularly:

"the fog which seems to spread over masses of letters and juvenilia just laid out on a table or in a book. It is partly the deadness of the dead. All these things dashed off in half a minute by a living hand and mind are served up to us as if they were carved in stone... But the main thing is the obvious fact that in letters and diaries people tend (a) much more often to write when they are miserable than when they are happy. Virginia noticed this somewhere in her diaries. (b) to exaggerate and dramatize their miseries. Not only our sweetest songs are those which tell of saddest thoughts, but they are also sweetest to the singer." [7]

Spotts then omits to quote Leonard's final paragraph in this letter:

"It is a curious fact that Pepys is almost the only intelligent diarist who does not go to his diary only or mainly when he is miserable. *His diary is extraordinarily objective and emotionally unbiased.*" (My emphasis.)

If we take this quotation as a whole, we shall immediately be confronted by the sort of difficulty that has to be faced when trying to portray

Leonard's character. By praising Pepys for being 'extraordinarily objective and emotionally unbiased', Leonard makes an *ex cathedra* judgement and thus raises Pepys's diaries above those of others, including Virginia's, which according to this judgment stand accused of emotional bias. But Leonard is here assuming an authority to which he is not entitled. In doing so, he reveals a very strong characteristic which runs through his life: that of making over-simple and provocative generalisations which are intensely judgmental, as though he occupied some exalted and exclusive position from which nobody could disagree with him. He promotes himself by diminishing the great majority of other people, whom he often termed collectively 'the human ant-heap'. Typical is Leonard's use of someone, in this case Lord Annan, whom he uses to form an exclusive triangle with an undeniably great man from the past – Pepys – together with Leonard himself. We shall find many examples of this type of intellectual games-playing in his writings: a mental sleight of hand at which he was extremely adept; and it was, no doubt, a stock-in-trade of his conversations.

Quite apart from assuming this superior attitude, how accurate are Leonard's judgments? In his reply to Lord Annan, for instance, he is incorrect in using Virginia's words to support what he calls 'the obvious fact' that in letters and diaries people tend much more often to write when they are miserable than when they are happy. When we find the reference in Virginia's diary, we discover that she is actually making quite a different point concerning the attitude of writers in their books – not in their diaries and letters. She says: 'An idea. All writers are unhappy. The picture of the world in books is thus too dark. The wordless are the happy: women in cottage gardens... Not a true picture of the world; only a writers picture. Are musicians, painters happy? Is their world happier.' [8] In *A Sketch of the Past* she wonders if she has painted too dark a picture of her father and takes the trouble to describe another side of him. [9] In both cases she was meticulously careful to reflect the truth of her perception and express her thought clearly.

By not checking his references, Leonard has thus misquoted Virginia. So what made him write to Lord Annan in this way? What was his motive? Whereas Virginia had nothing to hide, and was therefore able to express herself simply and truthfully, Leonard wanted to suppress many of his early writings, especially the collection of remarkably revealing letters he wrote to Lytton Strachey from Ceylon which he does not mention in his autobiography. Instead of admitting that his own early writings were an embarrassment to him, he hung his (false) generalisation onto the safely dead Virginia, while he presents himself to the admired Lord Annan as an equal to Pepys, who is 'extraordinarily objective and emotionally unbiased'. Only a close reading of Virginia's work, and the adoption of a wary and vigilant attitude concerning Leonard's autobiography, will enable one to correct such distortions as this.

Actually, letters and diaries tend to be very alive. There is no fog, no 'deadness of the dead' about a letter or note written in the intensity of the moment. In this instance, as in many others, when we examine one of Leonard's grand generalisations it falls apart, possibly revealing some less grand personal motive.

The major disaster of Leonard's early life, in early 1892 when he was eleven years old, was the death of his much admired father with whom he identified. Sidney Woolf was a successful lawyer who had been made a QC at a young age. During those years of success and prosperity the family occupied a large house in Kensington. On Sidney Woolf's death, their circumstances changed. Marie Woolf found herself with nine children whom she had to bring up single-handed. To survive financially she sold the Kensington house and moved her brood to a much smaller and therefore overcrowded house in the less fashionable Putney, where they all had to learn to live on limited means. Leonard reacted against the loss of his father and the despised environment of suburban Putney, by protecting himself with what he called his carapace, a hard shell which he used as a defence against the world. Part of this carapace was built out of pride, not for his immediate family but for his Semitic ancestors on his father's side. A pair of oil paintings, of his paternal grandfather and grandmother, hung memorably in the dining room:

"They – my grandparents – died before I was born, but their portraits which loomed over so many meals have indelibly impressed upon my mind their features and characters. I remember him as a large, stern, black-haired, and blackwhiskered, rabbinical Jew in a frock coat, his left hand pompously tucked into his waistcoat, while she... was the exact opposite: pretty, round cheeked, mild and forgiving. Yes, it was all, no doubt, as it should be – the male forbidding and the female forgiving." [10]

Leonard was the third surviving child in the large Jewish family headed by his mother, whom he saw as over-emotional. He insisted that he was the least loved of her nine children, although she always denied it. To others, Marie Woolf might seem heroic in her determination to do the best for them, all of whom were given a good education; but Leonard was determined to pull himself out of the 'softness' of his mother's influence and the well-meaning bourgeois conventions which ruled that stuffy house in Putney, by the bootlaces of intellectualism, reinforced by that image of his bewhiskered grandfather looming over every meal they ate at the communal dining table, who reminded him of his inheritance of tough Semitic ancestors from his admired father's (but not his despised mother's) side of the family.

Whereas the sensitive Virginia lacked a skin, and was never conditioned by being at school, Leonard acquired at least one skin too many as he determined not only to survive but to make his mark in a none-too-friendly gentile world. His sister Bella was three years older than himself and his brother Herbert one year older; they had recognisable positions in the family and were sure of themselves. But Leonard, the third child, an under-sized Jewish boy who had an arm that trembled, the trembling extending to his entire body in moments of excitement, had to cope with the rigours of home and school life. He had problems which he could not admit to even in his eighties. The carapace remained in place, and safely hidden within it he adopted a negative attitude – indeed, a savagery – towards the whole of humanity including himself. He wrote:

"It would be difficult to exaggerate the instinctive nastiness of human beings which is to be observed in the infant and child no less than in middle or old age... The fact is that at the age of ten, I was a fully developed human being, mean, cowardly, untruthful, nasty, and cruel, just as I was at twenty, fifty, and seventy." [11]

Some self-image. To picture Leonard in those early days, we need to see him as a hermit-crab under siege, carrying about with him the borrowed shell of his carapace from which he could make sweeping negative generalisations in a world he early decided was hostile, and then withdraw into his shell with the attitude 'nothing matters'. Only later could he afford to go on the hunt, like a fox or mongoose. But he never lost his stance of aggressive negativity, nor did he apparently ever realise the cost of it to others – or himself. Describing his school days, he says:

"I soon had an encyclopaedic knowledge of wickedness in man, woman, and child, both from the schoolmaster's point of view and that of the dirty and dirty-minded little boy. But by this time, I think, I had become inoculated against any feelings of personal guilt, for, though I often did things which I knew were considered to be wrong, I cannot remember ever to have felt myself to have been a sinner." [12]

He disowns all sense of guilt or sin rather too often, as Peter Alexander points out:

"In his account of his childhood... he was concerned to argue, repeatedly and with great earnestness, that religion had had little impact on him, and that he had never had any sense of sin or guilt. The very lengths he goes to in making this point partly invalidates it: a man with no sense of guilt does not go about loudly proclaiming that fact, nor does a convinced atheist rail against God." [13]

Leonard insists he was never bullied at school because of his prowess at cricket and other sports, although I take leave to doubt this. Again, his insistence is rather too obvious. His early memory of sitting on a prickly horsehair sofa until he could not contain himself any longer, crying and urinating, is no doubt admitted to as the ultimate horror scene, the horror of vulnerability, of the hermit crab without its protective shell, of losing control and consequent public shame. Carrying his carapace around with him was at least better than that, it protected him from the slings and arrows of outrageous fortune and insulated him from feeling, at least on the conscious level, any sense of guilt or sin. Hidden inside, it gave him the illusion of power and control which could carry him through any dangerous situation and enabled him to make judgements as from a fortress within which he did not need to question whether he was sometimes wrong. He describes his kindergarten, which was:

"presided over by a Mrs. Mole. Though the rest of the school was for girls only, co-education being in those days unknown, small boys were admitted to the kindergarten and entrusted to the incompetent Mrs. Mole. To the incompetent Mrs. Mole I was entrusted at the age of five or six. I cannot remember to have learnt anything at all in Trebovir Road except to take an early sexual interest in small girls." [14]

Here, carapace in place, he expresses male contempt for women's intellectual capabilities as typified by his description of 'the incompetent Mrs. Mole' who ran the kindergarten. One may question how, at the age of five or six, he knew that she was incompetent. But it was easy enough for him to make this judgment with hindsight, as with so many of those he makes in his autobiography.

At his next school, a Preparatory school for boys only, Leonard was initiated into the mysteries of sexuality by 'a particularly smutty individual at an early age':

"The only thing I learned thoroughly at Arlington House, other than cricket, was the nature and problems of sex. These were explained to me, luridly and in minute detail, almost at once by a small boy who had probably the dirtiest mind in an extraordinarily dirty-minded school. I was at the time completely innocent and I had considerable difficulty in concealing from him the fact that it was only with the most heroic effort that I was preventing myself from being sick. However I soon recovered; one had indeed to develop a strong stomach in things sexual to stand up against the atmosphere of the school when I first went there... I have never known anything like the nastiness – corruption is hardly too strong a word – of the minds and even to some extent bodies of the little boys in Arlington House when I first went there... I instinctively disliked it at the time and, when I look back on it, it rather horrifies me even today." [15]

First his brother Herbert who was 'something of a Puritan' and then he himself, when each in turn became captain of the school, managed to change the atmosphere: 'as we were both strict disciplinarians... from that of a sordid brothel to that more appropriate to fifty fairly happy small boys under the age of fourteen.' Thus Leonard learnt to wield power at an early age and taste the pleasures of being a 'strict disciplinarian'.

He went on to become an outstanding classical student at St. Paul's School, where he attended as a day boy. His success was achieved by unremitting, even obsessive, hard work in a limited subject and this characteristic remained with him for the rest of his life. From there, he won a scholarship to Trinity College, Cambridge, a remarkable achievement in itself. Not only this, but he was admitted as a member of an exclusive secret society, the Apostles, seen as the highest attainable level among the intellectuals of the University, within which both undergraduates and dons participated: an elite, where rituals abounded and non-members were doomed to outer darkness and written off as 'phenomena'. Members of the Apostles were 'brothers' of Plato and other great philosophers; they lived in the World of Reality and considered, according to Bertrand Russell, that 'the virtue of intellectual honesty was in our keeping'. Undergraduates in their first year who had a brilliant school record were considered as 'embryos' (possible members of the Apostles) and if they were elected then they were 'born'. After their days at Cambridge members who were successful 'took wings' and became 'angels' [16]. Their University training encouraged them to feel superior to everyone else; being an Apostle reinforced that belief.

Leonard's happiest years were surely spent at Trinity College, Cambridge. Here, he acquired a sense of destiny. He could dream his dreams. And these dreams were no less than changing the world, to replace modern capitalism with the democracy of Athens in about 400 BC. He called Lytton Strachey, himself and Saxon Sydney-Turner (his room mate, who went on to become a pillar of the establishment in the Foreign Office) the 'Trinity of Trinity', which they supposed to be even more exclusive than the Apostles. In his first published letter to Lytton he formed another triumvirate when he says that they must include Job at the top of their list of 'superlative people', along with Plato and Shakespeare, and then seeks to connect himself to them, referring to a copy of the *Book of Job* which Lytton Strachey had given him:

"I may be wrong & probably am – perhaps there really is Eastern blood in my veins which answers the cry of an ancestor – how splendid if one discovered that one was descended from Job! – perhaps that makes me partial but really it does seem to me to 'dwell apart'." [17]

We shall return to Job later, as Leonard wrote about him at length in one of his books. Meanwhile one can see a characteristic pattern in the way Leonard includes himself, not as a leader, but as a fellow-traveller among the best and most admired; one of a small group who 'dwell apart' from the rest of humanity.

Before going up to Cambridge, Leonard had renounced his Jewish faith as part of his distancing himself from his immediate family. At Cambridge he replaced religion with the philosophy of George Edward (G.E.) Moore, whose seminal book *Principia Ethica* became the bible for that generation of young men and especially those who were Apostles. Today, G.E. Moore's work appears to be almost unreadable. The following is by no means the most convoluted paragraph in his book:

"We cannot hope to understand what we mean, when we say that this is good or that is good, until we understand quite clearly, not only what 'this' is or 'that' is (which the natural sciences and philosophy can tell us) but also what is meant by calling them good, a matter which is reserved for Ethics only. Unless we are quite clear on this point, our ethical reasoning will be always apt to be fallacious. We shall think that we are proving that a thing is 'good,' when we are really only proving that it is something else; since unless we know what 'good' means, unless we know what is meant by that notion in itself, as distinct from what is meant by any other notion, we shall not be able to tell when we are dealing with it and when we are dealing with something else, which is perhaps like it, but yet not the same." [18]

Moore proceeds to nullify his own argument by deciding that 'good' could not be defined, it was intrinsic to itself. However, despite this, he pronounces that the 'greatest goods' are personal affection and aesthetic enjoyments, and in doing so provided the ethical basis for the Bloomsbury Group, which gave its members a licence to explore every type of sexual relationship both homosexual and heterosexual, provided one was 'honest' and told the 'truth' about one's feelings. In their philosophy it was permissible to steal the partners of one's friends. Thus Moore's ethics led to a remarkable sense of liberation. Lytton Strachey, a member of a large influential family and a key member of the Apostles, fell in and out of love with men and curiously used the judgmental Leonard as his confessor.

Quite suddenly, Leonard found himself in the top echelons of intellectual society, in a different world from suburban Putney and, arguably, he could now afford to come out from under his carapace, relax his trembling arm and participate much more directly in the life of Cambridge before the First World War, when such intellectual giants of the previous generation as A.N. Whitehead, Bertrand Russell and G.E. Moore were in residence. That he did not do so can partly be attributed to his effort to establish himself, despite what he felt to be the odds against him. He felt as though he were an outsider struggling against insuperable difficulties. Like some latter-day old testament prophet, he made grandiose judgements and he needed a select group around him within which to do so. He also needed a leader such as he found in Lytton Strachey. Michael Holroyd describes Leonard at this time:

"Having inherited a highly-strung intellect from his father, and rejected his mother's squeamish sentimentality, he was growing up a rather dry, nervously repressed young man, in appearance lean, with a long nose, sombre eyes and pale ascetic lips. The pendulum of his emotions appeared to swing through a fairly small arc, but in moments of stress they found an outlet in the involuntary trembling of his hands." [19]

That Leonard remained within a narrow circle can also be partly explained by the spreading of homosexuality through the Apostles, beginning with G.E. Moore himself. This set them apart, so that they were disliked by many other members of the University and therefore decided that they alone knew the 'truth' and were indeed supreme – the cream of the cream. Often, they would sit in complete silence, none of them daring to say anything because they would be jumped on by a member of their circle who challenged them with: 'And *what* do you mean by *that?*' They prized intellectual honesty and thought that they were the standard bearers of 'the good', that indeed they were the only true inheritors of civilisation itself. But their high-minded discussions were complicated by scandals and gossip among the fevered young men many of whom, including Lytton Strachey, saw themselves as female. Lytton would outrage the orthodox with his individual manner and style of dress, while paradoxically it was the masculinity of Thoby Stephen that enchanted him. As Holroyd said: 'Lytton idealized Thoby. Different in every respect from himself, he represented what was unattainable in life. He seemed the perfect human specimen, the aesthetic ideal.' And yet Thoby, admired by all of them including the despised Clive Bell, was not elected as a member of the Apostles. This group, together with Saxon Sydney-Turner, had formed another small circle called the Reading Club, known as the Midnight Society as they met late at night to read texts aloud and discuss them. Lytton, in singling out Leonard as his confessor to whom he confided his secret passions, found that their relationship was only partially successful; as Holroyd recounts:

"He had much to recommend him – a good brain, a lack of prejudice, a detachment of manner, an impressive honesty. But his puritanism stood as an obstacle to complete and spontaneous confidence. Often Lytton would tease him about it, suggesting that he should join a League for Social Purity... Leonard Woolf reacted indignantly to such jibes. But whenever Lytton tested him with some specially obscene piece of gossip, he would sense Leonard's fractional recoil. 'It is hopeless,' he told his brother James... 'what can one expect in even a remote future, when *Woolf* thinks that people ought to be 'punished' for incest?' " [20]

The heterosexual Leonard was in an equivocal position. Although he was one of the most devoted admirers of G.E. Moore's philosophy, which he relied upon as a replacement for his Jewish faith while providing him with a sense of his own pre-eminence above the 'human ant-heap', he was also, and always would be, both a strict disciplinarian and, as he admitted in his autobiography, 'mentally, morally and physically a coward'. [21]

That he tied this description of himself as a coward to the assertion that Virginia was 'mentally, morally and physically a snob', at which 'she was inclined to agree', is entirely typical of the man. However, we would do well to read her piece Am I a Snob? before making up our own minds as to whether he was writing accurately about Virginia's views.

If we are to trade degrees of snobbery, there was nothing more extreme than the intellectual snobbery that permeated the old Universities of Cambridge and Oxford at that time. When Lytton Strachey and Leonard wrote to each other, they gave themselves ridiculously great importance. In September 1904, Lytton says:

"Yes, our supremacy is very great, and you've raised my spirits vastly by saying so. I sometimes feel as if it were not only we ourselves who are concerned, but that the destinies of the whole world are somehow involved in ours. We are – oh! in more ways than one – like the Athenians of the Periclean Age. We are the mysterious priests of a new & amazing civilization... We have abolished religion, we have founded ethics, we have established philosophy, we have sown our strange illumination in every province of thought, we have conquered art, we have liberated love... Your letter was wonderful, and I was particularly impressed by the curious masculinity of it. Why are you a man? We are females, nous autres, but your mind is singularly male." [22]

The world seemed to be a much smaller place in those days, with the young men of Cambridge (in their own eyes) at its pinnacle. The narrow, classics-based education bred a form of intellectual snobbery that is today hard to credit but we need to make the effort if we are to comprehend the character and attitudes of the man Virginia Stephen committed herself to live with when, after several months of doubt, she agreed to marry Leonard Woolf. Leonard's political writings are at first glance easier to read than those of Moore's ethics but there is a lack of light and shade, an absence of doubt, in what he says. For whatever reason most commentators are content to portray him as the husband of Virginia Woolf – a hopefully benign character, even a 'saint' – who kept her alive during one of her 'mad' turns and otherwise got on with his own work. It is certainly time to question whether this view of Leonard is valid.

During his Cambridge years and for the rest of his life, Moore's philosophy was Leonard's faith. He wanted to be its chief exponent: to champion 'good' against 'bad' and to promote a form of idealised civilisation derived from the philosophies of classical Greece, against 'barbarism' in all its forms

– a word which stood for everything he disliked, or couldn't control, including his own family's bourgeois life-style and, later, Virginia's 'madness'. Leonard particularly admired what he and Strachey called the Periclean Age. Leonard identified himself with the great orator himself, Pericles, the 'founder of democracy', together with Job representing the Jewish side of his nature (another triangle). By the time he began to write his autobiography, he saw himself as descended from three disparate cultures which he described sitting at his window in Monk's House:

"I write this looking out of a window upon a garden in Sussex. I feel that my roots are here and in the Greece of Herodotus, Thucydides, Aristophanes, and Pericles. I have always felt in my bones and brain and heart English, and more narrowly a Londoner, but with a nostalgic love of the city and civilization of ancient Athens. Yet my genes and chromosomes are neither Anglo-Saxon nor Ionian... my Semitic ancestors, with the days of their greatness, such as it was, already behind them, were in Persia or Palestine. And they were already prisoners of war, displaced persons, refugees, having begun that unending pilgrimage as the world's official fugitives and scapegoats which has brought one of their descendants to live, and probably die, Parish Clerk of Rodmell in the County of Sussex." [23]

Thus Leonard felt even his roots to be divided into three: English, Jewish, and ancient (Athenian) Greek. In one sense he was making large claims for himself, in another he was able to adopt the role of a disadvantaged outsider with a fail-safe position, trying a little too hard. Leonard was something of a misfit even in the rarefied atmosphere of Trinity College, Cambridge. He set himself apart and took refuge in a bristly, argumentative stance which he retained for the rest of his life; he took pride in never admitting he was wrong and refused to give up whatever position he had adopted, merely despising those who disagreed with him.

At the end of this period of his life as a Cambridge undergraduate, during which there was no limit to the visions these young men conjured up, the real world struck Leonard a major blow: he did not do nearly as well as he had anticipated either in his final examinations or, after a fifth year, in his Civil Service results. He had expected, at least, a good enough grade to enter the Foreign Office and begin an upwardly mobile career as a diplomat. Instead he came out 65th in the Civil Service list and was only offered a job in the Colonial Service which, in his case, meant leaving England to help administer the British Empire in Ceylon.

He found his family's finances in a worse state than he thought, and turned down his elder sister Bella's offer to pay for him to study law. With no private means he had no alternative but to go. However, he left England an embittered man. His worst nightmare was, perhaps, that his disappointing results showed he did not have a first class brain after all.

As he set sail, Leonard decided he was an outcast from everything that mattered in life. He took with him into what he saw as the outer darkness of Ceylon his dog and his complete set of Voltaire, exaggerating the number of volumes. Hoping to improve his financial position, he became a small-time gambler. Leonard's chief link with his old life was his correspondence with Lytton Strachey; and, through those years of his exile, he retained a distant vision of the Stephen sisters, Vanessa and Virginia, when they attended a May Ball at Trinity College wearing long white muslin dresses and carrying parasols.

In Ceylon, Leonard found some relief through obsessive hard work. He drove himself, as well as the patient Tamils, from dawn until dusk, insisting that every possible letter should be answered on the day that it came and making everyone adhere strictly to the most pettifogging rules and regulations; in a word, he personified the belligerent, autocratic imperialist administrator and was able to indulge to the full the strict disciplinarian side of his nature. He hunted large and small game and had bouts of hard drinking and whoring. He frequently lost his temper and was generally irascible, with periodic depressions such as the occasion when he took out his gun with the intention of killing himself but did not get around to actually pulling the trigger. He wrote to Lytton Strachey:

"the drunker I get the more sober I am. Damn damn damn damn damn I took out my gun the other night, made my will & prepared to shoot myself. God knows why I didn't; merely I suppose the imbecility of weakness & the futility of ridiculous hopes. Whores & vulgar gramophones, fools & wrecked intellects... I am on the edge of death or of being sick so good night." [24]

At this period of his life Leonard was in many ways an unpleasant young man, arrogant and opinionated. Admittedly, he was showing off and dramatising himself in his letters to Lytton, yet it is clear that he despised the other civil servants who were his contemporaries or immediate superiors, while ingratiating himself with those who held power.

His attitude towards women is frankly horrifying. He lost his virginity but sex was seen as 'degrading' a word in frequent use by the disciples of G.E. Moore. Spater and Parsons in *A Marriage of True Minds* give an overview of the correspondence between Leonard Woolf and Lytton Strachey at this period. Leonard reports each episode of his various affairs:

"at one point observing: 'I am beginning to think it is always degraded being in love: after all 99/100ths of it is always the desire to copulate, otherwise it is only a shadow of itself, and a particular desire to copulate seems to me no less degraded than a general'." These authors continue:

"Leonard... managed to control things reasonably well by Victorian standards, seeking his satisfaction from the readily available prostitutes of Jaffna – but apparently small satisfaction it was since, as he reported to Strachey, he found galloping on a horse 'better I think as a pleasure than copulation'... It is plain that what Leonard found 'degrading' in his romances was the object of his affections. By both persuasion and nature Leonard was a G.E. Moore man to the core, and 'wherever the affection is most valuable' says *Principia Ethica*, 'the appreciation of mental qualities must form a large part of it'." [25]

In his letters to Lytton Strachey, written in 1905, Leonard says:

"I foresee dry rot of everything, no one to talk to & no time even to read: I shall go awhoring, I think, in desperation as women are so cheap & it doesn't matter if you do get syphilis in Jaffna." And again: "a thousand years ago I walked & talked with Gods! The 'society' of this place is absolutely inconceivable; it exists only upon the tennis court and in the G[government] A[gent]'s house; the women are all whores or hags or missionaries or all three; and the men are, as I told you, sunk." [26]

The diatribe in Leonard's letters to Lytton continues. He discusses with the Superintendent of Police 'whether a Singalese whore is better than a Tamil or a German better than both', to which Lytton responds:

"By God, don't you sometimes get a feeling of eminent satisfaction to see yourself towering above your loathsome companions? The thought of [Maynard] Keynes often acts upon *me* like a tonic. I whirl into the empyrean, and you must too... Do they bow down before you? I believe, if they don't, they will... You burn with a mystic unquenchable flame – a dark triumph, which circumstances may shake, but never shatter." [27]

Lytton was certainly bolstering Leonard up, telling him he 'burnt with a mystic unquenchable flame – a dark triumph, which circumstances may shake, but never shatter.' In some ways, he was quite right. Within

Leonard's carapace was a desperate determination to win at all costs, which apparently sits oddly with his cowardice: these two, the flame and the fear, were Leonard's 'engine', propelling him and at the same time preventing him from relating directly and openly with other people, who were seen as getting in his way, to be despised and thrown aside if he could not make use of them.

Although Leonard gradually came to appreciate both the country itself and the 'queer tortuous people', especially the Singalese, his views at this period of his life were conservative. When he heard from members of his family that women were trying to gain the vote in England, he replied: 'I don't think it really matters a damn whether they have votes or not... More women are fools, I believe, than men but there are so many men that are fools that I cannot see any harm in giving women votes if they want them.' [28] His cynicism annoyed his sisters and brothers, who were rallying to the cause; Leonard was behind the times and they wrote and told him so.

Although homosexuality is openly discussed in this correspondence with Lytton Strachey, indeed it is a major preoccupation between them, Leonard does not mention it in his autobiography. His letters reveal a fairly typical public school but, nevertheless, appalling attitude towards women, who are objectified. He writes:

"The most astonishing & sordid thing I have yet seen out here was last week in court, a rape case. An old hag of a woman charged a boy of about 18 with raping her. You should have seen her in the witness box with the grinning table of lawyers, it was absolutely the depths. She had to describe minutely the whole operation, the position of his & her legs & thighs & hands & mouth. It was quite plain that she had let him copulate with her & then got annoyed & charged him: but even *she* collapsed in the box when asked 'How do you know that the male organ entered the female organ, did you see it?' Eventually she said she had felt it. 'Have you ever felt the same thing in your dreams?' At last she gasped out, Yes." [29].

'O god, O god, it's absolutely & entirely incredible to what depths & madness one passes here... The only method of life I find when one is simply engulfed is to be absolutely unrestrained, to pile madness on madness & degradation on degradation...' And again: 'I suppose you want to know everything – well, I am worn out or rather merely supine through a night of purely degraded debauch. The pleasure of it is of course grossly exaggerated certainly with a half-cast whore.' [30]

As a result of Leonard's sexual experiences before he married Virginia it is unlikely that they would have been compatible, even without her own sexual problems. His alienated lust and her terrified frigidity were at opposite ends of the sexual spectrum.

Through the 'degradation' of his first year in Ceylon Leonard particularly remembered Vanessa and was upset when he heard that the despised Clive Bell was in love with her and had proposed marriage, although at first Vanessa rejected him:

"It's rather sad, certainly more so than I thought it was, for I always said that [Clive Bell] was in love with one of them – though strangely I thought it was the other [that is, Virginia]. In a way I should like never to come back again now... You think that Bell is really wildly in love with her? The curious part is that I was too after they came up that May term to Cambridge, & still more curious that there is a mirage of it still left. She is so superbly like the Goth [Thoby Stephen]. I often used to wonder whether he was in love with the Goth because he was in love with her & I was in love with her, because with the Goth." [31]

The news of Thoby's death in 1906 and the precipitate marriage of Vanessa to Clive greatly increased Leonard's sense of distance from England; it now seemed impossible that he would ever be able to return to the hopes and dreams of his previous life. He had spent well over a year in 'the stagnant pond of Jaffna'. The 'more than ordinarily furious heat' could reduce him to impotency, so that he sat silent in the presence of a prostitute, then gave the woman all his money and fled. [32]

In his desperation, Leonard's behaviour towards the Tamils hardened. He wore stiff white collars in the hottest weather to emphasise his superior position; and he became increasingly overbearing, on one occasion insisting that a man of high caste clean up his own spit. This evoked criticism from his superiors, so he thought he would be dismissed. Instead, he was promoted and moved to Kandy. Here he had more responsibility, including having to officiate at public hangings. He watched four men executed, in pairs:

"I saw the most appalling spectacle the other day... I have a strong stomach but at best it is a horrible performance... They are led up on to the scaffold & the ropes are placed round their necks. I have (in Kandy) to stand on a sort of verandah when I can actually see the man hanged. The signal has to be given by me. The first two were hanged all right but they gave one of the second too big a drop or something went wrong. The man's head was practically torn from his body & there was a great jet of blood which went up about 3 or 4 feet high, covering the gallows & priest who stands praying on the steps. The curious thing was that this man as he went to the gallows seemed to feel the rope round his neck: he kept twitching his head over into the exact position they hang in after death. Usually they are quite unmoved." [33]

In contrast, Lytton yearned for 'beauty – but absolute Beauty – reigning supreme in Cythera.' (Cythera: the island birthplace of Aphrodite, Goddess of love and beauty). Leonard realised all too clearly how entirely different, and how distant, his life had become:

"One thing you must understand & that is that I am done for as regards England. I shall live & die in these appalling countries now. If I come back for good now I should do nothing but loaf until I died of starvation. What else could I do? And as for happiness – I don't believe in being happy even in England." [34]

Underlining his commitment to the colonial life he was leading, Leonard continues this letter: 'I am really in love with someone who is in love with me. It is not however pleasant because it is pretty degrading, I suppose, to be in love with practically a schoolgirl. Also the complications are appalling when one has, as they say, to 'behave like a gentleman', when one does not intend to marry... Sometimes I think really I am only in love with silly intrigue & controlling a situation, & sometimes merely with two big cow eyes which could never understand anything which one said & look as if they understood everything that there has ever been, is or will be.'

Back in England, a court case threatened the magic world of the Apostles and their 'supremacy', as Lytton recounted. The mother of one of the young men found a letter that was 'rank with sodomy... She stormed and raved, and... wound up by accusing the Society, if you please, of being a hotbed of unnatural vice.' This incursion of the real world, where homosexuality even between consenting adults was still a criminal offence, set Leonard off on one of his life-long day-dreams: the yearning to drop out of one lifestyle and take up another; to go from being immersed in a particular existence to the point of obsession, to taking up a different one: 'To glide silently out of even one's own life... it would be like a re-incarnation, being born again into the world with all one's knowledge, all one's experience & all one's memories. One could not, I imagine, help being supreme; one could burst forth then unhampered & uncontrolled.' [35]

Leonard's hankering for an 'unhampered & uncontrolled' rebirth, to become a foot-loose 'Wandering Jew' who sloughed off one life before entering another, and then took into the new life his previous knowledge so that he would be 'supreme', was to be expressed in his second novel *The Wise Virgins*, and again in his play *The Hotel*. It was, in my view, a major factor in Virginia's death.

In 1908 Leonard, so far from breaking free, was 'hopelessly enmeshed in my surroundings.' Committing himself still further, he demonstrated his capacity to organise an event, putting on a show that impressed his superiors who made him Assistant Government Agent. After only four years in the Colonial Service, at an unusually young age, he was put in charge of Hambantota District, a large area of jungle in the south of the island inhabited by poor village communities living in mud-huts:

"And I suppose I am happy too, happier I expect as far as quantity goes than you. I work, God, how I work. I have reduced it to a method and exalted it to a mania... I am on my own in my district which is about 1000 sq[uare] miles with 100,000 people in it. So I live at the Residency Hambantota." [36]

Leonard was making a success of his career. He could have gone on to become Governor General and receive a knighthood, but that is not his story. From his Residency he made long journeys either on horseback, or in a horse-drawn cart, to inspect remote villages and exact a road tax from the often half starved and diseased people, who were fined or imprisoned if they did not pay. He was 'everything': 'policeman, magistrate, judge, & publican.' If there was a murder he had to go to the scene:

"The orders of the Government are that when a murder is reported you go straight to the spot & look at the body & take down the interminable evidence... A man had kicked the woman with whom he lived to death because she had not got his supper ready. They took me into the room of the hut where she was lying dead, & they stripped her naked for me to examine the wounds. Most women naked when alive are extraordinarily ugly, but dead they are repulsive & the most repulsive thing is the way the toes seem to stick up so straight & stark & dominate the room. But the most abominable thing was the smell." [37]

It is strange to think that, in the fullness of time, Leonard had to identify Virginia's corpse after it had been lying in the River Ouse for three weeks. Surely it must have brought that scene in Ceylon back to him with a vengeance, but he did not draw the parallel. It was indeed as though he slipped from one life to another without gaining in tolerance or what is called maturity. Since Leonard omitted all mention of this correspondence between himself and Lytton Strachey from his autobiography, he was unable to put in perspective his state of mind at the time. He did indeed remain a ten-year-old in his outlook; John Lehmann was to call it 'a flaw in his character', and this is something that commentators need to acknowledge. I am glad that our sources of information about his life, and even more about his relationship with Virginia, are not circumscribed by the carefully constructed and incomplete story of himself that he told in old age.

Leonard became more and more immersed as a civil servant leading an exotic life in the tropics, wielding power over large numbers of indigenous people on behalf of the British Empire; but he never quite lost touch with England and Lytton never abandoned him, continuing to retail tantalizing gossip about their friends. In the autumn of 1908 Lytton wrote that Clive, with Vanessa and Virginia, had gone to Italy together, adding: 'Don't you think it's the wildest romance? That little canary-coloured creature we knew in [Trinity] New Court should have achieved that? – The two most beautiful and wittiest women in England!' [38]

Saxon Sydney-Turner suggested Leonard might write something about Thoby. Leonard replied to Lytton, sympathising with him for losing Duncan Grant to Maynard Keynes: 'I detest Keynes don't you? Looking back on him from 4 years, I see he is fundamentally evil if anyone was. God! Fancy electing him [as an Apostle] and not the Goth. We shall never be able to answer for not electing the Goth. It is the one thing that I think is unpardonable.' [39] He reread Thoby's letters, but then wrote to Saxon pouring cold water on his plan to publish them: 'They make one weep with bitterness. He is complete in them for anyone who knew him, but I wonder whether they would convey anything to anyone who did not: for after all everything was in his character.' Was Leonard being sensible, or merely mean? He reacted just as negatively to the possibility of publication when Vanessa's son Julian died young.

This year, Leonard's gambling paid off: he won the Calcutta sweepstake of 690 pounds and sent some money home to his grateful family. His ties with England were growing stronger as his year's leave approached. By early 1909, the concerted efforts of Vanessa, Clive and Lytton to get Virginia married reached his ears. Lytton urged Leonard to return. He replied:

"The most wonderful thing of all would have been to marry Virginia. She is I imagine supreme & then the final solution would have been there, not a rise above all horrors but certainly not a fall, not a shirking of facts... It is undoubtedly the only way to happiness, to anything settled, to anything not these appalling alternations from violent pleasures to the depths of depression. I am sure of it for myself &, as I perpetually now live on the principle that nothing matters, I don't know why the devil I don't. But something or other always saves me just at the last moment from these degradations – their lasciviousness or their ugliness probably – though I believe if I did I should probably be happy. Do you think Virginia would have me? Wire to me if she accepts. I'll take the next boat home; & then when I arrived I should probably come straight to talk with you." [40]

Lytton answered, saying that he himself had proposed to Virginia but 'saw that it would be death if she accepted me'. He renewed his efforts to get Leonard to agree to marry her. He was also discussing this possibility with Vanessa, saying to Leonard: 'I told Vanessa to hand on your proposal'. Even his sister Bella, who had visited Leonard in Ceylon, writes to him regretting his loneliness and saying:

"You need a very special sort of girl... strong-minded & clever & a sense of humour. If you marry a weak character you'll squash her... You *must* marry someone who can hold her own with you & yet be good-tempered." [41]

Spotts considers that this letter from Bella may have been inspired by Lytton, who had recently met her. The plot thickens. Lytton then went a step further:

"Your destiny is clearly marked out for you, but will you allow it to work? You must marry Virginia. She's sitting waiting for you, is there any objection? She's the only woman in the world with sufficient brains; it's a miracle that she should exist; but if you're not careful you'll lose the opportunity... She's young, wild, inquisitive, discontented, and longing to be in love. If I were you I should telegraph." [42]

No wonder Virginia sensed that a conspiracy was being carried on behind her back by Vanessa, Clive and Lytton. Her own knowledge of Leonard had come mostly from Thoby's larger-than-life and rather lurid accounts of his friends – 'we talked of them by the hour' Virginia recalled, in a paper 'Old Bloomsbury' she read at the Memoir Club in 1928:

"And then Thoby, leaving me enormously impressed and rather dazed, would... tell me about another astonishing fellow – a man who trembled perpetually all over... he was a Jew. When I asked why he trembled, Thoby somehow made me feel that it was part of his nature – he was so violent, so savage; he so despised the whole human race... most people, I gathered, rather rubbed along and came to terms with things. Woolf did not and Thoby thought it sublime. One night he dreamt he was throttling a man and he dreamt with such violence that when he woke up he had pulled his own thumb out of joint. I was of course inspired with the deepest interest in that violent trembling misanthropic Jew who had already shaken his fist at civilisation and was about to disappear into the tropics so that we should none of us ever see him again." [43]

Leonard did not telegraph. In May 1911, he set sail for England. He left a girl behind in Ceylon who, according to the prevailing conventions, he should have married. She appears as Gwen in *The Wise Virgins*.

Immediately on his return Leonard visited Lytton Strachey and then went to a performance of Diaghilev's Ballets Russes to see Nijinski where, with a sense of unreality, he saw a dozen people in the audience whom he knew, including Virginia Stephen. He had dinner with Vanessa and Clive, and Virginia joined them later. Then he set out on a two-month tour of Sweden and Denmark with his younger brother Edgar who talked about 'the Insurance Bill & Education & Trades Unions', as Leonard told Lytton. This tour left an indelible impression on Edgar, during which he learnt more than he liked about his older brother. Many years later he wrote a long, furious letter to Leonard, which Leonard describes as 'the bitterest letter I ever received', part of which reads:

"As a boy you were mean and a bully – not that I ever allowed you to bully me, but Herbert and Harold did.

I saw little of you until I went to Sweden with you in 1911, when I realized how mean you were in your outlook. After that I have seen little of you." [44]

While they were together on holiday, Leonard talked to Edgar: 'about Virginia & your difficulty about proposing & the idea of the Ceylon Civil Service.' [45] But what did Leonard tell Edgar that made him complain about his 'mean outlook' that he remembered half a century after the event? and why did Leonard find the prospect of proposing to the virginal Virginia so difficult? It is worth considering these questions before we follow Leonard's fortunes as a suitor for Virginia's hand in marriage.

On the positive side marriage to Virginia Stephen would give him an excellent opportunity to get away from his successful, yet 'degraded' existence in the Colonial Service and be 're-born'; if he returned to Ceylon at the end of his year's leave, Gwen would be there waiting for him and he would have to marry her. Life with Virginia obviously provided a much better prospect. She was intelligent, and a key member of the Bloomsbury Group so that as her husband he would at once become a central figure in the Group. Marrying into an established family, he would gain a social position; and he would be provided with the finances he had always wanted, since Virginia's Quaker aunt had left her a considerable fortune and she also possessed other money. Thus Leonard would not have to work at a career to provide an income and his dreams of awakening the world to the wonders of Periclean Athens might yet be realised. If, with the help of Vanessa and Lytton, he could get Virginia to agree to marry him, the outlook was indeed rosy for Leonard. So what was holding him back?

On the other side of the equation, there was Virginia's 'madness', which Leonard knew about in general terms; and it is true that he had fallen in love with Vanessa and not Virginia. But there were some other problems. Sexually he would have to cope with a highly-strung, sensitive, beautiful woman of whom, despite himself, he felt somewhat in awe; and he would have to deal with her virginity, of which he was frightened, instead of bedding a very young, willing, submissive girl who was in love with him. He might miss the prostitutes in Ceylon, whose services he had been able to buy cheaply whenever he wanted. Among his problems was, perhaps, fear of impotence if he was unable to gain power over the woman until she threw herself at him, committed and abandoned. (We find out about this in *The Wise Virgins*.) From his childhood experiences, Leonard equated sex with dirt, and this was reinforced by his degraded sex life in Ceylon.

If Leonard, in Sweden, discussed the pros and cons of his future marriage prospects with Virginia in terms such as these, Edgar might well have thought him mean-minded. But there was something more. Leonard attributed his rapid advancement in Ceylon to his use of what he called 'the method', which he refers to in a letter to Lytton in November 1905, at the beginning of his term in Jaffna. He had passed his first law examination in record time and was already wielding some authority:

"All this I put down entirely to a persistent use of the method... It is only through the method that the other officials think me 'nice' & are so 'good & kind' to me that they say it is a shame that I'm overworked & help me to do things which 'as a rule it is a perfect scandal that a cadet be allowed to manage.' ... This is a phenomenal & degraded letter." [46] He describes 'the method' in detail in *Sowing*, quoting from two conversations he had written down and later rediscovered among papers, from his days as a Cambridge undergraduate. First there is a gruesome story about a cat with worms and a 'tall, big' woman catching and killing rats with her teeth. The second is an account of using 'the method' on the third member of 'the Trinity of Trinity' – Saxon Sydney-Turner. This story is not so obviously offensive as the first but is a good deal more sinister in its implications. Leonard explains:

" 'The method' referred to in the conversation had been invented by Lytton and me; it was a kind of third-degree psychological investigation applied to the souls of one's friends. Though it was a long time before we had any knowledge of Freud, it was a kind of compulsory psycho-analysis. It was intended to reveal to us, and incidentally to the victim, what he was really like; the theory was that by imparting to all concerned the deeper psychological truths, personal relationships would be much improved. Its technique was derived partly from Socrates, partly from Henry James, partly from G.E. Moore, and partly from ourselves. We had already applied the method with disastrous success to Saxon." [47]

There follows the transcript of a conversation following the successful use of 'the method', in which a sustained barrage of prepared questions had been asked by Lytton until the victim (not named) had broken down. Lytton is recounting the scene to Leonard:

"He's going – and that of course will be the ultimate – to give me the names.

God!

He began pacing again.

There's no hypnosis even, he went on. The touching and all that – that's not the important part. You see, I *can't* understand it.

But the questions, I said. How could you ask them?

Well, once I *did* think I was lost. But what's so awful for him, poor thing, is that however much he swears it's true, I can't believe him.

Well, you are cruel. I call it sheer brutality.

He stood and drummed on the table with my pen while I lay back in my chair and looked at him. The group round the fire was still silent. Suddenly he turned to go and as suddenly came back to the table. There's one thing more, he said. This has certainly been the most wonderful of all.

Then the door slammed."

That is the end of the transcript, dated 10 May 1903. Leonard continues:

"Let me return for a brief moment to Saxon. I have said that we applied 'the method' to him with disastrous success. Lytton and I were very fond of him – we had become intimate friends long before Saxon and I had the double set of rooms in Great Court. But the more intimately we got to know him, the more concerned we became about his psychological state. He seemed, even at the age of twenty, to have deliberately withdrawn himself from life... by spinning around himself an elaborate and ingenious series of cocoons... Lytton and I decided that we ought to apply 'the method' to Saxon, to try and make him tear up and break through the veils of life. One evening after dining in Hall we began to apply the third-degree psychological investigation to him about half-past eight and continued uninterruptedly until five in the morning; when at last he staggered away to bed, we had successfully uncovered the soul of Saxon, but had disastrously confirmed him in the determination to stifle it in an infinite series of veils. Twenty five years later, I amused myself by writing 'characters' of some of my friends."

Among the 'characters' was Saxon Sydney-Turner, who in Leonard's account spun a great web around himself and when they broke it open there was nothing there. However, Saxon did well with his exams and entered the Foreign Office and eventually became far more of a rounded human being than either Lytton or Leonard, who eventually described himself as a caged panther unable to see beyond the bars of his cage – in other words, Leonard turned out to be very much like the image he had invented of Saxon.

'The method' was a form of psychological attack, or brainwashing, which involved putting a person in the wrong and refusing to believe them when they replied; challenging their defences with unremitting questions for hours until they cracked. And it was all being done to reveal the 'soul' of the victim. This was carried out by a couple of highly neurotic amateurs, Lytton and Leonard, who had set themselves up as the arbiters of sanity. Here is yet another triangle, this time a potentially deadly one, with Lytton as instigator, Leonard as eager supporter not taking full responsibility, and Saxon as victim – so much for the Trinity of Trinity.

That Leonard did not forget 'the method' is evident, since he attributed his success in Ceylon to its use. It was now employed not so much to reveal the 'soul' of his victim, as to make his superiors think he was 'nice,' becoming 'so good & kind to him' that they wanted to help him in his career. Perhaps he told Edgar about it during their tour and his brother remembered his sense of horror for the rest of his life.

When Leonard returned to England in August 1911, he brought back with him a psychological weapon that he had concocted in Cambridge and perfected in Ceylon: a method of manipulating other people to his advantage. For years he had practised his technique of 'silly intrigue & controlling a situation'. Now he, the wary wily fox, prepared to hunt Julia's little goat.

LYTTON STRACHEY AND CLIVE BELL CTITICISING WORKS OF ART;
A DRAWING BY HENRY LAMB

Chapter Three

TYING THE KNOT

On returning from his tour to Sweden with Edgar, in August 1911, Leonard Woolf stayed with his family in Colinette Road, Putney. His youngest siblings Clara, Flora, Cecil and Philip had become young women, young men, during the seven years he had been away in Ceylon and all of them wanted to talk and ask him questions. But so far as Leonard was concerned, nothing had changed. There they all were sitting in their accustomed places around the dining room table as though he had never been away. His mother still refused to accept the shadow of guilt he laid on her for her husband's death, with her slightly nasal voice talking about the neighbours! And the servants! When she spoke, the others quietened. They called her Lady. We know some of their conversation because Leonard used it in his second novel *The Wise Virgins*.

Eagerly his brothers and sisters begged him to tell them about Ceylon – the wild animals he had shot; galloping through the jungle; the way he had made the natives do his bidding, and his impressive Residency house in Hambantota. All of them hanging on his every word. Until he caught Edgar's eye, watching him silently. And he knew it wasn't real. None of it was real. He'd been acting a part, out there, had taken them all in, the fools! And here was Bella, his elder sister, corroborating everything he said, believing every word. She had visited him, she knew something of the conditions, the heat, the work he had to do. Was that real – or this? Or neither? He let her talk. Sat back. Looked, as so often before, at his grandfather's portrait on the wall above them: bewhiskered, dark, even more fierce than he remembered. After all, what had he really done? He still had five hundred pounds of his sweepstake money, and another five hundred saved from his salary – a mere thousand pounds, after seven years! Maybe both of them, he and his grandfather, alone of them all in this over-crowded room, were descended from Job. His eyes took on a glazed look, his mouth set as his mother droned on, and his arm trembled until they all heard his hand knocking against the wood under the table. He glanced at the soft painted face of his grandmother, then at his mother, the lines on her face heavier, indulgent, proud of her brood. They had good jobs, they were actively campaigning to get women the vote, the younger ones were almost left-wing – 'Haven't they done well, Len?' He looked quickly away and got up abruptly: their words, their half finished sentences, hanging off him like torn party decorations. He strode out of the room, out of the house, where the air was tepid, thin; a hint of autumn made him shiver as he walked the absurd little streets lined with redbrick houses, each with its gate and hedge and minuscule front garden, named, numbered, net curtains behind the windows shifting as the hidden inmates noted his homecoming. God! He'd got to get out of there! And then a story came to his mind.

He would write about Ceylon as if he were already looking back into a life that was past. He would write exactly 500 words every morning, counting every word; nobody must disturb him. He decided to become a novelist.

He returned to the house, his eyes bright now, his trembling hand more or less under control, and went up to his room where he meticulously laid out paper and pen. He would call his first book *The Village in the Jungle*.

No doubt Lytton had already given Leonard all the gossip concerning Virginia, her removal to Jean Thompson's nursing home in 1910 for a month's 'rest cure', and Vanessa's keenness to get her sister married. He would have heard of the Thursday evenings when the Group met at No. 38 Brunswick Square, the London home of Virginia and Adrian, and of the suddenly widened scope of their conversations after Lytton walked into the room one evening and saw Vanessa sitting apart. Lytton noticed a stain on her skirt, pointed to it and said the one word: 'Semen?' From that moment on, their talk was not confined to 'truth' and 'beauty', or even 'the nature of reality'. Sex was now on the conversational menu. He would have seen the grotesque figure of his friend lolling in his chair, his very long arms and legs straggling at every angle, and been partly relieved to think that he was not a rival in wooing Virginia; but he was also wary, he no longer wanted to be as close to Lytton as before.

Once he had obtained a position in the Group, what might he not achieve? If his efforts to become Virginia's husband failed, then he knew that he would have no alternative but to return to Ceylon at the end of his year's leave. He was becoming increasingly reluctant to do this, despite the fact that he would probably end up as a Governor with a knighthood, since he was beginning to question the very basis of imperi-

VIRGINIA AND LEONARD WOOLF AT ASHEHAM HOUSE

alism. Besides, if he returned, he would certainly have to marry the unhappy Gwen. For Leonard, the key to reaching his goal in England must be the wooing and winning of Virginia Stephen. This was not going to be easy. It had to be planned carefully, with the help of Vanessa; she was essential to his success. But Vanessa was still in Turkey where she had had a miscarriage; for a while after her return she was too ill to see him.

Here was another possible life opening to him, only he would have to work hard to achieve it. With so much at stake he felt daunted by the prospect of proposing marriage to Virginia. She had written to her sister on a previous occasion, when a young man was on the point of popping the question: 'I shall write with friendliness – but I have no discretion – no kind of instinct in me, such as most women have, in affairs of sex'. [1] Impatient whilst biding his time, he visited every friend he could think of. Also, he wanted to catch up with the many plays and concerts that were being performed in London where he found all the arts were enjoying a remarkable flowering.

There was no problem meeting Virginia. She took the initiative and wrote to 'Mr Wolfe' (her spelling) inviting him to Little Talland House, her holiday home in Firle, Sussex, for the weekend of 16 September, together with Desmond MacCarthy (who had recently begun his career in journalism) and Marjorie Strachey. She suggested they use Christian names and warned: 'This is not a cottage, but a hideous suburban villa – I have to prepare people for the shock.' To Desmond she wrote an easy, chatty letter:

"Is there any chance that you would come here for the weekend on the 16th? L. Woolf is coming, and Marjorie Strachey, I think... And all this time you have been earning your 16 pounds a week... It makes me feel a perfect amateur – sitting here before white sheets, every now and then chuckling at my own jokes–" [2]

Virginia was leading a pleasant and relaxed social life which included inviting a few of her friends for weekends to Firle. As a committed writer needing sympathetic support and loyalty to provide a peaceful background to her writing, her circle of women friends could be relied on. There were her ongoing friendships with Violet Dickinson, Janet Case and Jean Thomas, all of whom visited her. She also enjoyed staying in her house on her own. In April she wrote happily to Clive: 'I've seldom enjoyed myself more than I have this fortnight... Perhaps one's proud of being a self-sufficient animal... I've found a new walk every day.' [3]

The advent of Leonard changed all that. When he came, she felt his intense eyes trying to penetrate her light-hearted manner. Did she remember Lytton's description of him, recounted by Quentin Bell:

"Lytton Strachey said that he was like Swift and would murder his wife. He despised the whole human race. He trembled all over, he was so violent, so savage; he had pulled his thumb out of joint in a dream; he was, in short a serious and powerful figure." [4]

If so, she didn't let it trouble her. During that autumn she felt pleasantly challenged and awaited with some amusement the well-heralded proposal of this dark Jewish man who had managed to control single-handed a hundred thousand natives in Ceylon.

Virginia was also receiving the attentions of two other men, Sir Sydney Waterlow who was still married to his first wife when he proposed, and Walter Lamb, the elder brother of Henry Lamb, the artist who painted a memorable portrait of Lytton Strachey. So Leonard had rivals.

Having saved her life, Roger Fry brought the sick Vanessa back from Turkey. He had fallen deeply in love with her; but her own affairs did not prevent both Vanessa and Clive waging a campaign against Walter Lamb's attempts to woo Virginia. Lamb became justifiably worried that Virginia was living in the centre of intrigues and told her that 'Clive blackened you with bitternesses' for which she, no doubt correctly, blamed Vanessa, saying: 'Kiss my snout, beloved, you did tap it.' [5] This was her way of telling her elder sister off when she behaved high-handedly.

Leonard saw Virginia as a beautiful, ethereal, perhaps unreachable and untouchable vision, as she entertained her guests with wonderful flights of imagination, a musical laugh and high good humour. How was he, the 'poor Jew' ever to get beyond the overwhelming sense of awe she inspired in him, that filled his daydreams and haunted his nights? He had need of allies who must pave the way before he could begin to woo her. Lytton was still useful, despite his now very evident homosexuality of which Leonard disapproved, while from Lytton's account Vanessa would choke off any other applicants in order to marry her sister off to Leonard as she wanted to keep him in her orbit. These two formed a powerful team. During that autumn Leonard was content to let them make the running.

When Leonard went to see Vanessa in October, we know at least some of what they talked about since she described his visit in a letter to Clive:

"At this point Woolf appeared and I have had a long visit from him. He is of course very clever and from living in the wilds seems to me to have got a more interesting point of view than most of the 'set' who seldom produce anything new or original. He thinks we ought to visit the East. The colour is amazing and one's animal passions get very strong and one enjoys one's body to the full. We discussed our set and young Cambridge and the neo-pagans." [6]

In this letter Vanessa does not mention other subjects she would have discussed with Leonard, such as Thoby Stephen's death; while Virginia must have provided a major topic of their conversation. Vanessa may have told him about the fortune Virginia had inherited from her aunt. She would have made no secret of Virginia's periods of 'madness'. She probably gave Leonard advice as to how to deal with them in such terms as: 'She's been like that since she was a child. Thoby and I knew how to set her off. A lot of it is play-acting to get her own way, which I must admit irritates me. Watch out for the danger signs: headaches, sleeplessness, over-excitement. I tell her she must rest completely and drink plenty of milk until she recovers. If things get too bad I call in Dr Savage, her nerve doctor. If she is a "mad genius" she is the only one in the family. There aren't many men who could make a success of being her husband, but I think you might manage it.'

Although unsympathetic to Virginia's breakdowns, Vanessa, having succeeded in getting her own way, had helped Virginia to get back on her feet and live her own life again as soon as possible. Leonard would not behave like Vanessa; his perspective, and his motives, were different.

As they sat talking, Leonard watched Vanessa closely. This was the woman he had fallen in love with over seven years ago, when he saw her at that May Ball in Trinity. Now she was Bell's wife with two children. He was not a man to forgive Clive Bell for 'stealing' Vanessa while he was away; how he loathed and despised Clive, who was obviously not good enough for her. 'She is maternal – and desirable'. This is how he was soon to describe her in his second novel. He probably considered her the dominant woman in the Bloomsbury Group, and therefore she was not only desirable but valuable to him.

Aloud, he talked about Ceylon, about the brilliant colours – something he never permitted to get onto the pages of *The Village in the Jungle*, where all is half-dead from drought and menacing thorns – and how the body awoke in the heat. And about the 'degraded' colonials. Then he would stare unblinking at her with his intense, bright-dark eyes, a true practitioner of his 'method' and watch her respond, watch her think:

'Woolf is lean and strong and dark and a little wild, just the opposite of Clive; we mustn't let him go back to Ceylon.'

"I shall have to go back to Ceylon after my year's leave," he said slowly, aloud, looking at her.

'I must get Virginia to marry him, so that he'll stay,' she thought.

And so they reached a most gratifying understanding. She told him about Rupert Brooke and the Neo-Pagans, as the Bloomsbury Group called this new, informal group of young people who went camping, swam naked together and were vegetarians. Virginia had joined them that August, bathing naked with Rupert Brooke who was famous for getting an erection in cold water. Lytton had found camping far too uncomfortable. The Neo-Pagans were heterosexual and disliked the Apostles' insufferable aura of superiority; also their Cambridge background and their homosexuality. Ka Cox was a Neo-Pagan – a no-nonsense young woman who from this time became friends with Virginia and, in 1913, would save her life.

In November 1911, Virginia and Adrian moved into a larger house in Bloomsbury: No. 38 Brunswick Square, where they lived and let out rooms to Maynard Keynes and Duncan Grant on a friendly share-alike basis. In December, Leonard took the top floor and thus became a lodger in Virginia's London house, where he could meet his quarry frequently.

Leonard began idealising Virginia as Aspasia, the foreign woman whom Pericles, his Greek idol, took as his mistress. (See *Appendix A* for details of their story.) Aspasia was admired by the great names of Leonard's beloved Athenians, with Menexenus saying: 'Truly Socrates, I marvel that Aspasia, who is only a woman, should be able to compose such a speech, she must be a rare one'. [7] We must not laugh.

Spater and Parsons help us to gain a valuable insight into the image Leonard had of Aspasia-Virginia at this time, by including in their book a personal account he wrote of her and then watched as she read it in front of the fire:

"I am in love with Aspasia... When I think of Aspasia I think of hills, standing very clear but distant against a cold blue sky; there is snow upon them which no sun has ever melted & no man has ever trodden. But the sun too is in her hair, in the red & the gold of her skin, in the glow of her lips & in the glow of her mind. And most wonderful of all is her voice which seems to bring things from the centre of rocks, deep streams that have lain long in primordial places beneath the earth. To drink once is to be intoxicated for ever. Whether she is walking or sitting there is always about her an air of quiet & clearness, but to think of her is to see her sitting, lying back in immense chairs before innumerable fires...

I see her sitting among it all untouched in her quietness & clearness rather silent a little aloof & then the spring bubbles up – is it wit or humour or imagination? I do not know but the thought has come from strange recesses, life for a moment seems to go faster, you feel for a moment the blood in your wrists, your heart beat, you catch your breath as you do on a mountain when suddenly the wind blows. The things that come are strange often fantastic, but they are beautiful & always seem somewhere far below to have touched even to have been torn from reality. Perhaps this is because her mind is so astonishingly fearless, there is no fact & no reality which it does not face, touch frankly openly. She is one of possibly three women who know that dung is merely dung, death death & semen semen. She is the most Olympian of the Olympians. And that is why perhaps she seems to take life too hardly. She does not really know the feeling – which alone saves the brain & the body – that after all nothing matters. She asks too much from the earth & from the people who crawl about it. I am always frightened that with her eyes fixed on the great rocks she will stumble among the stones.

'And her heart?' You ask. Sometimes I think she has not got one, that she is really interested in what will happen & in reality, that she is made from the eternal snow & the rocks which form the hidden centre of reality. And then I swear that this cannot be true, that the sun in her comes from a heart."

Virginia's reaction to this was recorded by Leonard:

"I showed Aspasia her character as I had written it. She read it slowly in front of the fire. I forgot she was reading it in the pleasure of watching her face & her hair: she must have been silent thinking for some time when I heard her say: 'I don't think you have made me soft or lovable enough'." [8]

Already there is a difference of perception between them. Whereas Leonard put Virginia, as Aspasia, among the Olympians in his Greek cosmology and saw her as a distant mountain top that he planned to climb, Virginia felt herself as lovable; she craved affection, devotion and support and gave herself the names of furry animals when writing to those she loved. The contrast between the cold top of a high mountain, and the immediacy of a soft furry animal is very great; indeed, it could not be greater.

I found a particular point of interest when I looked up Aspasia and Pericles in my leather-bound Smith's Classical Dictionary, (see *Appendix A*) and found that Pericles, who was active around 450 years BCE, was already a major figure in Athens, with a wife and two children, when he took as his mistress the 'outsider' and foreign woman Aspasia. Thus in Leonard's fantasy, his and Virginia's roles are reversed: the socially secure and somewhat elitist Virginia, as Aspasia, becomes the outsider who is dependent upon the great Pericles. It is important to realise that at this early stage in their relationship the almost penniless Leonard-as-Pericles gives himself a dominant position over Virginia-Aspasia. Thus in fantasy he overrides her in the very areas where in real life his position is inferior to hers – in social and financial status.

At night Leonard would lie half-awake in bed and dream his Greek dream. But we would be mistaken if we were to equate Aspasia with his anima, since we are at one remove upward: Aspasia was the anima of Pericles and so the earthly Leonard experienced 'love' at one remove both from himself and from Virginia. The original Aspasia was a high-class prostitute who would have been well versed in sexual stimulants and variants. If this was the vision Leonard thought he was marrying in Virginia then the reality, the 'frigid woman' whom he encountered on his honeymoon, must have come all the more of a shock to him.

Locked in his carapace, the hermit crab felt agonising passion fuelled by testosterone: but his inflamed feelings had little or nothing to do with Virginia herself, as a person, as she later began to realise. This whole performance was to be repeated, often with the same phrases used, at slightly less intensity when he became obsessed with Trekkie thirty years later – he even called Trekkie, Aspasia. The point is that Leonard never did change.

At this time Virginia gave up her house in Firle, having discovered Asheham House splendidly isolated under its chalk down. She shared the lease (she would have paid most of it) with Vanessa. Its regular facade with three upper-storey stone mullion windows and central front door, with a small gabled building on either side of the main building, gave Asheham House a classic beauty which delighted her. If anywhere, Virginia found her heart in this place. Here she could let her flights of fancy roam in the company of invited friends or, relaxing away from the excitements of London, she could go for long walks on the downs thinking about her book. She was envisaging a less structured life with few or no servants, although she had no intention of becoming a complete bohemian beyond the socially accepted boundaries, as Vanessa was already doing. Vanessa was writing affectionate letters to Roger Fry; soon they would be involved in a passionate affair.

George Bernard Shaw later wrote to Virginia telling her that Asheham House had inspired his play *Heartbreak House*. In Shaw's play, set just before the first world war, his characters have an unconventional, post-Victorian attitude to life and the formal relationship between servants and their employers is breaking down. There are two dominant sisters who can be broadly recognised as Vanessa and Virginia; but he, like Leonard in *The Village in the Jungle,* had to include a father – their necessary masculine 'I' figure; neither man could see the women as they were, without a dominant male of any sort, either father or brother. Although Shaw's two sisters are very different from Leonard's, reflecting the differences between the two men, in both Leonard's novel and Bernard Shaw's play we can recognise the originals. For good measure we have an off-stage Leonard-figure in Shaw's play. In Leonard's book there is a sincere Thoby-like young man who dies of typhoid fever.

Leonard's book tells the story of a village that dies and is overrun by the surrounding jungle; the jungle itself is a death force, grey and full of thorns, a place of starvation and overwhelming fear, the fear that he himself must have felt when he rode through Hambantota district, in the extreme south of the island, from one village to another.

An interesting aspect of his book is that the (twin) sisters, with their father, are members of the Vedda tribe, the original inhabitants of Ceylon. They are social outcasts, to be feared and reviled as devil-worshippers when disasters come upon the village. The sisters' father, a hunter and Leonard's chief 'I' figure in the book, is a Job character who loses everything. When he realises that the village head and the visiting moneylender have been plotting against him, he takes his gun and shoots them both; whereupon a surprisingly kindly British legal system commutes his death sentence for double murder to 20 years in gaol, as though the author could not bear to kill his alter ego. But he has no hesitation about killing the young Virginia-figure, who is described as 'mad'. Indeed, he lavishes every care on writing the scene where she watches the villagers stone her pet (male) deer to death, after which:

"She lay in the house, silent, resigned to die. She had even ceased to think or feel now. Life had no more hold upon her, and in the hour before dawn in deep sleep she allowed it to slip gently from her." [9]

Thus Leonard consigns his Virginia-figure to madness and an early death in his book, which never actually recovers from her loss, while the litany of misfortune and death continues. Her baby daughter, together with all the children in the village, had already died of fever. Eventually, only the Vanessa-sister survives (her child, too, has died) to become the last inhabitant of the village, existing alone in her crumbling hut as the jungle encroaches:

"In the day the hot air eddied through the hut, hot with the breath of the wind blowing over the vast parched jungle; at night she shivered in the chill dew. She was dying, and the jungle knew it; it is always waiting; can scarcely wait for death. When the end was close upon her a great black shadow glided into the doorway. Two little eyes twinkled at her steadily, two immense white tusks curled up gleaming against the darkness. She sat up, fear came upon her, the fear of the jungle, blind agonising fear... As she fell back, the great boar grunted softly, and glided like a shadow towards her into the hut." [10]

Leonard does not tell us that the Vedda's social customs are matrilineal, part of the old order, before patriarchal men took over as the dominant sex and alienated human beings from the rest of nature. If he had written his book from the point of view of the two women rather than their father, his story would have been more balanced and interesting. However, the fact that he sympathised with the Vedda, even as doomed people, shows he had moved beyond the imperial assumption that 'natives' could be treated as 'boys' to do the white man's bidding, and hanged if they transgressed his laws.

The overall effect of *The Village in the Jungle* is of extreme negativism in which the author evidently takes a perverse pleasure in controlling the lives and deaths of his characters. Where King Midas turned everything he touched to gold, Leonard turned everything he touched to aridity – dust, ashes, death – with another old man preaching fatalism, 'nothing matters'. Bernard Shaw did give his two sisters pride of place, with their father a doddering, dramatically effective old drunk; but neither he nor Leonard could envisage a true matriarchy. Seeing through the other eye, discovering the female truth, was left to Virginia Woolf and it took her a life-time to do so.

On the 7th of January Leonard recorded that he helped Virginia do her accounts, during which he must have discovered a great deal more about her financial affairs. He then went to visit a friend (rather improbably the

Vicar of Frome) in Somerset and from there, in a state of turmoil inspired, perhaps, equally by her beauty, her money, and the fear that she might accept Walter Lamb, sent her a telegram: 'I must see you for an hour tomorrow... if I can come to Brunswick Square 1.15 can I see you then. Leonard.'

The next day there took place a scene between Virginia Stephen and Leonard Woolf that we need to try and envisage, since it set the tone of their future relationship. Our guidelines as to what occurred are given in the long, self-justifying letters he wrote to her immediately afterwards and Virginia's cool replies; together with Vanessa's letter giving Leonard her complete support. We can recreate the scene:

On arrival, Leonard launched himself into a pleading frenzy. He knew he wasn't nearly good enough and he had so many faults he had decided never to marry anyone – he was cruel and mean and beastly and a liar – and she was so extraordinarily beautiful, that was it, beautiful. So beautiful. And untouchable. Like a snow-covered mountain. He was Pericles and she was the beautiful Aspasia, so beautiful – he could hardly say the words he had rehearsed to himself in the train, as the thought of actually having to penetrate her virginity made him tremble uncontrollably. Instead of grabbing the adored object in his arms and planting burning kisses on her upturned face (as P.G. Wodehouse was to recommend) Leonard relied on speech and words quite literally failed him. He had such a fixed idea, such a high ideal, of what he wanted to say but what came out was an irritable complaint. He had spent four hours in the train just to propose to her! He was an outsider! He was a penniless Jew! She must accept him! He grovelled, furiously, at her feet while Virginia looked down at him. Cold, indifferent. How could she love this – creature? She called him a wolf because of his name, but he was really a much smaller animal with his piercing bright eyes fixed on her. What had become of the husband she had imagined during those inspiring talks with Vanessa as they walked in the early autumn, discussing their future? That wonderful husband, who would give her everything she wanted including a child? A kindly man who got on with his life whilst she fulfilled her destiny as a famous writer? He was impossible to recognise in this little quivering figure who put her on a pedestal one minute and blamed her the next. Maybe Walter Lamb – what a choice, the wolf or the lamb! – she didn't know whether to laugh or cry. Only her schooling as a young woman at the family tea-table prevented her doing both. She tried to tell him that she too had faults, she was unsure of her own feelings, they were

so changeable; and she certainly wasn't Aspasia, she was a bag of monkeys –
he interrupted her, he hadn't listened. He needed an intelligent wife. With
her, he could be a novelist, writing 500 words every day. He recommended
that. She must write, too, after all, she had the advantage of her social background, her literary father. If she refused him, he would have to go back to
Ceylon and it would be her fault – he glared just like a mongoose! That was
it! Suddenly her calm broke and she laughed her mocking, musical laugh at
the absurdity of the scene they were both playing. But which of them was
the prey? Which the predator?

At this moment, in the silence, as words of dismissal trembled on her
lips that would have turned the gap between them into an unbridgeable
chasm, Walter Lamb walked in. Leonard scrambled up. He hastily retreated to the other side of the room and left soon afterwards to catch his
train, maintaining an air of shattered dignity as befits an Apostle who was
really Pericles, that great Athenian orator, in disguise.

Virginia recounted her version of the disaster to Vanessa, hoping for
sympathy, but as she was telling it she laughed and cried and Vanessa was
very annoyed with her, then promptly got in touch with Dr. Savage who
ordered complete rest at home. That same evening, from Somerset,
Leonard sent his first letter:

"I must write to you before I go to bed & can, I think, probably think
more calmly. I have not got any very clear recollection of what I really
said to you this afternoon but I am sure you know why I came – I dont
mean merely that I was in love but that that together with uncertainty
drives one to do these things. God, I hope I shall never spend such a time
again as I spent here until I telegraphed... I knew you would tell me
exactly what you felt. You were exactly what I knew you are & if I hadn't
been in love before, I would now. It isnt, really it isnt, merely because you
are so beautiful – though of course that is a large reason & so it should be
– that I love you: it is your mind & your character – I have never known
anyone like you in that – won't you believe that?

And now, I will do absolutely whatever you want. I dont think you
want me to go away, but if you did, I would at once. If not, I dont see
why we cannot go on the same as before – I think I can – and then if you
do find that you could love me you would tell me.

I hardly know whether I am saying what I mean or feel. I am extraordinarily tired. A dense mist covered the whole of Somerset & the train was
late & I had to crawl my way from the station for 3 miles to the house.

Don't you think that the entrance of Walter almost proves the existence of a deity?" [11]

Virginia replied with a cool, brief note: 'There isn't really anything for me to say, except that I should like to go on as before; and that you should leave me free, and that I should be honest. As for faults, I expect mine are just as bad – less noble perhaps. But of course they are not really the question. I have decided to keep this completely secret, except for Vanessa; and I have made her promise not to tell Clive.' [12]

She wrote rather desperately to Violet Dickinson: 'Do come to tea on Friday... I now live like the Tortoise in the zoo – once a day I make an excursion for food – otherwise sleep. But as you know, there was once a sleeping beauty, and some have been kind enough to hint – in short, I have no objection to being kissed.' [13]

In her following letter, to Katherine (Ka) Cox, whom she called the bear, or Bruin, she reveals why she calls herself and her friends animal names: 'you can't think how essential you are to the proper aspect of things; that is why animals are made; to balance human beings.' But she continues, using emphasis that is rare in her letters: 'the accounts from the zoo are *thoroughly satisfactory*. They've come to the stage, I am told, when *they must be taught habits*; and you know how important this is, so come back on that account.' [14]

Vanessa had evidently told Virginia off severely, as she realised that her carefully planned solution to the problem of what to do about her sister, together with her desire to keep Leonard in England, was in danger of falling apart; she immediately wrote to Leonard, doing her best to repair the damage:

"I am writing to tell you that Virginia has told me about her talk with you and also to say how glad I shall be if you can have what you want. You're the only person I know whom I can imagine as her husband, which may seem a rash remark, considering how little I know you. However I have faith in my instincts, at any rate as far as they imply what I think of you. Besides that, which perhaps isn't very important, I shall be so glad if you dont go back to Ceylon. It seems absurd that we shouldn't get the benefit of your existence." [15]

The following day, Virginia received Leonard's next missive:

"I can try & write about what, with you sitting there, it was so difficult to discuss calmly & dispassionately... it would be worth the risk of everything to marry you. That of course – from your side – was the question you were continually putting yesterday & which probably you ought to. Being outside the ring of fire, you should be able to decide far better than I inside it. God, I see the risk in marrying anyone & certainly me. I am selfish, jealous, cruel, lustful, a liar & probably worse still. I had said over & over again to myself that I would never marry anyone because of this, mostly because, I think, I felt I could never control these things with a woman who was inferior & would gradually infuriate me by her inferiority & submission... It is because you aren't that the risk is so infinitely less. You may be vain, an egoist, untruthful as you say, but they are nothing compared to your other qualities: magnificence, intelligence, wit, beauty, directness. After all too we like one another, we like the same kinds of things & people, we are both intelligent & above all it is realities which we understand & which are important for us." [16]

Leonard continued to plead his cause on paper with such passionate intensity that Virginia became over-stressed. To save herself, she wrote urgently to her women friends asking them to come and see her. She was evidently making a desperate attempt to maintain her autonomy in spite of Leonard's epistolatory onslaughts, which owe a great deal to 'the method' as he included her in his view of their relationship. He did not simply intend to marry her, but insisted on possessing her completely; whereas she wanted to be certain that he was in love with her so that she had the necessary support to get on with her writing. This question as to who would love the most, and who would captain the ship, became a dangerous source of tension in their relationship.

Virginia invited Leonard to Asheham House early in February, together with Adrian and Marjorie Strachey. The place was extremely cold and uncomfortable, without carpets or sanitation. If he had held any hopes of romance with 'Aspasia' on that occasion they were rudely shattered when she consulted him about where they should build an earth closet in the garden, a scene she recalls in her last completed book, *Between the Acts*. Whatever happened during this visit (apart from Marjorie's fear that she was going to get chicken pox), it was too much for Virginia, she was unable to sleep and, from being a semi-invalid at home, Dr. Savage once more ordered a fortnight's enforced rest in Jean Thomas's nursing home at Twickenham, while Leonard was told that he must neither visit her nor write to her. She wrote to Violet Dickinson shortly before being incarcerated:

"We went to Asheham on Saturday – my God! What a day: all pipes frozen; grates with false bottoms; no E.Cs... However, it was great fun... I am now rampant, feeding on bullocks blood and henbane; or the heads of red poppies, which make me dream wild dreams – about you, and alabaster pillars, and dogs defiling them." [17]

Evidently the 'heads of red poppies' were part of her medication, under whose influence she dreamed of (male) dogs defiling alabaster pillars.

Leonard spent a second weekend at Asheham House in Virginia's absence, when he helped Vanessa, Clive and Adrian to lay carpets. A major topic of conversation was the prospect of Leonard having to return to Ceylon in May at the end of his year's leave. Vanessa no doubt once more took charge of her sister's matrimonial affairs, promising him total support while she gave him comfort and reassurance. So the conspiracy to keep him in England was being put into action and any hope Walter Lamb had of marrying Virginia was finally squashed, the victim of Bloomsbury Group intrigue.

Leonard was amazed how like Thoby Vanessa looked, while Vanessa also told him he reminded her of her dead brother. He decided to take a few painting lessons. Vanessa evidently succeeded in her self-appointed task of reassuring Leonard. On returning to London he wrote to the Colonial Secretary for an extension to his leave; he also sent some of Lytton's letters and manuscripts to Virginia, from which she understood a great deal more about the Apostles. She wrote to him from the nursing home:

"I shall tell you wonderful stories of the lunatics. By the bye, they've elected me King... I summoned a conclave, and made a proclamation about Christianity... I avoided both love and hatred. I now feel very clear, calm, and move slowly, like one of the great big animals at the zoo. Knitting is the saving of life... Today Lytton came to tea, and was very charming and amenable to all the strictures I made about Cambridge life and [The Apostles]. He practically agreed with me that the Hearthrug was rotten, and the whales a-stink." [18]

The Hearthrug and the whales were two of the rituals involved in membership of the secret society. Leonard had to put up with having that sacred cow derided by Virginia. As always when she was experiencing her other reality, getting in touch with herself, there are sexual overtones; this time, she says she will spend five shillings 'on chocolates and a sleeping draught, if the shops are open, and I escape molestation. I shan't want the sleeping draught – in any case.'

This wasn't the sort of letter Leonard really wanted to receive from his future wife, except that it could be used later, if necessary, to prove her 'madness'. Already, Leonard is likely to have realised that his own reluctance to have children could be attributed to Virginia's supposed unsuitability as a mother; and that meant, in those days of uncertain birth-control measures, that there would not be so much emphasis on sex. He firmly believed that letting mad people breed was a threat to the future of the human race, and equated madness with decadence and barbarism.

Despite this drawback (or possibly partly because of it) Leonard remained committed to marrying Virginia, who could still provide the money and lifestyle he wanted. As the weeks went by and he was not allowed to press Virginia for an answer, other members of the Bloomsbury Group were told of his efforts to marry her and she was being blamed for not making up her mind and for causing him difficulties over his career. In March Virginia was once more living at 38 Brunswick Square, a 'semi-invalid life'. She writes to Desmond MacCarthy's wife Molly:

"I didn't mean to make you think that I was against marriage. Of course I'm not, though the extreme safeness and sobriety of young couples does appall me, but then so do the random melancholy of old maids. I began life with a tremendous, absurd, ideal of marriage, then my bird's eye view of many marriages disgusted me, and I thought I must be asking what was not to be had. But that has passed too. Now I only ask for someone to make me vehement, and then I'll marry him!... I feel oddly vehement, and very exacting, and so difficult to live with and so very intemperate and changeable, now thinking one thing and now another. But in my heart I always expect to be floated over all crises, when the moment comes, and landed heaven knows where! I don't really worry about W[Woolf]: though I think I made out that I did. He is going to stay longer anyhow, and perhaps he will stay in England anyhow, so the responsibility is lifted off me.

No, I shan't float into a bloodless alliance with Lytton – though he is in some ways perfect as a friend, only he's a female friend... I am now leading a semi-invalid life, and it is very nice, when the days are fine, doesn't that sound old!... Please go on being my friend, whatever I take it into my head to do." [19]

She again contacted her women friends, including Ka Cox, suggesting pleasant excursions: 'What I should like would be a great deal of eating in 18th Century houses by the river side, then a walk among daffodils and small blue flowers. Then more eating, this time in a great Inn on a hill with bow windows, where there is a nightingale outside.' [20] And describes her sister: 'Vanessa's character remains very hard, and calculated to outlast the sphinx'. [21]

Leonard wrote to the Colonial Secretary asking for a four-month extension to his leave, but when he was asked to give a reason for his request he refused and simply renewed his demand:

"In continuation of my letter of 30th April, I think upon consideration that I would prefer not to state more exactly the nature of my private affairs & that my resignation should be accepted." [22]

The last thing Leonard wanted was to be granted an extension of time, which would have relaxed the vice-like grip in which he and Vanessa held Virginia. Her escape into the nursing home may have provided her with a breathing space but any sense of freedom was both temporary and illusory, since it gave him time to mount his forces. The doubt about his return to Ceylon was precisely what put him at an advantage over her. As the days passed the feeling of urgency about coming to a decision increased; while, thanks to the efforts of Lytton and Vanessa spreading the word, he was backed by more and more of their friends. Virginia invited him to Asheham House, together with Vanessa and – not Clive, but Roger Fry. During this visit she told her sister she probably wouldn't marry anyone at all, and that she wanted to go on writing her novel, *The Voyage Out*. This coolness on her part drew a long, agonised letter from Leonard on his return to London: he still found it so much easier to write to her than plead his cause in person. He had read some of her work for the first time and he starts off with a remarkably high-handed comment which shows his judgmental arrogance – as though he is the professional writer and she the mere student:

"Dearest Virginia, I cant sleep not from desire but from thinking about you... I've read two of your MSS from one of which at any rate one can see that you might write something astonishingly good. I want to see you and talk with you & now, though I suppose I shouldn't, I'm going to write utterly miserable what I should want to say to you & probably couldn't.

Since yesterday something seemed to rise up in you against me. It may be imagination on my part; if it is, you must forgive me: I dont think even you realize what it would mean to me. God, the happiness I've had by being with you & talking with you as I've sometimes felt it mind to mind & soul to soul. I know clearly enough what I feel for you. It is not only physical love though it is that of course & I count it the least part of it, it isn't only that I'm happy with you, that I want to live with you; it's that I want your love too. It's true that I'm cold & reserved to other people; I dont feel affection ever easily: but apart from love I'm fond of you as I've never been of anyone or thing in the world. We often laugh about your lovableness but you don't know how lovable you are. it's what really keeps me awake far more than any desire. It's what worries me now, tears me two ways sometimes – for I wouldn't have you marry me, much as I love you, if I thought that it would bring you any unhappiness. Really this is true though it hurt me more than the worst physical pain your mere words that you told Vanessa that you probably would never marry anyone... I believe I know how you feel now & one should speak out what one thinks. I should like to say it to you, only when I'm with you all sorts of feelings make it so difficult to say exactly what I mean – so it's a good thing perhaps that I am writing to you... I dont think much of the physical part of it though it must come in – but it's so elusive. If one happens to be born as I am, it is almost certain to be very strong, but even then it becomes merged with one's other feelings. It was the least strong of my feelings for you when I fell in love & when I first told you. It has grown far more violent as my other feelings have grown stronger. I think we're reaching a point at which everything will tremble in the balance. Sometimes I suppose you don't know exactly what you feel & really unimportant things become magnified. I have faults, vices, beastlinesses but even with them I do believe you ought to marry me & be in love – & it isn't only because so often I feel that if you never are, the best thing in life will have gone. I shall never be like you, never anything like it, but you seem to purge my faults from me. And I have the fire in me at any rate & the knowledge. I want to live & get the best things in life & so do you. You are the best thing in life & to live it with you would make it ten thousand times more worth living. I shall never be content now with the second best." [23]

He is hammering at her, beating a tattoo as though Virginia, of all people, is blind and deaf. She recognises that his career is in danger but refuses to accept responsibility for this, replying on 1 May from Asheham House: 'You can't take the leave, I suppose if you are going to resign cer-

tainly at the end of it. Anyhow, it shows what a career you are ruining!'
She then continues:

"Well then, as to all the rest. It seems to me that I am giving you a great
deal of pain – some in the most casual way – and therefore I ought to be as
plain with you as I can, because half the time I suspect, you're in a fog
which I don't see at all. Of course I can't explain what I feel – these are
some of the things that strike me. The obvious advantages of marriage
stand in my way, I say to myself. Anyhow, you'll be quite happy with him;
and he will give you companionship, children, and a busy life – then I say
By God, I will not look upon marriage as a profession. The only people
who know of it, all think it suitable and that makes me scrutinise my own
motives all the more. Then, of course, I feel angry sometimes at the
strength of your desire. Possibly, your being a Jew comes in also at this
point. You seem so foreign. And then I am fearfully unstable. I pass from
hot to cold in an instant, without any reason; except that I believe sheer
physical effort and exhaustion influence me. All I can say is that in spite of
these feelings which go chasing each other all day long when I am with
you, there is some feeling which is permanent, and growing. You want to
know of course whether it will ever make me marry you. How can I say? I
think it will, because there seems no reason why it shouldn't – But I don't
know what the future will bring. I'm half afraid of myself. I sometimes
feel that no one ever has or ever can share something – Its the thing that
makes you call me like a hill, or a rock. Again, I want everything – love,
children, adventure, intimacy, work... So I go from being half in love with
you, and wanting you to be with me always, and know everything about
me, to the extreme of wildness and aloofness. I sometimes think that if I
married you, I could have everything – and then – is it the sexual side of it
that comes between us? As I told you brutally the other day, I feel no
physical attraction in you. There are moments – when you kissed me the
other day was one – when I feel no more than a rock. And yet your caring
for me as you do almost overwhelms me. It is so real, and so strange. Why
should you? What am I really except a pleasant attractive creature? But its
just because you care so much that I feel I've got to care before I marry
you. I feel I must give you everything; and that if I can't, well, marriage
would only be second-best for you as well as for me... We both of us want
a marriage that is a tremendous living thing, always alive, always hot, not
dead and easy in parts as most marriages are. We ask a great deal of life,
don't we? Perhaps we shall get it; then, how splendid!

One doesn't get much said in a letter does one? I haven't touched upon the enormous variety of things that are happening here – but they can wait." [24]

This is a crucial letter, since it decided Leonard to resign his career. Virginia evidently thinks she has regained her autonomy but her words show she has very little understanding of Leonard. She is treating him as an adult: reasonable, honest, sincere, well-intentioned. Whereas he wanted to possess her utterly, she needed space both for her sanity and her creativity. She also assumes she will have children and I think that Leonard had already decided against this: the very fact that he wanted to marry a gentile would have been part of his reluctance to become a father. If Leonard had been honest he would have written back explaining that he didn't want children. But he didn't do this. Denial of children was one of the tragedies of Virginia's life and later she realised that she had been cheated. Her letter reads far more responsibly, and truer, than Leonard's, because she had no axe to grind. She seems to be unaware of the dangers of being burnt by his ring of fire, his unquenchable flame, and at this stage is still confident that she will be able to make her own choices, because he 'cares' for her so much. But she does not feel any physical attraction for him – a potentially disastrous situation. She says she is 'half afraid of myself'. Actually, she should have realised that she was very afraid of him, and she was right to be. She could not recognise this because there seemed to be no reason for such a feeling. All she knows is that she wants to feel 'vehement' about a man and Leonard does not make her feel vehement.

Leonard was busily acquiring a valuable new shell to replace the carapace of his position in Ceylon. Possibly if he had actually been what he seemed, Virginia, paradoxically, would not have married him – or any man. The price she paid for doing so was enormous, and her first payment was immediate. In May, they began playing their game of animals, as the Stephen family had always done and especially Virginia. But now it was serious. In order to make sense of her suppressed fear of Leonard she saw him not as a man but as a Mongoose – an outwardly soft and furry creature but in reality sharp, bright-eyed, determined, and deadly to snakes because of its ability to dodge and pounce at lightning speed. She had recently been a whole lot of small playful monkeys, now she would be one large one. She visited the zoo and saw him – a Mandrill, the giant baboon with a brightly coloured snout and an obscene, swollen red and blue bottom. In this way she silenced her inner, warning voices and refused to acknowledge Leonard's as yet hidden but increasing power over her. Mongoose and Mandrill from now on formed the basis of their private world. Leonard's method was working; to his delight, he had nearly gained his objective – everything was as he had planned from the outset:

"Dearest & most beloved of all creatures! Have you ever had a letter beginning like that? At any rate you never have had one in which the words were so near the truth of the writer's feelings – or rather so far below them... I believe if ever you got to have a grain or particle of love for me, I shall be happy for the rest of my life. You don't know what a wave of happiness comes over me when I see you smile & the tone, I always hope for, of happiness comes into your voice – as it does when the sad & worried moods are chased out. God how I wish, I never caused them & that they could be chased out for ever. I must post this now. I hope the Mandril* went to its box early & isnt worried by anything in the world. The end is as the beginning was & it always will be, that's for me the dearest & most beloved creature in the world." [25]

Considering the determination with which she had promoted their alliance, Vanessa was surprisingly disconcerted when she saw them together. She wrote to Virginia on 2 May 1912:

"Well, I'm afraid I was very inexpressive today, but although I had expected it, it was somehow so bewildering and upsetting when I did actually see you and Leonard together that I didn't know how to say what I felt. You do know, however, Billy, and Leonard too, that I do of course care for you. I won't say more than for anybody, but in a way that's quite special to you. Your happiness does matter to me and I do now feel quite happy about you, which really means that I think Leonard one of the most remarkable and charming people I know. I am looking forward very much to having him as a brother-in-law.

Goodnight, my dear couple, before I get too doddering. It's a great blessing to think how happy you are. It does make the whole difference to one's life, doesn't it?" [26]

On the same day Leonard wrote to Lytton Strachey:

"Do you remember the year in which I was going to justify myself & my method of dealing with life? 1935 was it? I feel somehow that I've

---

* Leonard spells Mandrill with one 'l'.

done it in 1912 or at any rate life's justified itself to me. Virginia is going to marry me. I'm so happy that that's the only thing that I can say to you, simply that I am. Lord, it is difficult to put one's happiness into words & it was so damned easy to put the miseries of life into them from Ceylon. At any rate after 13 years & the silences in them, youre the person I turn to first in the world and try to tell you of either." [27]

Leonard thus admits that he had used his 'method of dealing with life' to conquer Virginia. In doing so, he may have been living in his 'ring of fire' but somewhere within the ring – or outside it – he was calculating his next move. His letters to her were part of a preconceived plan, which only Lytton knew about – he therefore wanted Lytton to be aware that his method had succeeded once more, as it succeeded in Ceylon; he would go on and use it again and again. Leonard's marriage to Virginia was only a means to an end, not the end in itself. Of this, Virginia had not the least conscious idea, but in her second novel she works through her deep feelings of doubt, as she wonders who it is that Leonard thought he had married? Lytton, busy with a love affair with Walter Lamb's younger brother Henry, had observed proceedings from a distance. He wrote to Ottoline Morrell after he heard their news:

"I've not seen either of them yet; but I know that he's in ecstasies of happiness. He had to besiege her a good deal before she accepted him. I feel rather a fool because I kept urging him to propose, while he was doing it all the time... There's a story that a week or two before the engagement he proposed in a train, and she accepted him, but owing to the rattling of the carriage he didn't hear, and took up a newspaper, saying 'What?' On which she had a violent revulsion and replied 'Oh, nothing!'" [28]

The next stage in Leonard's campaign was to get Virginia to write to her friends and relatives in a way that would enhance his importance. Her early letters giving her news do not do this, and he evidently criticised them. When Virginia wrote to Violet Dickinson, her tone is apologetic:

"I've got a confession to make. I am going to marry Leonard Wolf [sic]. He's a penniless Jew. I am more happy than anyone ever said was possible – but I insist upon your liking him too... He was a great friend of Thoby's, went out to India... You have always been such a splendid and delightful creature, whom I've loved ever since I was a mere chit, that I couldn't bear it if you disapproved of my husband... My novels just upon finished, L. thinks my writing the best part of me... the one thing that must be made plain is my intense feeling of affection for you. How I've bothered you – and what a lot you've always given me." [29]

She adds: 'my novel is getting on, in spite of interruptions, and L. wants me to say that if I cease to write when married, I shall be divorced.' [30]

I personally find that remark of Leonard's, apparently encouraging, actually intrusive since it takes over her initiative. The question of what effect, direct and indirect, Leonard had on her writing is a major study that has not yet been undertaken.

In the final chapters of her novel *The Voyage Out,* the Virginia-figure dies. Trevor, sitting by Rachel's death-bed, says: 'No two people have ever been so happy as we have been. No one has ever loved as we have loved.' [31] This was Leonard's impossible standard that he set for Virginia to live up to as the price she paid for marrying him. She quotes it in one of her suicide letters in 1941, as much as to say – 'I've tried my best'. And his response was in the last line of the note he wrote on the afternoon of her death that was found, crumpled and hidden, among his effects after his own death in 1969: 'There is no limit to one's stupidity & selfishness.'

Back in 1912, Virginia wrote to her Greek teacher and friend Janet Case:

"I want to tell you that I'm going to marry Leonard Wolf [*sic*] – he is a penniless Jew. He was a friend of Thoby's, – and I'm so happy – Its not at all what people say, but so much better. I dont think I'm nearly worth what he is. May we come and see you... I want you to like him. It has been worth waiting for." [32]

And a quick note to Lytton:

"Ha! Ha!

Virginia Stephen

Leonard Woolf." [33]

But the headaches and sleeplessness begin again. After her first visit to Leonard's family, she confesses to Violet Dickinson: 'My head goes on aching stupidly... Work and love and Jews in Putney take it out of me'. [34] She then gets down to the serious business of repeating impressive – and enhanced – stories of Leonard's life in Ceylon, rather as Desdemona might have retold Othello's stories. The writing is the pen of Virginia but the voice is the voice of Leonard. She is doing her best to compensate Leonard for giving up his career for her sake. That he made that choice is forgotten. She carries an unaccustomed burden of guilt and apologises for

herself, while promoting him, writing a series of letters that she says are
'too intimate even for her'. This to Madge Vaughan:

"how am I to begin about Leonard? First he is a Jew: second he is 31;
third, he spent 7 years in Ceylon, governing natives, inventing ploughs,
shooting tigers, and did so well they offered him a very high place the
other day, which he refused, wishing to marry me, and gave up his entire
career there on the chance I would agree. He has no money of his own.
I've only known him 6 months, but from the first I have found him the
one person to talk to. He interests me immensely, besides all the rest. We
mean to marry in August, and he wants to find out about labour and fac-
tories and to keep outside Government and do things on his own
account. He has also written a novel, and means to write as well as be
practical. We shall, I think, take a small house and try to live cheaply, so as
not to have to make money.

O what an egoist I am! but you asked for details...

At first I felt stunned, but now every day the happiness becomes more
complete – even though it does seem a fearful chance – my having found
any man who gives me what Leonard does.

You will come and see us, won't you, when we are married, and continue to be that eccentric but engaging animal, the Barbary Ape?" [35]

And to Lady Robert Cecil, from Leonard's point of view the most
important of these letters:

"I wrote to you, but the difficulty of describing my husband overcame
me, and I tore it up... I think you will like him – though you will probably wonder why on earth he should marry me – considering that he has
ruled India [sic], hung black men, and shot tigers. He has written a novel;
so have I; we both hope to publish them in the autumn... I am very very
happy." [36]

She explains to Violet Dickinson:

"At this moment we vaguely think of rooms in Grays Inn – they'd be
very small, but cheap, and sufficient for a start. However, we haven't let
these yet, and our plans depend on that... Leonard hasn't yet got a profession – the Board of Trade would give him a job, but we should have to
take it at once; and get no holiday till next June, and that doesn't seem
worth while... my novel is at last dying. O how sad when it's done! I
think some of its very, or rather, amusing; and as it gets shoved out of my
head, another begins; but next year I must have a child... My husband is
much too good for me, but I'm very happy." [37]

'But next year I must have a child' – becoming a mother is seen to be in conflict with her writing; they can't take rooms until they have let part of her Brunswick Square house: this is Leonard's restrictive view of their future. He could have taken a paid job at the Board of Trade but rejected this to live as a free-lance – on Virginia's money. Virginia finished her book according to Leonard's specification, writing 500 words a day, instead of going along at her own pace. Nevertheless, finish it she did. They intended to publish their two first novels together after their marriage but Virginia was so incapacitated by self-doubt that Leonard not only published his first novel but also his second before *The Voyage Out* made its appearance in 1915.

Virginia could very easily have joined the ranks of so many other creative, sensitive and valuable women who are submerged by their husbands – women whose energy is taken over and used to fuel yet another male ambition. That this did not happen in her case makes her writing true to her female perspective even more important because of its rarity. It is indeed so rare that we need to ask how it happened. Why is it that Virginia, on the brink of marriage and all too eager to adopt the part Leonard wanted her to play, became an exception?

One reason is that Leonard's work, after the publication of *The Village in the Jungle* which did quite well, met with remarkably little success. His budding career as a novelist ended abruptly when his second book, *The Wise Virgins,* was given a hostile reception by the critics and failed to sell. Another reason is that when Virginia's life became distorted by outside pressures she would collapse into 'madness', from which she emerged with a new sense of creative freedom. This was her way of surviving the psychic burdens laid on her by tragic events such as her parents' deaths, and by other people's obsessive personalities including Vanessa's and, for the rest of her life, Leonard's. Thus her so-called madness was a form of liberation, part of her creative process; but it gave Leonard dominance over every other aspect of her existence. Although Virginia Woolf is known as a feminist writer, her life with Leonard would be extremely circumscribed.

Until he had safely married her, Leonard was aware that Virginia could escape the net he was closing around her. She might realise he was intending to make use of her, to give him a position in society and live on her money. She could at any time discover the underlying mechanism of his 'method' by means of which he was propelling her towards a style of life that would benefit him. This was, therefore, both a testing and an exciting time for him and one he no doubt revelled in, since it held the spice of excitement and uncertainty.

They attended the inquiry into the sinking of the unsinkable *Titanic* that had occurred in April, with the loss of 1,500 lives. This tragic event symbolised the end of the halcyon Edwardian period in England – those long hot summers when tea was served on green lawns under the trees – that finally expired in the four-year massacre of Europe's young men in World War One.

He took her horse riding in Richmond. I see this as a momentous scene: Leonard, wearing his jodhpurs, mounted and showed off to Virginia demonstrating his mastery of the horse, celebrating his control, his dominance, his triumph. But at this moment of supremacy came fear, terrifying grey fear dimming the sunlit Richmond Park and turning it, like the Hambantota jungle, to dust and ashes: nothing matters. Virginia, watching, evidently did not identify her own situation with that of his mount; all she said was that: 'the horse was surprised'. [38] They returned to Bloomsbury by train.

Leonard now made a dramatic and characteristic gesture that changed forever his relationship with every member of his Jewish family and set the scene for his marriage. He refused to invite his mother to their wedding. At once, there were heated arguments in Colinette Road, Putney. Virginia wrote to Duncan Grant:

"we've had such rows with poor old Mother Wolf [*sic*], who says she never imagined such a slight as not being asked to the wedding, that it is doubtful whether anyone will come." [39]

Leonard's tactic is masterly. Virginia found visiting the Woolf family an ordeal, but instead of helping her to feel at home there he made a breach that never healed, and nor did he want it to. By dividing the two women, Leonard assumed control over both. Throughout their marriage, he refused to let Virginia make friends with his mother.

We can see Virginia as the new host for what amounted to the attack of a parasite. And we realise that she was peculiarly susceptible to precisely this type of takeover. Her father and half-brothers had aroused her defences against both individual men and maleness in general: she would not have considered any man who sent out similar signals of rage or rape. Leonard did neither. He did not obviously dominate her. When she found him 'foreign' – a foreign body who was physically repulsive to her

– he played down the sexual aspect of marriage and became 'caring', since that is what she needed and what Vanessa expected him to be. Between the two of them Virginia was permitted to be daughter and sister, even 'genius', but she never had the status of a wife or a fully adult woman. We can but speculate what would have happened if she had married Walter Lamb with whom she took a final long walk.

Virginia, who had not been to school, had not been inoculated against Leonard's type of attack, therefore she did not react negatively to this invasion of her autonomy. On one level she began to work for him, writing letters in response to his promptings that exaggerated the stories of his activities abroad; on another, she brought him into her world of animal pet-names by calling him Mongoose – an apparently adorable but actually vicious small mammal – while she was Mandrill, the largest and ugliest of monkeys. Leonard ended his letter to her of 24 May: 'I hope the Mandril [sic] went to its box early & isn't worried by anything in the world.' It is all there in this one sentence. On the grounds of protecting and caring for her he interposes himself between Virginia and the outside world. In this situation it would have been impossible for her to connect this apparently caring, mothering man to Swift, who, as Lytton Strachey said, 'would murder his wife'.

The main difference between them was that while Virginia was open and straight in all her relationships with other people, Leonard's apparent weaknesses concealed what was actually his underlying strength: a desperate, and ultimately quite ruthless, will to win – regardless of how long it took or what the cost to others. He said that all through his life he felt he was acting a part. He could therefore change the part he played to suit his objective. This was the carapace he presented to the world, which he felt to be necessary to protect his passionate and vulnerable inner self and enable him to play a winning game with the help of his 'method'. Marriage to Virginia was essential for his success; but it was a marriage of opposites, where one partner was manipulating the other.

The union between Leonard Woolf and Virginia Stephen was of hot with cool; of internal attack with external defence; of the man trying to narrow the distance between them, with the woman requiring all of that distance if she was to have any hope of retaining her sanity – for Virginia sanity was a balance that depended on neither loving nor hating, but Leonard with his 'unquenchable flame' was forcing her to do both; of the man who did not admit to feeling any guilt in himself but who managed to make those around him feel doubly guilty, with the woman who desperately tried to be fair-minded and who was apt to blame herself.

Virginia's position, her sense of herself and her autonomy as a committed writer, was being eroded even before marriage. She had begun writing to a timetable set by Leonard, and she had taken on the burden of financing them both so that he did not have to earn money. His part of the bargain was to look after her when she became over-tired, but this too became an important part of his control over her. Twice they had to put off seeing Violet Dickinson because: 'I've been rather headachy, and had a bad night, and Leonard made me into a comatose invalid.' ... 'My head goes on aching stupidly.' Some of these notes may have been excuses, since Leonard did not particularly want to visit Violet, but making Virginia write them meant that she was having to play his game against one of her closest friends.

Loss of self-confidence was starting to undermine Virginia before they attempted to have a sexual relationship. At the same time as putting herself down, Virginia was building up her image of Leonard. She says that he reminds her of Thoby: 'There is something very like Thoby about him, not only in his face.' He thus dons the mantle of her dead brother. In the summer of 1912, both Virginia and Leonard had become focused on each other but who or what, exactly, were they focused on?

Leonard was Pericles marrying his exotic mistress, Aspasia. On that upper level of what Alma Halbert Bond terms his super-ego, everything is clear, close to his Greek ideal, and simple. He needed to make Virginia reluctant to have the child she had always wanted, by persuading her that motherhood would get in the way of her writing and she would have to choose between them. A far more devastating reason would soon be provided by the unbearable stresses of sexuality. But the 'madness' this brought on, as we shall see, became the decisive step in Leonard's campaign not only to avoid having children but to enable him to take over as her legal guardian, so that he gained total control over her life and her money – and this could be presented as entirely her 'fault', just as her frigidity was to be seen as her 'fault'.

Who was Virginia marrying? She saw the physical man as unattractive to the point of repulsion, and she was frightened of the intensity of his passion, which found expression in letters while he stumbled over his words and was almost tongue-tied when he tried to speak directly to her. I think she married someone who, for all his educational advantages, she felt would not outshine her own natural talent. Marriage to Leonard was a challenge for her and one that she thought she could benefit from without losing autonomy. She had her vision of being a modern writer who was yet contributing to the mainstream of English literature, a woman among the 'giants' whose works she had been familiar with throughout her childhood; and if there were difficulties she thought she could surmount them. As she told Molly MacCarthy: 'in my heart I always expect to be floated over all crises, when the moment comes, and landed heaven knows where!' [40] This was the positive view. Perhaps she also hoped eventually to stand on her own feet with less need for someone else's support. If so, she entirely mistook the situation between herself and Leonard.

He must have been a puzzle to Virginia at this time, maybe a puzzle she never entirely resolved. On the one hand there was the gentle, caring Leonard to whom she was grateful, and whom she needed as a replacement for Vanessa and for Violet Dickinson – as a replacement, in short, for a woman. But on the other hand there was the Leonard who was described by Lytton Strachey as one who 'burns with a mystic, unquenchable flame – a dark triumph, which circumstances may shake, but never shatter', who 'towers above his loathsome companions' as he 'whirls into the empyrean'. It was only after her major breakdowns which lasted for most of World War One, during the first of which she almost died, that Virginia attempted to grapple with the problem of the two Leonards. They were about to climb aboard the matrimonial seesaw from opposite ends, each thinking they would reach the heights.

Leonard decided to tie the knot with a minimum of ceremony at St. Pancras Registry Office, leaving the date undecided until the last minute. There were only a handful of people present. He had asked one or two of his favourite siblings but they refused to go, out of respect for their mother. Three days before the marriage, on 7 August 1912, Marie Woolf wrote to Leonard with considerable dignity:

"My dear Len,

Thanks for [your letter]. To be quite frank, yes, it has hurt me extremely that you did not make it a point of having me at your marriage. I know full well that neither Virginia nor you had the least desire to slight me, why should you, but it has been a slight all the same.

You are the first of my sons who marries, it is one of *the* if not *the* most important day of your life. It would have compensated me for the very great hardships I have endured in bringing you all up by myself, if you had expressed the desire that you wished me before anyone else, to be witness to your happiness.

...It has been the custom from time immemorial that one's nearest relatives are paid the compliment of being invited to the marriage ceremony; to ignore that custom & to carry it so far as to leave out one's Parent, must strike one as an unheard of slight... However I will not say more; you have missed a great opportunity of giving me some happy moments – I have not had many lately!...

> With very much love
> Ever, my dear Len,
> Your devoted
> Mother" [41]

He had returned from Ceylon the prodigal son; now, within the space of a year, the son and brother of whom the Woolf family had been so proud kicked them in the teeth. He was never forgiven for not inviting his mother to his wedding, the hurt being intensified before long by his depiction of the all-too-recognisable Jewish family in *The Wise Virgins*.

We can find excuses for Leonard's refusal to invite his mother to his wedding. He was marrying a gentile and embarking on a very different kind of life, he therefore wanted to clarify his break with the past. He also found it necessary to separate his wife from his mother as completely as possible, and he continued this policy of separation. Virginia herself probably felt some pleasure at having whisked Leonard away from his Putney upbringing, as she still had some of the prejudice of her class against Jews. Nevertheless, we need to see this decision of Leonard's as part of a power game that he played with devastating effect, if we are to comprehend what living with Leonard was really like for Virginia.

The row spread to the extent that Virginia wondered whether anyone at all would come to their wedding. The only people to attend were Vanessa Bell, George and Gerald Duckworth and Aunt Mary Fisher from Virginia's family; Saxon Sydney-Turner, the third member of the 'Trinity of Trinity', was Leonard's representative; then there were the painters Roger Fry, Duncan Grant and Frederick Etchells. As well as the Woolf family, there were some notable absentees such as Lytton Strachey and Clive Bell; and Virginia's close friends Violet Dickinson, Janet Case, Emma Vaughan and Ka Cox. Virginia described the occasion a week later at the start of their honeymoon, writing to Janet Case from The Plough Inn, Holford, Somerset:

"Its really a very good way to be married – very simple and soon done. You stand up and repeat two sentences, and then sign your name. Nothing went wrong, the only disturbance was about Vanessa and Virginia, which the registrar, who was half blind and otherwise deformed, mixed hopelessly and Nessa upset him worse by suddenly deciding to change her son's name from Quentin to Christopher. [Quentin Bell remained Quentin.] It thundered all the time, but we enjoyed it all. Afterwards there was a very odd lunch party – George and Gerald in frock coats looking very suspiciously at Duncan [Grant], and an odd little painter [Frederick Etchells] who came in, and could only talk about pawning clothes. I suppose one oughtn't to enjoy one's wedding, but I did." [42]

Leonard gave his own account in his autobiography, written over fifty years after the event:

"Virginia and I were married on Saturday, August 10 [1912], at St. Pancras Register Office in a room which, in those days, looked down into a cemetery. In the ceremony before a Registrar one makes no promise 'to love and to cherish, till death us do part, according to God's holy ordinance', but in the St. Pancras Office, facing the window and looking through it at the tomb-stones behind the Registrar's head, one was, I suppose appropriately, reminded of the words 'till death us do part'." [43]

Whereas Virginia heard the thunder, Leonard chose to emphasise the tombstones and so the aura of death hangs over his memory of the occasion.

Twenty-nine years later Virginia's suicide by drowning cut the knot they tied that day; the only person present at her funeral was Leonard.

PART TWO

THE SERVILE STATE OF MARRIAGE

Chapter Four

LEONARD TAKES OVER

Leonard Woolf paid for their honeymoon with the remains of his winnings from the Calcutta sweepstake. He also planned it to suit himself. They were to spend their first night together at Asheham House and then, after a night at Brunswick Square, stay for a few days at the Plough Inn, Holford, in Somerset. After that they would take a boat to Spain and journey from place to place as their – or rather Leonard's – fancy took them, without reserving rooms in advance, as he had moved around Ceylon. He wanted to be footloose and free, the Wandering Jew. He had a taste for travel and his honeymoon gave him a good opportunity to indulge it.

I have no doubt that Virginia agreed to this scheme with delight. She too enjoyed travelling and seeing new places and now it would be even more exciting to be accompanied by her new husband instead of her tall friend, Violet Dickinson or her siblings. Not for a moment did she forget the illnesses members of her family had contracted abroad or the death of her brother Thoby after one of these trips. Nor did she forget the almost intolerable excitement, and envy, she felt when her half-sister Stella had left home on just such a honeymoon abroad with the inordinately sexually charged Jack Hills, only to return home to die. She would carry all these ghostly figures from the past with her as she set out on her own marital adventure.

Both she and Leonard had something to prove: whereas many of the Apostles enthusiastically adopted the ancient Greek idea that love between two men was superior to that between a man and a woman, she and Leonard would embody perfect heterosexual love and return triumphant. Their relationship would show to what heights of happiness the union of two intelligent people of the opposite sex could achieve: they would succeed where others had failed. Aspasia was no longer to be a distant, snow-covered mountain but the glowing-eyed, passionate mistress of Pericles the great lover. Or so they hoped.

What exactly happened when Leonard and Virginia faced each other in their bedroom at Asheham House on that first night we can never entirely know, although there are clues. Leonard had been accustomed to paying whores in Ceylon to do just what he wanted, whereas Virginia had

WALKING TOUR IN CORNWALL, 1916
MARGARET LLEWELYN DAVIES WITH LEONARD

VIRGINIA WEIGHING 12 STONE
AFTER FORCED FEEDING

spent her girlhood from the age of thirteen trying to avoid the unwanted attentions of her half-brother George. When Leonard tried to approach her she became very excited, jumping about and eluding him as she had done in her room at 22 Hyde Park Gate. When he held her, getting angry, shouting at her to lie still, she broke free, laughing and chattering with nervous fear – a terrified monkey – anything to put off the moment when this foreign man, for whom she felt no more than a rock, should... actually... she cowered, sobbing. It was all her fault – but was it? Leonard was not only terrified of a woman's virginity, he was determined not to father a child. Eventually they gave up, their dreams of perfection in ruins. He shot his bolt and fell asleep.

We get an insight into the Woolfs' sexual mismatch from Gerald Brenan, who was a comparative stranger to them when they visited him in 1923. Years later, in 1967, Brenan wrote to Rosemary Dinnage: "When in March 1923 they came out to visit me in my Spanish mountain village... Leonard told me that when on their honeymoon he had tried to make love to her she had got into such a violent state of excitement that he had to stop, *knowing as he did that these states were a prelude to her attacks of madness.* This madness is of course hereditary, but her early seduction by her half brother was no doubt a predisposing factor. So Leonard, though I should say a strongly sexed man, had to give up all idea of having any sort of sexual satisfaction. He told me that he was ready to do this *"because she was a genius".* [1]

I have emphasised these words because, in 1912, Leonard did not know from personal experience that Virginia was a genius; by then she had not published a single book; nor did he know that 'these states' may be a prelude to 'her attacks of madness'. She had retired to the Twickenham nursing home for a fortnight's enforced rest the previous spring, when his intense wooing became too much for her, but it is evident from their letters then that it was Leonard who became over-excited to the point of incoherence, while she remained all too cool, calm, collected and reasonable. If, on his honeymoon, he knew that states of excitement were a prelude to Virginia's 'attacks of madness', he must have gained this knowledge at second-hand from Vanessa.

We should not lose sight of the possibility that it was not Virginia but Leonard attempting to cope with a virgin, which he had always dreaded, who became over-excited and impotent. What we do know is that sexually they suffered from a fatal mismatch.

Any commentator has to be aware of this problem of Leonard's arguments which were inspired by hindsight. By 1923 he had adopted the face-saving story of 'Virginia Woolf the mad genius', together with the assumption that she had a hereditary taint of madness and that molestation by her half-brother George was a predisposing factor, while he could still be considered a strongly sexed man who generously gave up all thoughts of obtaining sexual satisfaction with the flawed and frigid Virginia.

Stories about Virginia Woolf's life and death have been told many times, but in my view nobody has adequately taken into account the nature, character and ambitions of her new husband, Leonard; nor the impact on those around him, including Virginia, when he applied the method he had developed at Cambridge to ensure that he was never blamed, as he fought his way to a position of power and dominance; and left other people to carry the burden of guilt, until they found it easier to adopt his point of view. However, it is possible to see through the cracks in that fiction if we wish to do so. Leonard's version of their matrimonial story was already in place when Virginia wrote her first post-marriage letter to her friend and old Greek teacher Janet Case, written on the second day of their honeymoon at Brunswick Square. She says:

"Well, I'm married – married since Saturday. We went down to Asheham and now we're staying the night here on our way through to Somersetshire. There we sit in the sun for a few days, and then go to Spain and Italy... I wish you were as happy as I am – and I am quite clear that I shall never really be ill again because with Leonard I get no chance!" [2]

The Plough Inn was small, old fashioned and outstanding for the quality of its home-cooked food. However, although it was August, the weather was not sunny; actually, it was unrelievedly chilly and wet, so the Woolfs spent much time reading. Virginia tried to learn Spanish, while Leonard wrote to Vanessa asking her to find rooms for them in the Temple in time for their return, then concentrated on writing articles on 'scientific management' despite knowing nothing about the subject. Virginia's second post-marriage letter to Janet Case, in which she describes the wedding (quoted in Chapter Three), has an interesting exchange between herself and Leonard:

'Leonard instructs the world upon scientific management, I think he's a fraud, but no one seems to know anything.' This is commented on, in

Leonard's handwriting: '*Virginia says I'm to say that I'm not* [a fraud]. *She is just dropping off to sleep in a chair in front of the fire or possibly she might say so herself.*'

Virginia did not do this, instead she adds: 'If you ever want a most comfortable Inn, delicious food, cream for every meal, quite cheap, come here. Please take a holiday some time.' [3]

Virginia evidently read her original letter to Leonard, with no suspicion that he might take offence at her teasing; but he couldn't tolerate her comment that he was a fraud, even as a joke. No doubt he explained at length how damaging to his reputation that sort of remark was, while she refused to rewrite her letter, telling him to add what he wanted; she then fell asleep to escape his censure and when she awoke she added her note praising the Inn in words Leonard, but not she, would have used: 'delicious food, cream for every meal, quite cheap.' Soon she would no longer dare to make such jokes.

While they were there Vanessa wrote to Virginia, first referring to her efforts to find rooms in the Temple as Leonard had asked her to do, then telling him he had been given the job of secretary to the second Post-Impressionist Exhibition that was to be held in the winter, in preference to Desmond MacCarthy who had been secretary for the first one. No doubt she persuaded Roger Fry to give Leonard, and not the more experienced MacCarthy, this paid job. She then says:

"I was also very much pleased by his letter [not published among Leonard's Collected Letters], extraordinarily false though his idea of my character seems to be. *Of course* I should have expected him to be in the 7th heaven of delight and happiness and would never think of quibbling in the way he suggests. As long as the ape [Virginia] gets all he wants, doesn't smell too much and has his claws well cut, he's a pleasant enough bed-fellow for a short time. The whole question is what will happen when the red undergrowth sprouts in the winter?

Are you really a promising pupil? I believe I'm very bad at it. Perhaps Leonard would like to give me a few lessons. But of course *some* people don't need to be skilful, at least that's my theory." [4]

This is not the letter of a kindly elder sister wishing her younger sibling well on her honeymoon. To suggest that Leonard might give her sex lessons is tactless to say the least, but underlying Vanessa's words is something even more damaging: a refusal to accept the validity of the Woolfs' relationship. She ridicules the possibility that Virginia was an attractive woman, calling her an 'ape' and hoping he doesn't 'smell too much and has his claws well cut', while perhaps he might be 'a pleasant enough bed-fellow for a short time', thus turning not only Virginia's sex but her animal fantasy against her – something Virginia never did to Vanessa: Dolphin, her name for her elder sister, was always lovingly used and meant. In stark contrast, Vanessa claims a close connection with Leonard as a fellow adult human being, whom she is helping to get both a job and the accommoda-tion he wants in London. Was the Woolfs' marriage doomed from the start because Vanessa laid claim to Leonard and only 'lent' him to Virginia for a short time? If so, she could have justified her action by remembering that Virginia had flirted with Clive while she was absorbed with her first-born son, Julian. As for Leonard, this would be an early example of his manipulating and controlling method played against both sisters, as well as Clive Bell. We cannot apply conventional standards to members of the Bloomsbury Group, since they were rebelling against Victorian constraints. Our guidelines are set by the available evidence.

Despite the delicious home-cooked food so plentifully provided at the Inn, Virginia was refusing to eat. Vanessa, at Asheham House, writes again to Virginia, saying that their servant Sophy Farrell: 'tells me what she thinks of you and Leonard – very flattering to *him* of course – and how she thinks you eat better when you are helped, and don't have to cut your own helpings... So tell Leonard to do the carving.' [5]

Now that she was his wife Leonard could let his highly developed left brain – his judgmental, controlling side – take over without any fear of losing her. He certainly reacted negatively when Virginia wrote that he was a 'fraud' and it is likely that he began criticising a number of aspects of her behaviour. He would not have been able to stop himself. From the evidence of *The Wise Virgins,* he found the sound of her voice 'irritating' and must soon have asked her not to talk so much. Fond of his food, he praised the ample meals to be found at the Plough Inn; and, when Virginia began to leave hers uneaten, his first reaction would have been to tell her not to waste food – he was paying for their honeymoon. He must have seen her refusals as a most annoying rebellion against him which he did his best to override; when this failed he would have immersed himself in work and ignored her, when he wasn't criticising her.

At first, Virginia cannot have believed what was happening to her. She, after all, had thought she was doing Leonard a favour by marrying him, the poor Jew. Her response was to have migraine headaches as well as refusing to eat. Only when he became seriously worried at the state she was in, did Leonard pay attention to her. He looked across the well-stocked table, sniffed the home-cooked ham and the boiled potatoes. Irritation rose in him. His arm, his body, trembled until his knife and fork rattled on the crockery. She must be sensible and eat her dinner! If she ate, she would settle down and not put on that absurd performance in the bedroom that caused him either to become impotent or ejaculate prematurely. Leonard related to sex as something 'dirty', to be carried out on inferior women who were sexually aware and therefore 'vile'. It would have been much more difficult for him to have had satisfactory sex with a woman whom he admired – as in these early days he admired Virginia for her beauty, intelligence and social position – the daughter of Sir Leslie Stephen bringing more than nine thousand pounds into the marriage.

For Virginia the Plough Inn, Holford, was to be remembered as a place of horror. Even before they began their wanderings through France and Spain, taking with them the burden of their failed sexuality, it should have been obvious that the physical exertions of such a trip were more than she could bear. Worse still, Virginia found herself travelling with a companion who did not listen to what she said, or discuss anything on her terms.

Leonard's way of dealing with their sexual problems was to take charge of Virginia as he had taken charge of the hundred thousand natives of Hambantota District. Concerning his treatment of them he was to admit, years afterwards, that his methods were 'too ruthless'; he was too much 'the strong man'. Now married, he organised everything to suit himself. In planning their future, he ruled out going back to shared living in their house in Brunswick Square, where Virginia felt at home with the other tenants who were her friends: no, they must be on their own, without servants, where he could assume complete control over her, until she had been forced to behave as he wanted his ideal woman to behave, without resistance, as obedient as a well-trained animal.

This pattern continued during their exhausting tour of Spain and Italy, with Virginia writing chirpily about their travels although they often found themselves in difficulties. They spent two days in one place, then a day travelling by train to somewhere else where they had to find accommodation for the night, all the while each avidly reading the books they had brought with them. Virginia writes to Lytton:

"When I tell you that the W.C. opposite our room has not been emptied for 3 days, and you can there distinguish the droppings of Christian, Jew, Latin and Saxon – you can imagine the rest." [6]

By 4 September Leonard was penning the first chapter of his second novel, *The Wise Virgins,* as Virginia told Ka Cox, a chapter in which he tears apart life in a London suburb in general and his own Jewish family in particular. Hidden in her letter is a disguised plea for Ka to help them let their two rooms in Brunswick Square. We can hear Leonard's voice prompting her: 'We have not let my two rooms. Being so far away, we feel helpless, and turn to you, not to do anything in particular, but if you could keep this in mind, please do. Possibly there are people coming down from Cambridge?' There was no need for this concern to let her rooms, since Virginia had sufficient means; but from the start of their marriage Leonard kept her in a state of anxiety about their finances, thus adding to her sense of strain and insecurity. Despite her courageous spirit, their travels exhausted Virginia, and this was eventually acknowledged by Leonard in his autobiography, where we get a startling picture of her ordeal:

"We were married, as I said some pages back, on Saturday, August 10, 1912. Then we went off on a long meandering honeymoon. In those days I had the *wanderlust* almost perpetually upon me. I suppose it was partly due to Ceylon: during my last three years there in the Hambantota District I was continually on the move, never more than two weeks at a time sedentary in my bungalow, continually travelling on circuit, sleeping anywhere in tents or in the bare circuit bungalows. I had got into the habit of thinking that one could go anywhere at any time, and rather on that principle we wandered about, first in Provence and then into and all over Spain. It was very pleasant, but of course we occasionally got into difficulties staying in pasadas off the beaten track and hiring mulecarts in out-of-the-way villages. I did not realise at the time that this kind of travelling was probably much too tiring for Virginia." [7]

Throughout Leonard's account we are given no sense of Virginia as an autonomous person. If she told him she was tired, or showed it, he was not going to change his plans. Leonard has taken charge as though his wife is part of the luggage. To continue his story:

"Eventually we got to Valencia, and there by chance I found a Hungarian ship on the point of sailing to Marseille and willing to take us as the only passengers. Not being able to make ourselves understood in English, French, Sinhalese or Tamil, and not understanding Hungarian, we did not realise we should have dined at 6.30. pm and that after 7.30 it was contrary to the laws of the Medes and Persians, and of the Hungarians and Austrians, to give any food to a passenger. We went to bed hungry; the Mediterranean was extremely rough; the boat bucked and rolled, creaked and groaned. In the middle of the night I woke up and realised that I was not alone in my bunk: three large cats had joined me. At 7.30 in the morning I staggered up on to the deck and found the Third Officer who spoke English. I explained to him that I was very hungry and why. He took me up on to the bridge and had breakfast sent to me there; the first course was an enormous gherkin swimming in oil and vinegar. One of the bravest things I have ever done, I think, was to eat this, followed by two fried eggs and bacon, coffee and rolls, with the boat, the sea, and the coast of France going up and down all round me."

Where, through all of this, was Virginia? Not eating, that's for sure. She has simply been omitted from Leonard's story of 'their' honeymoon. The enormous gherkin swimming in oil and vinegar perhaps gains a Freudian dimension from their unhappy sex life. It is not generally acknowledged that for the first few years of their marriage, Leonard took charge of their lives in ways that suited himself. He was doing the organising for them both. In a word, he was running the show. I believe Virginia's enforced sacrifice of initiative to Leonard was a major cause of her worst breakdown, whose first symptom was her refusal to eat; it almost ended in her death a year later. This is a point that has not been picked up by other commentators.

Two salient characteristics of the Woolfs' honeymoon were first that Leonard planned it to satisfy his 'wanderlust', not reserving rooms ahead and assuming he could command immediate service from servants and underlings; but Europe was not like that, and he had Virginia with him. The other characteristic was that their sexual relationship turned out to be what Virginia later described as 'a dismal failure'. Leonard's dream of marrying Aspasia, the intelligent whore, was shattered. Virginia, too, found that reality was very different from her expectations since she had married someone who could not make her feel vehement; thus neither of them had entered the realm of marital sex with any likelihood of success.

Belying the brave front she puts on in her letters at this time, Virginia had already become a prey to blaming herself, while Leonard was being over-active in making plans and getting others to help him. There seems to have been no relaxation between Virginia and Leonard; no letting up; no idling of his busy brain.

Virginia was not only exhausted by the travelling but terrified of being at the receiving end of the behavioural and sexual demands of her new husband. No wonder she was 'excited'. Not only this, but she was bereft of feeling, experiencing great waves of coldness towards Leonard because he was 'so foreign'. Her emotional flight was not intentional, but a desperate defensive reaction to terror – terror of death, as suffered by her half-sister Stella; terror of giving herself at long last after years of some sort of sexual abuse or stimulation without orgasm by her elder half-brother George; terror of 'losing herself' – her inviolable creative writing self. The only way she could gain the space she craved was to retreat into some inner distance where Leonard, much to his annoyance, couldn't reach her; and she became as cold and distant as a snow-covered mountain. The price she paid was to be denied children. And to be labelled 'mad'.

Leonard, busily starting a new stage of life, was exhilarated by the novelty of his situation as he always was when he was in the process of acting a new part. However, the shock of their sexual failure must have profoundly affected him, and this can be seen in the utterly different tone of voice with which he wrote *The Wise Virgins* compared to that of his first novel *The Village in the Jungle*. He complained to Vanessa (his letter is not published), who replied on 21 September:

"I charitably put down Mrs. W's silence to the fact that she's too happy with a really sympathetic and admiring companion to think willingly of wholesome discipline. But as for you, after your awful description of a night with the apes [Virginia] I can hardly imagine why you don't write to me. I am happy to say it's years since I spent a night in their company, and I can't conceive anything more wretched than it sounds. it would be bad enough to know they were in the next bed with all their smells and their whines and their wettings, but to have to change beds with them and all the rest of it – a coal hole would be more to my taste. So now you know what I think." [8]

Are we to take this literally, that in her misery and panic Virginia wet her bed? If so, at least she insisted on moving into Leonard's dry one. Whatever the situation, Leonard allowed himself to describe the most intimate details to Vanessa, who in turn gave him total support at the cost of being utterly disloyal to her sister. He saw Vanessa as both the sexual and the motherly female (Katherine in his novel), whereas Virginia was not permitted to be either. At this time Vanessa was carrying on an intense affair with Roger Fry, to whom she wrote: 'Oh, Roger, it was delicious today in spite of sordid surroundings... I have always had a taste for love-making in the midst of quite ordinary things. It turns them into something else. Not that it wouldn't be divine to do it in Asia Minor, too... you know Roger, I love you. Do you know how much?' [9] However when Fry, with his Quaker background, fell more and more deeply in love with her, Vanessa drew away and left him broken-hearted.

There is another description of the Woolfs' honeymoon, this time from Virginia herself. It is admissible in her case to read much of her creative writing as autobiographical, at least as something remembered because it was felt intensely at the time. Spater and Parsons in *The Marriage of True Minds* details many of these references. Because she did not invent characters, the people in her novels emerge as a transmutation of her own experiences both within herself and from her observations of her family and friends. We can therefore listen to Rhoda's speech in *The Waves*, published in October 1931, a book in which Louis has much in common with Leonard, and Rhoda with Virginia. In this novel we can hear poignant echoes of Virginia's agony in Spain in 1912:

" 'Oh, life, how I have dreaded you,' said Rhoda, 'oh, human beings, how I have hated you!... Now as I climb this mountain, from the top of which I shall see Africa... I left Louis; I feared embraces... I desired always to stretch the night and fill it fuller and fuller with dreams... Now I climb this Spanish hill; and I will suppose that this mule-back is my bed and that I lie dying. There is only a thin sheet between me now and the infinite depths. The lumps in the mattress soften beneath me. We stumble up – we stumble on. My path has been up and up, towards some solitary tree with a pool beside it on the very top. I have sliced the waters of beauty in the evening when the hills close themselves like birds' wings folded. I have picked sometimes a red carnation, and wisps of hay. I have sunk alone on the turf and fingered some old bone and thought: When the wind stoops to brush this height, there may be nothing found but a pinch of dust.

The mule stumbles up and on. The ridge of the hill rises like mist, but from the top I shall see Africa. Now the bed gives under me. The sheets spotted with yellow holes let me fall through. The good woman with a face like a white horse at the end of the bed makes a valedictory movement and turns to go. Who then comes with me? Flowers only, the cow-bind and the moonlight-coloured May. Gathering them loosely in a sheaf I made of them a garland and gave them – Oh, to whom? We launch out now over the precipice. Beneath us lie the lights of the herring fleet. The cliffs vanish. Rippling small, rippling grey, innumerable waves spread beneath us. I touch nothing. I see nothing. We may sink and settle on the waves. The sea will drum in my ears. The white petals will be darkened with sea water. They will float for a moment and then sink. Everything falls in a tremendous shower, dissolving me.

Yet that tree has bristling branches; that is the hard line of the cottage roof. Those bladder shapes painted red and yellow are faces. Putting my foot to the ground I step gingerly and press my hand against the hard door of a Spanish inn." [10]

In an explanatory note, the editor says:

'*I climb this mountain*: Rhoda is now in Spain. She has left Louis. This passage is rare in being in the past tense and bids farewell to her memories. She imagines her own suicidal fall yet enters the inn.'

The scene Virginia describes is clear: She would have liked to leave Louis-Leonard on their honeymoon, and in her novel Rhoda does so: 'I left Louis... I feared embraces'; or to have escaped through suicide. 'We stumble up – we stumble on': the mule is her bed, burdened with her own dying self. 'The sheets spotted with yellow holes let me fall through', until she sees the precipice and a plunge into the sea as an escape, a cleansing 'dissolving me'. But instead she goes on, stands on the ground and presses her hand on the hard door of a Spanish Inn, facing with desperation another night of sex with Leonard, her only possible reward to conceive – but she did not do so. During their wanderings Virginia lost her virginity, however Leonard must have taken care not to make her pregnant. On their return they consulted Vanessa – of all people – about Virginia's dislike of sex. Vanessa wrote to Clive, who remained in her orbit despite her affair with Roger Fry:

"the Woolves... seemed very happy, but are evidently both a little exercised in their minds on the subject of the Goat's coldness. I think I perhaps annoyed her but may have consoled him by saying that I thought she never had understood or sympathised with sexual passion in men. Apparently she still gets no pleasure at all from the act, which I think is curious. They were very anxious to know when I first had an orgasm. I couldn't remember. Do you? But no doubt I sympathised with such things if I didn't have them from the time I was 2." [11]

On their return to London, Leonard immediately began work as secretary for the upcoming exhibition of Post-Impressionist paintings at the Grafton Gallery. This meant that he entered the world of the visual artists. His closeness to Vanessa at this time was demonstrated when he grew a beard and she in sympathy altered her hair style, changes that would not have been lost upon Virginia. Whether Leonard actually gave Vanessa lessons in sex, as she had invited him to do, is anyone's guess. Given the permissive attitude of the Bloomsbury Group and his lack of sexual satisfaction with Virginia, I think it possible (even likely) that he did. Virginia might not have known for certain but she would surely have suspected and her sense of insecurity would have increased.

During the exhibition, Leonard bore the brunt of the fury of the outraged philistines who went to see it, which he probably enjoyed. However, he went too far with Vanessa when he wrote an article on visual art in which he declared that he could become an expert at anything in a few months. With the end of the show, Leonard's interest in art waned and he removed his beard; then he promptly adopted another persona, that of socialist politician, under the influence of Margaret Llewelyn Davies. He really was like a mongoose as he jumped in every direction, attaching himself to a dominant woman who became his confidante; but each time his compulsive leaps took him further and further away from Virginia. As he busied himself with one all-consuming interest after another, she must have felt that the passionate relationship between her two lovers in *The Voyage Out* was no longer relevant. If the book were launched it would have to venture out alone across a strange ocean without captain, crew or passengers, a terrifying prospect seen through the fog of her deepening depression.

The Woolfs rented rooms in Clifford's Inn, in the heart of the City. Here again, they were living in accordance with Leonard's vision. The old place reminded him of his years at Cambridge. He could once more dream his dreams of 'supremacy' that he had shared with Lytton Strachey. In his autobiography he described their new address:

"we went to live in Cliffords Inn in Fleet Street. It was still then the old Cliffords Inn, rather beautiful, our rooms incredibly ancient, also incredibly draughty and dirty, for 50 years ago in the City of London all day and all night long there fell a slow gentle rain of smuts, so that, if you sat writing by an open window, a thin veil of smuts covered the paper before you finished a page... The old buildings, the rooms, the court, was almost exactly the same as a Cambridge College and it was as though I had returned to live in the Great Court of Trinity. We felt wonderfully free. We had, of course, no servants; only a daily char came in and made the beds, swept up the smuts, and washed up the dishes." [12]

Leonard liked Clifford's Inn so much that he tried to live there again after Virginia's death; only he found it so changed for the worse that he soon moved elsewhere. Throughout the years of his marriage he must have harboured some resentment that he was forced to give up that apparently desirable life.

On one level, no doubt, Virginia saw living on their own as an adventure, she who had had numerous servants in that solid family house, 22 Hyde Park Gate; but she had to try and cope with household chores, at which she was very bad. She certainly did not share Leonard's dream of Cambridge and particularly Trinity as some godlike haven which was the high point of his life and which he longed to re-experience, at least partly, at Cliffords Inn. She had expressed her view forcibly the previous year, in a letter to Lytton Strachey:

"How difficult it is to write to you! It's all Cambridge – that detestable place; and the ap-s-les [Apostles] are so unreal, and their loves are so unreal, and yet I suppose it's all going on still – swarming in the sun – and perhaps not as bad as I imagine. But when I think of it, I vomit – that's all – a green vomit, which gets into the ink and blisters the paper." [13]

She was not only repelled by the homosexuality of most of the Apostles and their glorification of love between men, but also by their arrogant assumption of supremacy, their unbounded egotism as they fancied they were an intellectual elite, on a different and superior plane from everyone else. She also thought a University education ruined people's literary style, including Leonard's. However, whatever her views, she would never 'win' over Leonard's adulation of Trinity College or the Apostles, since they linked him with ancient Greece and with 'civilisation' itself, which he saw as the only defence against barbarism. His time at Cambridge was infinitely precious to him, and he was trying to recreate it at Clifford's Inn, though shackled to Virginia who had had no formal education whatsoever.

Every morning they would sit at work, with smuts floating down on their paper. Virginia wrote reviews to earn money, while Leonard, in a settled mood of cynicism, continued to write *The Wise Virgins*. His first novel, *The Village in the Jungle,* was due to be published in February the following year. By December 1912, Virginia was getting headaches and Leonard had a bout of malaria.

At the end of the year Leonard went through their finances. Virginia's fortune at their marriage came to rather over nine thousand pounds, together with some other assets including jewelry, but according to Leonard, her capital brought an annual return of less than 400 pounds. His total assets came to 506 pounds (their financial details are given in *A Marriage of True Minds*). As Virginia's husband, despite being far richer than he had ever been before, that first December of their marriage Leonard no doubt persuaded her to write reviews and articles for which she would be paid, and argued that she must limit her spending so that he would not have to look for a job. In this way, he interfered with her sense of herself as a creative author. He was writing the Woolf novels, not she.

The subject of whether or not Virginia should have a child would not go away. Virginia must have continually brought it up, trying to persuade him; pleading; cajoling; desperate. And the more she tried, the more he would have withdrawn, enjoying his power over her; no longer attempting to have sex – she was being punished – until she realised she might never become a mother. Migraine headaches prostrated her; she refused to eat; and now, since everyone agreed that she was a sexual failure, an even stronger argument was being mounted against her. With the suggestion that there was a 'weakness' in the Stephen family, he could use their sexual difficulties to demonstrate that there was something radically wrong with Virginia which meant that it was his duty as her husband not to let her have a child who might carry the taint into the next generation. Leonard had succeeded in turning his own refusal to father a child into a grievance he could use against Virginia; as he habitually used the grievance that began with the death of his father, by blaming his mother saying he was her 'least loved child', although Marie Woolf always denied this.

In January 1913 Leonard consulted Vanessa, asking her whether Virginia's mental health would permit her to become a mother. Vanessa suggested he should talk to Dr. Savage, Virginia's nerve specialist who had been treating her over the years; also Jean Thomas, who ran the Twickenham nursing home where Virginia had spent several periods undergoing enforced rest – the most recent occasion having been during the previous Spring, when she had been unable to cope with Leonard's persistent wooing. The advice of both these experts was that having a child would be good for Virginia. This was not what Leonard wanted to be told, he therefore set about finding different specialists who would agree with him. He searched until he found two specialists who backed his view that Virginia should not become pregnant due to her 'madness': it was this which became his ultimate excuse for denying her a child. And from now on he could put every aspect of Virginia's behaviour which annoyed him under the general heading of madness.

The records of this time in Virginia's life make pathetic reading when we see it from her point of view – a point of view that Leonard had entirely ceased to consider. Roger Poole in *The Unknown Virginia Woolf* and Stephen Trombley in *All That Summer She Was Mad* have given a detailed account of the horrors experienced by Virginia at the hands of those pompous, patriarchal doctors. T.B. Hyslop believed that:

"the new breed of intellectual women was sapping ancient energies, and that the women who wanted to do 'mental work', like writing and so on, 'would damage the general health of their offspring', while if a 'mad' woman had children she would contaminate the purity of British blood and undermine the Empire." [14]

Hyslop was one of the specialists brought in by Leonard to support his own anti-child prejudice; others were Dr Wright and Dr Head. He also consulted his doctor, Maurice Craig. Craig was younger and comparatively enlightened; later, he even wrote that: 'Emotion arising from whatever cause quickly affects the appetite and digestion, and if it persists there is a steady deterioration in the body weight and in the general health of the patient, and yet it is common to see these conditions being treated as if the error in the digestive system were the primary cause.' [15]

But according to Leonard, who consulted his doctor without so much as taking Virginia to see him, Craig sided with Hyslop and himself (another triangle). And Jean Thomas, who initially agreed with Dr. Savage's view that having a child would be good for her, changed her mind as a result of pressure from Leonard. In January 1913 Vanessa wrote uneasily to him:

"I am rather surprised at your account of Jean [Thomas]'s opinion, for she certainly told me the opposite. Why has she changed? I hope you'll get something definite from Savage. After all he does know Virginia and ought really to be the best judge. I suppose Craig can't tell as much without having seen her or knowing her at all. Do tell me what Savage says." [16]

It was essential to Leonard that Vanessa should support him during the negotiations that were taking place concerning Virginia's future, while he denied Virginia any opportunity to put her own point of view. Here was another conspiracy occurring behind her back, on an issue that was vital to her own future happiness and wellbeing, with Vanessa once again being a key player whilst she was being left out of the discussions. She was no match for any of them and simply tried to remain cheerful despite the odds stacked against her, as her end of the matrimonial see-saw dipped down and Leonard's soared higher.

Margaret Llewelyn Davies was originally a friend of Virginia's. It was through Margaret that Leonard became interested in the Co-operative Movement. Accompanied by Virginia, in March he travelled to the north of England visiting Liverpool, Manchester, Leeds, York, Carlisle and Leicester to look at the industrial situation. Margaret was strong, practical, part of the political scene and could assist Leonard on his upward climb into public life more effectively than his wife was able to do. His praise of this woman in his autobiography is fulsome:

"The vitality and inspiration of the [Women's co-operative] Guild – and also its organization – were mainly due to Margaret... She was that strange and usually inexplicable phenomenon 'a born leader'. Of course one could explain it by her immense energy and enthusiasm; by her laugh which was characteristically Margaret, a deep contralto spontaneous laugh; by the feminine charm which was also so spontaneous and unconscious... and by her beauty... the fresh English beauty of hair and eyes and skin, marvelously united with a chiselled classical beauty of Greek features... which perhaps should be called Roman rather than Greek. But when one has catalogued all these charms and powers, one feels that there was something beyond them which made her glow in the co-operative drabness so that she was able to inspire thousands of uneducated women with her own passion, both for 'sweetness and light', and also for liberty, equality, and fraternity. This something can, I think, only be described as a kind of virginal purity of mind and motive which – I am afraid it sounds rather absurd, but is nonetheless true – made her a kind of Joan of Arc to her cohorts of Lancashire and Yorkshire housewives in her crusade against ignorance, poverty, and injustice." [17]

No wonder Virginia wasn't well. She had to listen to Leonard's panegyrics about this 'Joan of Arc', this English, Greek or Roman beauty who was so inspiring him, and could feel herself being pushed further and further aside. She could see such journeys to the industrial north fuelling his ambition, stretching into the future: a future that was antipathetic and entirely alien to her, despite her sympathy with working women, whom she had encouraged during her time at Morley College. Dragged along in Leonard's wake, Virginia's health began to give way. As Quentin Bell recounts: 'a further political excursion was accompanied by a sudden deterioration in her health' [18] This later trip, in June, was to Newcastle-upon-Tyne to attend the Women's Co-operative Congress 'returning to London with Margaret Llewelyn Davies. Virginia not well.' Not only were these trips physically exhausting for her, although they undoubtedly were, as the honeymoon had exhausted her; but she was being dragged away from her creative centre. There was also the question of Leonard and Margaret's relationship. Margaret was the strong, active, politically aware woman that Virginia was not, surely she would make him a much better wife than herself? Her Greek-Roman beauty fitted her to be the central character in his vision of reviving classical Greek civilisation in contemporary Britain; whereas his wife, with her bouts of 'madness', was merely a useless failure: a member of a decadent family at the lower edge of the aristocracy, a barbarian.

One person who was anxiously watching the effect of marriage on Virginia was Clive Bell. Clive had recognised and encouraged Virginia's talent – or genius – very early and Leonard no doubt resented this, as he resented anyone or anything concerning Virginia over which he did not have complete control. Clive thought Leonard was:

"provincial and puritanical, an enemy to all that was charming and amusing in life. Moreover, his effect on Virginia was disastrous. She was, he declared, losing her looks, drifting away from her old friends and being led into the dreary routines of politics... He was vexed to see her carried into Committee rooms and Co-operative halls, wearing 'sensible' clothes and stout boots. And of course he might object, with a fair show of reason, that she had neither the abilities nor the stamina for such work." [19]

However worried Clive was he could only watch, appalled, and do nothing to help her.

Leonard's *The Village in the Jungle* came out in February 1913. He was now a 'published author' before Virginia's long-awaited book had even been sent to a publisher. It was only after the appearance of some reasonably positive reviews that he took Virginia's novel to Duckworth, a firm owned by Gerald Duckworth, her elder half-brother. (This was the man who in boyhood had explored her genitals when she was six.) The submission of her first book was thus left to Leonard, who timed it to suit himself. By launching himself as a novelist before Virginia, he had won the first round of the literary rivalry which continued throughout their marriage.

Quentin Bell uses Leonard's argument that her slide into depression was due to the acceptance for publication of *The Voyage Out*; at which point Bell says: 'It is fair to suppose that she immediately had misgivings', and goes on to blame the coming crisis on her fears about its reception. He gives no weight either to her agonised sense of deprivation that she was being denied motherhood or to the effect of those political trips during which Leonard gazed with open admiration at Margaret Llewelyn Davies, as a possible cause of Virginia's breakdown. Vanessa wrote to her sister with her familiar tactlessness on May 3rd, 1913, from Italy:

"Give my love to Leonard and tell him I think he might write to me soon even if he is a successful novelist." [20]

When the proofs were sent to Virginia, she panicked and publication was held up for two years, while she suffered the first part of her most devastating breakdown which gradually became worse during the spring and summer of 1913 and almost ended in her death in September.

It seems there were four main elements that precipitated Virginia's slide into mental breakdown, any one of which could easily have been disastrous; together, they were overwhelming. And all of them could have been avoided. First, there was her vulnerability as she thought she had not loved Leonard sufficiently and had let him down over sex; this led her to become a prey to the feeling that other women, including Vanessa and Margaret Llewelyn Davies, would be able to help Leonard more than she could; she therefore decided Leonard would be better off without her. Second, trips to political meetings not only tired and bored her but made her feel that she was being plunged into an alien world that broke into the quiet time she needed for her writing. Third, Leonard went ahead with publication of his first novel and the writing of his second, apparently unstoppable and invincible, while her own terror increased, of what the reaction would be to her intense love story, which now seemed quite irrelevant. In her weakened state she was apprehensive as to what the critics would say about her book, while she no longer felt herself to be strong enough to defend it. Fourth, Leonard refused to let her have a child; and every symptom she showed of her nervousness, her dismay, and finally and unwillingly her despair, strengthened his arguments that she should not have one. She finally lost the support of Vanessa, who wrote to Leonard agreeing with him that Virginia should remain childless.

One question that needs to be asked is: were the problems encountered by Virginia entirely due to her own sensitivity, or was Leonard plotting her downfall? Was he making use of the technique that he had developed at Trinity College, Cambridge, which he called the method, whereby he could bend any and everyone to his will? Most commentators including Quentin Bell, Virginia's nephew and official biographer, have seen Leonard as the innocent victim who did his best to save Virginia and rescue his marriage. If we adopt this line of thought Leonard does not emerge as a real person with his own drives, visions and ambition. Moreover, accepting that view, we have little alternative but to label him a 'saint' whose one aim and object in life was to do everything to aid and support his ailing wife. But it would then be necessary to try and explain why Virginia, as a committed writer at the outset of her career, inexplicably tried to kill herself in 1913 and almost succeeded.

In this book I am putting forward an alternative perspective: that Leonard was using his undoubtedly clever brain – his left brain – to better his own position in relation to all those around him, including Virginia herself, as he had done with such success in the civil service in Ceylon, where he worked obsessively and despised most of his colleagues. It was a winning formula. Back in England he was also working hard, whether writing his novels or becoming an instant authority on art, systems of industrial management, Fabian politics or international affairs. With the same intensity he set about consulting specialists on Virginia's health, going over the heads of doctors he disagreed with until he was given the answers he wanted. In each case he was using every opportunity to further his own interests without any regard for other people's point of view.

This is a believable description of a person who has learnt the hard way to gain what he wanted at whatever cost. He was a Jew in a gentile world and he grew up despising the softness of his mother's ancestry. If Virginia was soft, then she was dispensable. If she could stand the treatment he was dishing out to her, then she was worthy to be his wife. Not only Virginia and her social class were on trial, but all gentiles.

In contrast to Virginia, Leonard was busy, well, happy and running the show. She must have felt intensely that he as a man, with his University training, had all the advantages while she was struggling on her own. If she had indeed been on her own she could probably have coped, but from her perspective every effort she made was being opposed and frustrated, until she doubted even her right to exist. Leonard's elder sister Bella had written before their marriage, that he needed an intelligent wife if he was not to squash her: now he had a highly intelligent wife whom he was bent on squashing, pretending that it was for her own good as he tried to teach her how to be his ideal partner.

Roger Poole believes that there was a battle of wills going on between the Woolfs at this time, based on Leonard's rationalism as against Virginia's perception. Leonard was testing everything and everyone in terms of his idea of 'reality', while she experienced intuitive flashes of awareness which broke through the 'cotton wool' of daily existence. But Leonard never attempted to discover the conceptual space occupied by Virginia, so that she found herself isolated. Instead, he built up a picture of her apparent madness and found support from at least two medical specialists. Their efforts to persuade her that she was ill – finally subjecting her to forcible feeding – gave her the sense that she was the victim of a conspiracy; and indeed she was not consulted before decisions were made.

Caught in Leonard's trap, Virginia came to feel that her distress was not caused by illness, or madness, but by her 'faults'. Quentin Bell says 'she felt overwhelmed by a sense of guilt for which she should be punished'. [21] This sense of overwhelming guilt and inadequacy was exactly what victims of Leonard's method felt has he broke down their defences. What was Virginia's 'guilt'? From the evidence of Septimus Smith in *Mrs Dalloway,* she was trying to come to terms with her lack of feeling. We can now see that she internalised all her problems by deciding that she had married a man she didn't love in order to be a married woman, like Vanessa – and to have a child – again, like her sister; that she had used Leonard for her own selfish purposes, and that her dislike of sex was only the physical expression of a more basic failure. She would have seen his closeness to Vanessa, and his admiration of Margaret, in terms of punishment for her 'faults'. She had only got what she deserved, and the obvious solution was for her to kill herself, in which case Leonard would benefit from her money and in this way she could compensate him.

What she was unable to do was to stand sufficiently outside her predicament to ask what part, if any, Leonard was playing. In terms of cold calculation, he had gained both socially and financially by their marriage and would stand to gain even more by her death, since then she would no longer be either a trouble or an expense for him.

We need to ask why, if their sexual failure had been of prime importance, the Woolfs did not have the marriage annulled in the Spring of 1913. My view of Leonard's character and ambitions, of the power game he was playing and Virginia's response to it, answers this question. He would certainly not have seen an annulment, or divorce, as a preferable alternative to Virginia's death. First and most starkly, he would have lost control over her money. He would have had to begin again; his position in the Bloomsbury Group would have been equivocal at best, and some at least of the contacts he had made through Virginia would be lost. Many of their friends would have sympathised with her; while Vanessa, fearing that if they parted she would once more have to take responsibility for her sister, would certainly have been against it. Vanessa was in full flower – wife, mother, mistress, as well as artist who had begun to sell her pictures – she had no intention of spending her time helping Virginia, with whom she felt little sympathy. But she could and did continue to support Leonard, for whom she felt a great deal. Leonard had everything to gain by remaining where he was, and if Virginia succeeded in killing herself he would have received sympathy and practical help from everyone, while inheriting her money.

As well as despair, Virginia eventually felt rage. Rage at the loss of her autonomy. After all, she had not taken the initiative in being married: this was a plot devised by Lytton Stratchey and Vanessa, with Clive Bell's assistance, to keep Leonard in Britain and take her off Vanessa's hands. Perhaps the most damaging of Leonard's intrusions is that he appeared to be deliberately rivalling her as a novelist; he had jumped in and taken over from herself, whose dreams and ambitions since early childhood had centred on becoming a writer and who had undertaken a most exacting training to fit herself to be one. The metaphysical waters of 'insanity' were about to close over her head, as the physical waters of the River Ouse eventually engulfed her. This was her response to a situation she could not control: as the victim of his method she was unable to extricate herself. Her 'madness' was a sign of strength rather than weakness. She was fighting for the right to live, to write the work that was in her. And eventually, at enormous cost and some permanent damage to herself – she won. In doing so she frustrated what I believe to have been Leonard's objective, which was to dominate the Bloomsbury Group and become 'king', perhaps with Vanessa as his 'queen'; and from there move on to further triumphs as a major political influence in the world at large – the modern Pericles. The battle Virginia undertook was horrendous, but its successful outcome from her point of view meant that the Group remained a matriarchy with the two sisters at its centre; it did not revert to the boring pattern of patriarchal domination, and is therefore remembered as a most remarkable and creative period in English cultural life.

In his biography, Quentin Bell is informative about the relationship of Virginia and Leonard at this time. However, he has been a major influence on future writers as he projected the instability of Virginia's mind and contrasted it with Leonard's patience, without considering the catastrophic effect of Leonard's strong judgemental influence on Virginia and his drive for dominance. I believe that Leonard was indeed manipulating and controlling the situation and that Virginia resisted him in the only way she knew: to submerge and fight her battle internally, to the point of embracing death itself.

In her absence from the surface level, Leonard had a free run. He was able to create the image of their life at this time which has endured for so long and which now needs to be challenged. It was an image that Virginia herself rebutted in her writings, when she was strong enough to do so. But at the time her rebellion took the form of mental breakdown, this was her only possible way of escape. Leonard was in his element consulting Harley Street 'nerve specialists', discussing Virginia's symptoms and giving the doctors his version of her condition, then ensuring that their draconian prescriptions were carried out. In her fourth novel, *Mrs Dalloway*, Septimus Smith had 'committed an appalling crime and been condemned to death by human nature':

"Once you fall, Septimus repeated to himself, human nature is on you. Holmes and Bradshaw are on you. They scour the desert. They fly screaming into the wilderness. The rack and the thumbscrew are applied. Human nature is remorseless." [22]

Leonard may not actually have wanted a heroic sex life with an insatiable Aspasia, except in his fantasies. The grievance he acquired as the result of Virginia's 'failure', together with occasional sex as part of his power games, were more useful to him.

The only gentle way the Woolfs managed to relate to each other during these turbulent months was in terms of Virginia's pet names: she as Mandrill, who was male (she would have liked the word man-drill), and he as Mongoose. Unlike real life, in their games Mandrill was dominant and Mongoose her humble suitor. But even here there was an underlying battle between them, with hidden hostility on both sides.

That spring of 1913, the Woolfs stayed at Asheham House in Sussex, not at Clifford's Inn. They received friends there and made a number of visits. Virginia's increasing distress was a constant worry. Leonard's busy care of her as he tried to get her to eat, and drink great quantities of milk, was just what all their friends hoped of him. But he was also preparing to get rid of Virginia's medical team on whom she relied and substitute his own. His way of doing so was to undermine the positions of both Thomas and Savage. As recorded by Quentin Bell, seen through Leonard's eyes:

"one of the difficulties of the situation was that Jean Thomas felt an unconscious but violent homosexual passion for Virginia and was also devoted to Sir George Savage; this made her awkward and quarrelsome." [23]

Thus Leonard marginalised both until their positions became untenable, his actual objection to them being that they were in favour of Virginia having a child and that he could not exert control over them. In his black and white, rigid left-brain, this made them quite simply the enemy, whom he had to outwit. He was preparing the ground to replace them with his selected doctors who would certainly not agree to Virginia becoming a mother.

Leonard took Virginia to Newcastle-upon-Tyne in June to attend a Women's Co-operative Congress, where Margaret Llewelyn Davies was the leading light; she accompanied them back to London. Virginia cannot but have contrasted herself unfavourably not only with Vanessa but with that sterling character. On the long train journey back from the north Leonard doubtless managed to demonstrate his admiration of Margaret, while showing up his wife's ignorance. Margaret arranged for the Woolfs to have lunch with Beatrice and Sidney Webb, who were both committed Fabians and drew Leonard into their political orbit. In July he joined the Fabian Society and began writing for the *New Statesman*. And so he continued to pursue his own interests, which were leading him away from Virginia. In this way disaster, step by step, came upon them.

During July Virginia was depressed and unwell. Towards the end of that month, the Woolfs attended a Fabian Society Conference at Keswick, where Virginia became ill. On their return they consulted Sir George Savage and she entered Jean Thomas's nursing home at Twickenham, where she told Leonard 'awful things', after which he was not allowed to visit her. He wrote her frequent love letters addressing her as Mandy (Leonard's abbreviation of Mandrill) and signing himself M, for Mongoose. In these letters he emphasises how very well he is, and that 'it wont be any time before we're again having the best life that any two people can have'. He insists that they have had 'a perfect year' together:

"Oh, Mandy, Mandy dearest, I dont believe even you know how I can think of nothing but you, how you are everything in the world to me – Do trust me that it is only a matter of days for everything to be perfect again & that there is nothing to fear. We said so so often & now darling is the time to prove it... you can't imagine how you obsess me & how I long to see you – but in a way I believe it is better for you not to see me for a few days." [24]

Once again, as when he was wooing her during the previous spring, his letters and his presence were intolerable to her. He assures her he would stay at Asheham for a long weekend but only with Adrian (she evidently doesn't trust him). He ends this letter:

"I believe, Great One, you do want to take on your mongoose in service for another year – & if you'll only let him grovel before you & kiss your toes, he'll be happy. Goodnight, beloved, Your M."

And two days later:

"This is to tell you dearest that I won't believe you even if you tell me those dreadful things & I am happy because I *know* you love me."

Evidently Virginia had told him she didn't love him, perhaps that she no longer wished to be married to him. She wanted out. Like Rhoda who left Louis, she tried to get away, while he was fulsomely putting her on a pedestal and grovelling. But he was also refusing to take any responsibility for her breakdown. It was she who had to 'prove' that 'everything would be perfect' by renouncing her own sense of truth. He had no intention of changing his life-style. He was once again living at Clifford's Inn.

Their two visions were catastrophically in conflict. He would allow himself to be Mongoose to her Mandrill but he was not going to dilute that precious blood of his with the effete, pallid, gentile blood of the English upper-middle class aristocracy, that (having married into it) he was beginning to detest and despise. He would not plant his seed in a woman who was proving herself to be tainted with madness. Thus he rationalised their sexual failure and now, staying alone at Clifford's Inn, he wrote *The Wise Virgins* with all the fury of his frustrated testosterone (if indeed his testosterone was entirely frustrated during these months). In his novel he insists that *mens sana in corpore sano* – a healthy mind in a healthy body – is essential: thus seeking to prove that he alone is right and Virginia wrong. His sense of his own sanity depended on Virginia being mad and it seems that he did a great deal to madden her.

Yet before Leonard had come back from Ceylon, Virginia was capable of leading her own life, of staying by herself at Little Talland House and writing, finding her own feet. There is no doubt that Leonard was appallingly bad for Virginia as an independent human being. Even after she had survived this period of her life, he managed to reduce her to a regressed state of infantilism so that she became ever more dependent on him. This is the flip side of his obsessive caring for her.

Jean Thomas differed from Leonard in only partly blaming Virginia's breakdown on the fear of what the critics might say about her book:

"Her sleepless nights were spent in wondering whether her art, the whole meaning and purpose of her life, was fatuous, whether it might not be torn to shreds by a discharge of cruel laughter." [25]

Not only this, but Thomas also blamed her family and friends who, instead of supporting her, were 'teasing' her. Thomas wrote to Violet Dickinson on 14 September, 1913:

"It is the novel which has broken her up. She finished it and got the proof back for correction... couldn't sleep & thought everyone would jeer at her. Then they did the wrong thing & teased her about it and she got desperate – and came here a wreck. It was all heart rending." [26]

Who teased Virginia about her book? Leonard? Vanessa? If so, the devil take them.

As soon as Virginia came out of the nursing home the Woolfs went down to Asheham House but she was not well. On 22 August, Leonard took her to London to see both Dr Savage and Dr Head. In his account, she agreed to see these doctors after he promised her that they would go down to the Plough Inn in Somerset immediately afterwards: this was the very place where their sexual failure had become so obvious the previous year; it is likely that Leonard himself wanted to go there again to have the pleasure of eating their 'delicious' food. The Plough Inn was always to be remembered as a place of terror to Virginia and when they got there she simply refused to eat, insisting that she was not ill and that her distress was due to her 'faults'. She lost more weight, became listless and apathetic. He sat by the hour trying to persuade her to take a spoonful. She was now in a state of deep depression and was delirious. She must have spoken frequently of being a failure and wanting to die. Leonard sent for her reliable friend Katherine (Ka) Cox, but Virginia's state continued to worsen. A week later they returned to London by train. Leonard and Ka had to keep constant watch over Virginia, in case she threw herself out of the carriage. They all moved into 38 Brunswick Square – not Clifford's Inn.

The following day, Leonard took Virginia to see Drs Wright and Head. Virginia thought she would meet Dr Head on equal terms so that she could put her side of the case, arguing that there was no reason for her not to have a child; but Leonard had already had a private consultation with him describing his view of her condition. Here there was definitely a conspiracy between Leonard and the doctors; and Virginia, as she later realised, didn't stand a chance. She had to sit there, objectified, while they off-loaded their pompous certainties on her – No child... Officially declared mad... Mustn't contaminate the human stock, must we?... Should be grateful your husband is looking after you. As she says, 'The rack and the thumbscrew are applied. Human nature is remorseless.' She left that appalling interview, which she recorded in *Mrs Dalloway* in the knowledge that Leonard had engineered it, knowing there was no hope and the only possibility of escape was death. Not only this but he had disregarded the right of Dr Savage, her personal doctor, to be consulted. It seems that he was actually *exhibiting* Virginia to these new doctors, in her state of despair, as he was to exhibit her to Dr Octavia Wilberforce in 1941, to exonerate himself from all blame if she did kill herself. On both occasions she tried to end her life immediately after seeing the doctors of Leonard's choosing; on the latter occasion, she succeeded. Neither suicide attempt had any direct connection with the books she had written but were not yet published, *The Voyage Out* and *Between the Acts*; both had everything to do with her loss of autonomy as Leonard gained ascendancy over her, and her recognition (true or not) that he wanted her dead.

On each occasion Leonard would have thought that he had won their battle of wills, their conflict of visions, in which he had proved that his vision was reality, hers illusion; and that he had demonstrated his own ability as a writer, whereas she had failed. In 1913, he considered that in *The Wise Virgins* he had said everything that needed to be said about their relationship. He had summed it up and provided the only authentic record, as he had summed up his life in Ceylon in *The Village in the Jungle;* and, with a writer's egocentricity, he was ready to move on.

If Virginia had succeeded in killing herself in 1913, and *The Voyage Out* had been published at all (it is quite likely that Leonard would have refused to let it be published, as he refused to let Thoby's letters appear and, later, tried to prevent Julian Bell's poems), it would merely have been seen as a promising romantic novel left by yet another half-mad, suicidal woman. On both occasions – there are too many similarities in her situation between this time in 1913, and 1941 – the evidence of the doctors would provide Leonard with an alibi so that he was not blamed.

Returning to the house and putting Virginia to bed that evening, after their visit to the doctors, Leonard went out, accompanied by Vanessa, to see Dr Savage and try to explain his behaviour in consulting Dr Head without first getting the agreement of Virginia's own doctor. In doing so he left the box containing Virginia's Veronal (her usual sleeping pills, a type of barbiturate) unlocked and open by her side. Alone, Virginia took a lethal overdose of 100 grams, then lapsed into a coma. Ka Cox, who was in the house, came into the room and saw something was wrong. It was only through Ka's prompt action in immediately alerting those who could help, that Virginia's life was saved. We owe all of Virginia's subsequent writings not to Leonard but to a trustworthy woman – Ka Cox. Quentin Bell gives us this account of the events on the evening of 9 September, 1913:

"Dr Head, nurses, Vanessa, were sent for. Ka stood by. Lodging on the top floor was Maynard Keynes's younger brother Geoffrey, a house surgeon at St Bartholemew's. He drove Leonard at high speed through the London traffic shouting: 'Urgent! Doctor!' got a stomach pump from his hospital and raced back. The doctors and nurses pumped the veronal out of Virginia and then watched through the night. At 12.30 [am] Leonard went exhausted to bed and slept. At 1.30 Virginia nearly died; at six in the morning Vanessa woke Leonard to tell him she was better; at nine Dr Head returned and was able to say that she was practically out of danger. She remained unconscious all that day." [27]

Leonard recalled that dash to the hospital with pleasure, it was so exciting. He claimed that he felt no sense of guilt at having left the box of Veronal open beside Virginia, and he prided himself on being able to go to bed and have seven hours' good sleep that night, while others coped with the crisis. This was hardly the caring behaviour that one would have expected of 'Saint Leonard'.

Two decades later we might have called Leonard's carelessness in leaving the Veronal available to Virginia, a Freudian lapse. As the end of the brief, tragic marriage of Leonard Woolf, successful novelist and budding left-wing politician, to a failed, fatally flawed genius, the story would have been so perfect. And, provided he wasn't blamed, he would have attracted so much sympathy. He had certainly done enough by manipulation of the doctors and a remarkable act of carelessness on his part to make her death the most probable outcome. If we consider the possibility that his action was intentional, then he would have justified Lytton Strachey's prediction that he, like Swift, 'would murder his wife'. However, it is perhaps more accurate to see Leonard as a gambler who, although he failed on this occasion to win the jackpot of Virginia's wealth, did succeed in his dangerous power game against Sir George Savage and Jean Thomas. His consolation prize was that Virginia would never be a mother and she lost her supporting medical team. Leonard was now free to make decisions on her behalf in consultation with his selected doctors; Dr Head was in charge. He gave Dr. Wright a copy of *The Village in the Jungle*. [28] In October, Sir George Savage wrote a dignified letter to Leonard:

"Dear Mr Woolf

I was glad to get your letter. I recognize your anxiety & that of Virginia's relations & I also fully understand why you and they thought it well to seek further and younger advice. I am not professionally jealous but that, while I was supposed to be looking after her, several others were also being consulted without reference to me caused me pain. This was made greater when another specialist was called down & I heard nothing from anyone. Fees certainly never entered my mind but consideration did. My one desire is that Virginia should once more be her bright self and I do not mind by whose instrumentality it comes. I am Yours truly G.H. Savage" [29]

Sir George's letter raises some questions about what Leonard was actually doing during the evening that Virginia had taken the overdose. If he and Vanessa had indeed visited Savage, no doubt the good doctor would have said so in his letter – but he heard nothing until he received, eventually, a letter from Leonard which he is acknowledging. Ka Cox was at 38 Brunswick Square when she telephoned Vanessa at 6.30 pm. Where did she phone to? If Leonard and Vanessa had been with Dr Savage, why did the doctor not come back with them to attend Virginia in this emergency? Most likely, they were together at Vanessa's studio that evening. This makes one wonder about the state of Leonard and Vanessa's relationship, that he left Virginia to visit her sister in this crisis. If he had no idea he had left the box of Veronal open, then he was simply in a hurry to get away; but if he had not just been careless, then he needed to remove himself from the scene of a possible suicide – and to seek support and even bodily relief from the queen bee of the Bloomsbury Group. He refused to accept any responsibility for Virginia's condition, soon after telling Lytton Strachey that 'it is illness & nothing moral', [30] and Janet Case: 'One can see it is so purely a physical thing: she *cannot* believe.' Spotts editorially questions Leonard's use of the word 'physical', and suggests he meant 'psychological', but it is clear that he meant what he wrote and that he had been arguing with Virginia, insisting that her 'illness' was simply physical, and that therefore he was not in the least responsible. All she had to do was get better and they could live their ideal of matrimonial happiness.

On her return to consciousness Virginia's symptoms continued to be 'very bad', according to Quentin Bell. George Duckworth offered to lend them, free of charge, Dalingridge Place, his large house in Sussex, where she needed three nurses to attend her. Clifford's Inn was obviously unsuitable; she never lived there again and Leonard relinquished it with considerable reluctance in December.

While Virginia was making a very slow recovery at Dalingridge Place, undergoing a strict regime which included force feeding, she heard the birds outside her window sing in Greek and she also heard King Edward VII swear atrociously. Both events can be interpreted as part of her effort to grapple with the 'perfect' super-ego ideals that Leonard had thrust upon her. She had to destroy them in order to emerge in her own person, as the writer she knew she could be. The birds outside were free to get above themselves and sing in Greek, as King Edward was free to lower himself by swearing, which she also did; and fought with the nurses. She refused to see Leonard for weeks at a time, as she broke down the rigidities and boundaries that he had erected around her. Expressing her rage was actually a symptom of returning sanity but was interpreted as madness.

Leonard's friendship with Margaret Llewelyn Davies continued. During those years of Virginia's breakdown, he could rely on Margaret's womanly sympathy. In 1941 he wrote to her:

"It is over now. You know what it was like before and I can never forget what you were at that time." [31]

My alternative title for this book is *Getting Away With Murder.* However, no thanks to Leonard, this is not what happened in 1913.

From now on, Leonard took total responsibility for Virginia. He refused to have her certified as insane. If she had been certified, according to the law at the time, he would not have been able to obtain a divorce from her, whereas he retained the right to do so; but if Virginia had wished to escape from their marriage she would not have been able to divorce him. He was legally empowered to act on her behalf. And he was in control over her money as well as her health. Any freedom she did achieve had to be in another dimension, within herself and in her writing. She had begun to experience this other dimension, hearing the birds sing in Greek and the swearing king, above and below the limited mental straight-jacket within which Leonard operated. In her own creative world she was out of the reach of his third degree method of insistent, judgemental, obsessive, apparently rational Socratic dialogue, where repeated questioning without accepting the answers is designed to reveal the victim's ignorance and break down their sense of self.

Sensitive to different vibrations, tunneling beneath, flying above, Virginia's dead parents and brother would soon reawaken within her and she would bring them back to life. Leonard never understood that her so-called madness was in fact an extended and enriched sanity. According to his limited rationalist attitude she had been permanently invalidated. Not only this but he now had the rest of the world on his side, sympathising with him for being married to a mad wife who was suicidal.

MONGOOSE

Chapter Five

LEONARD EXPOSES HIMSELF

When Leonard sat down to write *The Wise Virgins* he was closely scruti-
nising his newly-won position as a Jew in the upper-middle class artistic
world of the gentile Stephen family and, in particular, the relationship
between himself and the two 'wise virgins', Vanessa and Virginia. He also
hoped to consolidate his intended career as a novelist. No doubt, with
that precise mind of his, he planned to publish one book a year and make
his name, if not his fortune. But, in fact, the fate of this book stopped his
budding career in its tracks – he never wrote another novel.

In *The Wise Virgins,* which is not readily available, we find close-up
contemporary portraits of Leonard himself as Harry, Virginia as Camilla,
Vanessa as Katharine, Clive Bell as Arthur and his own Jewish family as
the Davises located in suburban Richstead (Putney) next door to the gentile family of the Garlands. We are not faced with Leonard's hindsight and
can, in fact, indulge our own as we seek to enter the mind of its newly-
married author who describes his efforts to break away from what he felt
to be the boring, conventional existence of his own relatives by entering
the upper-class world of the Lawrence (Stephen) family – a world he both
admired and despised.

Sub-titled 'A Story of Words, Opinions and a few Emotions', this
book is a so-called *roman a clef*, literally a 'key' novel about real people
who are thinly disguised. Harry-Leonard, the Jewish hero, is not married
to Camilla-Virginia; indeed, Camilla rejects Harry when he asks her to
marry him. Camilla's sister Katherine (Vanessa) is also unmarried
although she 'looks like a mother', while Arthur (Clive Bell) is a rival
suitor for Camilla. There occurs as part of the disguise a too-simple
exchange of arts in that both Arthur and Camilla are painters and
Katharine is a writer. Despite these changes, the people themselves are all
too recognisable.

Leonard not only rides roughshod over his family (he saw this as a side
issue, thus compounding his 'crime' in their eyes), but also over Virginia
who was just beginning her own writing career: here she is, being encapsulated in Leonard's book. This is a problem women continue to face –
men's assumption that they have the right to envision 'reality' and to

HOGARTH HOUSE, RICHMOND

write about women as part of their story. For a woman to become the valid subject of her own life is still a struggle. In 1913 Leonard did not consider that Virginia's process of self discovery as a person and a writer would have been a great deal more difficult if his book had succeeded.

In his unkind, indeed almost vicious, portrayal of the Woolf family, and especially his mother as Mrs Davis, Leonard confirmed the hurt he inflicted in not inviting her to his wedding. Many of the family never forgave him and made further protests through the years, when Leonard repeated his views both in print and in a broadcast on the BBC in June 1959, on 'My Parents and Grandparents'. Leonard's treatment of his mother as Mrs Davis is indeed uncompromising. Harry sits listening as she repeats in 'her nasal, monotonously quiet voice' the names of servants: 'they seemed to be used with cynical mockery of him in the sordid, greasy chronicles of his mother':

"Mrs. Davis was now started upon a subject about which she really felt. You could hear it in her voice which, quiet and precise, seemed to fit so ill with her appearance. There was no doubt she had been a handsome woman – in fact, robustly and boldly, she still was a handsome woman. The big curved nose, the curling, full lips, the great brown eyes would have made a fine old woman of her, if she had been squatting under a palm-tree with a white linen cloth thrown over her head and drawn round her heavy oval face. The monotonous sing-song of her voice would have sounded all right if she had sung the song of Miriam... it came incongruously through the large nose in her quiet, precise, voluble and thin-sounding English. However, that was the voice in which for the next quarter of an hour she poured out the lore of servants, their follies, stupidities, and vices." [1]

Much later in the book Harry recalls his childhood when he was a small boy dependent on his mother, and reflects: 'It was strange that no finest strand of that relationship, one could hardly call it love or affection, remained to bind him to her. He wondered whether perhaps he was merely without human feelings.' [2]

Reading this book deeply hurt Marie Woolf and most of her other children. What of the portraits Leonard draws of some other figures? He is even more devastating about Clive Bell (Arthur) whom he disliked and despised when they were up at Cambridge, for having private means from his well-to-do, landowning family and for his warm, outgoing, social personality which he could not intimidate; and he never forgave

Bell for marrying Vanessa. In his novel Leonard plays with his victim as a cat plays with a mouse:

"Arthur Woodhouse [woodlouse!] tossed his fat, round little body and his little, round, fat mind from side to side... His mind and his body and his laugh and his feelings were all equally restless. Feminine charms moved him more easily and at random than he himself realised... he was one of those men so small mentally and morally that anything which took place in his little mind or little soul naturally seemed to him to be one of the great convulsions of nature. So he was very happy, when alone between the sheets, to recognise how susceptible he was and how virile, and still happier to believe that other people, including women, recognised it. It only remains to add that Arthur was a barrister who practised only as a literary critic, and earned a living by being neither one nor the other." [3]

Meeow!

Unlike the Woolf family, Clive did not retaliate. He was probably not surprised by Leonard's display of spleen since he had already won the 'prize' by marrying Vanessa and having two children with her; he had also had a lengthy flirtation with Virginia while Leonard was in Ceylon and had carried on a very positive and helpful correspondence with her about her writing. Understandably, Clive was seriously concerned about the effect Leonard was having on Virginia and, since he was a gentleman, would have said or done nothing to make her predicament worse.

Leonard makes a central point of Harry being a Jew. Harry sets himself to choose between two contrasting types of woman, both of whom are gentiles: there is the 'cold' ethereal Camilla, of whom he is in awe, who is beautiful and feeds his dreams, and there is the provincial Gwen, a member of the Garland family living next door to the Davises. Their two houses provide the opening mise-en-scene of the novel and are no doubt located in Colinette Road itself.

Harry deliberately shocks the simple, innocent Gwen, in order to 'wake her up', then anticipates with pleasure her 'dreams' of him. Gwen's character is drawn from the girl Leonard left behind in Ceylon; while Harry, who wears the stiff, starched collars Leonard habitually wore in Ceylon, is the egocentric, provocative and embattled outsider:

"She [Gwen] hadn't liked him, none of them had. He hadn't got on with them; he never did with people. They were so dull, so stupid. But she had been interested in him, he had seemed strange to her... But they couldn't understand him. Did anyone? Was he to wander up and down the world always between rows of cold, dull eyes? The intolerable dullness of life! And yet the interest! He almost laughed at himself. 'Egoism,' he thought, 'damned egoism! I never think of anyone except myself, or in relation to myself. But I *am* better than they are, for at any rate I know I am an egoist... The horror of the night is that we're alone with ourselves. No one to mop and mow before, to play the fool before. Only our miserable, naked selves – and we'd mop and mow and pretend before ourselves, if it were any good. And that's just what I'm doing.' He jumped up, flung his clothes off and huddled into bed. 'Damned fool! Damned fool!' he said aloud, as he settled himself to dream.

'They're Jews,' said May, when the front door was shut and they had wandered back into the drawing room.

'And what if they are?' said Gwen rather sharply.

'I hate Jews.'...

'I don't see anything to hate in the Davises, May,' said Mrs. Garland gently...' Gwen's fallen in love with Byron. I hope you'll make him wear different collars, Gwen dear.'

Gwen did not answer. She kissed her mother and went up to bed. She undressed at once, but slowly. She was dejected and discontented. Was he nice, that dark young man? Had he liked her? Had he despised them? He had thought her stupid, dull. There was something unpleasant, cynical about him. And yet he thought in a way in which none of the people whom she knew thought. Was she really stupid, and was life dull? She would ask him straight, next time she saw him, why he despised them. She, at any rate, had spirit. And she too settled herself to dream." [4]

Harry needs the stimulation of desirable females. Next morning he is on his way to the art studio, where he will meet Camilla:

"[Harry] grew still happier in the train among the crackling newspapers and red shaved faces and the cheery, masculine jokes. He manoevred in order to sit facing a fresh, pink-faced girl preening herself in colours among the many males." [5]

We see his meeting with Camilla-Virginia from Leonard's idea of her point of view:

"She smiled thoughtfully. He interested her; she wanted to find out what he was like. He was so different from the other boyish students, so open in their poses and soft in their minds and faces. He was so obviously hard and clever, and there seemed under the crust to be something intricate and perhaps violent. She wanted – it was purely curiosity – to see, if possible, what it might be. And it must be added that she got some personal pleasure from noticing his interest and admiration.

She certainly did interest him... Ever since he had been a child he had found the need of something romantic for the thoughts that were never spoken and for the dreams that he was accustomed to dream by day... He liked to recall the purity of her face and her voice: the remoteness of a virgin, he said to himself. When one knows the coarseness and tortuousness of one's own mind, the foulness and ignobleness of one's own thoughts, he used to think to himself, such purity of beauty is almost frightening. One longs to be intimate with it, but is there any point of contact? She seemed to be in another world from his, and that attracted him all the more. Sometimes in that sentimental quarter of an hour before sleep she seemed to belong to two worlds, to bring, in what she said or might say, the fragments of songs and sights of a stranger and more beautiful world into the stupid tangle of Sainthills and Graysons and Garlands." [6]

In order to make a 'point of contact' Harry's (and no doubt Leonard's) gambit is to make generalised negative judgements, usually about other people. With Camilla, he inveighs against spinsters:

"He stopped painting, and stood, with his brush lifted, looking at her. 'They appeal me sometimes, those spinsters drifting on through life to be dried up into disappointed, soured middle-age. There they sit in a great circle round London, waiting, in the suburbs – the suburbs are full of them. It's horrible.' "

Leonard must have argued this point with Virginia before their marriage. In his book, Camilla disagrees: 'I daresay they're tragic, but there *is* something fine, almost noble, in them. I like their point of view. It's alive, they're alive – so much more alive than those cow-like married women.' Whereupon Harry comes back: 'But they miss something immense; not only children, I mean, and child-bearing. The – the romance of life. It gives me the horrors sometimes to think of it. *I* may miss it too; *you* may even – though I don't suppose you will. It all seems so purposeless, so futile, idiotic. That's what dries them up mentally, just as their breasts and bodies are dried up. And little hairs sprout under their chins.' " [7]

There is the irony here that Harry-Leonard saw having children as one antidote to the dreaded state of dried-up spinsterhood, while in reality he prevented Virginia from having any. Later in the novel, when talking to Gwen, Harry even says: 'It's the one thing that I regret in not being a woman, that I can't bear children.' [8] He could not, indeed, *bear* children, especially the possibility of Virginia becoming a mother. This would have given her the initiative in their marriage and taken attention away from his insatiable masochistic egocentricity. It is clear that he argued for 'the romance of life' in which Virginia must avoid dried-up spinsterhood by playing her part in his drama. Returning to Harry's first scene with Camilla:

"His voice was dull and passionless. His dark view of life seemed to her to throw a gloom over the bright day. She fought in herself against that view. He had not said what those dried-up spinsters missed, what he was afraid for him and her missing. In his mind it had meant what the male wants, a certain fierceness of love, mental and bodily; something which romance and civilisation and all the generations which lie behind mankind have made, at least in our hopes and imaginations, a flame that shall join and weld together and isolate from the rest of the world... Among men, as among animals, it is the young male who is fierce and dangerous, and roars and bellows and makes all the noise.

She burst out: 'Life's so wonderful.'

'And so damnably disappointing.'

'Don't. I won't believe it – it's untrue. There's not a minute of my life that I don't enjoy, and I *will* enjoy it.' " [9]

Throughout her life Virginia wanted every day to be happy and relaxed, this was the necessary state for her to be fully creative. Yet here was Harry-Leonard demanding that 'a flame shall join and weld' them together and isolate them from the rest of the world. She had realised that if her father had lived it would have prevented her writing; now, the threat came from Leonard's 'flame' and his drive to isolate her from the very world of which she was part and needed to respond to her work. She had to resist him, even at the cost of a life-threatening nervous breakdown. Death itself would have been preferable to being subjugated by a man and losing her creativity.

This was the stark choice that faced Virginia, together with the knowledge – which she only admitted when she was 'mad' – that she had been trapped into a marriage with a man she did not love, to whom she felt indeed entirely cold, as a result of a conspiracy by Vanessa, Lytton Strachey and Leonard, each for their own motives. Descent into 'madness' was her way of escape from an intolerable situation; but Leonard was quite incapable of seeing beyond the devouring egocentricity of his day-dreams, and his sense of destiny, that he was the cause of her breakdown.

In *The Wise Virgins*, Leonard contrasts Vanessa with Virginia. Harry says of Camilla, who understands with her imagination: 'Bare truth she might misunderstand; she is more female than Katharine. But Katharine's the only woman I've ever met who understands the bare truth.' Whereupon Harry says he 'would give all the understanding in the world for a little imagination'. [10] Understanding 'the bare truth' that Leonard shared with Vanessa was surely an important factor in Virginia's breakdown: it led her to believe she was holding Leonard back, getting in his way when he could have been doing so many things which he could discuss with Vanessa but not with her.

Here we are in a hall of mirrors where the glancing reflections illuminate Leonard and Vanessa, and leave Virginia-Camilla isolated, a beautiful icy mountain in shadow.

Contrasting the qualities of Jewish and gentile women, Harry, talking with his friend Trevor, says:

" 'I admire your pale women with their white skins and fair hair, but I despise them.'

'Do most Jews feel like that?'

'All of them – all of them. There's no life in you, no blood in you, no understanding. Your women are cold and leave one cold – no dark hair, no blood in them. Pale hair, pale souls, you know. You talk and you talk and you talk – no blood in you! You never *do* anything.'

'Why do you think it's so important to do things?'

'Why? Because I'm a Jew, I tell you – I'm a Jew!' " [11]

Katharine tells Camilla that she will have to decide whether she is going to marry Harry, although, she says, 'I don't think anyone ought to marry you... he would have to be very much in love with you,' to which Camilla replies:

" 'There's no reason in nature, is there, why he shouldn't be that?... Attractive: love therefore enduring until death do us part. *Mens sana in corpore sano* ['a healthy mind in a healthy body' – something Leonard did not think Virginia had] so that all the marriage service can be read without blushes. And a mind on wings! Katharine, I'm simply made for marriage... You admit that I'm simply the ideal woman for marriage, so why go on croaking your nevermore at me?'

'I imagine a husband might not always be content merely to be in love with you. It isn't a normal male idea of the ideal wife.'

'...But do you honestly think I'm as cold as all that, Katharine dearest? You know I love you far more than you love me.'

'That's hardly the point we were talking about, is it?'

'But I'm not cold, am I? I couldn't be so very attractive if I were. I'm very affectionate, you know that, don't you? I like silk and soft things and strokings. I was told the other day that I was like hills with virgin snow on them; but that's nonsense, isn't it?' "

This is a direct reference to the piece Leonard wrote about Virginia and read to her in the spring of 1912 [12]; parts of this passage, and maybe the whole of it, are evidently taken from life:

" 'It does sound like it, certainly. But that wasn't what I said... I shall marry, however, and I shall be in love with my husband,' said Katharine with impassive conviction, and it was quite clear that she would be." [13]

Virginia read *The Wise Virgins* for the first time in January 1915. She must have felt that Leonard was writing it not only to her, but at her. Most of what she thought she kept to herself, only saying that it was a writers' book and that the bad parts were not so very bad. But a deeper reading must have reinforced her semi-conscious awareness that the dark, more vital Katharine-Vanessa is obviously more sympathetic to Harry than the pale 'cold' Camilla.

In the novel Katharine is both unmarried and childless (the other 'wise virgin') and Leonard stretches credulity when he wants to describe her. He does it through Camilla who looks at her sister and thinks: 'Her face was already that of a mother's; her own would always retain something of the virgin's.' The author contrasts the two sisters:

"When you saw [Katharine] for the first time you thought her darker, deeper, and more beautiful than she really was. Yet she was dark and deep and beautiful enough, those who had seen her oftenest would have told you. By her side Camilla seemed stranger and fairer than she really was. Even when she was sitting now motionless and silent thinking, her eyes seemed to have to dart quickly to keep pace with her thoughts. Middle-aged and elderly ladies... called her most erroneously a sweet young woman; young women and many young men found her fascinating but frightening; old men felt like a father to her without noticing that they had fallen in love with her. Harry was right, you did not think of innocence in Camilla's face; you thought perhaps of purity, coldness even, of hills and snow, of something underneath, below the surface, that might at any moment break out destructive of you – of her?" [14]

Leonard attempts to sum up what Camilla-Virginia thought:

"She was quite certain she was not in love with Harry, and somehow or other she did not see how she ever would be. She liked his sensibility, his vigour, and his violence; she liked his hardness, and it repelled her; the sombreness of his mind and his yellow face repelled her. If nothing else were asked of her, she might, she felt, love him as a friend; but to live in one house and close to him, which after all one must envisage in marriage... And then too he left her cold." [15]

Camilla entertains them at their country house (Asheham House) with one of her flights of fancy, deciding she would keep hens despite other people's objections: 'They are wonderfully beautiful in troops on green fields, each with a noble cock, all in their different colours, yellow and blue, and glossy black and snowy white. I'll have them marshalled in their glossy troops in the field in front of the house, and I shall sit all day long upon the terrace, watching them and the pattern they weave on the field as they strut about.' Camilla's flights are famous in the novel, just as Virginia's were in the Bloomsbury Group, but Leonard's comments on them are sobering:

"The flights intoxicated Harry... in the timbre of a woman's voice, when it was beautiful, there seem to be mysteriously harmonised all the desires and enchantments both of the spirit and the body. He, at any rate, seemed to hear a deep and rare note in Camilla's voice as she sat there very still and fair and smiling, abandoning herself to something outside herself, to another world from which ideas welled up and formed themselves upon her lips into the beautiful sounds of words. To those who loved or desired her... this abandonment to something outside herself, something which seemed to belong not to the ordinary constituents of humanity and femininity, caused fear and a curious catch at the heart. *To those who had to live with her it often caused irritation. She had eluded them, slipped from their grasp and from their power to inflict human feelings of pleasure and pain; she was so intolerably far from them! Who in this world can ever quite forgive a near relation for not being like himself, for touching anything in which he cannot share, for being in any way not in his power?*" [16] (My italics)

And there we have it. The free-flying woman with her positive energy and ability with words, shackled to a man who demands the power 'to inflict human feelings of pleasure and pain' and, when she eludes him by entering her own creative space: *'For those who had to live with her it often caused irritation'*. Had Vanessa told Leonard she was 'irritated' by Virginia's imaginative flights? Did he feel irritation sitting in a big arm-chair while Virginia was talking? As Jean Thomas said, 'they' teased Virginia about her first book. Now we find that 'they' were irritated by her gift for words. In Leonard's novel he was trying to teach Mrs. Leonard Woolf the intolerable lesson that she could no longer let her imagination soar as a free spirit. And he often did not permit her to talk at all.

Camilla is present during a verbal contest between Harry and Arthur:

"She compared them: Harry so cold and with that air of concentration and wariness that animals possess when they are seeking their own food or trying to avoid becoming the food of others; Arthur with all his pleasantness and follies and pettinesses bubbling out of him. Harry clearly would never give himself away, as Arthur was doing even now. Was there something ungenerous in not being able to give oneself away? They seemed matched unequally, and instinctively her sympathy went out to the weaker. Harry himself felt something of what she was feeling: it made him shrink all the more into himself; he felt physically the weight of self." [17]

Harry-Leonard decides that it is going to be a very long weekend indeed with the Stephen family at Asheham House (to give them their real names) and when he went to bed:

"he would dream there, dream deliberately before he settled to sleep, dream of what he wanted to have and what he wanted to be... He thought of himself standing up on some raised platform above a crowd, a hostile crowd threatening him. Stones were thrown, there was blood on his face, but he stood there shielding – someone, from the stones. His arm fell limply to his side, but he stood up straight still." [18]

Surely this was a basic fantasy of Leonard's. While he is standing there shielding someone (that cowering hermit crab within his own carapace, not anyone else) from the stones being thrown by the hostile crowd, one of his arms would have trembled violently as it did when he was tense or excited. Freud would have seen his dream as sexually-inspired, complete with erection and detumescence.

Leonard's emphasis on 'doing things', as opposed to merely talking, which he identifies as a Jewish trait, provides an important pointer to the almost frenetic activity that was characteristic of him as a schoolboy and during his years in Ceylon. By means of obsessive work he had climbed out of Colinette Road and into Trinity College, Cambridge. A similar dedication to work, often of the most pettifogging sort, helped him climb up the Civil Service ladder in Ceylon in record time, while he made sure that he gained the sympathy of the people who were in a position to help him. He was doing exactly the same thing after his return to England.

In his book there is a very explicit passage in which he describes the motivation underlying the Jewish temperament, including a sense of superiority over other people who are then belittled: – it is essential to go for what one wants whether the objective is money as a means of power, or any other goal, and how different this is (in his eyes) from the attitude of gentiles. Thanks to this passage, we realise in what spirit of acquisition Leonard decided to marry Virginia: he was 'doing something' with a vengeance. Harry is speaking to Camilla:

" 'I expect I can let myself go much more than you or any of those down there, but I only do it when there's something worth letting oneself go for... That's because I am a Jew. Oh yes, you see what I mean, of course. We wait hunched up, always ready and alert, for the moment to spring on what is worth while, then we let ourselves go. You don't like it? I see you don't; it makes you shrink from me – us, I mean. It isn't pleasant; it's hard, unbeautiful. There isn't sensibility, as they call it, in us. We want to *get*, to feel our hands upon, what's worth while. Is it worth while? Is it worth *getting*? That's the first and only question to buzz in our brains.'

Camilla was silent. She believed what Harry was saying. It made her sad. She distinctly did not want him to be like that... She wanted to enjoy the gayness of sun and wind and the song of larks...

'We're born that way; I suppose we were born that way twenty thousand years ago in Asia. Personally I'm proud of it. I like it... I don't like softness. I'm different from Arthur... and – good Lord! – I'm different from you, and always will be... I'm still looking out to get hold of things which – which are worth while.'

'And what is worth while?' said Camilla very slowly and wearily.

Harry hesitated. He had been speaking almost angrily, with a desire to hurt her, to expose himself and to justify himself. What was worth while?

There was one thing which at the back of his mind he had all through half believed that he meant as worth while. But he only half believed it, and he shrank from, did not dare the putting of it into words.

'Money,' he said, 'money, of course. That's the first article of our creed – money, and out of money, power. That's elementary. Then knowledge, intelligence, taste. We're always pouncing on them because they give power, power to *do* things, influence people. That's what really we want, to feel ourselves working on people, in any way, it doesn't matter. It's a sort of artistic feeling, a desire to create. To feel people moving under your hands or your brain, just as you want them to move! Admiration, appreciation, those are the outward signs. They make you swell with pride and happiness. You feel you're doing something, creating things, not being tossed and drifted through life with a few million other imbeciles. Then of course we get an acquired pleasure in the mere operation of doing things, of always feeling oneself keyed up and absolutely alive. You don't like this? You don't like my picture of us? But you must admit that our point of view implies imagination?'

Camilla remained silent.

'You don't know what life is,' he went on. 'You live in a world of your own; it consists mostly of clouds. By God! I wish I could take you to Richstead and show you that. That's how nine hundred and ninety-nine people live out of every thousand in this, my world, like caterpillars. The males crawl out to their offices in the morning, and crawl back to their houses in the evenings. The females crawl about their own and other people's houses all day. They are crawling after food and eggs – food to keep themselves alive, and eggs to keep the race of caterpillars alive. They don't know what they're after; they haven't got the imagination for it. But we have, even in the worst sink we know we're crawling and after what. The lowest pawnbroker in the Whitechapel Road has enough imagination to get himself an ideal; he knows what he's after, what is worth while.' "

Camilla refuses to commit herself, whereupon Harry tells her he is going away – as Leonard must have told Virginia that he would return to Ceylon if she did not make up her mind to marry him:

"Camilla felt strangely impersonal, and yet interested, even excited, as to what was coming next.

'I expect that's it,' he said in a voice in which there was now no trace of heat or anger. 'You want me to change my groove. You would hate to change yours; you want to go on as you've always gone on. I mean all of you. Well, so do I. It doesn't do, it is not worth it – not when you see what's going to happen, and that you'll never get what you want, if you want it. You don't like me.'... 'You know that isn't true,' she said. 'This is simply silly, Harry. We all like you.'

'Not as I am. You may like me as you are, and of course I could become so – but I won't, I never will, you know.'

'That's absurd. We like you as you are.'

Her voice was affectionate, almost pleading now. Harry sat down by her side. His anger left him suddenly; he looked back nervously over what he had said to see whether he had not been making a fool of himself, and he was inclined to think that he had...

They spent the morning walking together over the hills. Harry forgot that he might be in love with Camilla, and Camilla forgot that she ought to make up her mind. They became intimate and happy together for a few hours like the lower animals or unintelligent people – which meant that, forgetful of the past and unsuspicious of the future, they took each moment that came as one isolated point of living and feeling, and enjoyed it." [19]

The emphasis, then, so far as Leonard was concerned, was in both *doing* and *getting*. Indeed, *doing* in order to *get*. And, helped by Lytton and Vanessa, when he married Virginia he succeeded in both. The problem was, having done and got, what was he to do with his acquisition? One solution would have been for her to die so that he could start again, unimpeded by her, and helped by the status and money he had acquired through his marriage. This very nearly happened in 1913.

In his novel Camilla turns down Harry's proposal of marriage, whereupon Harry realises he has failed and plays his negative game with the 'foolish virgin', Gwen, the suburban young gentile girl. He had already wound her up during a boat trip on the river, by making generalised, derogatory and provocative remarks:

" 'Lord, Lord! You foolish virgins!'

'What do you mean?' asked Gwen without turning round...

'That's what's wrong with you all,' Harry went on. 'You're only half baked. There's something wanting here and there' – he touched his forehead and left breast. 'You are like village idiots, a little wanting. One half of life you never can understand, the male the female, and the female the male. The Greeks were wiser than we; they initiated the young men and women into the mysteries. Well, they lost what they lost and gained the whole world...'

'But are you – have you gained the whole world, as you call it, Harry?'

Harry looked at Gwen's back, hesitated and then smiled. 'Yes, thank God,' he said...

Gwen was frightened, frightened of the new violence of her feelings and of the way in which the veils seemed to be torn from life for her by Harry." [20]

Harry kisses Gwen ('ineptly'), then tries to draw back, which makes her realise he doesn't love her. But she, instead of licking her wounds in the bosom of her now-despised family, comes into his bedroom in the hotel where both families are staying:

"Harry rubbed his eyes with his hand; it seemed unreal. He looked at Gwen. She seemed to him extraordinarily beautiful with her flushed, excited young face, and with the wonderful waves of hair falling around it. A little movement of desire, cruel and brutal, ran through him. It was stifling in the room; his body was damp with sweat. He could see her bare throat through the open nightdress. He turned away his eyes.

'You can't come here,' he said huskily. 'You don't know what you're doing. Go away, for God's sake.'

She still stood by the door, smiling, as if eager to feel the full power of her passion and exaltation.

'Listen to me, Harry,' she said in a whisper. 'You must listen to me now. I love you, Harry, Harry darling, I love you. And – Harry – all you said was true... It's my chance... How can I live like that again with mother and Ethel? I can't, I won't. I'm yours absolutely. I don't mind if you don't love me; I'll make you. But – but – I can't live without you.'

Harry stared at her, motionless; her excitement carried him away. It seemed to him that, somehow or other, even for Gwen his words had been true...

Harry struggled with himself, trying to get back to reality, to a sense of ordinary life...

The next moment he felt her arms around his neck, and her kisses on his face. He caught her in his arms, and pulled her down onto the bed by his side, kissing her hair, her lips, her throat.

'Say it's true, Harry,' she panted.

'You darling, darling Gwen,' he whispered, kissing her mouth, and pressing her to him." [21]

If we take this scene as one that Leonard actually experienced, and I think we can – not only Gwen, but the tropical heat of Ceylon has migrated to a hotel on the South coast of England – in order to rouse him sexually, Leonard needed the total giving of the woman who must abandon her own way of life and adopt his. He will make no commitment to love her in return, or adapt himself to her lifestyle. But when she commits herself to him and he sees her bare throat he feels a surge of cruelty, a hint that he could put his hands round her neck and strangle her. Then he feels power without the risk of encountering the detachment of a woman's independent thoughts. Harry is even pleased that he has driven Gwen 'mad':

"It was intolerable that Gwen was crying upstairs. *Could* he marry her? After all, Camilla would never love him. It might be comfortable with Gwen – but God! how tired he would grow of that child's face at the breakfast table, and the dinner table. And yet it was his fault. She might do anything; she was mad, over the border." [22]

Gwen's 'madness' excites Harry, who has deliberately pushed her 'over the border'. Did Leonard deliberately goad Virginia into that 'madness' of 1913? – Did he push her 'over the border' for the sake of the excitement and sense of power as she became another victim of his 'method'? But Virginia resisted being either strangled or torn apart by Leonard's psychological games playing. She didn't want to end up as the prey of an emotional junkie in scenes where he was only aroused by driving her to desperation. She wanted to talk, to write, and to hear the echo of her books from the outside world which, unlike Leonard, she did not belittle or feel to be hostile. They inhabited different worlds, she and Leonard; and even though she had been driven down into the depths of depression, she never abandoned her world for his sake. Perhaps we may dare to consider whether Virginia was more sane than Leonard. She certainly needed to be extremely strong in order to cope with him.

It was evidently not possible for Leonard to interrelate with people on equal terms. A large part of his defence was to despise and diminish them, for then they seemed less dangerous. When he watched other people they seemed unreal, they were so small and inferior to him, they seemed like mere marionettes being pulled by hidden strings. He wanted to know how those strings worked, to pull them himself and watch those diminished people react differently because he had pulled their strings. It was only when he was doing this that his pervasive sense of boredom was relieved. As Harry says:

"The truth is that he was bored, and it is difficult to find in such a condition that which is as important as air to the healthy life of each individual, the secret and sentimental contemplation of oneself as a hero." [23]

By reducing the importance of those millions who make up the rest of the human population, the outer world gains a magic intensity: 'The sense of unreality persisted; it was a picture, a play on the stage. He felt enormously himself in a ring of automata, little figures, marionettes worked by wires – there they were jumping about in the gilded room, and outside the great world, wild, passionate, unrestrained.'

The dream-life of Harry-Leonard (it really is difficult to tell them apart) grew ever more compelling but remained distant and unattainable. Harry is: 'the wandering Jew, the everlasting Jew. Only I don't wander – I wish I could... I am one, and proud of it too. And the everlasting one. And the point of him is that there never is any kingdom for him to find.' [24] This theme of the Wandering Jew recurs twenty-eight years later in *The Hotel*, the only play Leonard wrote.

As the everlasting Jew in *The Wise Virgins*, Leonard-Harry identifies himself with Jesus while Harry's father, Mr Davis, is likened to God. At a late stage in writing the book, Leonard changed this figure from that of Harry's elder brother to Harry's father; but he was really describing his own elder brother Herbert, when he wrote that he was 'what God intended the human species to be – he accepts his environment and the universe, absolutely. Consequently he is happy, consequently he is the fittest, consequently he will survive. Damn him!' [25]

Leonard was a deeply discontented man and Virginia took on more than she could cope with when she married him. No wonder she wanted out. Leonard needed a woman who was not only able to shoulder the heavy burden of his own unfinished business with his family but also his melancholia which he saw as essentially Jewish. Only a strong, passionate woman could have carried this enormous load; however, Leonard did not seek out such a woman for the good reason that he could not have controlled her. Arthur (Clive Bell) speaks words that Leonard must have strongly believed: 'I wonder if any woman understands what it is to be a man. They don't realise that we've got bodies. That's what makes it so intolerable: unless they are loose and vile they have no passions. What's noble in us is vile in them.' Then Arthur says of Camilla, again no doubt Leonard's view:

" 'She is one of the few women who can see clearly. She wants to be desired like all of them; but she sees that that isn't enough. She wants so much. What she really wants, only she doesn't know it, is to be a man; and – damn, damn, damn – she never will be.' " [26]

Leonard has distorted the character of Arthur in making him speak those words and also their target, Virginia. Virginia did not want to 'be a man', she wanted to explore both sides of her female brain. That is, she wanted to grow to become what she was to call an androgynous writer. In 1913 this seemed an unattainable vision. She was faced with an almost impossible task when she decided to devote her life to using her own creative energy. She could only do so by remaining a 'virgin' – that is, by refusing to let her deeper sexual feelings become involved. In *The Wise Virgins* it is the foolish virgin, Gwen, with whom Harry has his only sexual experience and Leonard's account of their night together amply demonstrates the dangers Virginia would have had to cope with if she had become passionate.

His book ends when Harry, having been rejected by Camilla and after his sexual experience with Gwen, reluctantly commits himself to the girl:

"He looked at Gwen, saw her childish face, her eyes blank... and then he saw Camilla. He had failed, failed, failed.

He looked again at the curve of the hill; it was fading away as the train rattled on. As it disappeared it seemed to him that the answer came to him. A kind of wave of happiness passed over him. He had known Camilla: he had loved her.

'Nothing matters,' he cried to himself...

Half an hour later he stood on deck with Gwen. There was no wind, but the air was keenly cold. The sea lay without a wave or ripple, smoothed out to a sheet of silver by the moon. Gwen put her arm through his and drew him close to her.

'Dearest', she whispered.

He looked down at her face so close to him, and, shutting his eyes, kissed her."

THE END

In the original version of *The Wise Virgins,* Gwen and Harry discuss having children; however, Leonard's publisher asked him to delete these passages. This is made plain in a letter by Leonard to his publisher, Edward Arnold, attributed to mid-February 1914, written from Asheham House where Virginia was moved early in the year to be looked after by two nurses. He agrees to a number of exclusions but argues for leaving certain passages unchanged, in particular:

"The passages... in which the question of children is discussed by Gwen & Harry, and I consider that if they are omitted the whole conception of the book & the psychology of the characters is altered. If they are cut out, Gwen's act at the crisis is one of mere lust, an act completely incongruous with her character. Further the whole moral significance of the book vanishes, & the moral significance is this: Harry is living in a circle of somewhat unnatural cultured persons & like them he indulges in a habit of wild exaggerated talk which he believes that he believes. The effect of such talk upon Gwen who is half in love with him is that her *imagination* (not her mere desires) is fired & she really believes & proceeds to act upon her belief. When the reality is as near to Harry as that, he finds that *he* dare not act upon his talk, because it is more talk than belief." [26] (Leonard's emphasis.)

Leonard eventually agreed to remove this passage and some others. Its omission means that we do not have an important statement concerning his attitude towards children. It would be interesting to know whether these excluded passages still exist. His insistence that the moral significance of the book relies on Harry believing that he believes in 'a habit of wild exaggerated talk' which he picked up from 'a circle of somewhat unnatural cultured persons', means that Leonard is prepared to objectify both the Apostles and the Bloomsbury Group as he makes every effort to try and get his novel published, despite his promise to his family not to do so, In 1953, his brother Edgar wrote to Leonard:

"You showed what a cad you were when you published the Wise Virgins – after solemnly promising not to! ...Unfortunately people know that I am your brother & I have the greatest objection to other people being given a lying and utterly caddish picture of our parents & our home. And I believe on good evidence you have done the same thing before.

Having always been the lickspittle of greater intellects, you suffer from the deformity of the little man, who thinks it makes him greater to cry out 'See how I have risen above my degraded beginnings.'

Unfortunately with your mean nature you'll go on the same way and delight in causing pain to all of us. But Virginia's Diary* shows you up for what you are better than any words of mine. Edgar" [27]

---

* 'Virginia's Diary' is a reference to *The Writer's Diary*, edited and published by Leonard in 1953, giving a selection of quotations from her diary.

Was Leonard mean, a bully and a cad as his brother says? Or was he a 'saint' as many commentators have tried to portray him after Virginia's death? Our best opportunity for making up our own minds is by considering what he says in *The Wise Virgins*, begun on his honeymoon and completed during the year after his marriage.

Early in 1914 Leonard went to stay for a week with Lytton Strachey at The Lacket near Marlborough, where he suffered a mini nervous breakdown with bad headaches. His near-breakdown has been attributed not to his difficulties in trying to his book published, or to the major criticisms he received from those to whom he showed his manuscript, or to his treachery to his family, but to looking after Virginia. The editor of Leonard's *Letters* provides a footnote: 'Although VW was much improved, the unremitting strain of caring for her nearly broke LW's own health. With Janet Case and Ka Cox standing in for him at Asheham, he spent ten days with Lytton Strachey, who had withdrawn to a country cottage in Wiltshire.' [28]

Lytton was beginning what was to be his most famous book, *Eminent Victorians*. He wrote to Henry Lamb on 12 March 1914, that Leonard: 'has been having a nervous breakdown in a mild way, and seemed to want repose... Virginia is apparently all right now, and there are no nurses any more.' [29]

We need to ask why the 'unremitting strain' Leonard was experiencing at this time is blamed entirely on his caring for Virginia although she was much improved. Yet every commentator, including and especially Leonard himself throughout his autobiography, blames Virginia's breakdowns on fears concerning her about-to-be-published books and not on her relationship with Leonard. It is time we questioned this discrepancy which is necessary for those who want to present Leonard as a selfless husband without ambitions of his own.

At The Lacket Leonard was in the company of Lytton Strachey, the friend who helped him fan the fire of their visionary ambition to bring the ancient civilisation of Athens in its heyday to modern Britain. A few months before the so-called Great War broke out, such great ideals still seemed to be achievable. There was Lytton living and writing in his cottage and able to travel when he wanted, enviably free to pursue his plan to demolish Victorian pretensions, as Leonard had envisaged his own life. And it was Lytton who had persuaded him to marry Virginia. No doubt Leonard tried to get his friend to sympathise with him but he evidently failed. Lytton sided with Virginia, whom he admired. The weather was atrocious. Within a short time, there were considerable strains on their friendship.

Virginia and Leonard wrote to each other every day. From these (on one level) loving letters in which they used their pet names, we realise Virginia felt a sense of relief that she was able to relax with Janet Case and Ka Cox; but Leonard was uncomfortable. He writes:

"There is no doubt of one thing, beloved, & that is that we do suit each other in some amazing way. I've never been alone with anyone else for a few days without irritating & being irritated. And yet you can day after day & all day give me perfect happiness... We argue & talk about books & Vanessa & Clive & Roger... He thinks Ness by nature a virgin... He has a tremendous opinion of Mistress Mandril... I think sometimes he is rather jealous of your old Mongoose...

"I think I shall go to Bella. I dont think it does to stay too long here. Lytton is very nice but he is exacting. I very nearly enraged him this morning because I said I saw no reason to believe that the Greeks didn't love women! Also this isn't really a very comfortable house: there's only one comfortable chair & no sofa, so that it's rather miserable if one is not feeling well.

"You cant realize how utterly you would end my life for me if you had taken that sleeping mixture successfully or if you ever dismissed me." [30]

In some ways his need for Virginia was greater than hers for him; she hastens to reassure him:

"Dearest,

If you could have seen my sorrow after you went you would have had no doubts about my affection... Make Lytton take care of you – and stay in bed if your head aches, and dont get into long arguments but rest your poor pate...

Old Mandril does want her master so badly and last night his empty bed was so dismal, and she went and kissed the pillow... Be careful, and come home cured to your dear Brute, and we shall have a happy spring. J[anet Case] says 'V. is a model of virtue, discretion, and reasonableness' Ha ha!" [31]

And again:

"Do come back a brisk well mongoose, with a feather in your cap.

My pet, you would never doubt my caring for you if you saw me wanting to kiss you, and nuzzle you in my arms. After all, we shall have a happy life together now, wont we?" [32]

To make matters worse for Leonard, a book by the despised Clive Bell had just been published and was praised by Roger Fry. Leonard dismisses it with: 'We have not discussed Clive's book very much – it is condemned.' Bell's *Art* puts forward the most important artistic theory to emerge from the Bloomsbury Group, the theory of significant form.

The Group's visual artists were very active, with Fry running the Omega Workshops producing furniture, ceramics and cloth featuring characteristic designs. Left to herself, Virginia would have had close links with these artists but she was being isolated by Leonard. His wife's job was to learn to love him, to learn politics at which she was no good, to earn money to pay for her doctors' bills and to make him 'perfectly happy'. She was once again trying to take on an impossible burden. She had a bad relapse shortly after his return to Asheham House, evidently not being able to cope with his presence, and once more her friends were asked to stay with her while he travelled in the North of England where he saw plenty of Margaret Llewelyn Davies. In May he drew up, and Virginia signed, a 'contract' committing her to rest, eat and sleep properly and to be wise and happy. There is apparently no balancing contract in which Leonard undertakes not to pressure her with his efforts to make her live according to his ideals while refusing to adapt to hers.

His admired elder sister Bella sent him a nine-page critique condemning *The Wise Virgins*. Finally she wrote:

"I have been thinking a great deal about our conversation on the subject of your book, & the more I think about it the less I am convinced by your point of view. I understand that you do not want to hurt people's feelings & you asked me if I thought it would do if you went carefully through the book & eliminated what was likely to do so. I gathered from what you said the other day that you are only altering a few names.

I suppose that other people's criticism has outweighed mine... and Virginia thinks the book better than *The Village in the Jungle*." [33]

Virginia could have had no reaction to Leonard's second novel in November 1913, since she didn't read it until the end of January 1915. Leonard's mother, Marie Woolf, wrote to her son:

"I am now returning you the Manuscript... by Registered Post, the reading of which has given me more pain than evidently you intended... You thought fit to hold us all up... to ridicule, contempt and pity... You have not convinced me one jot that the people at Richstead are one bit less valuable to the common working of the Universe, than the people at

Bloomsbury. I don't know what the Lawrences [Stephens] are developing into in your next chapters but as far as I have made their acquaintance I have discovered nothing especially attractive, useful or great... No Leonard, this style of writing is unworthy of you, you can do better, if only you would give first preference to the finer part of your nature and intellect. If you publish the book as it stands, I feel there will be a serious break between us." [33]

Criticism was not universal. Edgar Woolf was outraged. Adrian Stephen disliked it. Ka Cox praised it, and Leonard's younger brother Philip enjoyed the book but found it depressing; he 'considered the portrait of Marie Woolf deadly accurate and doubted that criticism by the family should be taken seriously'. Leonard turned to Lytton Strachey:

"Will you read it & let me have it back at the very earliest possible? And will you really be absolutely candid? Your opinion cannot possibly be more damnatory than all I have had except one. This is the position. My family think it a rotten bad book & forbid me to publish it. Now if it is rotten or even poorly, it isn't worth bringing all these people about my ears, obviously. But if it's otherwise worth publishing, I shouldn't mind, I think, telling the whole lot of them to go to Hell. I am so sick of the whole affair... I shall never write another book after these damned Virgins." [33]

Lytton suggested that Leonard should put the book aside for at least six months, a letter which Leonard called 'splendid & very encouraging'. Vanessa commented that 'although the story would be bound to offend some of those portrayed in it... feelings, after all, *arent* very important'.

Apparently on the road to recovery Virginia, at Asheham House, wrote to Leonard while he was moving their things from Clifford's Inn, where she never stayed again:

"D'you know, I believe I like you better and better? Feelings arise in me, such as I have not had for long.

I keep thinking that you ought to be an independent man, doing things, instead of wasting your life – but you'll be bored by this...

Dearest Mongoose, I wish you would believe how much I am grateful and repentant. You have made me so happy."

And:

"Would it make you very conceited if I told you that I love you more than I have ever done since I took you into service, and find you beautiful, and indispensable? I am afraid that is the truth.

Goodbye Mongoose, and be a devoted animal, and never leave the great variegated creature. She wishes to inform you delicately that her flanks and rump are now in finest plumage, and invites you to an exhibition." [34]

This year of uncertain health for Virginia, during which the first World War began, proved to be only a lull before the devastating storm of her second major post-marital breakdown beginning in February 1915, in which rage almost destroyed her.

On publication of *The Wise Virgins* in December 1914, and the hostile reviews that greeted it, Leonard blamed the war for its failure to sell complaining that he only made twenty pounds in royalties. But other books flourished; indeed, there was an avid reading public which he failed to tap. It is, no doubt, a bad novel, whose very badness sheds floods of light on key members of the Bloomsbury Group from Leonard's point of view. And the light strikes none of them with a clearer shaft than Leonard himself.

In *Orlando*, Virginia was to write a portrait of her friend Vita Sackville-West not only without offence or animosity but in a spirit of love that delighted Vita, who generously gave permission for her to write and publish it; and it has continued to delight its many readers world-wide. Where Leonard, with his thinly veiled portraits of living people, stole and diminished, Virginia caressed and enhanced. His novel was anathematised and would have been forgotten but for those with a special interest in the Bloomsbury Group, while hers remains loved and admired for its own sake. There is thus a striking contrast between the Woolfs as novelists.

Peter Alexander tries to excuse Leonard's book by saying that he intended it as an anti-Semitic caricature. I see no indication that Leonard tried to draw any sort of deliberate caricature. Surely he wrote exactly what he wanted to write, criticising both Putney and Bloomsbury with considerable zest, and his attempt to do so back-fired and burnt the author. The book lacks a dimension, as Leonard himself lacked a dimension in his determination to grab people and try and make them fit his world-view instead of attempting to comprehend theirs: it is this that makes it a bad novel. His account is certainly very difficult to accept at face value by anyone who insists on seeing Leonard as a 'saint'. The dynamics of the book appear to derive from applying his 'method' to his puppet characters; in real life his manipulations eventually had fatal results for Virginia.

The First World War had surprisingly little effect on the members of the Bloomsbury Group. Most of the men became conscientious objectors and worked on farms run by sympathetic friends. When Leonard was called up in 1916 he trembled so violently at his medical examination that he was given complete exemption. To him the war meant that 'civilisation' was being replaced by 'barbarism'. No longer a novelist, he turned his attention more and more to left-wing politics, with Margaret Llewelyn Davies as his Etheria, from whom in Roman folklore King Numa received his instructions. [35] Margaret, as his new strong woman, could help him realise his political aspirations better than either Virginia or Vanessa. Thus he formed another of his triangles between the mythical King Numa, Etheria-Margaret and himself, while Virginia continued to struggle for years to find her balance on the dangerous see-saw of their marriage.

MANDRILL

Chapter Six

BEGINNING AND END OF THE GOOD WIFE

Virginia began her diary, published in six volumes as *The Diary of Virginia Woolf*, on the first of January 1915. She continued writing it for over twenty-six years, until her death in March 1941. However, some six weeks after she began there is a major gap. Volume One stops abruptly on the fifteenth of February 1915 and she does not resume until August 1917. During those two and a half years she suffered the second major nervous breakdown of her marriage, the first being characterised as melancholic and the second as manic.

Diaries and letters are written as part of the ongoing life-process of their author. Despite Leonard's attempt to invalidate them, it is to their great advantage. Virginia herself was experiencing the events she records and as soon as we begin reading the entries for those first six weeks we get a close-up account of the lives of the Woolfs and the relationship between the two of them at that time, seen from Virginia's point of view. The initial entries help us gain an insight into a period of their marriage before a pattern of life was established between them which enabled her to write.

Her early entries show that she was trying to cope with different and more immediate stresses than those which Leonard blames for her second post-marriage mental breakdown. He blames it either on fear of the critics' reaction to her first novel, delayed from its original date in 1913 and now due to be published in March 1915, or on 'purely physical' causes. He never considers the possibility that he himself is putting pressure on her to play the 'good wife', while he attempts to pursue a career in left-wing politics hoping to specialise in international affairs, a field that is particularly unsympathetic to her.

The Woolfs are staying in rooms overlooking the Green at Richmond while they searched for a house in the area able to accommodate a staff of servants that was necessary for Virginia. Leonard had to accept the necessity for this, although it was very different from his own preference for a small house without servants and a wandering existence, while living cheaply so that he did not need to earn any money. Hogarth House was one of the properties they considered.

SNAPSHOT BY OTTOLINE MORRELL OF VIRGINIA
AT GARSINGTON, JUNE 1923

At this time Richmond was still a village, with its own history. It had not yet become a suburb of London, as it is today, although it still retains some of its earlier character. The Woolfs selected this locality because it provided a quiet retreat for Virginia while being within reach of London by rail, an important consideration in the days before cars.

Reading these early diary entries gives one a strange impression of emptiness, of thinness. At the outset Leonard laid down certain rules and restrictions concerning what Virginia could and couldn't write in her diary – it was to remain a light account of their activities which he could read at any time; she was not to discuss her 'soul' in it; and she was not to criticise him, in contrast to the letter she wrote on her honeymoon to Ka Cox: 'Except for a sustained good humour (Leonard shan't see this) due to the fact that every twinge of anger is at once visited upon my husband, I might still be Miss S.' [1] By 1915, there was to be no anger against him and no teasing. Her autonomy – Leonard accused her of egotism or vanity – had evidently been under continuous attack ever since she married and she took refuge in believing that her husband was 'much too good' for her. At this time they were neither colleagues nor equals – nor even literary rivals. He was writing articles for the New Statesman, often spending his days in central London and elsewhere, while she must stay in their lodgings in Richmond where she copy typed for him and other people.

Virginia began her diary as therapy, as we should now say. It is full of good intentions, the account of the stay-at-home wife who is being taught how to behave by her husband. She soon describes how Leonard gave a course of lectures:

"5th January: L. went off to Hampstead to give the first of his lectures to the Women's [Co-operative] Guild. He did not seem nervous. He is speaking at this moment."

"6th January: L. went off at 10 A.M. to give his second lecture at Hampstead. The first was a great success, as I knew it would be. He finds the women much more intelligent than men; in some ways too intelligent, & apt on that account, not to see the real point. He has another to give this afternoon, so he is staying up at Hampstead, lunching with Lilian [Harris, a friend and companion of Margaret Llewelyn Davies] & perhaps seeing Janet [Case]. No one except a very modest person would treat these working women, & Lilian & Janet & Margaret, as he does.

Clive [Bell] or indeed any other clever young man, would give himself airs; & however much he admired them pretend that he didn't." [2]

So speaks the good wife, criticising Clive Bell to please her husband. Leonard goes to see the editor of the *New Statesman*, and on the 11th February he visits the London Library:

"He has to write an article of 1200 words by Wednesday noon, on Diplomatists – a wonderful subject anyhow.

On the 12th: 'L. is now writing his article upon diplomacy, & I must go & typewrite.'

14th: 'L's article on diplomacy is to come out on Saturday. He was, of course, convinced after sending it that it would be rejected (this is a note, for future use & quotation).'

16th: 'We wrote this morning. L's article by the way reads very well in the New Statesman... L. went to the L[London] Library; I took Max along the River, but we were a good deal impeded, by a bone he stole, by my suspenders coming down, by a dogfight in which his ear was torn & bled horribly. I thought how happy I was, without any of the excitement which, once, seemed to me to constitute happiness. L. & I argued for some time about this. Also about the worthlessness of all human works except as a means of keeping the workers happy. My writing now delights me solely because I love writing & dont, honestly, care a hang what anyone says. What seas of horror one dives through in order to pick up these pearls – however they are worth it.'

So Virginia gets over her fear of having her work published; it was not this that brought on her second post-marital breakdown. On the afternoon of the 18th February they went house-hunting:

"which has led to a long discussion about our future, & a fresh computation of income. The future is dark, which is on the whole the best thing the future can be, I think. L. went to the Webbs, & I came home... as I began this page, L. stated that he had determined to resign his commission [with the New Statesman] and write a pamphlet about Arbitration – & now I shall stop this diary & discuss that piece of folly with him... I want to see what can be said *against* all forms of activity & thus dissuade L. from all his work... Of course it is absolutely essential that L. shd. do a work which may be superbly good."

After the fiasco of *The Wise Virgins* it is seen as 'absolutely essential' for Leonard to produce something that 'may be superbly good' and Virginia does her best to support and encourage him, although she does not want him to spend his life as a political writer. Their relationship is uneasy; it is Leonard who is depressed and annoyed with Virginia:

19th: "L's melancholy continues, so much so that he declared this morning he couldn't work. The consequence has been a rather melancholy day... All I can do is to unsay all I have said; & to say what I really mean... after praising L's writing very sincerely for 5 minutes, he says 'Stop'; whereupon I stop, & there's no more to be said. When I analyse his mood, I attribute much of it to sheer lack of self confidence in his power of writing, his melancholy sinks far deeper than the half assumed melancholy of self conscious people like Lytton, & Sir Leslie [Stephen, Virginia's father] & myself. There's no arguing with him."

We now arrive at an interesting point. Virginia had only recently been rescued from a suicide attempt from the depths of melancholy, that would have been fatal but for the immediate efforts of Ka Cox and the doctors, while her father wore out both his wife Julia and step-daughter Stella with his alternating tantrums of melancholy and rage. Yet Virginia is now saying that Leonard's melancholy 'sinks far deeper'! Things rapidly get worse. The weather, too, is appalling. It loses, as Virginia writes, 'all sense of self restraint'; while the maid at their lodgings, 'this House of Trouble', puts them through ordeals of flood, fire and a near-explosion besides breaking china. Leonard comes back from Hampstead late on several occasions. There is a feeling of impending disintegration which is held in check for a day on Virginia's birthday. She was thirty three.

25th January: "L. had sworn he would give me nothing, & like a good wife, I believed him. But he crept into my bed, with a little parcel, which was a beautiful green purse. And he brought up breakfast... & a square brown parcel, with The Abbot in it – a lovely first edition – So I had a very merry & pleasing morning – which indeed was only surpassed by the afternoon. I was then taken up to town, free of charge, & given a treat... I don't think I've had a birthday treat for 10 years; & it felt like one too... In fact I dont know when I have enjoyed a birthday so much – not since I was a child anyhow. Sitting at tea we decided three things: in the first place to take Hogarth, if we can get it; in the second, to buy a Printing press; in the third to buy a Bull dog... I am very much excited at the idea of all three – particularly the press. I was also given a packet of sweets to bring home."

Hopefully, when Leonard crept into her bed they had sex. I do not agree with Spater and Parsons that they never did so, only these were rare occasions and they had to be in a certain mood. Here, she was acting the role of a child and he had bought her a present; there was nothing heroic about it. Virginia reacts to her birthday presents with the pleasure of a child, which is how she was treated for that one day. It doesn't last. Indeed, it is all too obvious that Leonard habitually behaved very differently towards her, trying to mould her into the 'good wife' he wanted her to be.

We can assume that Leonard brought back with him from his daily trips to London and Hampstead the heavy atmosphere of negative energy that so many men know all too well how to project onto their isolated wives who have spent their day alone at home while he concentrated on his 'important' work, instead of entering into her world when he opened the front door. This assumption can be made because Virginia herself was soon to portray just this situation in her agonised and agonising short story *Lappin and Lapinova*. This story expresses with gut-wrenching awareness the pulling apart of a married couple when the man refuses to continue to live his wife's fantasy-world in which they are both rabbits, or hares. The wife, Lapinova, notices that King Lappin's nose no longer twitches when he returns home from work. Instead of changing into a hare, her husband remains the businessman Ernest, with the businessman's alienated and judgemental reactions. At that moment their private dream that protects them against the outside world is shattered and Lapinova is desolated:

"He came in and switched on the light. There he stood tall, handsome, rubbing his hands that were red with cold.

'Sitting in the dark?' he said.

'Oh, Ernest, Ernest!' she cried, starting up in her chair.

'Well, what's up now?' he asked briskly, warming his hands at the fire.

'It's Lapinova...' she faltered, glancing wildly at him out of her great startled eyes. 'She's gone, Ernest. I've lost her!'

Ernest frowned. He pressed his lips tight together. 'Oh, that's what's up, is it?' he said, smiling rather grimly at his wife. For ten seconds he stood there, silent; and she waited, feeling hands tightening at the back of her neck.

'Yes,' he said at length. 'Poor Lapinova...' He straightened his tie at the looking-glass over the mantelpiece.

'Caught in a trap,' he said, 'killed', and sat down and read the newspaper.

So that was the end of that marriage." [3]

Was this story pure imagination, or had Virginia realised that she had been caught in a trap and (very nearly) killed? I think she did realise this and found a way of escape through awareness of the characteristic brain difference between women and men. This awareness was her vision that she expressed in her writing. But first she had to burn through the horror of realisation in uncontrolled rage.

A note of autobiography may be found in a passage in one of Virginia's short stories, precursor to her fourth novel *Mrs Dalloway:*

"But then she remembered how on their honeymoon Dick had shown her the folly of giving impulsively. It was much more important, he said, to get trade with China." [4]

Here is the difference between the female individual witness, who is trying to effect a change in some particular circumstance by 'giving impulsively', and the arrogance of the male as he makes his apparently more important generalisations about 'trade with China'. With her beautiful wit, Virginia expresses it exactly. Generalisation does not invalidate the particular; the sense of truth of oneself as an individual witness is at least as great, if not greater, than the apparently impersonal generalisation that can so easily be used as a weapon.

But through the early years of her marriage Virginia Woolf's individual viewpoint was being systematically discredited as Leonard repeatedly told her what she must not do, such as spend money, and how he wanted her to behave. He was trying to train her, forcing her into the position of a suburban wife, while he spent time with other women.

To return to Virginia's diary, on 26 January 1915, she sees a characteristic difference between a 'female' and a 'male' mind:

'L. went up to the School of Economics this morning... After lunch, I met L... He has already grasped his Arbitration – such is the male mind – & will, I see, go through with it straight off & (here I make my prophesy) it will be a great success, & lead to as much work as he wants.'

On the 29th January: 'we came back early, so that L. might have tea before he went to a Committee at Hampstead.' An editorial footnote tells us: LW went to see Janet Case, and then to a meeting with Margaret Llewelyn Davies and Lilian Harris at the offices of the Women's Co-operative Guild.

And on the 30th: 'He was kept late at Hampstead: didn't get home till 10.15. when we had hot chocolate over the fire.'

And then it happens. The Woolfs have a major quarrel, after which Virginia read *The Wise Virgins* for the first time:

Sunday 31 January: 'O dear! We quarrelled almost all the morning! & it was a lovely morning, & now gone to Hades for ever, branded with the marks of our ill humour. Which began it? Which carried it on? God knows. This I will say: I explode: & L smoulders. However, quite suddenly we made it up, (but the morning was wasted) & we walked after lunch in the Park, & we came home by way of Hogarth, & tried to say that we shan't be much disappointed if we don't get it... After tea... I started reading The Wise Virgins, & I read it straight on till bedtime, when I finished it.' She comments on Leonard's novel:

'My opinion is that its a remarkable book; very bad in parts; first rate in others. A writer's book, I think, because only a writer perhaps can see why the good parts are so very good, & why the very bad parts aren't very bad... I was made very happy by reading this: I like the poetic side of L & it gets a little smothered in Blue-books, & organisations.'

Virginia does not say what they actually quarrelled about on the morning of the 31st January. We can perhaps guess that she argued against Leonard committing himself to a political career, 'smothered in Blue-books, & organisations', taking him further and further away from her, while he blamed her for having had to spend money on doctors and nurses so that he couldn't do the work he wanted and this made their future 'dark'. One result of this quarrel was that she read *The Wise Virgins* immediately after it, so they probably also argued about their relationship with Virginia, perhaps, once again pleading to have a child, whereupon he would have told her that if she wanted to write she couldn't also be a mother. But underlying this type of disagreement was something far more serious. As she wrote in a period of lucidity to Lady Robert Cecil later that year: 'I am 33, and have decided that I am completely misunderstood'. [5]

Virginia came to realise she was not like the person Leonard thought he loved, This was to become the central theme of her second novel *Night and Day* where her two main characters agonise over what they call their 'lapses' from loving each other. Leonard would have told her that she didn't love him as much as he loved her (he continued to say this through the years) and that she had an irrational fear of what the critics would say about *The Voyage Out*. In his autobiography Leonard writes negatively about the publication of her book, saying that it 'only' sold

2000 copies and that she 'only' received 120 pounds from sales (six times what he earned from *The Wise Virgins*). We should consider the possibility that, smarting from his own failure, he insisted she should review other people's books and get short articles published instead of wasting time trying to write novels which would not earn money. If she had to cope with such attitudes, intensely stated, she would indeed have exploded, possibly accusing him of preferring Margaret Llewelyn Davies to herself, to which he would have accused her of being jealous and obstructive since Margaret was helping him with his work. There was certainly plenty for them to quarrel about and, since Leonard was never known to give way in an argument, Virginia must have been reduced to an exhausted silence.

We are almost at the end of this section of Virginia's diary. There is a ten day gap, from 3rd to 13th February, when the Woolfs went away to Ryde and Hastings. On their return Leonard continues with his work, while Virginia wanders about London. Her clothes are falling apart: 'I have some mending to do, my entire skirt having split in two yesterday'. Her last entry for two and a half years is on the 15th February:

"Then I had tea, & rambled down to Charing Cross in the dark, making up phrases and incidents to write about. Which is, I expect, the way one gets killed.

I bought a ten & elevenpenny blue dress, in which I sit at this moment."

On that final day before her long silence – a least, so far as her diary is concerned – she had wandered about central London feeling like an outcast: 'Then I had tea, & rambled down to Charing Cross in the dark, making up phrases and incidents to write about. *Which is, I expect, the way one gets killed.*' Virginia must have considered suicide many more times than she actually attempted it. Absent-mindedness while thinking creatively was one possibility. Perhaps curiosity about how her first book would be received, so far from making her suicidal, helped to keep her safe on this occasion. Her creative fire burned within her, she needed to use words in ways that only she could do. This need was frustrated by her enforced role as the good wife which superimposed upon her the woman Leonard wanted her to be while he, feeling impeded by her, tried to get on with his life.

During those weeks before her second and even more serious postmarital breakdown, Leonard's 'melancholy' was, according to Virginia, even deeper than her own or her father's; she tried to encourage and reassure him, and was told to 'Stop'. She also called him 'modest', about his lecturing. It seems she did not understand that this was his way of getting on his side the people who could help him enter a world of which he wanted to be part – he was using his 'method' to endear himself to a group of prominent women who were able to promote his interests; and indeed they soon did, since he was invited to hold a position in the Fabian Society.

Margaret Llewelyn Davies was an important figure in left-wing politics. She had been up at Girton College, Cambridge and was General Secretary of the Women's Co-operative Guild, 1889–1921. At this time she was living with her father in Hampstead; he died in 1916. According to Leonard:

"She was that strange and usually inexplicable phenomenon 'a born leader'. Of course one could explain it by her immense energy and enthusiasm; by her laugh which was so characteristically Margaret, a deep contralto spontaneous laugh; by the feminine charm which was also so spontaneous and unconscious, and sometimes among her regiment of working women, and Co-operative stores so endearingly incongruous; and by her beauty, which remained even when she had grown fat and almost an old woman, the fresh English beauty of hair and eyes marvellously united with a chiselled classical beauty of Greek features." [6]

In contrast to the paean of praise Leonard lavishes on Margaret, he gives an off-hand description of Virginia and ridicules her clothes.

Alone in digs in Richmond, Virginia must have sensed Leonard's transference from herself to the much admired 'Etheria' who combined English beauty with Greek features and Roman leadership. She must have particularly disliked the male tradition of making myths about women based on Greek and Roman stories, taught as part of their expensive school and University Classical education: these are at the opposite end of the spectrum from her own animal familiars. Virginia no doubt feared that Leonard was transferring his admiration from herself to Margaret.

So she argued not only against his 'Blue-books, & organisations' but his doing any sort of work, preferring his 'poetic' side; and thus attempted to hold him back and away from Margaret. That is, she understandably wanted to keep him focused on herself and their lives together. Simply to know that another woman was taking on this role of confidante to her husband would have made Virginia feel insecure, whether or not they were having a sexual relationship. She paid a brief visit to Hampstead. There was her long-time friend and tutor, Janet Case, helping Leonard and Margaret. Virginia must have felt ignorant and superfluous. She was indeed battling with the fear that she was losing Leonard at this time, and in an important respect she was right. She did lose a large part of him as he made an exalted image of Margaret. Virginia was no longer his dream-woman, his Aspasia: she was flawed by 'madness' and proving expensive to keep. She was losing her looks. Her clothes were a mess and he gave her a pitifully small allowance out of her money to spend on herself. The buying of the blue dress costing a few shillings represented a hard-won victory on her part – the real cost being in nervous energy that she could not afford. But he was also tantalised by living with a woman he needed to possess fully. For her, a full commitment meant having a child and this he was not willing to do. Indeed, we can gain an understanding of the strength of Leonard's repulsion against pregnancy in the following account he gave in a letter to Lytton Strachey in 1918 when Adrian Stephen and his wife Karin, carrying their second child, visited the Woolfs at Asheham House:

"I dont like these pregnant women. Karin and Adrian (who is by no means pregnant) have just left us. Karin has the appetite of ten horse-leeches. For seven days I tried to fill her up and make her refuse something. I increased the helpings until I thought no human being could possibly stand it. She blew and puffed and heaved and swelled but it all went down; so I told V. to order a very heavy suet pudding for lunch and when it appeared I heaped Karin's plate... Half way through she stopped and gazed out the window, sighed heavily, and a curious twitching appeared to take place about the stomach and abdomen. We sat expecting either an explosion or a premature birth, but after another deep sigh, she finished her plate of suet. Next day she went to Brighton and bought a bottle of liquid cascara which broke in Adrian's pocket." [7]

The expenses of Virginia's medical treatment must have been constantly held up before her as a reason why she could not spend any money and why Leonard could not live as he wished. Thus in these early years did the little donkey stagger under the burden Leonard laid on her back. This unnecessary stress became one of the causes of her coming breakdown which paradoxically cost more money and prevented her earning anything. She was being made to feel the powerlessness of a typical dominated and possibly-about-to-be-cast-aside wife who didn't enjoy sex and wasn't fit for motherhood. All that mattered was Leonard's 'important' career, while another woman had become the dominant, admirable female figure to him. Trying to cope with this situation would have made her nervous about the forthcoming publication of her book, whose romantic story now seemed irrelevant. Thus she was suffering not so much from jealousy as from an extreme sense of insecurity.

Virginia's suppressed rage at having been trapped in this inferior position where she could not write; her yawning sense of insecurity at the withdrawal of Leonard's support, together with his refusal to listen to her point of view and the sense that she was being completely misunderstood, were all major causes of her eruption into uncontrolled so-called mania.

The reception by critics and public of *The Voyage Out* was of crucial importance to Virginia. Failure would have meant that she would have been in an even weaker, indeed utterly intolerable position in relation to Leonard whose arguments would have gained overwhelming weight; while the impressive Margaret was becoming an ever brighter star in his sky. In the event, the reviews of *The Voyage Out* were generally favourable and most of their friends, particularly Lytton Strachey, thought highly of it. It proved indeed to be a successful first novel. But by then the rage in Virginia was erupting with great violence and she no longer cared. We can be fairly sure that concern for her book was not the chief reason for her breakdown and that her relationship with the melancholy, irritable Leonard who was having an increasingly close relationship with Margaret, was the major factor.

Only the state of mania (that is, uncontrollable rage) into which Virginia now plunged rescued her from a diminished lifetime playing second fiddle to 'Leonard the politician', whom she suspected of being a fraud. Apart from suicide her so-called mania was indeed her only remaining way of escape since he would not have considered giving her the grounds to divorce him. During the coming lengthy breakdown her anger was liberated and for months she refused to speak to Leonard or let him anywhere near her.

Lacking Virginia's own contemporary record of the following two and a half years, we can get some idea about what this second bout of 'madness' was like from Quentin Bell's account in his biography of her, as well as from letters. We need to remember that Bell was using Leonard and Vanessa's recollections in old age as the basis of his account and that he needed to gain Leonard's permission to publish his authorised biography of Virginia. Bell says:

"[*The Voyage Out*] was to appear at the end of March; in the middle of February Leonard took Virginia to the dentist... the following day he came home to find her with a bad headache. He began the usual treatment; rest, seclusion, veronal at night; and, as before, recorded her progress in his diary.

But one morning, while she was breakfasting in bed, Virginia began to talk to her mother; she became very distressed and more and more excited and incoherent. A day or two later she seemed – to herself at any rate – to have stepped back from the abyss and, remembering the nightmare of the previous year, tried to express something of what she owed to Margaret Llewelyn Davies:

17. The Green, Richmond

Thursday [25 February 1915]

My dear Margaret

...I want just to tell you how wonderfully things have changed in the last few days. I am now all right though rather tired. It is so wonderful that I can hardly believe it. And I wanted to say that all through that terrible time I thought of you, & wanted to look at a picture of you, but was afraid to ask! You saved Leonard I think, for which I shall always bless you, by giving him things to do. It seems odd, for I know you so little, but I felt you had a grasp on me, & I could not utterly sink. I write this because I do not want to say it, & yet I think you will like to know it. Our happiness is now something I cannot even think about.

Please come... I can't do much but lie still, but I should like immensely to see you...

Dear Margaret, I so often think of you, & thank you for what you have done for us both, & one cd do nothing to show what it meant. Yrs V.W.

I wanted to tell Janet [Case] what I have told you but Leonard thought better not. Her goodness was so great." [8]

Quentin Bell continues:

"This letter, rather hurriedly, rather wildly but quite firmly written in pencil, may possibly express a sentiment of rational guilt and remorse resulting from agonies of irrational fury, and the reason why Margaret Llewelyn Davies should inspire such feelings need to be explored. She had indeed saved Leonard and, during the past two years had become, after Virginia, the most important woman in his life. She was, as

Leonard has said, a born leader, energetic, enthusiastic, likeable and handsome; she brought Leonard into the work of her own particular organisation – the Women's Co-operative Guild; Virginia came too and was indeed very much impressed. Nevertheless it must have been clear from the outset that Leonard would move further and faster on this excursion than Virginia. With Margaret as his guide, Leonard had soon adventured deep into politics and, as Virginia realised, this was what he needed at a time when her illness would otherwise have driven him to despair.

But the influence of this wholly benevolent, altogether virtuous, 50-year-old Egeria cannot have been wholly welcome. Virginia was never drawn to female politicians and Margaret, with all her fine qualities, was something of a bore. That Leonard should be so dependent upon her – and Virginia too, for Margaret's kindness was such during Virginia's illness that Leonard found his gratitude too deep to express – was not altogether a recommendation."

When one reads Bell's defence of Leonard as being somehow the victim of Virginia's 'madness', a man who has to be 'saved', with no hint that he himself might have been even partly responsible, one can well see why Virginia did not improve. Bell continues:

"Virginia believed that she had recovered when she wrote to Margaret on 25 February, but it was no more than a respite... in fact she grew rapidly worse. It was quite unlike the first phase of her madness when she was depressed, languid and, though sometimes violent, more often quietly suicidal. Now she entered into a state of garrulous mania, speaking ever more wildly, incoherently and incessantly, until she lapsed into gibberish and sank into a coma." [8]

Considering the disaster that followed Virginia's writing that letter to Margaret, it is reasonable to suppose that Leonard insisted on her doing so and indeed stood over her while she wrote it. Her one escape from a life distorted by Leonard's demands that she should support him in all he did until her own sense of truth and power of creativity became lost to her, was to break the bounds of reason and go 'mad'. Thus, driven to the extreme of desperation, she rebelled.

Virginia was taken to a nursing home, where she remained for a week while Leonard moved from their lodgings into Hogarth House. She was then installed there under the care of four mental nurses when she showed even more harrowing symptoms, as Bell recounts:

"for now Virginia was violent and screaming, and her madness culminated in virulent animosity towards Leonard himself. On 20 May Leonard's diary reads: 'Exc. & irritable all day but not as bad as yest. Margaret [Llewelyn Davies] came to tea... Did not see V.' For almost two months he scarcely saw her. Vanessa reported to Roger Fry: 'Woolf himself seemed to have reached a state when he didn't much care what happened which was rather dreadful; & one couldn't say anything much.' " [8]

Quentin Bell says:

"Very, very slowly Virginia began to improve. That is to say there were fewer moments of violence and excitement. She became more lucid and more rational. But it seemed that there would be no real recovery from this second bout of the disease; it had inflicted a wound which appeared to be incurable... it was not only her mind but her entire personality which had deteriorated. At the end of June Vanessa wrote:

'Ka had been to see Virginia & thinks she's really getting better slowly, but it sounds most depressing as she seems to have changed into a most unpleasant character. She won't see Leonard at all & has taken against all men. She says the most malicious and cutting things she can think of to everyone & they are so clever that they always hurt... it looks as if she had simply worn out her brains.' "

(NOTE: The quotations from Vanessa's letters given by Quentin Bell are not included in the *Selected Letters of Vanessa Bell;* a serious omission.)

Saying 'malicious and cutting things' was just what Leonard had already done to his family and to Clive Bell in *The Wise Virgins*, and no doubt also to Virginia when he was alone with her, but he was not considered mad.

Bell concludes:

"Thus by the summer of 1915 it was clear that Virginia, however completely she might seem to recover from her insanity, could easily relapse into madness, and each attack seemed worse than its predecessor. After two years of intermittent lunacy it appeared that her mind and her character were permanently affected." [8]

This, with a vengeance, was the end of the good wife.

The Voyage Out was published the day after the onset of Virginia's rage. No doubt, in 1913, Virginia had been terrified at the prospect of her first novel being published, especially as 'they' – supposedly Vanessa and

Leonard – jeered at her; but now it was far worse: feeling that Leonard wasn't really interested in what she wrote. His apparently flattering comparison between her work and that of Jane Austen had nothing to do with the way she felt about her book or what she was saying in it; while he was being guided by his 'Egeria', his political goddess who was there to comfort him and to lead him along paths that took him away from her. No wonder she fell into a fierce and uncontrollable rage against him personally and against all men. In this dire situation, it is not surprising that she cut off from him and spoke to her mother: she would have recognised her own predicament in Julia's difficulties living with Sir Leslie Stephen and spoken across the grave to her after she had died worn out at the age of forty nine. Virginia was rebelling not only against Leonard himself – when she married him she thought he was an exception because he 'cared' for her – but against what she saw as a male characteristic of not listening and of erecting defensive barriers around and against the women they lived with.

In her fifth novel *To the Lighthouse*, Virginia was able to bring both her parents back to life but it took her many more years to understand Leonard's devious psychology; this she only managed to write about extensively in her last completed novel, *Between the Acts*.

To learn to speak in her own right as herself, without pretending to be academic, Virginia simplified the very quality of her language and this turned her into the sharp and witty modern writer she became. She was no longer going to compete with Leonard, or men in general, on their terms: she was going to carve, with infinite difficulty, her own mode of expression that corresponded with her own particular female brain and sense of truth. Her ungovernable rage had more than one focus; however, underlying it was the sense that she had been betrayed, as women are betrayed by having to live in a world made in the shape that suits men but not women.

Vanessa also betrayed Virginia by being irritated by her breakdowns and sympathising with Leonard, absolving him of all responsibility; she was what we would call nowadays a patriarchal woman. On reading her sister's newly published book in April 1915, she wrote disparagingly to Roger Fry:

"I expect I agree with most of what you say about Virginia's novel, and I suppose it's true that she has genius. I'm not sure I should call it so. Can Stephens produce a genius? I doubt it. I don't think Jane Austen's art is the only kind of art and I only compared them because Woolf has always done so – of course to Virginia's advantage, or at any rate equality... But of course she's an artist, though she mayn't have produced a work of art... most of the minor characters seem to me more interesting than the principal ones." [9]

Leonard was apparently displaying the endurance of Job while Virginia from the 'mad' depths of her soul cursed him; but he acted in his own best interests as the long-suffering innocent husband, a role he managed to sustain for the rest of his life and which still clings to his memory. Roger Fry understood that Virginia was an individual writer working out her own creative destiny; however, Roger himself was in a similar situation to Leonard Woolf in that he also had a 'mad' wife; however, Roger accepted an ongoing responsibility for his children. Leonard must have congratulated himself on refusing to have any. And he had not had to face looking at his wife's 'repulsive' pregnant body. Nowadays, we can sympathise with Virginia in her forced deprivation; at least we do not have to choose between motherhood and creative writing: we can do it all.

Driven too far down on the marital see-saw Virginia became submerged, entering some region beneath the familiar earth level of human intercourse, and here something happened: she took root: she connected with the upward energy and became an autonomous person. In Jung's word, she individuated. And in doing so she brought back with her the seeds of all her novels, together with a determination to write directly about women's situation under patriarchy, as she did in *A Room of One's Own* and *Three Guineas*. In the agony of 1915 to 1917, Virginia Woolf herself was born.

As she very slowly returned to this world, the Woolfs started the Hogarth Press from the smallest of small beginnings. In different ways, this activity was to be far more beneficial to them both than they could have imagined at the time; I think that it was the major factor that enabled their marriage to continue although there were occasions when each of them wanted to abandon the Press. They bought a small hand machine and began printing in the most primitive way: Virginia's task was to set each individual letter of lead type, as Leonard's trembling arm made the fiddling work too difficult for him; while he printed off one page at a time on the machine. Theoretically, Leonard and Virginia were equal partners but, needless to say, Leonard kept a complete hold on expenses and insisted that everything they published should make a profit, however small. The Press became known as Leonard's 'mistress' and even after they began to employ a few people to help them run it Leonard remained in control of the management, while Virginia took on the job of reading manuscripts; it was largely thanks to her that the Press became important, publishing much of the significant work being written by modern writers.

From 1921 onwards, all Virginia's books were published by the Hogarth Press. This meant that Virginia could avoid the soul-destroying process of sending out manuscripts to uninterested, and uninteresting, publishers. She is a standing example of the advantages of what was virtually self-publishing; Leonard was the only person who read her work before publication and for ten years he was generally positive and supportive about her work; however, his attitude changed in the early nineteen thirties and it was then that she should have moved on to being published by other firms that were eager to take it. Leonard, on the other hand, had not intended to self-publish and it was only the difficulty of getting his own books accepted that brought him back to the Hogarth Press.

So, almost despite themselves and from a most unpromising beginning, the marriage of Virginia and Leonard Woolf continued. However, there was a major cost to pay. Nothing changed Leonard's settled conviction that his wife was 'mad'; while the lack of both children and sex made Virginia feel that she was disembodied. In *Mrs. Dalloway*, Clarissa describes this feeling:

"But often now this body she wore... this body, with all its capacities, seemed nothing – nothing at all. She had the oddest sense of being herself invisible; unseen; unknown; there being no more marrying, no more having of children now." [10]

"Like a nun withdrawing, or a child exploring, she went, upstairs." [11]

The nun withdrawing, the child exploring – this was Virginia Woolf. In these two aspects she had found a way to exist, while Leonard provided the security and the constricting boundary. They were neither of them religious believers – there was no omnipresent god beaming (or frowning) down on their sanctuary – yet there was a radiance within, shining from the nun-child, which somewhat awed Leonard and kept his destructive 'nothing matters' at bay for much of the time. And he insisted that she did create, for without this the nunnery with the child within would have been but an empty shell; from which Leonard the manipulative would have moved away to begin his life again, as he did twenty years later. It was only by her writing that Virginia managed to delay what was always going to be the inevitable end of her marriage – her death. As she foresaw quite clearly in the death of Rachel in *The Voyage Out*, which she re-read in February, 1920, and noted in her diary:

"The mornings from 12 to 1 I spend reading The Voyage Out. I've not read it since July 1913... The failures are ghastly enough to make my cheeks burn – & then a turn of the sentence, a direct look ahead of me, makes them burn in a different way." [12]

The truth was that with the fineness of her female perceptions and the quality of her writing, Virginia managed to realise much of her vision despite (perhaps, indeed, because of) the fact that Leonard refused to share it. Throughout their partnership he embodied the heavy rock walls that were never able to confine her spirit. That free spirit was able to descend down the column of upward energy when the walls he erected around her loomed too ominously over her head; and in this way Virginia escaped from him to find enrichment in the darkness below, in the nether world – the world that Leonard called madness and patriarchal society calls hell – the place, to refer in our turn to one of the Greek myths, where Persephone ruled for half the year while winter froze the earth above her and turned it into barren land.

Virginia was eventually able to describe some of her inner experiences during these years and write about them in *Mrs Dalloway*, where the shell-shocked Septimus Smith expresses some of what she went through. But the grief and rage at not having been able to persuade Leonard to have a child and complete her globe of happiness in that way, remained with her for the rest of her life.

During her gradual recovery through 1916 and onwards, Virginia began to write again. At this transitional stage her creative writing was in the form of short stories as she explored different ways of expressing herself, different styles which could be tried and dropped without the major commitment necessary for a novel. To read *The Complete Shorter Fiction*, where the stories are arranged chronologically, is to watch Virginia at work. The editor, Susan Dick, quotes Virginia as saying in 1917 how 'frightfully clumsy and overpowering' the novel as a form of writing was, adding 'I daresay one ought to invent a completely new form. Anyhow its very amusing to try these short things.' [13]

In 1917 *The Mark on the Wall* was written 'all in a flash, as if flying' and was included among the eight pieces in *Monday or Tuesday*, the only collection of short stories Virginia published in her lifetime. In 1921 this little book was appallingly produced by the fledgeling Hogarth Press using an outside printer, a decision taken by Leonard, while at the same time three of his own stories entitled *Stories of the East*, were lavishly and carefully produced by the Hogarth Press, with Virginia's assistance. Leonard in his autobiography acknowledged the disaster of her book, calling it 'one of the worst books ever published', while refusing to take any responsibility, and gives a long and amusing account of the vicissitudes it encountered; but says nothing at all about *Stories of the East*. To have mentioned this would have drawn attention to the favourable treatment his little volume enjoyed. So once again the Woolfs were literary rivals, as they were in 1913, with the cards stacked heavily in favour of Leonard. It says a great deal for Virginia that she was not upset by this discrimination, although she was worried that her work 'might be dismissed as negligible'. She seems to have been chiefly interested in seeing how the reviewers, and her friends, reacted to her early attempts at a new writing style and was not too disappointed by their response.

In 1918 Virginia wrote *Night and Day,* her second novel, in which she questions the experience of love. When one feels love for someone, to what extent if at all is this related to the personality of the love object, or is it simply evoked by the sensation of their beauty or their attractive aura? This is a question many women ask when a man 'falls in love' with them. We can see *Night and Day* as Virginia's answer to Leonard's *The Wise Virgins*. It is dedicated to Vanessa and her main female character is named Katharine, as Vanessa was named in Leonard's novel. However, Virginia's Katharine is not simply an attempt to portray her sister. We have here the first of her 'double' characters since there is also much of Virginia included in Katharine Hilbery, especially when she is relating to Ralph-Leonard in the most intense passages in the book. In a letter to Ethel Smyth written in 1931, Virginia sums up her attitude towards both her 1915 breakdown and the writing with which she began her recovery:

"After being ill and suffering every form and variety of nightmare and extravagant intensity of perception – for I used to make up poems, stories, profound and to me inspired phrases all day long as I lay in bed, and thus sketched, I think, all that I now, by the light of reason, try to put into prose... – after all this, when I came to, I was so tremblingly afraid of my own insanity that I wrote Night and Day mainly to prove to my own satisfaction that I could keep entirely off that dangerous ground. I wrote it, lying in bed, allowed to write for only one half hour a day... I shall never forget the day I wrote The Mark on the Wall – all in a flash, as if flying, after being kept stone breaking for months... I saw, branching out of the tunnel I made, when I discovered that method of approach, Jacobs Room, Mrs Dalloway etc – how I trembled with excitement; and then Leonard came in, and I drank my milk, and concealed my excitement, and I wrote I suppose another page of that interminable book Night and Day (which some say is my best book)." [14]

Towards the end of *Night and Day* Katharine is worried about 'lapses' in love which she discusses with Ralph. It is evident that a 'lapse' means a very different thing to the two of them. Ralph gives way to a desperate, physical 'wanting', which blinds him to a sense of the other person; while Katharine 'lapses' into detachment, indeed into frozen indifference or even hostility:

" 'It's only marriage that's out of the question,' Katharine replied.

'But if I find myself coming to want you more and more?'

'If our lapses come more and more often?'

He sighed impatiently, and said nothing for a moment.

'But at least,' he renewed, 'we've established the fact that my lapses are still in some way connected with you; yours have nothing to do with me, Katharine,' he added, his assumption of reason broken up by his agitation, 'I assure you that we are in love – what other people call love. Remember that night. We had no doubts whatever then. We were absolutely happy for half an hour. You had no lapse until the day after; I had no lapse until yesterday morning...

'Reality – reality,' she ejaculated... 'I cease to be real to you. It's the faces in the storm again – the vision in a hurricane. We come together for a moment and we part. It's my fault too. I'm as bad as you are – worse, perhaps.'

They were trying to explain, not for the first time... what in their common language they had christened their 'lapses'; a constant source of distress to them... What was the cause of these lapses? Either because she wore something different, or said something unexpected, Ralph's sense of her romance welled up and overcame him either into silence or into inarticulate expressions, which Katharine, with unintentional but invariable perversity, interrupted or contradicted with some severity or assertion of prosaic fact. Then the vision disappeared, and Ralph expressed vehemently in his turn the conviction that he only loved her shadow and cared nothing for her reality. If the lapse was on her side it took the form of gradual detachment until she became completely absorbed in her own thoughts, which carried her away with such intensity that she sharply resented any recall to her companion's side. It was useless to assert that these trances were always originated by Ralph himself, however little in their later stages they had to do with him. The fact remained that she had no need of him and was very loth to be reminded of him. How then, could they be in love? The fragmentary nature of their relationship was but too apparent." [15]

Taking this at face value, it seems that Virginia did consider that her 'trances', in which she drew away from Leonard, were caused by him. Did she withdraw as a defence against his romantic image of her, in contrast to her feelings of physical repulsion? Or against his attempts to train her, his irritability and judgementalism? For whatever reason: 'The fact remained that she had no need of him and was very loth to be reminded of him.' This is a remarkable admission. Some sort of resolution is attained by the end of the book when they begin to speak only what they feel:

"he persuaded her into a broken statement, beautiful to him, charged with extreme excitement... making him feel that he had stepped over the threshold into the faintly lit vastness of another mind, stirring with shapes, so large, so dim, unveiling themselves only in flashes, and moving away again into the darkness, engulfed by it... They were victors, masters of life, but at the same time absorbed in the flame, giving their life to increase its brightness, to testify to their faith." [16]

They make their way by bus towards a river (the Thames):

"She felt him trying to piece together in a laborious and elementary fashion fragments of belief, unsoldered and separate, lacking the unity of phrases fashioned by the old believers. Together they groped in this difficult region, where the unfinished, the unfulfilled, the unwritten, the unreturned, came together in their ghostly way and wore the semblance of the complete and satisfactory. The future emerged more splendid than ever from this construction of the present. Books were to be written, and since books must be written in rooms, and rooms must have hangings, and outside the windows there must be land, and an horizon to that land, and trees perhaps, and a hill, they sketched a habitation for themselves." [17]

In *Night and Day* Virginia left far behind Leonard's account of their relationship as he described it in *The Wise Virgins*. With great difficulty, as she lay in bed and 'hid her excitement' from Leonard who brought her glasses of milk, she found a way of reconciling their extreme differences at least in the pages of her novel. In 1938 she commented to Vanessa that 'marriage, as I suddenly for the first time realised... reduces one to damnable servility.' [18] Perhaps it is as well – although somewhat surprising – that she did not realise this earlier.

Whilst Virginia was laboriously writing *Night and Day*, she also wrote *Lappin and Lapinova,* that agonising short story which gives a very different picture; she revised it in November 1938 ('& all my courage needed' [19]). When she first conceived this story she had very good reason for being 'mad' – to escape from the dark bar of Leonard's intense, obsessive 'I' which demanded her acceptance of his view of the world: his destructive yearning to possess her on his terms destroying her fantasy in the process. Precisely, Leonard was not content to be the caring 'saint' of a husband looking after his wife while she got on with her novels. While pursuing his own ambitions outside, at home he inflicted on Virginia a close psychological grappling that permanently damaged her autonomy. She must quite often have felt the grip of his hands tightening at the back of her neck.

All her periods of so-called madness were self-protective breakdowns in response to intolerable stress: and from those depths she brought back the treasures of her creative writing, to be worked upon in a state of extended, intensified and enriched sanity.

MONK'S HOUSE, 1919

PART THREE

VIRGINIA LEARNS TO RIDE THE SEE-SAW

VIRGINIA WOOLF IN THE 1920s

Chapter Seven

BRINGING THE DEAD TO LIFE

Leonard read *Night and Day* in the spring of 1919. His 'verdict' as Virginia calls it in her diary, gave her 'immense pleasure'. However, she also says that Leonard found the book's philosophy very melancholy. She could easily have been depressed by this, but instead argues against his view. She was not nervous then or later when the book was published, thus giving the lie to Leonard's claim that her breakdowns were due to exhaustion after finishing a book and terror at what the critics would say. This did not happen with *Night and Day*, nor indeed with any of the books she published in the following decade: those ten years of amazing creativity which brought her considerable fame and a modest fortune. She writes:

"In my own opinion N. & D. is a much more mature & finished & satisfactory book than The Voyage Out... L. finds the philosophy very melancholy. It too much agrees with what he was saying yesterday. Yet, if one is to deal with people on a large scale & say what one thinks, how can one avoid melancholy? I don't admit to being hopeless though – only the spectacle is a profoundly strange one; & as the current answers don't do, one has to grope for a new one; & the process of discarding the old, when one is by no means certain what to put in their place, is a sad one... I don't suppose I've ever enjoyed any writing so much as I did the last half of N. & D... & if one's own ease & interest promise anything good, I shall have hopes that some people, at least, will find it a pleasure... Is the time coming when I can endure to read my own writing in print without blushing & shivering & wishing to take cover?" [1]

Self confidence in her book carried Virginia through its publication and the response of friends and reviewers not only with equanimity but with pleasure. Theoretically, she should have been able to continue her literary career without further breakdowns, mental or physical. For the first time she was riding high on their marital see-saw; but, as with all see-saws, when one person is up aloft the other person is down; and when that person was Leonard, Virginia had to suffer his melancholy. He saw himself as a failure, his strong atmosphere of discontent conflicting with her need to be happy and relaxed when she was at work on her novels.

There is a note of warning in her diary of 28 December 1919: 'Isn't this 'reputation' the deepest of all masculine instincts?' During this time Leonard's reputation was suffering from the closure of the International Review of which he had been editor for a year. However, he was appointed editor of Contemporary Review while two of his many working documents, *Co-operation and the Future of Industry,* and his *International Economic Policy,* came out in December. Despite these publications, there is no doubt that Virginia and not Leonard was the centre of attention. In her new-found security, Virginia basked in the positive responses of Vanessa, Clive Bell and a column of praise in The Times; and was not upset when Katherine Mansfield criticised her book for having been written as though 'the war had never been' and for being 'so tahsome'. Publishers in America began to show an interest in her work. She had written the book to vindicate her sanity and she felt that she was on her way.

Leonard's melancholy was not of the passive kind. If Virginia had taken the limelight as a budding novelist, he would consolidate his position as the owner of the land beneath his feet. When the lease on Asheham House came to an end Virginia promptly purchased the Round House in Lewes; since it was her money she felt she had the right to make this decision. But Leonard at once insisted that she resell, and buy Monk's House in the village of Rodmell at auction for 700 pounds. Leonard liked Monk's House for two reasons: it's name (although he discovered that no monks had ever lived there); and its large garden. He, the landless Jew, now owned land. This was the third of his three 'roots', the first in ancient Greece, the second as a Semite, and now having a territorial right to a small part of Sussex.

Virginia agreed to buy Monk's House for the sake of peace with Leonard, although from the beginning she had doubts about it. Doubts that were well-founded. The house was actually a cottage consisting of a jumble of small rooms, with no sense of scale. Its location with its front gate opening from a lane and its back wall beside a church and churchyard, was too close to the village of Rodmell, thus she was frequently disturbed. She always remembered with regret the style and detachment of Asheham House at the other end of a driveway from the road, with no nearby buildings.

From the beginning there is a note of worry in Virginia's account of their move, although she attempts to make the best of it. But she already calls the place an 'island.' She soon records that Leonard 'runs out like a child allowed to get down and go', as he begins his love affair with the garden that lasts the rest of his life, whereas Virginia was much more interested in the walks up the downs and along the river.

Thus the Woolfs settled down after the war, albeit somewhat uneasily, to get on with their lives in the changed world which meant very different things for the two of them. For Virginia the early nineteen twenties meant an opening out, a new beginning with an increase of health and strength. She broke away from conventional prose and, with infinite difficulty, forged a new way of writing that put her in the forefront of modern thought. Leonard, on the contrary, was looking back, mourning what he saw as a lost civilisation and anticipated the world overwhelmed by barbarism. She had to do everything she could to reduce his negative atmosphere so that she could go on writing. In the country, this meant making the best of a holiday home she never really liked. In London they still lived in Richmond, where she had to put in long hours to make the fledgeling Hogarth Press flourish.

Virginia's third novel, *Jacob's Room*, was taking shape in her mind: this was the first of a series of novels whose living germ she brought back with her from her other world that she had explored with such dangerous intensity during her last breakdown and whose discovery had given her such 'exquisite' happiness. She remembered those experiences when she came to leave Hogarth House in 1924. In this year they moved the Press and themselves into 52 Tavistock Square, in central London. She certainly liked this large house, just as she adored London itself:

"London, thou art a jewel of jewels... music, talk, friendship, city views, books, publishing, something central and inexplicable, all this is now within my reach, as it hasn't been since August 1913, when we left Clifford's Inn, for a series of catastrophes which very nearly ended my life, & would, I'm vain enough to think, have ruined Leonard's... I am grateful. Nothing could have suited better all through those years when I was creeping about, like a rat struck on the head, & the aeroplanes were over London at night... Moreover, nowhere else could we have started the Hogarth Press, whose very awkward beginning had rise in this very room, on this very green carpet. Here that strange offspring grew & throve; it ousted us from the dining room, which is now a dusty coffin; & crept all over the house.

And people have been here, thousands of them it seems to me...

Postscript by VW: I've had some very curious visions in this room too, lying in bed, mad, & seeing the sunlight quivering like gold water, on the wall. I've heard the voices of the dead here. And felt, through it all, exquisitely happy." [2]

Among the dead was her brother Thoby who succumbed to typhoid in November 1906. His death is commemorated in *Jacob's Room* mainly as absence, as emptiness, through the actions and reactions of others. Jacob Flanders himself remains a somewhat isolated, fugitive figure. In this book Virginia explores the tantalizing sense of not knowing what it would be like to be the other person. The waiting characters who circle just beyond Jacob's range experience the desire to know, and are frustrated, as Virginia and all Thoby's friends were frustrated when he died, with a desire that could never be satisfied: as the families and friends of the many thousands of young men who died during the first world war were similarly frustrated. What would he have been like in this new post-war world that he had not lived to see, to experience? This is how Virginia coped with the war: not in *Night and Day* but in *Jacob's Room*. To write this novel Virginia had to revisit her own childhood both subjectively and objectively and the result is a strange, spare novel making no concessions to the more 'human' and romantic style of her earlier two books.

Virginia's third novel remains dry, brilliant but dry. Stylistically, what she does is to leave out the transitions between one event and the next. It is an iconoclastic text in its criticism of Cambridge University basking in its arrogant, exclusive attitude 'we are the sole purveyors of this cake' [3]; and the love affair of the young men with ancient Greece, which is regarded as a male domain and the foundation of their superiority over women:

" 'Probably,' said Jacob, 'we are the only people in the world who know what the Greeks meant'... A strange thing – when you come to think of it – this love of Greek, flourishing in such obscurity, distorted, discouraged, yet leaping out, all of a sudden." [4]

That exclusive university life is immediately contrasted with:

"At this moment there shook out into the air a wavering, quavering, doleful lamentation which seemed to lack strength to unfold itself, and yet flagged on; at the sound of which doors in back streets burst sullenly open; workmen stumped forth.

Florinda was sick."

Here, confident of what she is saying, in her own voice, Virginia clashes common life against the rarefied air of Cambridge.

The polarities of female and male, each left unsatisfied by the other, are deftly portrayed. The writing style employed by Virginia in this novel is pointed and humorous; the fractured treatment reflects, and is reflected by, impressionist art. Sue Roe says in her perceptive Introduction:

"It is in this novel that Virginia Woolf clearly determines the direction of all her future thinking, makes her final break with the conventional novel and brings us face to face with the intangible but not inexpressible vagaries of loss, longing, recollection and desire." [5]

Jacob's Room is the first novel by Virginia Woolf that does not include a major romantic character who can be likened to Leonard; not only this, but she has rejected the writing method Leonard used in *The Wise Virgins,* where the author assumes total knowledge of everything his characters think and all their motives. Here, the characters have to fend for themselves and are often isolated and alone or, like Jacob, reflected in the eyes of others.

In July 1922, Virginia records Leonard's comments when he was confronted with her manuscript:

"On Sunday L. read through Jacob's Room. He thinks it my best work. But his first remark was that it was amazingly well written. We argued about it. He calls it a work of genius; he thinks it unlike any other novel; he says that the people are ghosts; he says it is very strange: I have no philosophy of life he says; my people are puppets, moved hither & thither by fate. He doesn't agree that fate works in this way. Thinks I should use my 'method', on one or two characters next time; & he found it very interesting, & beautiful, & without lapse (save perhaps for the party) & quite intelligible." [6]

She had found her own writing voice which was not only very different from Leonard's, it was speaking from the opposite pole. This was the insight she gained as a result of her life-threatening rage, at both Leonard himself and maleness in general that had so recently been expressed in a devastating war. She had begun to mine some of the raw energy she had located during her journeys to the underworld, her creative centre. Not only this but she was staking out a very considerable area of internal landscape which she made her own. It was a landscape shaped and illuminated by the female brain: from this perspective the maleness both of individual men and as a generality was under examination as never before.

In August 1922, Virginia took stock of her situation:

"Twice a year I make good resolutions – in August & October. My good resolution for August is, to work methodically, yet with the grain not against it. Often, my wisdom teaches me, good resolutions wither because forced... I should make one of my little addings up of days, since there is a break. On the whole a good summer; by which I mean that pleasures – dining out, seeing people, – were rather successfully combined with reading & writing & staying at home. On the whole, L & I are becoming celebrities. L. would deny this... Reputation seems to accumulate, though we published nothing this year, Mrs Nicolson thinks me the best woman writer – & I have almost got used to Mrs Nicolson's having heard of me. But it gives me some pleasure. Again, I am on freer terms with my little world, & have the chance I think to expand it, only no money to buy clothes." [7]

This is her first reference to Mrs Nicolson – Vita Sackville-West, who would become the great love of her life. The two women did not meet until December this year, when Clive Bell invited them both to dinner; their relationship developed slowly from that time. We see that Virginia's day to day existence was full of petty difficulties and restrictions:

"I should very much like to account for my depression... At Brighton I saw a lovely blue Victorian dress, which L. advised me not to buy. Sydney [Waterlow] reproduced in his heavy lifeless voice exactly the phrases in which [Middleton] Murry, dismisses my writing 'merely silly – one simply doesn't read it – you're a back number.' Then Squire rejected Leonard's story; & perhaps I don't like seeing new houses built all about; & get edgy about our field... I now add my spending 10/6 on photographs, which we developed in my dress cupboard last night; and they are all failures. Compliments, clothes, building, photography – it is for these reasons that I cannot write Mrs Dalloway." [8]

Leonard is determining their lives, deciding what will and will not be bought with Virginia's money which she was not allowed to spend. She also becomes aware of similarities between herself and her brother-in-law Clive Bell – in contrast to Vanessa and Leonard who were in alliance, working out ways of destroying Clive's passionate love affair with Mary Hutchinson:

"Nessa, who concentrates upon one subject, & one only, with a kind of passive ferocity which I find alarming, took L. off primarily to discuss her attitude to Mary. Clive & I are much alike in our haphazard dealings with people. We do not concentrate; we are easily gulled & flattered; we expand & contract; we chatter & gossip; there is something much more fell, stable & determined in the characters of my sister & husband. Really, they can both determine a relationship & hold to it." [9]

Virginia was never a match for Vanessa's 'passive ferocity' (Marjorie Strachey, when she read Vanessa's hand, called her inconstant and cruel), or for her husband and sister's 'fell, stable & determined' personalities. When she was their target we need to be afraid for her, not of her. However, through the rest of this decade Virginia was able to escape with ever more confidence, no longer into madness but into her creative writing. The following year, she describes her method of bringing her characters to life that she explored in all her future novels:

"my discovery; how I dig out beautiful caves behind my characters; I think that gives exactly what I want; humanity, humour, depth. The idea is that the caves shall connect, & each comes to daylight at the present moment." [10]

Thanks to her 'madness' Virginia, as an individuated woman, connected with the upward life-energy in the present moment, something Leonard never achieved. In doing so, she changed the emphasis of her fourth novel from a male to a female orientation. In first draft, entitled The Hours, Leonard is objectified as the Scallywag and the structure is held rigid by the chiming of London's clocks during the course of the single day during which the story takes place. There is also an important Prime Minister. These two characters, the Scallywag and the Prime Minister, provided a hierarchical structure in terms of male social roles, which were abandoned in the second draft in favour of the female characters. In the completed text of *Mrs Dalloway* the magic reversal of energy from male to female is everywhere present and glowing.

This reversal is reflected in Virginia's life. During the early stage of planning her book, Leonard stood for a seat in Parliament as Labour candidate for the Combined English University Constituency – in the days when University members had more than one vote. The CEUC represented the other Universities, not Oxford or Cambridge. Virginia says in her diary that she did her best to ruin his political career, with which she had little sympathy and considerable fear that it would take him away from her more and more; but it died its own death without her assistance when he failed to win the seat by a wide margin at the General Election in November 1922. Failing to get elected led to long-term depression for Leonard: his dreams of becoming a politician had to be abandoned. He would no longer be Pericles, the orator. Also, his part-time job on the Nation was in jeopardy. Virginia dates their 'misery', which began with Leonard and not her, from the 3rd of January 1923:

"Leonard thinks himself a failure. And what use is there in denying a depression which is irrational? Can't I always think myself one too? It is inevitable." [11]

With the failure of Leonard's political career Virginia changed the emphasis of *Mrs. Dalloway,* reducing the importance of the Prime Minister and dropping the Scallywag completely, leaving Clarissa Dalloway as the central, connecting character.

Clarissa is partly an embodiment of Kitty Maxse, a society hostess (an 'awful snob') whom Virginia had known as a child: 'Not that I ever felt at my ease with her. But she was very charming – very humorous. She got engaged at St Ives... They sat on the seat by the Love Corner... I keep going over this very day in my mind.' Kitty Maxse died after falling over the banisters in her home, with the suggestion that she did so deliberately. With an admixture of the social, party-loving side of Virginia herself, she was a good candidate for resurrection. The diary entry of 8 October continues:

"Mrs Dalloway has branched into a book; & I adumbrate here a study of insanity & suicide: the world seen by the sane & the insane side by side – something like that. Septimus Smith? – is that a good name? – & to be more close to the fact than Jacob: but I think Jacob was a necessary step, for me, in working free. And now I must use this benignant page for making out a scheme of work."

At last Virginia feels strong enough to tackle the themes of madness and suicide, and the brutality of doctors, that she avoided in *Night & Day.* In contrast to the party held by Clarissa Dalloway, for which she prepares throughout the day, there is the under-level of Septimus Smith and his frightened Italian wife Rezia, who feels both isolated and embarrassed at his strange behaviour as he sat on a bench in Regent's Park:

" 'Septimus!' said Rezia. He started violently. People must notice.

'I am going to the fountain and back,' she said.

She could stand it no longer. Dr. Holmes might say there was nothing the matter. Far rather would she that he were dead! She could not sit beside him when he stared so and did not see her and made everything terrible... and he would not kill himself; and she could tell no one... To love makes one solitary, she thought. She could tell nobody, not even Septimus now, and looking back, she saw him sitting in his shabby overcoat alone, on the seat, hunched up, staring... She put on her new hat and he never noticed; and he was happy without her. Nothing could make her happy without him! Nothing! He was selfish. So men are. For he was not ill. Dr Holmes said there was nothing the matter with him... It was she who suffered – but she had nobody to tell...

I am alone; I am alone! she cried, by the fountain in Regent's Park (staring at the Indian and his cross) ...such was her darkness; when suddenly, as if a shelf were shot forth and she stood on it, she said how she was his wife, married years ago in Milan, his wife, and would never, never tell that he was mad! Turning, the shelf fell down; down, down she dropped. For he was gone, she thought – gone, as he threatened to kill himself... But no; there he was; still sitting alone on the seat, in his shabby overcoat, his legs crossed, staring, talking aloud." [12]

Septimus experiences what Virginia must have experienced during her breakdowns, and we also feel the embarrassment of the watcher, the carer, in a public place. We are let into the secret thoughts of the 'mad' person, thoughts from which the 'sane' are so carefully protected when the 'mad' are confined within the deaf walls of an institution. Virginia's words are as exposed in her book as Septimus's body is exposed sitting on a bench in Regent's Park. What does this 'mad' person say?

"Men must not cut down trees. There is a God. (He noted such revelations on the backs of envelopes.) Change the world. No-one kills from hatred. Make it known (he wrote it down). He waited. He listened. A sparrow perched on the railing opposite chirped Septimus, Septimus... [as a sparrow must have chirped 'Virginia', or 'Ginia', to her in 1913] ...four or five times over and went on, drawing its notes out, to sing freshly and piercingly in Greek words how there is no crime and, joined by another sparrow, they sang in voices prolonged and piercing in Greek words, from trees in the meadow of life beyond a river where the dead walk, how there is no death.

There was his hand; there the dead. White things were assembling behind the railings opposite. But he dared not look...

'What are you saying?' said Rezia suddenly, sitting down by him.

Interrupted again! She was always interrupting." [12]

Rezia reacts to Septimus as Leonard reacted to Virginia, interrupting her with unwanted glasses of milk when she was absorbed in her inner world that we now know was often intensely pleasurable to her, she could become 'exquisitely happy'. Those journeys to the underworld brought her into the rich but dangerous present moment – the now – that the 'sane' step over from past to future, hardly knowing of its existence. And she returned with a sense of understanding that was sexual in its nature.

Was it wisdom she had discovered, or simply the ravings of lunacy? She was never sure. To evoke the dead, to lower the barriers between the dead and the living and then, when 'white things were assembling', to be too terrified to look, gave Virginia the problem of letting the dead live again in her books without being taken over by them. This task she had taken on was a tremendous burden and responsibility.

What was it the birds sang to her in Greek? *They told her there was no crime and no death.* It was not her job to make judgements (for there was no crime). Instead, she must help those who had died to live again (for there was no death) and discover deeper meanings in their truncated lives. In *Mrs. Dalloway* she shares with the deceased Kitty Maxse the now that escapes from the tyranny of the ticking clock and gave to the dead woman some aspects of her own life: the 'sane' Virginia who loved London and enjoyed parties (which Leonard as a rule did not):

"As if to catch the falling drop, Clarissa (crossing to the dressing-table) plunged into the very heart of the moment, transfixed it, there – the moment of this June morning on which was the pressure of all the other mornings, seeing the glass, the dressing-table, and all the bottles afresh, collecting the whole of her at one point (as she looked into the glass), seeing the delicate pink face of the woman who was that very night to give a party; of Clarissa Dalloway; of herself... She pursed her lips when she looked in the glass. It was to give her face point. That was her self – pointed; dart-like; definite." [13]

A magical flood fills the text. Virginia said the book grew like a pearl in an oyster. This is a potent image: the irridescent sheath that forms to protect the oyster, submerged in the ocean, from the pain and damage done to its soft body from an alien and intrusive particle of grit.

Leonard is splintered between Richard Dalloway, Clarissa's reliable but boring husband, and the agonized Rezia, the wife of Septimus Smith (Rezia was partly modelled on Lydia Lopokova, a Russian dancer who married John Maynard Keynes). Virginia never stopped hoping for a union with Leonard on another level, in which they could 'mount together, if we could perceive from a sufficient height', to share a unique perspective, as Rhoda in *The Waves* says of Louis before she commits suicide [14]; but that hope, that vision of Virginia's, never came to fruition in their relationship. Leonard resisted her vision which he equated with madness and barbarism, in opposition to his determined sanity and dream of an ideal civilisation. Although she sometimes relied on him for reassurance in daily life, when she brought him into her writing he shattered into surrounding walls and sharp shards, the grit in the oyster.

His comments on this book, as recorded by her, are both predictable and perfunctory:

"L. read it; thinks it my best – but then has he not *got* to think so? Still I agree. He thinks it has more continuity than J[acob]'s R[oom], but is difficult owing to the lack of connection, visible, between the two themes." [15]

Interestingly, Vanessa enters *Mrs. Dalloway* in the form of an ornament. For years Virginia had called her sister Dolphin. Here, on the mantelpiece of Clarissa Dalloway's drawing-room, stands a crystal dolphin. Lucy, the helpful maid, comes in with a tray of clean silver for the party:

"All was for the party.

(And Lucy, coming into the drawing-room with her tray held out, put the giant candlesticks on the mantelpiece, the silver casket in the middle, turned the crystal dolphin towards the clock...)

'Oh, Lucy,' [Clarissa] said, 'the silver does look nice!'

'And how,' she said, turning the crystal dolphin to stand straight, 'how did you enjoy the play last night?' " [16]

The maid turns the dolphin towards the clock – that male image – as the chiming of the hours continues to punctuate the novel but not to dominate it; whereupon Virginia-Clarissa 'straightens' the dolphin and turns her to face outwards towards herself. Vanessa was too close to Leonard to be a trustworthy support for Virginia, hence she is not a warm, breathing flesh-and-blood dolphin but a crystalised ornament. There is no evidence that either Leonard or Vanessa took Virginia's hidden messages seriously.

Early in *Mrs Dalloway* we see Clarissa as a nun, with her narrow single bed, her sense of disembodiment; but as the book progresses she gains corporeality. In the earlier version, when it was still called The Hours, Virginia had assumed that Clarissa would die at the end. Instead, in the final version it is Septimus Smith who dies and Clarissa hears of his death while she lives on, triumphant. Clarissa's survival was an enormous effort, a tremendous achievement. And her party has been a success. For the first and perhaps only time Virginia manages to embody herself centrally:

"Then (she had felt it only this morning) there was the terror; the overwhelming incapacity, one's parents giving it into one's hands, this life, to be lived to the end, to be walked with serenely; there was in the depths of her heart an awful fear. Even now, quite often if Richard had not been there reading *The Times*, so that she could crouch like a bird and gradually revive, send roaring up that immeasurable delight, rubbing stick to stick, one thing with another, she must have perished. She had escaped. But that young man had killed himself.

Somehow it was her disaster – her disgrace. It was her punishment to see sink and disappear here a man, there a woman, in this profound darkness, and she forced to stand here in her evening dress... but... with the clock striking the hour, one, two, three, she did not pity him...

Fear no more the heat of the sun. She must go back to them. But what an extraordinary night! She felt somehow very like him – the young man who had killed himself. She felt glad that he had done it; thrown it away while they went on living. The clock was striking. The leaden circles dissolved in the air. But she must go back. She must assemble... And she came in from the little room."

The book ends triumphantly when Peter Walsh, an old flame of Clarissa's whom she had once rejected and now persuaded to come to her party, watches her enter:

"I will come, said Peter, but he sat on for a moment. What is this terror? What is this ecstasy? he thought to himself. What is it that fills me with extraordinary excitement?

It is Clarissa, he said.

For there she was." [17]

There is an almost wholly 'black' character, Miss Kilman, who many commentators see as an alien and unnecessary part of the story. But she is a very important, indeed essential, element so far as Virginia is concerned. Doris Kilman, an ugly middle-aged socialist woman, with a grudge against the rich and beautiful such as Mrs Dalloway, wields the destructive power Margaret Llewelyn Davies represented to Virginia. In this book, she had to be faced and destroyed. Whatever Virginia feared, or knew, about Leonard's relationship with Margaret she provides an agent for her destruction by giving a daughter to Clarissa and Richard Dalloway: Elizabeth, a young girl with dark hair and oriental eyes, has the strength to have tea with the sinister woman and then leave her, to live her own life. These scenes convey a very strong message, especially as Richard Dalloway does not even recognise his daughter throughout the party with which the day, and the book, ends.

Most of the narrative and the comments are carried by the characters themselves; however, Virginia in her own person makes an appearance in the text, to say:

"And Richard and Elizabeth were rather glad it was over, but Richard was proud of his daughter. And he had not meant to tell her, but he could not help telling her. He had looked at her, he said, and he had wondered, who is that lovely girl? and it was his daughter! That did make her happy. But her poor dog was howling." [18]

Lack of a child, of a daughter, was the most painful experience Virginia ever had to suffer; and this deprivation is part and parcel of her difficult relationship with Leonard. Her poor dog never stopped howling. She records in her diary at this time:

"We came back from Rodmell yesterday, & I am in one of my moods, as the nurses used to call it, today. And what is it & why? A desire for children, I suppose; for Nessa's life; for the sense of flowers breaking all round me involuntarily. Here's Angelica – here's Quentin & Julian… Years & years ago [in 1909], after the Lytton affair, I said to myself… never pretend that the things you havent got are not worth having; good advice I think. At least it often comes back to me. Never pretend that children, for instance, can be replaced by other things. And then I went on… to say to myself that one must… like things for themselves or rather, rid them of their bearing upon one's personal life. One must throw that aside; & venture on to do the things that exist independently of oneself. Now that is very hard for young women to do. Yet I got satisfaction from it. And now, married to L., I never have to make the effort. I do it, if I enjoy doing it. Perhaps I have been too happy for my soul's good? perhaps I have become too cowardly & self-indulgent? And does some of my discontent come from feeling that? I could not stay at 46 [Gordon Square, London] last night, because L. on the telephone expressed displeasure." [19]

She gives an unusually upset account of Leonard's high-handed treatment of her when she wanted to stay with Vanessa at 46 Gordon Square, and he phoned her preventing her from doing so:

"Late again. Very foolish. Your heart bad – & so my self reliance being sapped, I had no courage to venture against his will. Then I react. Of course it is a difficult question. For undoubtedly I get headaches or the jump in my heart; & then this spoils his pleasure, & if one lives with a person, has one the right – So it goes on."

Thus Leonard was capable of being heavily negative to Virginia. In large decisions and in small he had the power of veto, and he was not above misusing this when he argues with apparent rationality simply because he has set his will for or against something, while her needs and wishes are regularly overborne.

When they had the opportunity to purchase Asheham House, Leonard refused to consider doing so saying that the house was cold and damp; it often was, especially in winter, but Monk's House was also cold and damp, as well as being very inconvenient. Virginia frequently saw other places that she would have preferred to live in, on one occasion wanting to build a house; but Leonard said they were 'too old' – they were in their early forties. Instead, her money was spent purchasing the field adjoining Monk's House garden, together with two cottages, which consolidated Leonard's territory and made it much more difficult for them to consider any other lifestyle. To the end of her life Virginia dreamed of escaping from the confining village of Rodmell and from Monk's House. So was Virginia really 'too happy for my soul's good'? Assuredly she was not. In contrast to Vanessa and her family, she saw Leonard in particular becoming rigid as they grew older:

"I'm afraid we're becoming elderly. We are busy & attach importance to hours. I have my correspondence to finish, says L. today. I don't laugh. I take it seriously... L., I think, suffers from his extreme clarity. He sees things so clear that he can't swim float & speculate... Nessa... rides much more freely than we do... We have to make money – that is true. We have to have a house; 2 houses; 2 servants; a press... Yet most of this is for my sake; & am I honest in wishing it otherwise? Dont I feel (mainly) that I must ease the strain of circumstances in order to write? – that interruptions bore me: put gross matter on my fire?

I will leave it here, unfinished, a note of interrogation – signifying some mood that recurs, but is not often expressed. One's life is made up, superficially, of such moods; but they cross a solid substance, which too I am not going to hack my way into now."

In large part Leonard accepted her books because they demonstrated that he was married to a significant modern writer, a 'mad genius'; and because they began to make money. But he consistently refused to try to understand or benefit from what she was saying, hence he failed to grow as a person; while she no longer depended on his reactions to feel confident about the value of her texts.

When, in March 1924, the Woolfs moved from Richmond to 52 Tavistock Square, the basement became a hive of industry. Virginia was to be seen in a large back room, known as The Studio, surrounded by books and papers, with her pad on her knee, writing *Mrs Dalloway*. While writing, Virginia could 'rub stick to stick, send roaring up that immeasurable delight, one thing with another', as she connected with the up-from-below, creative female subterranean energy and let the channel of life flow upwards through her body, into her work. Having perfected her method, she had no fears at finishing it and no terror at what her friends or the critics might say:

"The reviewers will say that it is disjointed because of the mad scenes not connecting with the Dalloway scenes. And I suppose there is some superficial glittery writing. But is it 'unreal'? Is it mere accomplishment? I think not. And as I think I said before, it seems to leave me plunged in the richest strata of my mind. I can write & write & write now: the happiest feeling in the world." [20]

Virginia became freer to explore her inner world, to write as she wished and enjoy her relationship with Vita Sackville-West, once Leonard had begun to write the first of an ambitious series of books on 'communal psychology'. Volume One was not published until 1931, at the same time as Virginia's *The Waves*. *After the Deluge* was Leonard's attempt to put the 'catastrophe' of the 1914–18 war in perspective – that is, his perspective. He believed that the war was a disaster without parallel and marked the end of civilisation itself. He thought the causes of the first world war were psychological and argued that civilisation, weakened by the war, would inevitably break down completely into barbarism if there were to be a second. He would therefore be the prophet of doom, and warn whoever read his book that disaster was both imminent and inevitable. But by introducing a number of his pet bugbears such as royalty and 'privilege', as well as quoting extracts from the Bible, he blunted the force of what it was he wanted to say.

Perhaps Leonard's main difficulty was that he was a short-term writer without an underlying depth of thought. He could make himself an 'authority' on anything in a few months; indeed, he wrote a report for the Fabian Society that was taken into account when the League of Nations (precurser to the United Nations) was set up. But that was very different from embarking on what became a trilogy of volumes which he did not complete until 1953, spending thirty years on them. He says in the Preface to *After the Deluge*, Volume One:

"Its plan, if it is ever completed, will require a good many volumes... In this first volume I have not yet finished the study of the communal psychology of democracy, but I have decided to publish it as it stands, partly because it ends at a point of real transition in the enquiry, and partly for the not very good reason that it has already taken a good many years for me to reach even that point."

This was not an introduction that was likely to inspire confidence in his readers. Duncan Wilson, in his 'political biography' of Leonard, found it impossible to give an overall picture of Leonard's philosophy and was surprised that he had not read some basic books on the subject, which he put down to his doing too many other things. He then says:

"It is more surprising to find him in the early 1950s still busy at constructing philosophical systems without testing and perhaps strengthening the original foundations. And it is hard to avoid the conclusion that this failure was largely due to a sense of having received an incomparable revelation at Cambridge early in the century." [21]

Leonard's 'incomparable revelation' was to achieve a rebirth of ancient Greek ideals in modern life. As this vision became more and more obviously unrealistic, he predicted that everything would be swept away in another 'deluge' of 'barbarism'. Thus he diminished the importance of the twenty years between the two wars.

Virginia, on the other hand, revelled in those wild years of the nineteen twenties, with their wonderful parties and the excitement of throwing off the old Edwardian literary styles to discover her own style as part of the modern movement. The pleasure for her was precisely to discover and explore the meanings she found in abundance. But then she had a far more flexible and enquiring mind than Leonard. He never overcame his rigidity of thought and a negative attitude towards others. After the second world war, he wrote with hindsight:

"In the terrible years between 1919 and 1939, everything in international affairs was dominated by the emergence of fascism in Europe and the menace of another war. To make up one's mind what seemed to be the right foreign policy and, where passions and prejudices became more and more violent, to keep cool and have the courage of one's convictions was a difficult, often an agonizing business. Even today it is difficult to write truthfully and objectively about those years and the part one played in them, for the passions and prejudices persist and distort history." [22]

He also thought that despite his thousands of hours spent on committees, he had achieved virtually nothing. However, at least he had found a preoccupation on which he could vent his 'appalling resistance and persistence', which he described many years later to Trekkie Parsons:

"the appalling resistance and persistence which I know I possess & cannot control, which is due to some horrible fire in my entrails & must be a weariness of flesh & mind to other people... It makes things obsess me. But only once before in my life has it made a person obsess me." [23]

That Leonard was obsessed by Virginia throughout the years of their marriage is, I think, undeniable. There are really two questions: Why was he so obsessed by her? and How did his obsession affect her? Both questions can be answered, however briefly and incompletely, by understanding more about Leonard's character. He himself suffered from deep depressions and a sense of being a failure, together with an unreal sense of his mission in life. His difficulties were partly due to his being a Jew in a gentile society, at a time when European Jews were increasingly successful but also increasingly distrusted; however as an Apostle, one of the chosen few, he could not accept that the 'human ant-heap' had any significance in his life. He was determined to consolidate his position within the limited framework of his life with Virginia – while also despising her class and her pedigree. This made him a very difficult man to live with, since she must support him emotionally as well as financially while realising, on occasion, that he was damaging her position and undermining her self confidence. Both escaped from this central conflict into their writing.

Leonard's vision was comprehensive in scope. It subsumed everyone else who thus became subject to his will, as the Ceylonese were subject to his will in Hambantota, while he despised his white colleagues whom he felt were a threat to him. In his vision everyone had to be brought together to form a perfect democracy, a new dawn of civilisation based on the ancient Greeks and the Semites, that necessitated the downfall of the English aristocracy – which Virginia supported and Clarissa Dalloway personified. Intent on his unattainable vision he was perpetually disgruntled, and dissatisfied with the contemporary world. If Leonard had had the courage of his opinions he could have been a dangerous man. Perhaps fortunately his centre of power remained almost entirely confined to the

Bloomsbury Group, while much of the hard work of which he was capable was spent on the Hogarth Press where his sudden tantrums and penny-pinching led to frequent changes in the staff, especially among the young men who took on the job of assistant manager hoping it would lead to a more important position in other publishing firms.

Virginia's developing relationship with Vita Sackville-West became increasingly necessary to her as an antidote to the limited, constricted company of Leonard. The threat of her move away from him towards Vita, who was married to the tolerant Harold Nicolson – both of them were bi-sexual and part of the English aristocracy – increased Leonard's sense of insecurity and intensified his obsession with Virginia. His reaction was to determine to spend even more time at home on his writing at the cost of giving up his part-time paying job, thus laying on Virginia an even heavier burden of having to earn more money for them both; a burden that was necessary to keep Leonard balanced on their precarious marital see-saw. In September 1924, she wrote:

"We have lost 100 pounds a year, & he need no longer attend the office – a great gain. Now I hope for his book. I also begin to cherish dreams of retiring to a lovely house in the country, & there writing – once we get the press on its feet." [24]

Her dreams of 'retiring to a lovely house in the country' remained just that – dreams, vetoed by Leonard because he didn't want to move away from Monk's House and its garden. And he never did allow the Press to get on its feet. It was, after all, his 'mistress'. Whereas Virginia wanted to make life 'fuller and fuller' Leonard complained and constricted, while possibly carrying on an independent sex life of his own which he kept secret from Virginia. She describes her upset when he returned very late from London:

"I meant to record for psychological purposes that strange night when I went to meet Leonard & did not meet him. What an intensity of feeling was pressed into those hours! It was a wet windy night; & as I walked back across the field I said Now I am meeting it; now the old devil has once more got his spine through the waves, (but I cannot recapture really). And such was the strength of my feeling that I became physically rigid. Reality, so I thought, was unveiled. And there was something noble in feeling like this; tragic, not at all petty... after the last likely train had come in I felt it was intolerable to sit about, & must do the final thing, which was to go to London. Off I rode, without much time, against such a wind; & again I had a satisfaction in being matched with powerful things, like wind & dark. I battled, had to walk; got on; drove ahead; dropped the torch; picked it up, & so on again without any lights. Saw men & women walking together; thought, you're safe & happy I'm an outcast; took my ticket; had 3 minutes to spare, & then, turning the corner of the station stairs, saw Leonard, coming along, bending rather, like a person walking very quick, in his mackintosh. He was rather cold & angry (as, perhaps was natural). And then, not to show my feelings, I went outside and did something to my bicycle. Also, I went back to the ticket office, & said to the man there, 'Its all right. My husband caught the last train. Give me back my fare' which he did. And I got the money more to set myself right with Leonard than because I wanted it. All the way back we talked about a row (about reviewers) at the office; & all the time I was feeling My God, thats over. I'm out of that. Its over. Really, it was a physical feeling, of lightness & relief & safety. & yet there was too something terrible behind it – the fact of this pain, I suppose; which continued for several days – I think I should feel it again if I went over that road at night; and it became connected with... death... But I have not got it all in by any means." [25]

How wonderful if Leonard had hugged Virginia and reassured her! But no. Why was he so angry? Because he had been with another woman and didn't want Virginia to find out? – Anything was better than facing her distrust of him. He obviously decided his best means of defence was attack, so that Virginia went and fiddled with her bicycle to hide her feelings. She draws a veil over what he actually said but it must have been enormously upsetting since she remembered this traumatic event the following year, when she was again at Monk's House:

"Here I am waiting for L. to come back from London, & at this hour, having been wounded last year when he was late, I always feel the old wound twingeing. He has been seeing Nancy Cunard, so I expect a fair gossip. Vita was here for Sunday, gliding down the village in her large new blue Austin car, which she manages consummately... Vita... is like an over ripe grape in features, moustached, pouting, will be a little heavy; meanwhile, she strides on fine legs, in a well cut skirt, & though embarrassing at breakfast, has a manly good sense & simplicity about her which both L. & I find satisfactory. Oh yes, I like her; could tack her on to my equipage for all time; & suppose if life allowed, this might be a friendship of a sort... Vita... took us to Charleston... it all looked very grey & shabby & loosely cut in the light of her presence. As for Monk's House, it became a ruined barn, & we picnicking in the rubbish heap. And then I regained my zest for life about an hour later. Now to the house, waiting for L." [26]

By the summer of 1924, Virginia knew better than to worry about where Leonard had been when he returned late. This time, he was apparently with Nancy Cunard who was 28 years old, 'the extravagantly rebellious and capricious daughter of Lady Cunard', according to an editorial note. Her poem Parallax was accepted by the Hogarth Press this June and published in April 1925. A number of women's names have been linked with Leonard. It is possible that he lived like a monk through the years of his marriage but I think it unlikely, given the sexual climate of the times and Virginia's later reference to his 'habits'. Virginia says in *Old Bloomsbury*, a Memoir read to the Bloomsbury Group in the early nineteen twenties:

"I should be sorry to tell you how old I was before I saw that there is nothing shocking in a man's having a mistress, or in a woman's being one." [27]

She had the courage to break away sufficiently to pursue her relationship with Vita Sackville-West, which she called:

"a spirited, creditable affair, I think, innocent (spiritually) & all gain, I think; rather a bore for Leonard, but not enough to worry him. The truth is one has room for a good many relationships."[28]

I doubt if Virginia would have felt so carefree about sharing her sexuality with Vita if Leonard had remained faithful to her. That their affair actually disturbed him far more than she admits, will be considered in the following chapter.

We can see that the life the Woolfs led during this decade was often turbulent and insecure for Virginia, although she did not suffer any major bouts of mental breakdown. In many ways she relied on Leonard, but his proneness to depression 'took the wind out of my sails' and spoilt her enjoyment. She was constricted by his determined negativity. On one occasion, in June 1924, after a week with the Apostles and a disillusioned party, he 'contemplated, seriously, some scientific form of suicide'. Her escape was not to a different country house or life-style, although she would have liked both, but into her creative writing. She triumphantly brought her dead back to life in three stylistically explorative books that laid the foundations for her reputation as a major modern novelist.

Virginia never invented a character who was not based either on herself or on someone she knew well. She objected when anyone assumed that she had taken her characters entirely from life, although this was in fact what she did, using some thin disguises and sometimes combining elements of different people. In her fifth novel *To the Lighthouse,* despite giving oriental eyes to Lily Briscoe and transporting the story rather improbably to Scotland, from her childhood holiday home in St Ives, Cornwall, we should not be misled into thinking that here is a cast of characters who have nothing to do with Virginia's own family and friends. Vanessa was under no illusion on that score, as she wrote to Virginia:

"it seemed to me that in the first part of the book you have given a portrait of mother which is more like her to me than anything I could ever have perceived possible. It is almost painful to have her so raised from the dead... It seems to me the most astonishing feat of creation to have been able to see her in such a way. You have given father too I think as clearly...

I wonder how Adrian will like James! Perhaps you will finish his psycho-analysis for him. I shouldn't be surprised." [29]

Sir Leslie Stephen as Mr. Ramsay occupies the dominant male role and the main tension is between Lily-Vanessa and Mr. Ramsay. Lily is also partly Virginia who, as author, ensures that Mr. Ramsay does not succeed in climbing up the rock on which the lighthouse stands since, if he had, Lily-Vanessa-Virginia would have faded into the background. In this way, Virginia was a true feminist but she was curiously blind – or preferred not to see – how the balance between herself and Leonard was continually being eroded by him, to his advantage. In the same diary entry she notes that she will:

"write a bunch of 'Outlines' to make money (for under a new arrangement, we're to share any money over 200 pounds that I make)."

Financially, their new arrangement actually increased Virginia's responsibility to earn money for both of them. Previously, Leonard had assessed their likely expenditure at the end of each year and then they divided the remainder between them, each having their 'hoard' theoretically to spend as they wanted – although Virginia only received pocket money and had to ask Leonard's permission to spend anything more.

Under their new agreement Virginia kept 200 pounds of her earnings, an amount they thought of as their basic income for one person, and halved the rest with Leonard which became his by right. As he earned less than she, they relied more heavily than before on her earnings, and she had no right to say how Leonard's half of her money was spent.

With the money she made from the publication of *To the Lighthouse* Virginia bought their first motor car, a second-hand Singer, in 1927. She assumed that, like Vita and Vanessa who were already driving around the countryside during those carefree early days when there were few vehicles on the road, she would learn to drive. But the car, like all the other benefits that came through the money she earned by her writing, became Leonard's and she was relegated to the passenger seat.

For once, his enjoyment of the freedom it gave him was unstinted and, from this time on, he was never without a car.

LEONARD WOOLF AT CASSIS

Chapter Eight

A BREATH OF VITA

Looking back to Britain in the earlier years of the twentieth century we are reminded that, although it was a time of discovering freedoms after the moralising Victorian and the softer Edwardian years, so brutally ended by the first world war, creative women were still battling both a general and an individual view of the world that was essentially male. Men's voices were heard: whether they praised or blamed, their opinions counted for far more than those of women. Those women who did speak were in a small minority, it took courage for them to experience and interpret life in their own right. Perhaps it was even more remarkable when they became friends and shared their feelings, their discoveries. That Vita Sackville-West, a member of the aristocracy with a shaky grip on her ancestral inheritance, and Virginia Woolf, who saw herself as 'shabby middle-class' in comparison with her new acquaintance, did so was due to the fact that they were both committed writers who were willing to reach out towards another interesting woman. And this is still a rare event. In Virginia's case there was a great need to do so, for Vita enabled her to take a few faltering steps beyond the walls of her marriage.

Vita was born Victoria Mary Sackville-West, in 1892. She was the only child of the third Baron Sackville and Victoria, illegitimate daughter of the second Baron Sackville and a Spanish dancer, Pepita. Vita had married Harold Nicolson in 1913, early in his diplomatic career. They had two boys, Benedict and Nigel.

Virginia saw in Vita a strong, free-striding aristocrat, well-known, daring and adventurous, a woman determined to live her own life as she wished to the point of attracting scandal, such as the occasion when, with Violet Trefusis, she travelled around the Continent dressed in male clothing. Their husbands followed them and Harold persuaded Vita to return to their delightful property in Kent, Long Barn. On that occasion Vita had gone too far for even Harold to turn a blind eye, but in general both Nicolsons took pride in their tolerant, open marriage which permitted great sexual freedom.

Vita was flattered by Virginia's growing interest in her; she only gradually came to realise that this was not just another conquest on her

VIRGINIA AT MONK'S HOUSE, JUNE 1926
PHOTOGRAPH BY VITA SACKVILLE-WEST

VITA SACKVILLE-WEST BY HOPPÉ

part, to be enjoyed and cast aside as she had done with other women; indeed her last affair had been with a man who left his marriage because of her and was then dismissed. Her friendship with Virginia (who was six years her elder) was especially valuable to her because she recognised the depth of her creativity and her ability to work with complete concentration at whatever she undertook. Virginia, in a word, was as good for Vita as Vita was for her: Vita's somewhat heartless, snobbish attitude to life was challenged by that very special woman who was Virginia Woolf. In September 1925, three months before their relationship became physical, Vita wrote to Virginia:

"You are a very, very remarkable person. I have only tonight thoroughly and completely realised how remarkable you really are. You see, you accomplish so much. You are one perpetual Achievement; yet you give the impression of having infinite leisure... One may not, for reasons of health, come to see you: you write divine letters, four pages long. You read bulky manuscripts. You advise grocers. You produce books which occupy a permanent place on ones bedside shelf. You cast a beam across the dingy landscape of the Times Literary Supplement. You change people's lives. You set up type. You offer to read and criticise one's poems – criticise meaning illumination, not the complete disheartenment which is the legacy of other critics. How is it done? Do you do it by concentration? Do you do it by organisation? I want a recipe so badly." [1]

Vita had sent her letter by messenger, because 'I was frightened of Leonard. I knew he would look disapproving if I appeared at the house. He would look the more disapproving because he wouldn't know how much I approved, – of his care of you, I mean.'

In November, Vita described Leonard to her husband as being 'a funny grim solitary creature', who is 'perfectly happy with a crowd of puppies.' Virginia is 'an angel of wit and intelligence.' While at the same time she reassured Harold about her increasingly intimate relationship with Virginia, which had not yet flowered into sexuality: 'not to worry, though. It is all right.' [2]

For most of this autumn Virginia lived the life of a semi-invalid. She had seen few visitors while staying with Leonard at Monk's House for their annual summer stay of eight or nine weeks. – Those long summers, when the Woolfs were living together at Rodmell, were often characterised by Virginia's ill health. In August she collapsed at Charleston where she had had to cope with the 'fell' combination of Leonard and

Vanessa. On the evidence, we could say with some justice that living with Leonard during their annual retreat in the country was more of an ordeal for her than finishing a book. However, others will say that Virginia was always prone to 'summer madness'. She only improved when Vita became her friend.

Let us try and find out why it was so difficult for Virginia to live in close proximity to Leonard; and in what ways did her relationship with Vita provide an essential antidote?

The key to why Virginia was not able to develop into an independent woman lies in Leonard's attitude to those people whom he called 'sillies', a word he acquired from Tolstoy. In his opinion not only was Virginia a 'silly' but so was Sophocles and G.E. Moore; also Lydia Lopokova, the Russian dancer who married John Maynard Keynes in August, 1925. (Leonard must have detested this union since he liked Lydia, while he and Lytton had always hated the increasingly successful Keynes). According to Leonard the novelist E.M. Forster was a 'silly' and so was Lily, a servant the Woolfs employed just before the first world war of whom Leonard gives a detailed account in the third volume of his autobiography, *Beginning Again*:

"Quite apart from Virginia's madness, life in Hogarth House during the first six months of 1915 acquired a curious atmosphere of wild unreality. Strange, ridiculous scenes took place. Here is one, a kind of tragicomedy inserted in the tragedy. In the previous year when we were at Ash[e]ham [House], we had engaged a house parlourmaid called Lily. Lily was one of those persons for whom I feel the same kind of affection as I do for cats and dogs [*sic*]. She was an extremely nice character, but temperamentally born to certain disaster... We took up the reference and a nun came out to see us. She told us that Lily had been seduced and had had an illegitimate child. She was not a Roman Catholic, but the convent had taken her in and cared for her and the child. The nun said that she was in many ways a very nice girl, but weak... she had passed from the category of respectability into that of disreputability... These 'sillies', as Tolstoy called them, are terribly simple and at the same time tragically complicated. You could almost see this in Lily's face; she had a long, pale, weak, rather pretty, sad face. There was a gentleness in her voice and manners which was certainly unusual in country girls of her class in 1913. And in 1913 in Haywards Heath fate had marked her down for disaster no less certainly than it had marked down the House of Atreus for disaster nearly 3,000 years before in Mycenae. [see *Appendix A*]

One night at 3 o'clock in the morning I was suddenly woken up by Annie, the cook, bursting into my bedroom and crying aloud: 'There is a soldier in the kitchen; there is a soldier in the kitchen – and Lily's there.' I went down to the kitchen in the basement and found that indeed a soldier – a sergeant – was there and Lily too in some disarray. When I opened the door, the soldier dashed past me down the passage, through the door into the garden – leaving behind him in the kitchen his cane. I told Lily that she had better go up to bed and that I would talk to her in the morning. Our conversation in the morning was very distressing. It was a moment at which Virginia was still terribly ill; it was essential that she should be kept completely undisturbed and unexcited, and one could not risk her being startled by soldiers dashing about the house and garden in the early hours of the morning. I told this to Lily and she was miserably contrite, saying that she had no excuse and had behaved abominably and had no right to expect to be kept on." [3]

Leonard told Lily he would consult the nun, who asked Leonard not to dismiss her as she had 'learnt her lesson'. Leonard agreed and Lily stayed, but 'she was very depressed and I was hardly surprised when she came to see me after a few weeks and said that she thought she should go and try to find another place. It was not because I had in any way reproached her after I had agreed to her remaining, she said, because I hadn't done so; it was that she reproached herself. The nun, consulted once more, agreed, saying that Lily had better go as she had worked herself up into such a state of contrition and unhappiness that she would never settle down again with us in Richmond. So Lily left. There is no doubt that she was tragically sensitive and in Haywards Heath 'born to disaster' which had been regulated by me and the nun on the highest principles and with scrupulous decorum... We never saw or heard from her again. Her epitaph has been written by two poets, one of the 17th and the other of the 18th century. "When lovely woman stoops to folly, and finds, too late, that men betray, what charm can soothe her melancholy?" "There is no armour against fate."

In the story of Lily we once again have a triangle, this time with Leonard (in control), the nun, who is in a superior position but must agree with him, and the victim – Lily, who is doomed. He surely used a sledge-hammer to crack a nut when he compared the legend of the fall of the House of Atreus, which involves incest and murder through several generations and the eating of human flesh, to the pleasure of one young parlourmaid in the arms of a soldier (a sergeant who forgot his cane) as a relief from the tedium of domestic work in the basement of Hogarth House, Richmond.

It is to be noticed that Leonard, in imposing this category of 'silly' on a curious mixture of people, has excluded himself – along with Vanessa, Vita, Harold and Margaret Llewelyn Davies, to name a few. Thus, for Leonard, 'sillies' are 'the other'. Perhaps we should ask whether his categorisation may be telling us more about Leonard Woolf than about the people he sets apart in this way. He professes both to admire and despise 'sillies': they are terribly simple and unworldly, yet tragically complicated, doomed to disaster: whom he, as a man of the world (and in contrast extraordinarily sane), can choose either to assist or leave to their fate. What he could not do was enter their world, therefore he was unable to give any real help either to Lily or Virginia.

Early in December 1925, Virginia and Leonard went for a walk around Ken Wood, in Hampstead, where Leonard criticises Lytton for having changed from being a 'silly' when they were up at Cambridge together. Virginia records their conversation:

"Morgan [E.M. Forster] is I think naturally more congenial to L. than Lytton is. He likes 'Sillies'; he likes the dependent simplicity of Morgan and myself. He likes settling our minds, & our intense relief at this. Well, well." [4]

As Leonard's wife, there was never a chance for Virginia to develop into a complete human being despite the immense effort she made in Mrs Dalloway to do so. He would never allow her to change into 'not a silly', as Lytton had done, since such a person was either a potential or an actual threat to him and would thus become a candidate for his lethal power games – either drawn in on his side, like Vanessa, or seen to be against him and therefore an enemy. The cage he had built around Virginia not only confined her, but protected her from his devastating ability to destroy a person using his 'method' However, protected as his 'mad genius' and made to work for a tiny amount of money in exchange for being looked after, she must remain within those parameters where she confirmed his own sanity. For 'sillies' he feels the same sort of affection as for cats and dogs – because they don't challenge him. As he watches them, his pets gambolling about on his land, he takes the pride of ownership in them.

Quentin Bell comments that there was no doubt Leonard infantilised Virginia. But Vita never made this mistake: she was awed by her and respected her. According to her younger son Nigel Nicolson, who has done such an excellent job of editing and publishing the great quantity of letters written by Virginia Woolf, as well as by his parents, Vita was surprised that: 'Virginia could embark at the age of forty-four upon the only love affair of her life without trepidation, as if she didn't want to go to her grave without having done something really wicked.' [5]

It is indeed remarkable that Virginia, after twelve years of living with Leonard, in her forties, had the stamina to experience love and sexuality. I believe her courage was due to the recognition that Vita was an essential antidote to Leonard. Loving Vita (whose name means 'life') she was choosing life over death.

In December 1925, she went to stay for three nights at Vita's house, Long Barn. Leonard wrote a letter to Vita, as from one grown-up to another, in which Virginia is treated not as a person but an object:

"Dear Vita,

I enclose Virginia & hope she will behave. The only thing I ask is that you will be adamant in sending her off to bed not 1 minute later than 11 P.M. She ought not to talk for too long at a stretch at a time. It is good of you to have her. I hope to be able to come for a night.

Yours

Leonard Woolf" [6]

During this visit the two women began their sexual relationship, committing themselves to each other without any fear or mistrust on Virginia's part. To relate fully to Vita in this way must have been a wonderful relief for her – the relief of the caged bird at last stretching its wings and soaring free into the wide sky. But her sense of freedom was illusory. She was more like a bird with a string tied to its leg, pulled sharply back to earth whenever Leonard's controlling hand decided to do so. This is a scene I watched with horror in Kashmir as a crow was again and again thrown skyward to fly for a brief moment of apparent freedom before being tugged down to fall heavily on the ground until at last it lay still, dying, while the sky was black with hundreds of crows flying overhead, calling and crying. (See *Claudia's India*.) Was the crow a 'silly'? Had it deserved its fate? Was its doom sealed by the gods? Or was it simply a victim, made a plaything by a group of sadistic Kashmiri men whose sport was to release it and tug the string?

Virginia and Vita spent the first two nights of her visit on their own together, on the second night staying excitedly awake until 3 am, despite Leonard's strictures. On the third day he went to Long Barn and remained there for the night. He quickly realised the nature of Virginia's love for Vita. His first reaction was to make sure that Vanessa and other members of the Bloomsbury Group knew what was happening. He needed to have some members of the Group on his side, particularly Vanessa, watching with approbation as he held the string and tugged. Vita had dared to breach the nunnery walls that he had erected so carefully around Virginia, while Virginia had glimpsed freedom, reached out towards a pleasure that he had not permitted her, and she had humiliated him. With the consummation of the women's love for each other, he suffered a loss of control that had to be turned to his advantage. We have a new triangle, of Virginia and Vita in the dominant positions and Leonard as a poor third, something he would never accept. He would certainly not further weaken his position by ranting or raging at them, he would watch and wait, hiding his 'fell' determination. Very little, if anything, showed on the surface of his behaviour. This allowed Virginia to believe – or hope – that he would sanction their love so long as she did not exclude him.

The Bloomsbury Group theoretically lived according to G.E. Moore's ethic of free love; this, and Leonard's rejection of suburban values, did not allow him openly to try and prevent their relationship. Also, he could not be seen to be less tolerant than Vita's husband Harold Nicolson, whose career in the Foreign Office was just what he had wanted to achieve. Nevertheless, we can recognise his changed attitude towards Virginia from this time onwards. His prized possession was now a threat to him. This she did not fully understand until the final months of her life when she wrote *Between the Acts*, although it is implicit in *The Waves*. His first recorded remark, distancing himself from Virginia and Vita, was typically micro-effective. In an incident recounted by Quentin Bell in his authorised biography of Virginia:

"The Woolfs spent Christmas that year with the Bells at Charleston. Vita drove over from Brighton to lunch on Boxing Day. 'How beautiful she is,' said Clive to Virginia after the guest had gone. 'An aristocrat of ancient race,' said Virginia to Clive. Leonard turned to Julian. 'What snobs they are,' he said." [7]

Julian Bell, Vanessa's eldest child, was seventeen at the time. No doubt over the years Leonard did his best to persuade Julian to adopt his own political stance against the aristocracy in favour of left wing ideals; in which case he would have helped to influence the young man when he made his headlong, and fatal, dash into the Spanish Civil War in 1938.

Vita commented to Harold about her visit to the Bells: 'I lunched at Charleston – very plain living and high thinking. I like Virginia's sister awfully... Oh my dear, they do live in such squalor!' [8]

Leonard knew he had an ally in Vanessa, since she had been active in steering Virginia away from lesbianism in 1910 and had carried out a successful campaign to get her to marry him on his return from Ceylon. Vanessa wrote opaquely to Duncan Grant about this visit (how fascinating to be able to perceive the same event from so many different angles of vision) in a letter dated 27 December, 1925:

"Leonard has gone today and Virginia goes tomorrow, when I hope we shall return to normal existence. I thought she'd stay longer, but she really can't bear to be parted from him a moment. To tell you the truth, though I have very much enjoyed having them, I shall find it a relief when they're gone, as one always does. Also I get very tired of the perpetual personal conversation that always goes on. Yesterday Vita came to lunch. Afterwards we all sate in the studio and Virginia held forth in her usual style which you know and I cannot describe, very amusing but also most uneasy, at least to my mind. The whole evening afterwards was spent in her making mock apologies for having talked so much. It is brilliant of course and I suppose one sounds curmudgeonly for finding any fault, but one simply gets exhausted and longs for some quiet talk that will lead nowhere for a change. I even think how refreshing some of the pure male speculations, to which as you know I cannot attend, would be. However, it's worth it of course, and I daresay it's family feeling that makes me restive." [9]

Vanessa does not detail the personal conversation that took place, nor does she say what 'family feeling' was causing her so much discomfort; however, Leonard must have talked about his wife's burgeoning affair with Vita and we should not be in any doubt about her prejudice against it. The following year, when Vita returned from her trip to Persia, Virginia wrote to Vanessa: 'Vita is back – that will bore you.' and 'Vita is now arriving to spend nights alone with me... I say no more; as you are bored by Vita, bored by love, bored by me, and everything to do with me... but such has long been my fate, and it is better to meet it open eyed. Still, the June nights are long and warm; the roses flowering; and the garden full of lust and bees, mingling in the asparagus beds.' [10]

No wonder Virginia left Charleston that Christmas of 1925, not because she couldn't bear to be separated from Leonard but because she wanted to escape from the destructive atmosphere. Vita was not a member of the Bloomsbury Group and had with good reason been alarmed at the prospect of that brief visit to Charleston. Clive Bell must have been present since he, when he met Vita a few days later at a New Year's country house party, asked her directly if she had slept with Virginia. Both Vita and Virginia had hoped to be discreet and keep their affair secret. Horrified at Clive's challenge, she at once wrote to Virginia:

"My darling Virginia

I write to you in a state of extreme perturbation – I'll tell you why, when I see you.

I was taken off my guard.

It's early morning in the new year. I'll write you a proper letter – but I am upset now – it is Clive who is responsible.

The house is full of children and noise.

Your bewildered

Vita" [11]

An editorial note explains that 'Clive Bell, another guest, asked Vita whether she and Virginia had slept together. Vita firmly denied it.' Vita blames Clive – but was he responsible? Or were Leonard and Vanessa using him, playing the same game the three of them had played against Virginia in 1910? I think it likely.

Two days later Vita wrote once more, this time admitting 'I was rather indiscreet, all the same'. Virginia reassures her: 'I want to know *why* you were so perturbed, and wrote in such a whirl, and *what* your fire talk was about – oh and crowds of things.' [12]

Here are the first tweaks on the string that bound Virginia to Leonard while she tried to fly in the open, life-giving air of her relationship with Vita. His needle-sharp mongoose teeth were already plunged into the neck of their affair.

The two women had so little time together. In January 1926, Virginia fell ill with suspected German measles, while Vita suffered from the effects of the inoculations she had before her journey to Teheran (the capital city of Persia, modern Iran), where she was to join Harold. However, they met several times and Clive was restored to favour. He gave Virginia his version of his conversation with Vita, and 'raved, with such warmth and emotion, about you, that my heart was touched.' [13]

Parted, the two women began a correspondence that was slightly nervous, yearning, yet perhaps it allowed them to get to know each other better
than they would have done at close quarters, as they kept in touch through
the four months of their separation. Vita wrote with excitement of her
journey by sea and overland to Persia, a country she loved, and of her life as
a diplomat's wife having to take part in ceremonial functions, although she
did this as seldom as possible. There were moments of opulence, pouring
priceless gems through her fingers, contrasted with unromantic England.
In the end the ritual became tedious, her days routine and she longed to
travel with Virginia whom she constantly thought about.

Virginia for her part was quite frightened by the strength of her feelings at the temporary loss of Vita. She wrote to 'dearest Towser' (now,
Vita was a dog, later 'donkey West') complaining of her friend's 'dumb'
letters that were neither passionate enough nor fired with sufficient creative imagination; but travelling abroad with her was out of the question:

'It is all very well about Bloomsbury being a rotten biscuit, and me a
weevil, and Persia being a rose and you an Emperor moth – I quite
agree... what is Bloomsbury, or Long Barn either, but a contortion, a
temporary knot; and why do I pity and deride the human race, when its
lot is profoundly peaceful and happy?... I extract by degrees a great deal
from your letters. They might be longer; They might be more loving.
But I see your point – life is too exciting.' [14]

They establish a balance, Vita living a fascinating adventure from
which will emerge a travel book, while Virginia is the more creative
writer. Vita:

"I don't know whether to be dejected or encouraged when I read the
works of Virginia Woolf. Dejected because I shall never be able to write
like that, or encouraged because somebody else can?... What I should
really like to do would be to take you to some absurdly romantic place –
vain dream, alas! what with Leonard and the Press – Besides, by romantic
I mean Persia or China, not Tintagel or Kergarnec. Oh, what fun it
would be, and Virginia's eyes would grow rounder and rounder...
Goodnight, darling and remote Virginia."

Virginia calls Vita 'truly a picture maker' while she is more concerned
with writing style; it 'is a very simple matter, it is all rhythm. Now this is
very profound, what rhythm is, and goes far deeper than words... Then
there's my character. I agree about the lack of jolly vulgarity. But then
think how I was brought up! No school; mooning about alone among my

father's books; never any chance to pick up what goes on in schools – throwing balls; ragging; slang; vulgarity; scenes; jealousies – only rages with my half brothers, and being walked off my legs round the Serpentine by my father... Yes, dearest Vita: I do miss you; I think of you: I have a million things, not so much to say, as to sink into you.' [15]

Vita replies:

"Like a little warm coal in my heart burns your saying that you miss me. I miss you oh so much. How much you'll never believe or know. At every moment of the day. It is painful but also rather pleasant, if you know what I mean. I mean, that it is good to have so keen and persistent a feeling about somebody."

Vita, aged thirty-four on the 9th of March, wrote: 'How is it that one can never communicate? Only imaginary things can be communicated, like ideas, or the world of a novel; but not real experience... I should like to see you faced with the task of communicating Persia. How I wish I could bring you here; couldn't you and Leonard come next spring? No, of course you won't: what, leave the press?... I wish I had a photograph of you. It is a torment not being able to visualise when one wants to. I can visualise you as a matter of fact surprisingly well, – but always as you stood on your door-step that last evening, when the lamps were lit and the trees misty, and I drove away. Think kindly of your exile, distant but very very loving. And very constant. I must write you a letter about constancy.'

Vita's desire was to adventure with Virginia, without Leonard: 'And I had galvanised you into asking Leonard to come to the South Sea; but, darling Virginia, that wasn't the point *at all*. The point was that you should come to Persia with *me; that I* should waft you to those brown plains; not that you should matrimonially disappear for a year out of my ken. Or were you teasing me?' [16]

Virginia in her happiness teased and played pranks on Vita. She talked about the 'He-brides' – a pun on the Hebrides, north of Scotland, where she had located *To the Lighthouse*; and she sent a copy of the book to Vita with all the pages blank, saying it was the best novel she had ever written – then worried in case Vita thought she was boasting.

Vita described her life in Teheran, sometimes unflatteringly: 'I am sure the Shah will come to the coronation in tennis-shoes... Harold in uniform and gold lace, little sword getting between his legs; Vita derisive, but decked in emeralds... everything is very shoddy here... Then once a fortnight the muddy car comes in, and there are letters: the only rift opening on the outside world. Otherwise it is all very self-contained, – what with the old white horse who goes his rounds every morning, bringing two barrels of water to every house in the compound, and the Sanitary Cart, which drawn by a donkey performs a sordid emptying function hencefor-ward unknown at Rodmell.'

That spring the Woolfs installed a bathroom with hot water and two flush lavatories at Monk's House, paid for with the money Virginia earned from *Mrs Dalloway* and *The Common Reader*. For eight years they had had to use an outside earth closet.

Virginia dared to comment on a draft of Vita's long poem *The Land:* 'I imagine it wants a little central transparency. Some sudden intensity.' To which Vita replied: 'you upset me dreadfully about the central trans-parency. Because it is what I have always felt myself. Only how to do it? ... What fun it will be to sit on your floor again and stick on stamps. And to carry you off in the little blue motor. If you knew what you meant to me, you might be pleased.' Vita returned to England earlier than originally planned. Virginia notes:

"How odd it is – the effect geography has in the mind! I write to you differently now you're coming back. The pathos is melting. I felt it pathetic when you were going away; as if you were sinking below the verge. Now that you are rising, I'm jolly again." [17]

When the two women met they miraculously managed to maintain and, indeed, deepen their relationship, despite both being very busy with their own lives and writings. There were limits. Neither of them would risk their marriage; yet, while little changed between Harold and Vita except that she now wanted him to give up his career and devote his time to writing and gardening, something had occurred between Virginia and Leonard. He would continue to care for Virginia, lay down the law on what she could do and not do and ensure that she had more work to get through than even she could manage. But from now on she was a 'silly' who had erred, a dangerous pet, whom fate would deal with as she deserved in due course of time. He could afford to wait. Meanwhile, he continued to write the first volume of *After the Deluge*, on which he was no doubt pinning his hopes of emerging into the political limelight and to be 'up' on their marital see-saw. As for Vita, both Virginia and Leonard persuaded her to change to The Hogarth Press, where one of her books was a best seller. Leonard was now her publisher and in con-trol; he reserved his coup de grace until after Virginia's death in 1941, when he rejected Vita's latest manuscript and published nothing more of hers.

Despite the boundaries to their relationship, Virginia's physical attraction for Vita gave her new energy and gradually transformed her. Her friend's absence, not her presence, could cause illness. She delighted in sexual references: 'You have written enough, let us now talk about copulation.' [18] The energy she found enabled her to write *To the Lighthouse* 'all in a flash', 'Never never have I written so easily, imagined so profusely.' [19] Alma Halbert Bond gives prime importance to their relationship:

"The unwritten story of the Woolf-Sackville romance, in my opinion, is that Vita was the love of Virginia's life. Whereas Vita had many loves besides Virginia, Vita, the rampant 'sapphist,' in reality was unable to love. In effect, she seduced Virginia, who lived a life as insulated, passive, and protected as 'a weevil in a biscuit' [20]... Once sexuality became conscious, it was probably far more enjoyable for Virginia than her biographers have been willing to admit."

And again:

"Vita instigated the flowering of Virginia's growth and creativity... Vita was the catalyst who enabled Virginia to resume her emotional development. Unwittingly, Vita contributed to the maintenance of Virginia's health and sanity for over eighteen years." [21]

Quentin Bell was much more cautious in his assessment:

"There may have been – on balance I think that there probably was – some caressing, some bedding together. But whatever may have occurred between them of this nature, I doubt very much whether it was of a kind to excite Virginia or to satisfy Vita. As far as Virginia's life is concerned the point is of no great importance; what was, to her, important was the extent to which she was emotionally involved, the degree to which she was in love. One cannot give a straight answer to such questions but, if the test of passion be blindness, then her affections were not very deeply engaged." [22]

Bell misses the point here. Physical love-making reinforced the intensity of the Vita who lived inside Virginia's imagination, illuminating and inspiring her. Vita was immensely valuable to her in this way. She had considered the quality of this inner relationship when she wrote *Night and Day*, and found romantic love unsatisfactory; in effect, in that book she criticises Leonard for using her for his dreaming vision, as Aspasia, regardless of the person she actually was. Leonard had long ceased to inspire Virginia – if he had ever done so, rage had burnt him out of her creative inner being; it was her timid, childish self who clung to him for reassurance. The woman in her, seeking public recognition and emotional development, reached out to Vita but she always saw her friend clearly for what she was – and wasn't. It was on these terms that the women continued their relationship through 1926, visiting each other while doing their best to take Leonard's feelings into consideration. Vita gave them a spaniel puppy, Pinka (or Pinker), who became Leonard's pet.

It was, however, an uneasy arrangement. This becomes evident in a succession of entries in Virginia's diary during the long weeks of summer when she and Leonard were once more living at close quarters in Monk's House. A wooden lodge (an earlier building than the present one) was built outside, so that Virginia could isolate herself and get on with her work, hoping to make some money that she could spend. But early in September she became depressed, in the night waking in a panic that Vanessa had children and Maynard could buy carpets, for which she begins by blaming herself:

"my own gifts & shares seemed so moderate in comparison; my own fault too – a little more self control on my part, & we might have had a boy of 12, a girl of 10. This always makes me wretched in the early hours. So I said, I am spoiling what I have. I like to have space to spread my mind in. Whatever I think, I can rap out, suddenly to L. We are somehow very detached, free, harmonious. I am immensely busy. Hence I come to my moral, which is simply to enjoy what one does enjoy, without teasing oneself oh but Nessa has children, Maynard carpets... talk with L.: a sense of great happiness & ease. Went & looked at the stars, but could not get quite the right sense of amazement because L. said 'Now come in. Its too cold to be out." [23]

Thus Virginia communicates. She reminds herself of her deprivation while also, despite being determinedly cheerful, revealing the bars of her cage. Ten days later she had a mini nervous breakdown that in my view was caused by Leonard's negative atmosphere, but he put it down to finishing *To the Lighthouse*. She describes her states of mind in headed notes. 'A State of Mind' gives an account of the horror:

"like a painful wave swelling about the heart – tossing me up. I'm unhappy unhappy! Down – God, I wish I were dead. Pause. But why am I feeling this? Let me watch the wave rise. I watch. Vanessa. Children.

Failure. Yes; I detect that. Failure failure. (The wave rises). Oh they laughed at my taste in green paint! Wave crashes. I wish I were dead! I've only a few years to live I hope. I cant face this horror any more – (this is the wave spreading out over me)... The wave again! The irrational pain: the sense of failure, generally some specific incident, as for example my taste in green paint, or buying a new dress, or asking Dadie for the week-end, tacked on." [24]

The three incidents she gives, the green paint, buying a new dress, and the inviting of George (Dadie) Rylands, were all things that Leonard would have opposed since he didn't want her to spend money, didn't want visitors. With an effort, Virginia tries to control her night's horror: '& then hear L. in the passage & simulate, for myself as well as for him, great cheerfulness, & generally am cheerful, by the time breakfast is over.' But by the 18th September:

"Intense depression: I have to confess that this has overcome me several times since September 6th... It is so strange to me that I cannot get it right – the depression, I mean, which does not come from something definite, but from nothing... Of course I was interested; & discovered that, for the first time for many years, I had been idle without being ill. We had been walking, expeditioning, in the fine hot weather. I was writing the last pages of To the Lighthouse (finished, provisionally, Sept. 16th). Somehow, my reading had lapsed. I was hunting no hares... This is a warning then; never cease the use of the brain. So I used my brain. Then, owing to mismanagement, no one came to stay, & I got very few letters; & the high hot pure days went on & on; & this blankness persisted, & I began to suspect my book of the same thing; & there was Nessa humming & booming & flourishing over the hill; & one night we had a long long argument. Vita started it, by coming over with Plank [George Plank designed the cover for Vita's poem The Land,] L. (I say) spoilt the visit by glooming because I said he'd been angry. He shut up, & was caustic. He denied this, but admitted that my habits of describing him, & others, had this effect often. I saw myself, my brilliancy, genius, charm, beauty (&.&. – the attendants that float me through so many years) diminish & disappear. One is in truth an elderly dowdy fussy ugly incompetent woman vain, chattering & futile. I saw this vividly, impressively. Then he said our relations had not been so good lately." [25]

For a moment Virginia's internal mirror shows her not what she usually sees of herself but, thanks to Leonard's gloom, the negatives. To him, in his own dark mirror, she often did look like an 'elderly dowdy fussy incompetent woman vain, chattering & futile'. Tired of her voice, trying to keep her quiet, he would put up with her for the sake of the money she earned so that he could increase his empire at Monk's House, as he wrapped himself in his mantle of self-importance and laboured over the first volume of his trilogy that he hoped would change the world. Now all this was in jeopardy because Vita was leading her away from him. What were they not planning behind his back? Freedom? Independence? From him! Hadn't he turned is wife into the writer she was by looking after her? Without him she might have spent her life raving and screaming like her half sister Laura, still alive and incarcerated in an asylum. No wonder their relations 'had not been so good lately'.

That summer the almost silent battle between them was intense and it drove Virginia into a nervous collapse. But at least she managed to cope with the stress. She even expresses dismay at the way Leonard is taking over at Monk's House, while the place was overrun by dogs:

"I admitted that I had been irritated, first by the prevalency of the dogs (Grizzle on heat too.) Secondly by his assumption that we can afford to saddle ourselves with a whole time gardener, build or buy him a cottage, & take in the terrace to be garden. Then, I said, we shall be tying ourselves to come here; shall never travel; & it will be assumed that Monks House is the hub of the world. This it certainly is not, I said, to me; nor do I wish to spend such a measure of money on gardens, when we cannot buy rugs, beds or good arm chairs. L. was, I think, hurt at this, & I was annoyed at saying it, yet did, not angrily, but in the interests of freedom. Too many women give way on this point, & secretly grudge their unselfishness in silence – a bad atmosphere. Our atmosphere decidedly cleared, after this."[26]

Virginia managed to stand up to Leonard thanks to the strength she was able to draw from her friendship with Vita, and her (illusory) hope of driving a car. 'With my motor I shall be more mobile.' She also gained further insights into her creative depths: 'It is always a question whether I wish to avoid these glooms. In part they are the result of getting away by oneself, & have a psychological interest which the usual state of working & enjoying lacks. These 9 weeks give one a plunge into deep waters; which is a little alarming but full of interest. One goes down into the well & nothing protects one from the assault of truth.' She makes a good resolution to 'be much more considerate of L.'s feelings; & so keep more steadily at our ordinary level of intimacy & ease: a level, I think no other couple so long married, reaches, & keeps so constantly.' She thus attempts to objectify her relationship with Leonard in order to protect her creative centre. However, she remained quite unable to 'make plain even to my own eyes, my season of profound despondency.'

Two days later, she foreshadows a new novel: 'All I mean to make is a note of a curious state of mind. I hazard the guess that it may be the impulse behind another book.' And she adds a later note: 'Perhaps The Waves or moths'. She had a revelation of a fin breaking the surface of a flat calm sea which she remembered and referred to as a major event the following year. The 'assault of truth', made Virginia more self-protective in her relationship with Vita; and it made her doubt the depth of Vita's love for her. Back in London, she writes:

"But you dont see, donkey West, that you'll be tired of me one of these days (I'm so much older) and so I have to take my little precautions. That's why I put the emphasis on 'recording' rather than feeling. But donkey West knows that she has broken down more ramparts than anyone. And isnt there something obscure in you? There's something that doesn't vibrate in you: It may be purposely – you dont let it: but I see it with other people, as well as with me: something reserved, muted – God knows what. Still, still, compare this 19th Nov – with last, and you'll admit there's a difference. It's in your writing too, by the bye. The thing I call central transparency – sometimes fails you there too. I will lecture you on this at Long Barn." [27]

Vita quoted this letter to Harold, adding:

"Damn the woman, she has put her finger on it. There *is* something muted. What is it, Hadji? Something that doesn't vibrate, something that doesn't come alive. I brood and brood; feel that I grope in a dark tunnel, persuaded that somewhere there is light, but never can find the way to emerge... it is the thing which spoils me as a writer; destroys me as a poet. But how did V. discover it? I have never owned it to anybody, scarcely even to myself. It is what spoils my human relationships too, but that I mind less." [28]

Vita continues to quote from Virginia's letter: 'Do you know this interesting fact: I found myself thinking with intense curiosity about death. Yet if I'm persuaded of anything it is of mortality. Then why this sense that death is going to be a great excitement? – something positive, active?'

Harold became worried that Vita might get into too intense a relationship with Virginia and trigger 'madness', but Vita behaved with unwont-
ed restraint. We realise the depth of love was greater on Virginia's part
than on Vita's, who nevertheless grew increasingly to respect and value
her friend: 'I don't think she is accustomed to emotional storms, she lives
too much in the intellect and imagination... Fortunately she is the sensible sort of person who pulls themselves together and says, "This is
absurd." So I don't really worry. (Rather proud, really of having caught
such a big silver fish.) I look on my friendship with her as a treasure and a
privilege. I shan't ever fall in love with her, *padlock*, but I am absolutely
devoted to her and if she died I should mind quite, quite dreadfully. Or
went mad again.' The Nicolson's private word 'padlock' can be translated
'not open to renegotiation'. Harold replied:

"No, my sweet – it doesn't annoy me that you talk so much about
Virginia... my dominant idea is one of pleasure that the rich ores of your
nature should be brought to light... I think you are very akin – the marriage of true minds to which I will not allow myself... to admit impediment... [I] shall never forget how she was kind to me when I was smarting from Lytton's rudeness... So at the bottom of my terror of her glim-
mers a little white stone of gratitude. Which can only be increased by her
loving you." [29]

The 'marriage of true minds' is a quotation from Shakespeare's sonnet
No. 116, where the poet vows: 'Let me not to the marriage of true
minds/Admit impediments.' Harold Nicolson, on 17 December 1926,
uses these words correctly in relation to Virginia and Vita, as he promises
that he himself will not interfere. In my view George Spater & Ian
Parsons misused them when they entitled their book about the Woolfs *A
Marriage of True Minds* (first published in 1977); it would have been more
appropriate if they had referred to two later lines in this sonnet:

Love alters not with his brief hours and weeks
But bears it out even *to the edge of doom*. (My italics)

Both Vita and Harold grew to question whether Virginia was actually
'mad'. They each in their own way call her sensible and speak about her
sanity. They apparently asked themselves what effect Leonard, that 'funny
grim solitary creature', as Vita had described him, was actually having on
his wife. Harold generously wrote to Virginia from Teheran early in

1927: 'I am glad that Vita has come under an influence so stimulating and so sane... You need never worry about my having any feelings except a longing that Vita's life should be as rich and as sincere as possible. I loathe jealousy as I loathe all forms of disease.' [30]

Harold the career diplomat, himself free of jealousy, must have questioned whether Leonard was suffering from that insidious disease. He may have been right. Their son Nigel Nicolson states in his Introduction to the last volume of Virginia's letters that she 'was not mad' when she died.

Vita's bounding energy and her conviction that life was to be lived at its fullest is to be sensed in all of Virginia's work through the middle and late nineteen twenties, culminating in *Orlando*; it is evident that Vita lived and glowed in Virginia's creative centre, displacing for a time Leonard's restrictive and gloomy atmosphere. These were the most creative years of her life, before Leonard regained his power and control over her and she once again had to cope with his negativity within herself.

Virginia continued her efforts to achieve some limited personal independence, although she reluctantly abandoned any dreams she may have had of fundamentally changing her life-style. In February 1927, she had her long hair cut short. In this month she planned to 'have a fling at my book on fiction; & make all the money we want for Greece & a motor car'. In June she deliberately set apart a few weeks to money making 'so that I may put 50 pounds in each of our pockets by September. This will be the first money of my own since I married. I never felt the need of it till lately. And I can get it, if I want it, but shirk writing for money.' [31]

For the first time since her marriage, Virginia was attempting to earn some money that she could spend as she liked. How pathetic this is. No wonder she told her audience of women undergraduates in 1928, that they would need five hundred pounds a year and their own room if they wanted to write. These lectures formed the basis of her first resounding feminist work, *A Room of One's Own*. She did not tell those young women that she herself had only achieved a wooden hut in the garden and had had to fight to earn a few dollars for herself. Perhaps, with Leonard in the audience, she could also have told them not to marry a man who siphoned off half of all the money she earned and prevented her from spending the other half as she wished.

While Vita was once more in Persia, Virginia planned several trips that she wanted to make. She tried to go on holiday to Europe with George

(Dadie) Rylands but cancelled it 'for private reasons' (we may legitimately guess that Leonard managed to prevent her). A projected visit to America, where she had been invited to lecture, was also cancelled – Leonard told her they would have to pay some of the expenses and therefore she would not make money, so they didn't go. As so often, her disappointment was relieved by creative inspiration. In March ideas for two new books came to her, another experimental book and an 'escapade', at first envisaged as the Jessamy Brides:

"I feel the need of an escapade after these serious poetic experimental books whose form is always so closely considered... I think it will be great fun to write; and it will rest my head before starting the very serious, mystical poetical work which I want to come next. Meanwhile, before I can touch the Jessamy Brides, I have to write my book on fiction, and that wont be done until January, I suppose. Anyhow this records the odd hurried unexpected way in which these things suddenly create themselves – one thing on top of another in about an hour. So I made up Jacob's Room looking at the fire at Hogarth House, so I made up The Lighthouse one afternoon in the square here." [32]

That book on fiction, which Leonard wanted her to write, was an albatross around her neck for years.

This spring the Woolfs travelled by train to France and Italy, visiting Vanessa and her family in Cassis. Vita wrote to Virginia saying 'dont let Leonard take you away'. She was worried that he would use this holiday to make a break between them. But Virginia greatly enjoyed the trip: 'I dont think I've ever enjoyed one month so much.' Clive was at Cassis, trying to get over his long affair with Mary Hutchinson and his depression reminded Virginia of her own: 'Suppose one woke & found oneself a fraud? It was part of my madness – that horror.' However, she had finished To the Lighthouse and her own appreciation of parts of it, together with its rapturous reception, gave her confidence. She admits:

"I think I am now almost an established figure – as a writer. They dont laugh at me any longer. Soon they will take me for granted. Possibly I shall be a celebrated writer. Anyhow, The Lighthouse is much more nearly a success, in the usual sense of the word, than any other book of mine." [33]

This was another occasion when she did not have a breakdown on publication of one of her novels, although Leonard thought that both of them would be depressed since he had published a book of essays and

Hunting the Highbrow the previous month, both unnoticed by the critics, hence his own depression. The dangerous gap between Virginia's success as a writer and Leonard's failure was widening.

In July, Virginia managed to visit Ethel Sands and Nan Hudson in Normandy for three days, on her own. Leonard wrote to her:

"Dearest, it was melancholy to see you fade away in the train, and Pinka cannot understand what has happened. She insisted upon going in at once to your room this morning to see whether you were or were not in bed... I am looking forward to Saturday and the return of all animals... Love from the two solitary animals.

M[ongoose]

P[inka]" [34]

So heavy. The contrast between being with Leonard, and Vita, must have been a constant reminder to Virginia of just how unnecessarily constricted her life had become. However, the Woolfs' usual long stretch of living closely together in Monk's House during the summer months was relieved for the first time this year by the advent of the motor car. In August Leonard was learning to drive. Virginia writes with delight:

"Yes, the motor is turning out the joy of our lives, an additional life, free & mobile & airy to live alongside our usual stationary industry. We spin off to Falmer, ride over the Downs, drop into Rottingdean, then sweep over to Seaford, call, in pouring rain at Charleston, pass the time of day with Clive, return for tea, all as light & easy as a hawk in the air... After a week here, Leonard has become perfectly proficient; I am held back by insufficient lessons, but shall be expert before September is half through." [35]

Virginia assumed she would soon be as free as Vita and Vanessa, who were both driving their own cars; it was another of her hopes that was not fulfilled.

One hot September day, Vanessa took her daughter Angelica, Duncan Grant and Angus Davidson in her car, while Leonard drove Virginia and Pinka, to Michelham Priory. Virginia describes the scene as part of her annual summer assessment for this year, in which she once again looks at her life with Leonard in the confines of Monk's House. She recalls her experience of the previous year when she was visited by 'the spirit of delight', from a song by Shelley:

" 'Rarely rarely comest thou, spirit of delight.' That was I singing this time last year; & sang so poignantly that I have never forgotten it, or my vision of a fin rising on a wide blank sea. No biographer could possibly guess this important fact about my life in the late summer of 1926; yet biographers pretend they know people.

A happy summer, this? Well, a striving working splashing social summer. Many meetings; & one or two gaieties. I amuse myself by watching my mind shape scenes. We sat in a field strewn with cut grass at Michelham Priory the other day. It was roasting hot... nothing much is said on these occasions; but the memory remains: made of what? Of coloured shirts; the pink roof of the Gateway against a grey blue sky; & Pinker; & my being cross about my book on fiction; & Leonard silent; & a great quarrel that hot night; & I coming up here to sit alone in the dark; & L. following me; & sharp hard words; right & wrong on both sides; peace making; sleep; content." [36]

Instead of doing her own creative work, Leonard was forcing her to write about fiction with all the power of his sterile, rationalist mind.

That September, Vita drove Virginia to Loughton Place, where they saw the remains of an isolated sixteenth century moated house that had been converted into a farmhouse in the eighteenth century. Together the two women broke in. Virginia records: 'It seemed, that sunny morning, so beautiful, so peaceful; & as if it had endless old rooms. So I came home boiling with the idea of buying it; & so fired L. that we wrote to the farmer.' But when she went with Leonard to see the house: 'it turned out unspeakably dreary; all patched & spoilt; with grained oak & grey paper; a sodden garden & a glaring red cottage at the back.' [37] With Vita, the place was full of possibilities; with Leonard it 'turned out unspeakably dreary'. So, of course, they didn't take it.

Writing *Orlando* provided Virginia with the satisfaction real life so often denied her. In this book she could fully experience her love for her friend and involve her in its creation, at a time when Vita had begun to see other women. The first germ came to her in September 1927, as one of a series of sketches of her friends 'It might be a way of writing the memoirs of one's own times during people's lifetimes. It might be a most amusing book. The question is how to do it. Vita should be Orlando, a young nobleman.' The following month, she wrote to Vita:

"Yesterday morning I was in despair: You know that bloody book which Dadie and Leonard extort, drop by drop, from my breast? Fiction, or some title to that effect. I couldn't screw a word from me; and at last dropped my head in my hands: dipped my pen in the ink, and wrote these words, as if automatically, on a clean sheet: Orlando: A Biography.

No sooner had I done this than my body was flooded with rapture and my brain with ideas. I wrote rapidly till 12. Then I did an hour to Romance. So every morning I am going to write fiction (my own fiction) till 12; and Romance till 1." [38]

This wonderful letter continues, full of energy. *Orlando* is 'all about you and the lusts of your flesh and the lure of your mind (heart you have none, who go gallivanting down the lanes with Campbell).' Virginia goes on to ask Vita's permission to write it, since she will no doubt be identified. Vita replied: 'My God, Virginia, if ever I was thrilled and terrified, it is at the prospect of being projected into the shape of Orlando. What fun for you; what fun for me... You have my full permission. Only I think that having drawn and quartered me, unwound and retwisted me, or whatever it is that you intend to do, you ought to dedicate it to your victim'. [39] Virginia did indeed dedicate *Orlando* to Vita. She hoped to 'dash this in for a week,' but:

"I have done nothing, nothing, nothing else for a fortnight; & am launched somewhat furtively but with all the more passion upon Orlando: A Biography. It is to be a small book, & written by Christmas. I thought I could combine it with *Fiction,* but once the mind gets hot it cant stop; I walk making up phrases; sit, contriving scenes; am in short in the thick of the greatest rapture known to me; from which I have kept myself since last February, or earlier. Talk of planning a book, or waiting for an idea. This one came in a rush; I said to pacify myself, being bored & stale with criticism & faced with that intolerable dull Fiction, 'You shall write a page of a story for a treat: you shall stop sharp at 11.30 & then go on with the Romantics.' I had very little idea what the story was to be about. But the relief of turning my mind that way about was such that I felt happier than for months; as if put in the sun, or laid on cushions; & after two days entirely gave up my time chart & abandoned myself to the pure delight of this farce: which I enjoy as much as I've ever enjoyed anything; & have written myself into half a headache & had to come to a halt, like a tired horse, & take a little sleeping draught last night: which made our breakfast fiery. I did not finish my egg." [40]

Without too great a degree of speculation we can guess at some of the things that were said by Leonard over breakfast, her half-eaten egg congealing between them, in their upstairs flat in Tavistock Square. They had returned to London on the sixth of October. Virginia had begun writing *Orlando* in a rush, on her own, without Leonard's consent or agreement, and she had broken her time chart in order to do so. *Orlando* was therefore an illegitimate offspring of her creative imagination as well as having been inspired by Vita. Now she was ill, she was not eating, she had a headache, and it was all her fault. I believe Leonard used this occasion to tug the string he had tied to her leg and brought her heavily down to earth. Releasing his pent-up fury, he told her she was wasting her time writing about aristocrats, who were irrelevant in the modern world. Britain should have had a revolution and got rid of them, like the French (he wrote about this in his second volume of *After the Deluge*). She must read his latest book *Imperialism and Civilization*. Vita was a bad influence on her; she should have been writing that book on fiction, as she had promised. As it was, the Press would lose money. In fact, he said, trembling all over – he knocked the salt pot onto Pinker whining at his side – it is not suitable for The Hogarth Press, I do not wish to publish it. At which point, with her new-found courage, Virginia told him she was an equal partner and insisted on the book appearing. Let him publish *Imperialism and Civilization* next April and *Orlando* in October, then no-one would draw comparisons. Going down to her Studio, she thought: he had no need to worry, because her book was saying goodbye to Vita. To sex. To life itself. No wonder she had a headache.

That Leonard was not in a good mood that October was immediately demonstrated by a farcical scene at the Press. He quarrelled with Angus Davidson, one of the best of the unfortunate procession of young trainee managers who started working for the Press with high expectations, only to crawl out of that decrepit, untidy basement a few months later. Leonard complained he was five minutes late and Davidson demonstrated that Leonard's watch was wrong; whereupon Leonard gave him notice to quit. Virginia came in and asked the time:

" 'Leonard can tell you' said Angus very huffily.

'Ask Angus. I dont seem to know' said Leonard very grumpy. And I saw Mrs. C[artwright] lower her head over her typing & laugh. This was the tail of a terrific quarrel about the time between them. Angus was dismissed... A bad year this, financially, for the Press: yet prospects seem flourishing." [41]

The next trainee manager to be appointed was Richard Kennedy who drew a most amusing sketch of Leonard with pipe in mouth and Pinker on a leash, his left hand firmly in his pocket to stop it trembling, haranguing the small workforce while Virginia sets up type in the printing room.

Vita describes to Harold one of Virginia's attempts to drive:

"Then I went and met Virginia, who had come down with Leonard to Richmond Park where V. was to have a driving lesson. Leonard and I watched her start. The motor made little pounces and stopped dead. At one moment it ran backwards. At last she sailed off, and Leonard and I and Pinker went for a walk at 5 miles an hour. Every five minutes Leonard would say, 'I suppose Virginia will be all right.' ...when we got back to the trysting place there was Virginia taking an intelligent interest in the works of the car." [42]

Virginia bought their second-hand Singer with the money she earned from *To the Lighthouse*, and paid for each succeeding vehicle, for which she gains no credit in Leonard's account. He says:

" 'certainly nothing ever changed so profoundly my material existence, the mechanism and range of my everyday life, as the possession of a motor car." [43]

Leonard's *Imperialism and Civilization* was published in April 1928, together with his *The Way of Peace*. Nobody took much notice of either book.

In *Orlando,* Virginia focuses on the changing spirit of the age from the year 1500, to: 'the twelfth stroke of midnight, Thursday, the eleventh of October, Nineteen Hundred and Twenty Eight' – the moment that saw its publication. Vita, immortalised, strides through the centuries first as one sex, now the other. Virginia draws on her wide knowledge of English literature to present her friend in each age. She suggests that, until the Romantic Age, the sexes might only have been distinguishable by the clothes they wore:

"Her modesty as to her writing, her vanity as to her person, her fears as to her safety all seems to hint that what was said a short time ago about there being no change in Orlando the man, and Orlando the woman, was ceasing to be altogether true. She was becoming a little more modest, as women are, of her brains, and a little more vain, as women are, of her person... The man looks the world full in the face, as if it were made for his uses and fashioned to his liking. The woman takes a sidelong glance at it, full of subtlety, even of suspicion. Had they both worn the same clothes, it is possible that their outlook might have been the same." [44]

Vita's sex changes through *Orlando* are reminiscent of Shakespeare's comedies. In Elizabethan drama the female parts were all played by men and they moved from male to female and back again with a change of clothes. In Virginia's book there are, in particular, echoes of *As You Like It*, where the hero is actually called Orlando; but it is Rosalind, the girl he loves, with her changes of sex and her energy, who is in fact more like Virginia's Orlando. She can get by without much difficulty in the rationalist eighteenth century, but it is harder in the early nineteenth:

"She had just managed, by some dexterous deference to the spirit of the age, by putting on a ring and finding a man on a moor, by loving nature and being no satirist, cynic, or psychologist... And she heaved a deep sigh of relief, as indeed, well she might, for the transaction between a writer and the spirit of the age is one of infinite delicacy, and upon a nice arrangement between the two the whole fortune of his works depends." [45]

Virginia had a sense of being many different selves which she describes:

"these selves of which we are built up, one on top of another, as plates are piled on a waiter's hand, have attachments elsewhere, sympathies, little constitutions and rights of their own, call them what you will (and for many of these things there is no name) so that one will only come if it is raining, another in a room with green curtains, another when Mrs. Jones is not there, another if you can promise it a glass of wine — and so on; for everybody can multiply from his own experience the different terms which his different selves have made with him — and some are too wildly ridiculous to be mentioned in print at all." [46]

The chiming of a clock breaks in on all these selves — and her interconnected, creative world is sharply awoken from the semi-trance state in which she wrote by the mechanical sound of the clock, as the alienated logic of Leonard's hard, sharp brain would painfully wake her up. We need to read Virginia Woolf's work in our own semi-trance state.

During 1928 Virginia's relationship with Vita changed in the aftermath of Vita's grief for the death of her father and the loss of Knole, the great ancestral home she had hoped to inherit and would have done if she had been a man. Virginia gives herself a new animal name, Potto, as she comforts her friend and perhaps herself, too:

"Dearest Honey;

Here is Bosman's Potto and the Pinche Marmoset, and some other of Virginia's animals — which will you keep for her till Friday.

Lord! how I look forward already to seeing you again!...

Friday's Vita: orange and rose, tipped with amethyst–

Please see to it that its a fine day, that there's a bun for tea, a porpoise in the fishmongers: and darling, write me something – a little poem: prose if nothing else, and we'll sit and talk and talk and talk: or walk. Only be well and glad to see me: or Noodles [butler] will have to wipe me up.

Love a thousand times. V" [47]

In February she noted, first, that Leonard was with Margaret Llewelyn Davies; then that Pinker had lice, and then: 'L. never makes a penny; I mean tries to: & I could almost wish we were more lavish in our ways.' [48] She regrets her inhibited life in comparison to that of Vanessa with her children and her free life-style at Cassis. She and Leonard spent a week there in March 1928, motoring on the Continent for the first time. When Vanessa returned in May, Virginia wrote:

"Mercifully, Nessa is back. My earth is watered again... She is a necessity to me – as I am not to her. She is also very cheerful, solid, happy. And how masterfully she controls her dozen lives; never in a muddle, or desperate, or worried; never spending a pound or a thought needlessly; yet with it all free, careless, airy, indifferent: a very notable achievement." [49]

In the spring of 1928 Virginia was awarded the Femina Vie-Heureuse Prize for *To the Lighthouse*. It was the only prize, or honour, she accepted and she took no pleasure in it. She wore a cheap black dress in which she felt uncomfortable:

"The prize was an affair of dull stupid horror: a function; not alarming; stupefying. Hugh Walpole saying how much he disliked my books; rather, how much he feared for his own... Afterwards there was the horror of having looked ugly in cheap black clothes. I cannot control this complex. I wake at dawn with a start. Also the 'fame' is becoming vulgar & a nuisance. It means nothing; & yet takes one's time. Americans perpetually." [50]

I find it upsetting that Virginia was not able to enjoy her achievement, and believe this was due to the necessity of coping with Leonard's envy by adopting his negative arguments about awards – after her death, he accepted several. At this ceremony the Woolfs met the American actress Elizabeth Robins, who specialised in Ibsen. A dynamic older woman, her appearance may have increased Virginia's feeling that she looked plain in her cheap black coat. Elizabeth approached them because she admired Virginia's work, but this was the start of a friendship between herself and Leonard.

Leonard read *Orlando* in May, when they evidently reached a compromise, with Virginia saying the book was not 'important' among her work and promising to write 'some very closely reasoned criticism' as well as the book on fiction. Leonard calls it a 'satire'. He: 'takes Orlando more seriously than I had expected, thinks it in some ways better than The Lighthouse; about more interesting things, & with more attachment to life, & larger... He says it is very original.' [51]

Leonard pleased Vita by writing in support of a controversial lesbian book, *The Well of Loneliness*. However, she clearly recognised his meanness and joked about it to Harold. Leonard suggested he should keep the Singer car in Virginia's studio when in London, to save paying garage fees. Vita recounts this farce to Harold, in July 1928:

"Darling, really the Wolves are funnies. You see, they haven't got a garage, and it goes to Leonard's heart to pay garaging fees for the umbrella [as they named the car]. So for some time past he has been saying what a good garage Virginia's studio would make, but she didn't respond very well because she didn't want her studio taken away from her. So Leonard didn't *quite* dare to suggest taking it away altogether, but finally he said, did she think they could poke a hole in the wall and get the motor in that way, if it wouldn't disturb her to work with a motor in the room?... A funny pair." [52]

That spring Vita seduced Mary Campbell, the wife of the poet Roy Campbell. Virginia was shocked – she even made her friend cry. Campbell was so enraged when he found out that he swore to murder Mary; he did in fact beat her. As Virginia comforted her friend for the loss of Knole, and upbraided her for once more playing a dangerous sexual game, she emerges as the stronger character. Their physical closeness was either ending or had ended, although she stayed at Long Barn in July:

"a good rather happy visit. I'm interested by the gnawing down of strata in friendship; how one passes unconsciously to different terms; takes things easier... scarcely feel it an exciting atmosphere, which, too, has its drawback from the 'fizzing' point of view: yet is saner, perhaps deeper." [53]

Virginia now admits that she no longer wants children: 'Children playing: yes, & interrupting me; yes & I have no children of my own; & Nessa has; & yet I dont want them any more, since my ideas so possess me... & almost dislike peoples bodies, I think, as I grow older; & want always to cut that short, & get my utmost fill of the marrow, of the essence.' [54] She felt physically colder 'the sun just going off one.'

Shortly before *Orlando* was published, Virginia and Vita planned to take a holiday together in Burgundy. This projected trip, coming too late after they had for so long dreamed of going away together, worried Virginia:

"This is written on the verge of my alarming holiday in Burgundy. I am alarmed of 7 days alone with Vita: interested; excited, but afraid – she may find me out, I her out... I'm afraid of the morning most; & 3 o'clock in the afternoon; & wanting something Vita does not want. And I shall spend the money that might have bought a table or a glass. What one buys in foreign travel is a series of scenes." [55]

Virginia was right to be alarmed, not about the holiday itself but about Leonard's reaction. Vita records in her diary that the Woolfs had 'a small and sudden row that morning about her going abroad with me.' This upset Virginia, who uses baby talk in her first letter to him from Paris:

"We had a cold but calm voyage – except that the poor mots [marmots] sobbed for Dadyka the whole way and so did Mandrill. Lord, how I adore you, and how little you do! I believe you are glad to be quit of us! and to read all the evening without having beasts all over you." [56]

His letters are burdened with guilt-inducing regret at Virginia's absence. In his first he quotes Harold who asked her to look after Vita (what an excellent suggestion, why didn't Leonard think of that?), then:

"I was terribly sad to see you go and moped with the Pinka family for some time [the spaniel had recently given birth] – it was the summer dying out of the year...

I think I must catch the post with this to make sure of your getting it... One Mongoose, Pinka, four puppies, all sad, send their love. L. [57]

Virginia did not receive this letter from Leonard, nor the next, written on the following day which ends: 'I hope you wont make a habit of deserting me'. It seems he delayed posting them. Not hearing any word from him ruined the early part of the holiday for Virginia. On the 27th, she wired in a panic: 'No letters anxious wire Hotel de la Poste Vezeley', and then wrote apologising for having done so: 'But I admit I was ready to bother you any amount to be put out of my misery'. His answering wire reassured her and after that the trip was a success.

The two women didn't 'find each other out'. Virginia bought a green corduroy jacket for Leonard and they visited Ethel Sands and Nan Hudson, where Vanessa and Duncan Grant were painting a loggia; Virginia read to them her memoir of Old Bloomsbury: 'the two old virgins bridled with horrified delight'. [58] Vita wrote to Harold: 'Virginia is very sweet, and I feel extraordinarily protective towards her. The com-

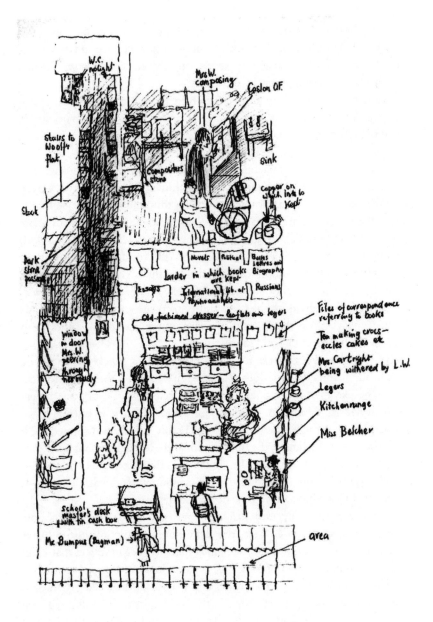

THE HOGARTH PRESS, C. 1928,
AS SKETCHED BY RICHARD KENNEDY

bination of that brilliant brain and fragile body is very lovable. She has a sweet and childlike nature, from which her intellect is completely separate. I have never known anyone so profoundly sensitive, and who makes less of a business of that sensitiveness.'

Some commentators including Quentin Bell have said, wrongly, that this was the only time Virginia stayed abroad without Leonard (there were two previous occasions; there would have been more if she had been able to have her way). Bell believed that this holiday was 'innocent' because Vita and Virginia inhabited separate rooms. A note in Vita's Diary for 27 September, records: 'In the middle of the night I was woken by a thunderstorm. Went along to V's room thinking she might be frightened. We talked about science and religion for an hour – and the ultimate principle – and then as the storm had blown over I left her to go to sleep again.' Vita, unlike George Duckworth earlier, or Leonard during the horrors of their honeymoon, could pad along the passage to her door and enter her bedroom without alarming her. Having separate bedrooms was no barrier. Vita obviously had the ability to relate to Virginia in a non-intrusive way; it was she and not Leonard who behaved throughout this holiday with perfect tact and kindness.

By 1928 the Woolfs were relatively prosperous. *Orlando* was the book that brought their income into a bracket that enabled them to afford an annual holiday on the Continent, and substantial building work was undertaken at Monk's House. A ground floor room, planned as a sitting room for Virginia, became her bedroom; it remarkably lacks a door connecting it with the rest of the house, the only way in and out being through the garden. An upstairs sitting room was also added. Thus Leonard continued to spend Virginia's money consolidating his position in Rodmell. In the chapter entitled Downhill to Hitler, he described his attitude:

"To live perpetually in a kaleidoscope of which the kaleidoscopic changes are always more or less the same bores and depresses me. After four years as literary editor of the *Nation* I already began to feel that I had had enough of this kind of journalism and talked to Maynard about giving it up. He wanted me to stay on and eventually I agreed provided it was arranged that I spent less time in the office, my salary being reduced from 400 pounds to 250 pounds... In 1929 I told Maynard that I could not stand any more of it and resigned early in 1930.

My resignation from the *Nation* was made possible by our financial situation which was revolutionized in the years 1928 to 1931... The turning point in Virginia's career as a successful novelist came in 1928 with the publication of *Orlando*... After 1928 we were always very well off. In the next ten years our income was anything from twice to six times what it had been in 1924. Neither of us was extravagant or had any desire for conspicuous extravagance; we did not alter fundamentally our way of life, because on 1,000 pounds a year we already lived the kind of life we wished to live, and we were not going to alter the chosen pattern of our life because we made 6,000 pounds in the year instead of 1,000 pounds. But life is easier on 3,000 a year than it is on 1,000. Within the material framework which we had chosen for our existence we got more of the things we liked to possess – books, pictures, a garden, a car – and we did more of the things we wanted to do, for instance travel, and less in the occupations which we did not want to do, for instance journalism." [59]

Leonard was, as so often, speaking for himself. We may justifiably take leave to disagree that their 'material framework' suited Virginia. She had earned enough to be able to break out of it and move to a country house, perhaps a larger version of Asheham House, with spacious well-planned rooms, but was prevented from doing so by Leonard. Nothing would make him shift from Monk's House and its garden. Her carefully managed but none the less very loving relationship with Vita, with its hopes for the future, had shown her that her life in this cottage was unnecessarily constricted. Not only were the small rooms claustrophobic and inconvenient, but she was constantly being disturbed because the property was too close to the village of Rodmell. Instead of considering moving, Leonard now employed a gardener, Percy Bartholemew, who was installed with his family in one of the two cottages they had acquired together with the field they purchased. Thus the spending of increasing amounts of Virginia's money only served to consolidate Leonard's growing 'empire'.

In November 1929 he decided to give up his part-time job on The Nation, whereupon Virginia had a dream. This is how she recounts it:

"I dreamt last night that I had a disease of the heart that would kill me in 6 months. Leonard, after some persuasion, told me. My instincts were all such as I should have, in order, & some very strong: quite unexpected, I mean voluntary, as they are in dreams, & have thus an authenticity which makes an immense, & pervading impression. First, relief – well I've done with life anyhow (I was lying in bed) then horror; then desire to live; then fear of insanity; then (no this came earlier) regret about my writing, & leaving this book unfinished [*The Waves*]; then a luxurious dwelling upon my friends sorrow; then a sense of death & being done with at my age [Virginia was 47]; then telling Leonard that he must marry again; seeing our life together; & facing the conviction of going, when other people went on living. Then I woke, coming to the top of all this hanging about me; & found I had sold a great many copies of my book [*A Room of One's Own*]; & was asked to lunch... the odd feeling of these two states of life & death mingling as I ate my breakfast feeling drowsy & heavy." [60]

In her next entry she says 'L's freedom draws near'. Evidently her dream was a warning that Leonard's 'freedom' would mean more pressure on her with more strain on her heart. Now entirely dependent on the money she earned, he would be omnipresent around the house. Her response to having lost even more of her limited freedom, while he gained his, was to dive down into her creative self and begin another book, to be published as *The Waves*.

Virginia Woolf was a feminist who never in practice gained the degree of autonomy she deserved with her writing, her fame, and the money she made. She never had five hundred pounds a year to spend in the ways she wished, as she advocated in *A Room of One's Own*. Moreover, the 'fell' combination of Leonard and Vanessa prevented her from growing to her full stature as an individual person. With the ending of her physical relationship with Vita, a light died that she could only re-ignite in memory.

MR HUGH WALPOLE MAKING THE FORMAL PRESENTATION OF
THE *FEMINA-VIE HEUREUSE* PRIZE TO MRS VIRGINIA WOOLF
(*The Times*, May 3, 1928)

Chapter Nine

WATERSHED

Virginia's excursion outside the framework of the cage Leonard had built around her, and into the world of Vita Sackville-West, was brief and fraught with difficulties. But Vita succeeded in breaking down many of the 'ramparts' behind which she had hidden from life; she had experienced the glow of physical love with another woman, and she immortalised her strong, free-striding friend in *Orlando*. Although Virginia retained her friendship with Vita, the loss of intimacy in the centre of her life was very great and the suffering this gave her is at the heart of *The Waves*. In this book she would return to her past, submerge into the ocean of her childhood with its deaths and its sense of loss; of regret.

Virginia also felt frustrated at the difficulties women experienced as they tried to express themselves, to live their lives in a male world. In October 1928 she gave two lectures to women undergraduates. At the first of these, to the Arts Society at Newnham College, Cambridge, she was accompanied by Vanessa, Vanessa's third child Angelica, and Leonard. This lecture, published as the first part of *A Room of One's Own*, begins by telling Leonard why she did not want to write that book on fiction:

"When you asked me to speak about women and fiction I sat down on the banks of a river and began to wonder what the words meant... The title women and fiction might mean... women and what they are like, or it might mean women and the fiction that they write, or it might mean women and the fiction that is written about them, or it might mean that somehow all three are inextricably mixed together... which seemed the most interesting.' However, 'I soon saw that it had one fatal drawback, I should never be able to come to a conclusion... The need of coming to some conclusion on a subject that raises all sorts of prejudices and passions, bowed my head to the ground. To the right and left bushes of some sort, golden and crimson, glowed with the colour, even it seemed burnt with the heat, of fire. On the further bank the willows wept in perpetual lamentation, their hair about their shoulders." [1]

Thus she contrasts the burning bushes on the near bank lined with men's colleges in Cambridge, with the weeping willows across the river where Newnham, one of only two all-women colleges, lay out of sight. A little thought, given the right conditions, can grow to something 'very exciting, and important', only it dies when she trespasses on that hallowed male preserve, the area of grass in the centre of the Court, and: 'instantly a man's figure rose to intercept me... he was a Beadle; I was a woman.' As a woman, she was not even allowed to enter the library: 'a guardian angel barring the way with a flutter of black gown instead of white wings.' Because the male world in general has risen up and prevented women through the ages from letting the light 'half-way down the spine, which is the seat of the soul' shine with female vision Virginia, instead of talking about women and fiction, concentrates on the practical difficulties faced by women writers and comes to the conclusion that they must have some basic independence and a comfortable life-style if they are to be able to express themselves creatively on their own terms:

"One cannot think well, love well, sleep well, if one has not dined well. The lamp in the spine does not light on beef and prunes." [2]

In Virginia's life Vita had provided the good food and comforts at Long Barn, lighting that lamp in her spine; Leonard doled out the beef and prunes in Monk's House.

By emphasising the importance of material comforts in the process of creative writing which were enjoyed by University men, but not women, Virginia warned the young women in her audience about the overwhelming power of the patriarchy. She delivered her famous dictum that women writers must have five hundred pounds a year and a room of their own if they are to stand any chance of succeeding – she, who in 1927 was struggling to earn fifty pounds that she could call her own, and who worked in a wooden hut in the garden when she was at Monk's House, Sussex, or a dusty room in the basement of 52 Tavistock Square that she shared with growing stacks of unsold books from the Hogarth Press while in London.

Virginia gave her lectures in autumn. For the second one, at Girton, she was accompanied by Vita; but she imagined the spring, when Manx cats once had tails: 'It is strange what a difference a tail makes.' She was telling her audience not to give up, telling those young women that Shakespeare had a sister called Judith who comes back in every generation and struggles to express herself, to use the particular shape of the female brain – it is a brave speech. She is handing on her sceptre to women of the future, just as she herself was about to return to the 'nunnery', where she would lose her autonomy to Leonard and submerge beneath *The Waves*.

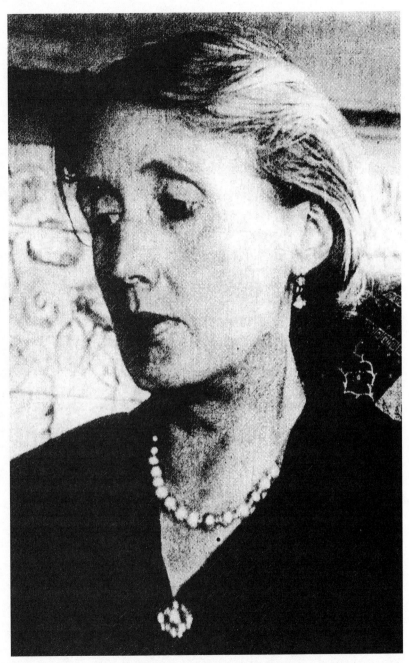

VIRGINIA AT TAVISTOCK SQUARE

On publication, *A Room of One's Own* divided Virginia's close friends and family; it was seen as provocative, even subversive, yet she managed to control the anger she felt at the discrimination and poverty suffered by women and succeeded in getting her message across. The book sold over ten thousand copies and attracted a new readership who discovered Virginia Woolf the feminist.

Before we dip down with Virginia beneath the Waves, we should glance at the changing circumstances of some part of her surface world.

Leonard increased his own comfort at Monk's House by having yet more building work done that would give him a large study upstairs. Vita wrote to her husband Harold in August 1929, incidentally underlining Virginia's loss of intimacy with her:

"They are really making Monk's House very nice. Leonard has thrown three rooms into one, and made himself a lovely room to work in. He invited me gravely upstairs to come and see it. I *do* like Leonard." [3]

The triangle between Vita, Leonard and Virginia has now changed to the more familiar pattern of Virginia occupying the lower third point, while Leonard gets Vita on his side by becoming her publisher. *The Edwardians*, issued in 1930, was a best seller that earned both Vita and the Press a good deal of money.

In March 1930 Margaret Llewelyn Davies, together with her friend Lilian Harris, visited Monk's House. Virginia describes the woman who had loomed so large during those traumatic early years of her marriage:

"My impressions were of great lumps of grey coat; straggling wisps of hair; hats floppy & home made; thick woollen stockings; black shoes, many wraps, shabby handbags, & shapelessness, & shabbiness & dreari-ness & drabness unspeakable... I doubt if they have enough to eat... Something has blunted Margaret's edge, rusted it, worn it, long before its time. Must old age be so shapeless?... M. has her tragic past. She is pathet-ic to me now – conciliatory & nervous where she used to be trenchant & severe." [4]

So Leonard's magnificent Etheria ends her life poverty-stricken in lodgings; as Miss Kilman also did, no doubt.

Harold Nicolson consulted the Woolfs on whether he should give up the Diplomatic Service and become a journalist on the *Evening Standard*. If he remained in the Foreign Office he would eventually have become an Ambassador and probably a Minister, a man at the top of his tree. Both Vita and Virginia thought he should resign, since neither wanted their husbands to devote themselves to a career. Whether Leonard had Harold's best interests at heart when he also advised him to resign, is open to doubt: he himself had tried unsuccessfully to get into the Foreign Service; his dislike, and envy, of the British aristocracy amounted almost to hatred and here was a wonderful opportunity to pull down Harold Nicolson, who had had all the advantages of birth in a gentile society that he lacked. Maybe Harold half wanted to become a 'He-bride'. After his resignation, he wrote a number of books and became a Member of Parliament. In 1930 Leonard, perhaps hoping to get a job in the Foreign Office, set up a meeting between Harold Nicolson, himself and Hugh Dalton, then Parliamentary Under-Secretary at the Foreign Office. Harold in his diary acknowledges there was discrimination against Jews by the Government:

"We go on afterwards to the Woolfs. Hugh Dalton is there. I attack the nomination board at the Foreign Office, not on the grounds that it rejects good men, but on the grounds that its very existence prevents good men from coming up for fear they may be ploughed for social reasons. The awkward question of the Jews arises. I admit that is the snag. Jews are far more interested in international life than are Englishmen, and if we opened the service it might be flooded with clever Jews. It was a little difficult to argue this point frankly with Leonard there." [5]

We need to remember that while Virginia was discriminated against as a woman, Leonard was discriminated against as a Jew. We are entering the decade that made it possible for the Holocaust to be imagined and carried out.

The first glimmer of what was to be *The Waves* had come to Virginia in 1926 during the depression she suffered that summer:

"I wished to add some remarks to this, on the mystical side of this solitude; how it is not oneself but something in the universe that one's left with. It is this that is frightening & exciting in the midst of my profound gloom, depression, boredom, whatever it is: One sees a fin passing far out... All I mean to make is a note of a curious state of mind. I hazard the guess that it may be the impulse behind another book... I want to watch & see how the idea at first occurs. I want to trace my own process." [6]

Her first idea for the book, to be called The Moths, originated in a letter from Vanessa written in May 1927 from Cassis. Vanessa describes her attempts to capture and kill a great Emperor moth to give to her sons. There is something atavistic, heartless, in her account:

"I sit with moths flying madly in circles round me and the lamp. You cannot imagine what it is like. One night some creature tapped so loudly on the pane that Duncan said 'Who is that?' 'Only a bat.' said Roger, 'or a bird.' But it wasn't man or bird, but a huge moth – half a foot, literally, across. We had a terrible time with it. My maternal instinct, which you deplore so much, wouldn't let me leave it. We let it in, kept it, gave it a whole bottle of ether bought from the chemist, all in vain, took it to the chemist who dosed it with chloroform for a day, also in vain. Finally it did die, rather the worse for wear, and now – here is another! A better specimen. But though incredibly beautiful, I suspect they are common, perhaps Emperor moths. Still I know how one would have blamed one's elders for not capturing such things at all costs, so I suppose I must go through it all again... What a lot I could say about the maternal instinct." [7]

Virginia had described Vita as an Emperor moth when she was in Persia, and saw herself as striving to become one. She may well have thought initially about contrasting the two women, Vita the glorious moth, Vanessa the maternal moth-catcher; how fascinating if she had done so. As it was she changed the title and the angle of her book, because, according to John Lehmann, she realised: 'Moths, I suddenly remember, don't fly by day'. [8] That may have been part of the reason. But she needed Vanessa to 'water her earth' and it would not do to criticise her sister for her maternal efforts at killing moths when she herself was childless.

The first page Virginia wrote in preparation for the book that began as The Moths and became *The Waves* has survived, thanks to J.W. Graham who published it as Appendix A, in his *Virginia Woolf – The Waves – The two holograph drafts*. According to Graham it was written either late in 1928 or in the first three months of 1929. Once again that stultifying subject, women and fiction, blocks her creativity:

"But I cannot write anything more about fiction.
What I want to do is to write the first words of the Moths
~~More~~
It was a silent b
No; I am superstitious & will not write another word.
Then the day fell into the sea: the sun went down.
& those who watched it saw no green light:
...our heads were burning

All the world seemed like a pit of darkness into which
their lives, which were as hot as coal, were dipping...
Also, there were the graves behind them.
The graveyard was always sickly. Flowers withered. No one
came at the right moment to replace them. Tomb after
tomb, like the white faces of dominoes, stood
upright, reflecting the suffused rose.
Between the sun & the churchyard was a strip of lawn;
on this they could walk, as a shipman walks his
deck. It was green, like ~~sea or~~ an unruffled
water. & at one end stood two elm trees, blotted
with dark nests." [9]

The scene set by Virginia in this initial draft, of the lawn and the graveyard and the two elm trees, evokes not the garden at Talland House in
Cornwall, to which she returned in *The Waves,* but Monk's House garden here and now before her eyes. Two great elms 'blotted with dark
nests' actually stood between the garden and the floodland, through
which flowed the River Ouse. The elms were named by the Woolfs
'Virginia' and 'Leonard' respectively and on their deaths their ashes were
to be scattered each under their own designated tree. The tombstones
were on the other side of the churchyard wall, where the flowers were
withering because 'no-one came at the right time to replace them.' And
what of the sun?

"Then the day fell into the sea: the sun went down.
& those who watched it saw no green light."

Here, on this piece of paper that was not intended for publication,
Virginia faces the desolation she felt at the loss of Vita. There was no-one
to give her comfort. Leonard, in control in Monk's House, must have felt
more triumph than sympathy as he had successfully separated the two
women, while he continued to believe that the implacable Greek gods
would eventually punish his wife for the pleasure she had experienced in
indulging in a guilty liaison with Vita.

In her emptiness, all Virginia had to comfort her was the power of her
own words. The sickly graveyard with the dead flowers, and no-one
bringing fresh ones, was all too real. The day fell into the sea when she

lost the 'fizz' of her affair with Vita and there was no compensating green light – her favourite colour. Thus she admits to her loss, her grief. But nothing of this remains in the final version, where the sun is a lamp held aloft by a female figure as yet couched invisible beneath the horizon. In this way she changes the bleakness of her earlier despair into a dynamic image of promise and hope for herself and all women:

"...as if the arm of a woman couched beneath the horizon had raised a lamp and flat bars of white, green and yellow spread across the sky like the blades of a fan. Then she raised her lamp higher." [10]

At first, she was not going to concentrate on individuals. Abstract attitudes were to be expressed: in the garden generalised children catch butterflies, not directly reminiscent of her own childhood at St Ives. But soon the children become individuals and emerge as familiar figures. Here once again is her dead brother Thoby (now named Percival), who does not express his own point of view but is the catalyst for all the others, as Jacob is the catalyst in *Jacob's Room*. Here is Vanessa as Susan, a rather distant figure as Vanessa was absent for several months of the year living at Cassis. Here too is Virginia herself divided into several of the characters, most poignantly as Rhoda.

Leonard is recognisable as Louis who enters the garden of her childhood although he is not part of the scene where children flit about catching butterflies in their nets. In all drafts, Louis meets Jinny who initiates him into sex. Jinny is based on Mary Hutchinson, the great love of Clive Bell's life. Neville is a homosexual, with perhaps some aspects of Duncan Grant. Bernard is the most mixed of all the characters with aspects of Clive, Desmond and Virginia herself. Thus this book evokes members of the Bloomsbury Group (which Virginia thought of as 'dead' at this time). The reflections of these close family members and friends, who lived within Virginia, emerge to tell their own stories each from their own unique angle of vision, to provide the main text. In doing so, the possibility of any single, ultimate truth is denied together with the supremacy of an author's viewpoint.

Wrapping their stories, putting them in context, is the rising and setting of the sun. The scope of Virginia's expression gains in both immensity and intensity as she grapples with the great issues of life and death. This book is the direct successor of *To The Lighthouse,* but her earlier image of the lighthouse standing on a rock flashing its warning beacon to heedless mariners was too limited to survive in this larger, more inhuman landscape. Suppose there is no warning light that can be relied on to protect and defend? What of the waves themselves? What of the sun? The fin breaking the surface of the smooth sea seems like the death pole; while the soul, lit halfway up the spine that Virginia spoke about in *A Room of One's Own*, is the internal creative life pole. In this work she seeks to encompass the two, the opposite poles of life and death, devoid of both egotism and fear. She compresses the whole of time into the present moment that moves through time, where there is only solitude, and in doing so manages to net the fin. *The Waves* is a difficult, mysterious book, unreachable for many. But for some women it is an endless and limitless resource.

While Virginia was at work, Leonard was completing the first volume of his *After the Deluge* (from Louis XV's 'Apres moi le deluge'). The Woolfs were once more in direct competition with each other. This time, their rivalry was for the highest stakes: to write a book that would continue to be read and influence people after their deaths. Surely now, at long last, their conflicting visions could at least run parallel and maybe even, at certain points, unite?

There are no aristocrats in *The Waves*, it was to be 'the life of anybody – life in general'. Virginia's initial intention to generalise can be seen as something Leonard advocated. But if we look at the very different ways the two of them used their 'watery' titles we realise that their visions were inescapably their own and were, indeed, diverging.

For Leonard, the 'deluge' of his title meant the first world war, an event that in his eyes was different in kind from all other, previous wars and entirely destructive. He saw it as a catastrophe that had fatally damaged, and would ultimately destroy, 'civilisation' bringing in its wake the imminent threat of barbarism. This was the major theme in all three volumes of his trilogy; he wanted to warn the world of the seriousness of its position and to contrast what he saw as the imperfections of modern democracy with the ideal democracy of the Age of Pericles: modern life would descend into barbarism if there was another world war, as the Golden Age of Greece gradually declined and descended into barbarism after the Peloponnesian War. This was his message, based on a revelation he had experienced at Cambridge in the early years of the century. He must stand up, attacked by all, to deliver his message. He never modified his position, or questioned it throughout his life; he tried to argue his case in his numerous books with more and more desperation as the political climate darkened and Germany came under the shadow of Nazism.

Thus the 'deluge' was to Leonard a two-stage disaster, the first part of which had already occurred. He wanted to prevent a second world war, the seeds of which he realised, as did others, lurked in the harsh terms of the Versailles Treaty which impoverished Germany as the country struggled to make financial reparations for the so-called Great War. The 'deluge' was outside himself; its power was negative, and threatened what he wanted to protect.

We may consider it strange that a war fought with metal weapons delivering unprecedented fire and explosive power, should be equated by Leonard with this basic, life-giving liquid. However, to the arch rationalist, a large body of water is the ultimate irrational force, as barbarism was the ultimate irrational force threatening 'civilisation'. No doubt he also saw water in biblical terms as 'the flood' that would sweep everything away. He was Job arguing against God, battling to replace God with his own (apparently) rationalist image.

For Virginia, water was certainly not a symbol of any outside, destructive or irrational force. For her it was both within herself and part of the world, its powerful ebb and flow: the gathering together of waves breaking on the shore when the hidden undertow drags them back, to rise and break again and again. That swelling of the waves, those tides, were felt in her own body and influenced the way she wrote; the restless shifting of ocean was instinct in the very rhythm of her language.

We can therefore see that even so basic an image as water meant very different things to Leonard and Virginia. Their views would never run parallel, never merge. Their underlying aims and motives, as well as their visions, were entirely different. But they were coming to a point of connection in time: the publication of their two books in 1931.

Leonard, like Pericles, was not a pacifist; he was in favour of the French Revolution because it swept away that country's aristocracy, and he would have liked the same thing to have occurred in Britain. Throughout all of his work Pericles remained his ideal, occupying centre stage both in his later *Barbarians at the Gate* and in Volume Three of *After the Deluge* which he called, with a misplaced sense of importance, *Principia Politica*. In Volume One Pericles is referred to, in company with other great men, as part of Leonard's criticism of historians for seeing:

"the history of each country or era as a necklace of great men and famous or infamous names... I call these people biographers or psychologists rather than historians." [11]

No actual words of Pericles himself survive. His assumed words are quoted by the historian Thucydides in the first of a series of pronouncements on democracy entitled: '431 B.C. Pericles in the Funeral Oration in Thucydides, Book II'. [12] Leonard uses a speech purporting to be by Pericles in support of his own view that modern democracy is defective:

" 'Liberty', said Pericles, describing what he thought to be Athenian democracy, 'is the principle of our public life and in our every-day life we are not mutually suspicious or angry with our neighbour because he pleases himself, nor do we look upon him with that kind of disapproval which, though harmless, is annoying.' " [13]

Leonard adds:

"The words describe admirably a democratic psychology which gives free play to individuality and individual liberty. It is a psychology which cannot be said to be characteristic of the modern democracies in which the State is too often a menace to individual liberty and the man who pleases or thinks for himself is the object of suspicion and anger. But here... the discussion, which began with equality, has insensibly led us to the third and most elusive member of the democratic Trinity – liberty."

His 'democratic Trinity' gives us a triangle, this time equality, democracy, liberty.

Leonard's quotation of words by a famous man (Pericles) to support his case contradicts his premiss that one can discuss 'communal psychology' without considering either the influence of important individuals on their societies, or the influence of societies on such individuals. One wonders, indeed, whether such an omission is possible. But he leaves the reader floundering when he does not question the validity of the apparently ideal democracy enjoyed by Athenian citizens in the fifth century b.c., that gave 'free play to individuality and individual liberty', when Socrates, their most renowned philosopher, was arrested, tried and condemned to death. This event actually occurred thirty years after the death of Pericles, when Athenian democracy was in decline, but Leonard does not make the point. He tries to excuse the forced suicide of Socrates first, by arguing that the philosopher was limited by the society in which he lived:

"The life that he lived, the thoughts that he thought, and the feelings that he felt ran between very narrow lines which were ruled for him by

Greek civilization, and with all his strange originality it was rarely that he succeeded in crossing them. The whole background of his life, beliefs, and aims was determined for him by the political and economic structure of Athenian society and by the vast complex of communal beliefs and aims of which he was himself so persistent a critic." [14]

He then complicates his argument by contrasting the lack of a sense of sin in relation to Athenian law compared to mediaeval law: 'there was a leniency and humanity in the administration of the criminal law which is almost unintelligible to Christianized Europeans even today. Legal torture, tolerated for centuries in Christian law-courts, was abhorrent to the Athenians; the traitor, convicted of treason, whom every Christian State to-day shoots or hangs, was banished or, if condemned to death, allowed to escape'. It was no pedantic scruple, Leonard would have us believe, but the 'habit and devotion of a life-time... which made Socrates indignantly reject his friends' suggestion that he should escape from prison'. In support of his view he quotes from a lawyer, Sir John Macdonnell: "If the prosecution and condemnation of Socrates were acts of State, they were at least done decently and in order, and with no desire to stifle the voice of the victim, and there are none of the circumstances of brutality which I shall often have to note in medieval and modern trials." [15]

It is difficult to know how one can kill someone without stifling their voice. However glad one might be that Socrates was not tortured, hanged, drawn and quartered, or made to feel guilty for his opinions, Leonard has still not answered the point that his condemnation and death contradicts the words he attributes to Pericles. Nor do brutal methods of killing those convicted of treason in medieval times – in societies which were not democratic – have any bearing on comparisons between different democratic systems. Above all, he compares a theoretical ideal on the one hand, with what occurred centuries later in practice on the other.

We may ask whether individuals are indeed as influenced, as Leonard wants us to accept, by the societies in which they live? He needed to put forward this argument because he believed that the concept of individuality only emerged in the world about two hundred years ago. His purpose is to trace the importance of communal and not individual psychology through different periods of history, but it may be that he was trying to write about a non-subject, made even more difficult if one views human populations as 'swarming ant heaps': 'History should be little concerned with the Socrates's and Shakespeares... its facts are not to be sought for in the lives of famous men, but in the swarming ant-heaps that rose in Mesopotamia, Athens, Rome, or London.' [16] So far from dismissing biographers and psychologists in his discussion of history, as he does, Leonard's political writings could perhaps have been better balanced and enriched by including these, together with the work of anthropologists, geneticists, economists and artists, among others. Duncan Wilson, after quoting from *After the Deluge*, adds in brackets a revealing comment:

"What I said could be summarised in a single sentence: a society which accepted and practised the one scale of values [Woolf's own] would be civilised, a society which accepted and practised the other would be barbarous." [17]

In other words, whoever does not agree with Leonard Woolf is inevitably a barbarian.

Having divorced his argument from any context, Leonard's chosen subject provided him with an opportunity to play generalisations off against each other championing 'civilisation' against 'barbarism' as though he is playing with white and black pieces on a drafts-board. He evidently preferred the idea of 'freedom' (his definition of freedom is so involved as to be incomprehensible) to authoritarianism, especially religious authoritarianism, which we may well applaud; but what can one make of this? Wilson says:

"Woolf went on to reach a conclusion which is a common-place of religious rather than atheist thought. It is the sense of freedom rather than freedom itself, which is most valuable for the individual; and 'in order to be free' the individual 'must learn how to lose his freedom'... Woolf illustrated his point from his experience as a trainer of animals over many years. His conclusion was that the 'permanent pattern of [children's] social behaviour is largely determined by the way in which they are conditioned to society in their first contacts with it, i.e. by the way in which... they are taught to control their instincts, to adapt them to the exigencies of social life, to regard authority and use freedom.' " [18]

Leonard's argument that individuals must suffer loss of freedom in order to control their instincts justifies every tyrant and dictator that has ever lived, from the patriarchal father claiming the right to control every member of his family including his wife, children and any servants he may employ, to the monsters who slaughter millions in the name of God, patriotism, or any other end for which the means is exerting power and control over others. He wanted to be in control of the 'human ant-heap' by blaming everyone else for not living in an ideal democracy while he remained an outsider. At home, freedom through the loss of freedom was Leonard's prescription for Virginia – twice she had escaped into madness and now, returning from her affair with Vita, it was a burden she was forced to endure for the rest of her life. Wilson sums up:

"Woolf's view of history, moreover, was indeed very partial. He did not mention, for example, the darker side of fifth century Athens... His sympathies and antipathies blinded him to a good deal of experience and made him seem an unreliable champion of tolerance. Moreover, the combination of these defects with a claim to write history more meaningfully than professional historians was hard to stomach even for his fellow amateurs.

It is hard to claim for Woolf that he left behind him the torso of a great systematic work either on the interaction of 'communal psychology' and history, or on the 'eternal struggle' between democracy and authoritarianism, the forms of government conducive to true civilization and those incompatible with it." [19]

In 1953, when he published *Principia Politica*, Leonard's trilogy received such trenchant criticism that instead of writing a fourth volume he decided to begin his autobiography, which was less open to challenge. By this time, Virginia was dead and he could say what he liked about her and their lives together. We should take the views he expressed with just as much doubt, distrust and suspicion as is necessary with his political writings: he was a man with a fixed attitude to 'good' and 'bad', 'white' and 'black', a proselytiser who sought to convert the world to his view. Leonard was a clever man who used rationalisation rather than a balanced reasonableness to support his convictions, and he never changed. Virginia's autobiography is in her owing writings, in her diaries, letters and novels; this is where we find her. It is left to those who come later to take a view of their life together which should not be defined by the attitude Leonard takes in his autobiography.

In the late nineteen twenties Virginia, at the age of forty-seven, with the onset of menopause and any possibility of motherhood closed to her, went back to the only escape left to her – her creative writing, whose deep springs came from the submerged world of her childhood. Included in her cast of characters in *The Waves*, are some members of the Bloomsbury Group. Her triumph was to contain Leonard himself, as

Louis, within her inner world. But the price she paid was to allow him to gain ever more control over her in the real world, where she was not allowed to spend the money she had earned in her own way, or to live where she would have preferred to live.

Sacrificing autonomy, Virginia's days were enriched by the people who inhabited her inner being, as she allowed her genius to bring them to life. This is nowhere more evident than in *The Waves* which, in its early drafts, was written as poetry. In Draft 1 distant children are bathed in a mystical sense of 'moth', and 'wave', and 'plant', to be discovered in an instant in the fold of a tablecloth or the leaf of a plant:

> "And there in that little crease of the napkin was a corner of a
> garden shadowed by leaves like the outstretched hands of giants.
> Here the enormous snails drew their thin track of
> iridescent slime; & the peacock butterfly
> settled on the flowers. Here came – but none of the
> children can have been ten years old yet – like
> in single phrases;
> as on a quiet day, when there had been a storm perhaps out at sea,
> & one huge wave rolls in, by itself, & crashes on the beach.
> solitary phrases, interrogations, a growly voice; love;
> an extended branch – Death; & tumult of leaves–
> shivering; hiding, showing, something
> dazzling; as if it were the red heart laid bare." [20]

Very soon a few of the children come into focus and begin to speak their stories. A scene is enacted between Louis and Jinny that also recurs in the second draft and is to be found in the final text:

> "~~Among these children was one there was Louis was~~
> some sense of the awful duration,
> of life, & such power to open the heart & close it; &
> to do as it liked
> with the heart...
> And yet it is not our doing; – Louis said in the
> corner of the garden, where the leaves
> were so prodigiously broad; & the shadows of the peacock
> butterflies were as black/ like clouds; and the spirally marked snail shells

were visible to the last grain. ~~So saying~~ he snapped a leaf off
viciously. ~~Far away~~ The other children hooted & catcalled,
chasing, seeking, skimming the flower tops, all
glittering & nodding flowers, the black & gilt, with their
nets, creasing together like folds of
glistery silk the cream, the lustre: for him shrivelled. There
Jinny & he together ~~killed a~~ saw a dead rat – the innumerable
maggots. And kissed there; on the seat by the white greenhouse."

Suddenly we have a scene, and a violent one, of love and death. Louis
does not see the beauty of nature 'for him shrivelled', and refuses to take
responsibility for the 'awful duration of life... to do as it liked with the
heart.' 'It is not our doing, Louis said... he snapped a leaf off viciously'.
He kisses Jinny in the garden beside a dead rat full of maggots. Susan-
Vanessa sees the kiss and suffers, squeezing her handkerchief in a ball and
running into a beech wood. She passes a shed within which are Bernard
and Neville (as they will be named). Bernard sees Susan and follows her,
taking with him Neville's knife.

Only Percival and Rhoda were not involved in this seminal scene, which
remains with the other five characters and is recalled throughout their lives.
In both the second draft and the text Louis becomes plant-like and rejects
responsibility for Jinny kissing him. Draft II has a deleted passage:

" 'I am standing in the corner by the wall among the flowers'
said Louis...
I am the plant. My roots go down to the
middle of the world, through the hot earth through the
damp earth...
...down there my eyes are the lidless
eyes of a stone figure in the desert by the Nile...
Up here my eyes are not open; I am eyeless...
here Bernard Neville, Jinny & Susan skim
the flower beds with their nets... I hear
them brush the surface of the world. I am
Their nets full of fluttering wings. Let them
pass me. Let them shout Louis! Louis!
& pass me on the other side of the hedge. They cannot see: I am
green as a yew tree in the shade of the hedge.

There are only little eyeholes among the leaves...
{I stand as still ~~as a~~ hemlock; I am this
hemlock; ~~but~~ I press the stalk. And a sticking drop oozes; &
Jinny, with her eye pressed between the leaves sees me; & she cries
Louis! Louis! & she flashes ~~on h~~ & she kisses me – it is
there is the crash of steel on the nape of my neck!}"

Then:
"She has kissed me! it is broken. The line is cut. The globe is
broken.'
It forms ~~sticky~~ at the mouth. There is a flash of pink past
the hedge. Now it stops Now she looks. I am
~~caught~~ She is here – she is on me – her kiss has
shattered the whole world. Down it falls broken
like glass. I have had a blow on the nape of the neck."
[21]

The first experience of sex for Louis, then, is something that shatters
his onanistic world with his lidless eyes open in the past, eyeless in the
present. He is not the active participant, Jenny's kiss is something that is
done to him. This is the same type of sexuality, with the man passive or
reactive, that Leonard described between Gwen and Harry in *The Wise
Virgins*. This scene survives in the final text, now in prose:

"Up here Bernard, Neville, Jinny and Susan (but not Rhoda) skim the
flower-beds with their nets. They skim the butterflies from the nodding
tops of the flowers. They brush the surface of the world. Their nets are
full of fluttering wings. 'Louis! Louis! Louis!' they shout. But they cannot
see me. I am on the other side of the hedge. There are only little eyeholes among the leaves... But let me be unseen. I am green as a yew tree
in the shade of the hedge. My hair is made of leaves. I am rooted to the
middle of the earth. My body is a stalk. I press the stalk. A drop oozes
from the hole at the mouth and slowly, thickly, grows larger and larger.
Now something pink passes the eye-hole. Now an eye-beam is slid
through the chink. Its beam strikes me. I am a boy in a grey flannel suit.
She has found me. I am struck on the nape of the neck. She has kissed
me. All is shattered." [22]

In this final version, Jinny describes the same scene from her point of
view:

"I was running, said Jinny, after breakfast. I saw leaves moving in a hole in the hedge. I thought 'That is a bird on its nest.' I parted them and looked; but there was no bird on a nest. The leaves went on moving. I was frightened. I ran past Susan, past Rhoda, and Neville and Bernard in the toll-house talking. I cried as I ran, faster and faster. What moved the leaves? What moves my heart, my legs? And I dashed in here, seeing you green as a bush, like a branch, very still, Louis, with your eyes fixed. 'Is he dead?' I thought, and kissed you, with my heart jumping under my frock like the leaves, which go on moving, though there is nothing to move them. Now I smell geraniums; I smell earth mould. I dance. I ripple. I am thrown over you like a net of light. I lie quivering flung over you."

I find fascinating the changes in these three versions of the same scene. In the first and second drafts we only experience it from Louis's point of view, he blames Jinny for seeing his plantlike masturbatory ejaculation (in the earliest version he is hemlock), and shattering the whole world with a kiss. In the final text the reader also enters the scene through the eyes of Jinny. The flow of the text – the rhythm of the waves – continues with Susan seeing the kiss, which is her agony that never abates, as she loves Louis; while Bernard follows Susan to try and comfort her.

Together these two, Bernard and Susan, run away and find Elvedon, a secret place where a woman sits writing and where in the first draft a gardener sweeps (he becomes more than one gardener in later versions). Thus arguably we discover Virginia the writer sitting between two tall windows at Elvedon, the country house she longed for, with gardener(s) sweeping the lawn:

"I see the lady writing. I see the gardeners sweeping,' said Susan. 'If we died here, nobody would bury us." [23]

Here is a hint of immortality. Immortality gained by dying in a gracious country estate, a secret place inhabited by a writer. But there are dangers in remaining there. Bernard sees Elvedon as hostile, they must escape back to the beech wood if they are not to be shot by the gardener in a black beard. (As Leonard the gardener prevented Virginia from living in a gracious country estate).

In *The Waves* the present moment is filled with a superabundance of life, of many lives, of towns and cities, of the complete span of memory, like some drop or sphere that excludes nothing. The characteristic phrases and images with which each member of the group begin their journey remain with them and are often repeated:

" 'I see a ring,' said Bernard, 'hanging above me. It quivers and hangs in a loop of light.'

'I see a slab of pale yellow,' said Susan, 'spreading away until it meets a purple stripe.'

'I hear a sound,' said Rhoda, 'cheep chirp; cheep chirp; going up and down.'

'I see a globe, said Neville, 'hanging down in a drop against the enormous flank of some hill.'

'I see a crimson tassel,' said Jinny, 'twisted with gold threads.'

'I hear something stamping, said Louis. 'A great beast's foot is chained. It stamps, and stamps, and stamps.' "

Rhoda, who is associated throughout with water ('the nymph of the fountain, always wet'), expresses alienation even from the circles and globes seen by the others: 'The world is entire, and I am outside of it, crying, 'Oh save me, from being blown forever outside the loop of time!' [24]

Virginia's method of writing this book ties the characters together and reduces the extent to which they can change or develop over time. Sitting in her 'nunnery' writing, the walls that separated her from her friends became thin; aspects of people familiar to her merge with others and become part of herself as she becomes part of them. The intensely sensitive, creative part of her became Rhoda. Leonard is central to Louis although he acquires some of the trappings of T.S. Eliot, who worked in a bank (Louis's father was 'a banker in Brisbane') and wrote poetry; the adult Louis lives in an attic and writes poetry. Louis and Rhoda share a relationship which is fractured and uncomfortable. In Draft II, begun in June 1930, Bernard wonders which of their lives was best:

" 'Louis & Rhoda, the conspirators ~~as~~ I sometimes
called them... Louis, with his
bony hands, seemed to clasp them, as the sides of a
dock close themselves with a slow anguish of effort,
compressing painfully the enormous tumult of
waters... he proceeded to rule
straight lines for this infinitely various, vagulous &
uncharted & unsounded life – to rule straight lines
with red ink & a fine nib.
Rhoda would then say to him, remembering

Percival, Away! The moor is dark beneath the
moon – Away! The gathering winds will
call the darkness soon – I am quoting [from Shelley]... I am
trying to suggest to you the flight & the abandonment, the
stricture & the anguish, the folly & the
insoluble discomfort & dissatisfaction of that
relationship; also its simple childishness, its consolation,
its little anecdotes; & how they talked
a little language, broken words, Rhoda & Louis, before
in a moment of extraordinary rashness, in [the date is missing]
she killed herself. An open window had always
presented to her an extraordinary attraction.' "
[25]

A tantalising passage, this. But 'the flight & the abandonment, the stricture & the anguish, the folly & the insoluble discomfort & dissatisfaction
of that relationship' and the efforts they make to try and cope with it,
with their 'little language, broken words', ring true. Virginia has dared to
describe the Woolfs' marriage of incompatible opposites and has closely
related this to Rhoda's desire for death by suicide. It is plain that her relationship with Leonard was not the 'truly fortunate, prosperous and happy
alliance' [26] that Anne Bell, the editor of Virginia's *Diary*, would have
her readers believe. Virginia says that in *The Waves* she 'tried to speak the
truth... wrung it drop by drop from my brain.' [27] However, since
Leonard read all of her final texts, her confession in Draft II is no longer
there. Rhoda's agony is implicit as she leaves Louis and dies 'seeking
some pillar in the desert' [28]

The majority of the characters in *The Waves* find that the barriers
between each other grow thin, while others do not:
    " 'Louis and Neville,' said Bernard, 'both sit silent. Both are absorbed.
Both feel the presence of other people as a separating wall. But if I find
myself in company with other people, words at once make smoke rings –
see how phrases at once begin to wreathe off my lips. It seems that a
match is set to fire; something burns... I do not believe in separation. We
are not single... I fill my mind with whatever happens to be the contents
of a room or a railway carriage as one fills a fountain-pen in an inkpot. I
have a steady unquenchable thirst.' " [29]

Leonard, like Louis, with his dominant left brain, must often have felt the presence of other people, including Virginia, as an alien presence against which he erected a separating wall of silence. Hence his dislike of most parties and very obvious boredom when he was in uncongenial company.

Jinny is clearly a portrayal of Mary Hutchinson, who was married to Jack Hutchinson but had a long-term affair with Clive Bell. Lady Ottoline Morrell noticed this similarity. [30] Clive did his best to bring Mary into the Bloomsbury Group but she was eventually ejected by the combined efforts of Vanessa (who painted an extremely unflattering portrait of her), Leonard and, somewhat more equivocally, Virginia who tried to tempt her into a lesbian relationship. The break came when Mary fell in love with a 'mysterious man'. This could have been Leonard's contribution to the plot. Jinny is a femme fatale to whom men come when she calls. Night excites her, it is her time. Susan thinks of her as she sits sewing in the evening: 'They dance in London. Jinny kisses Louis'. Jinny tells her own story:

" 'night is beginning. I feel myself shining in the dark. Silk is on my knee. My silk legs rub smoothly together. The stones of a necklace lie cold on my throat. My feet feel the pinch of shoes. I sit bolt upright so that my hair may not touch the back of the seat. I am arrayed, I am prepared...

People are arriving; they do not speak; they hasten in. There is the prelude, this is the beginning. I glance, I peep, I powder. All is exact, prepared. My hair is swept in one curve. My lips are precisely red. I am ready now to join men and women on the stairs, my peers... I feel a thousand capacities spring up in me. I am arch, gay, languid, melancholy by turns. I am rooted, but I flow. All gold, flowing that way, I say to this one 'Come'. Rippling black, I say to that one, 'No'. One breaks off from his station under the glass cabinet. He approaches. He makes towards me. This is the most exciting moment I have ever known. I flutter. I ripple. I stream like a plant in the river, flowing this way, flowing that way, but rooted, so that he may come to me. 'Come,' I say, 'come'...

I do not care for anybody save this man whose name I do not know. Are we not acceptable, moon? Are we not lovely sitting together here, I in my satin; he in black and white? My peers may look at me now. I look straight back at you, men and women. I am one of you. This is my world...

I fill my glass again. I drink. The veil drops between us. I am admitted to the warmth and privacy of another soul. We are together, high up, on some Alpine pass. He stands melancholy on the crest of the road. I stoop. I pick a blue flower and fix it, standing on tiptoe to reach him, in his coat. There! that is my moment of ecstasy. Now it is over.

Now slackness and indifference invade us. Other people brush past. We have lost consciousness of our bodies uniting under the table... Here is my risk, here is my adventure. The door opens. O come, I say to this one, rippling gold from head to heels. "Come', and he comes towards me.' " [31]

This free, ironic passage has something of the stride and dash of *Orlando*. But Rhoda enters this scene and suddenly we get a tragic dramatic contrast:

" 'I shall edge behind them,' said Rhoda, 'as if I saw someone I know. But I know no one. I shall twitch the curtain and look at the moon. Draughts of oblivion shall quench my agitation. The door opens; the tiger leaps. The door opens; terror rushes in; terror upon terror, pursuing me. Let me visit furtively the treasure I have laid apart. Pools lie on the other side of the world reflecting marble columns... the moon rides through the blue seas alone. I must take his hand. I must answer. But what answer shall I give? I am thrust back to stand burning in this clumsy, this ill-fitting body, to receive the shafts of his indifference and his scorn, I who long for marble columns and pools on the other side of the world where the swallow dips her wings.' " [32]

The intensity of this book, whether in the shortened lines of the drafts or the final prose text, is a very sensitive expression of Virginia's right brain and it is to our right brain that she speaks. We are in an entirely different world from that of Leonard's analytical *After the Deluge*, to the extent that it is difficult to make the transition from one to the other.

Throughout *The Waves* each character expresses her or his own experiences which are interconnected like the petals of a flower whose non-speaking centre is Percival. His death in India scatters the remaining six 'petals' of the other characters who come together occasionally and speak to each other with increasing difficulty. On a more universal level Percival's death represents a threat to all of life: as Thoby's death left a permanent shadow on Virginia which she re-experiences in her deepest novels. But this does not explain why the weight of tragedy in *The Waves* so overlays the lightness and energy that had animated *Orlando*.

The most frequent image for Rhoda is her attempt to float white petals like a fleet of ships in a brown bowl and to stop them becoming over-whelmed. She loves. She hates. She gives, but – 'Oh, to whom?' We can well be worried that Virginia is under great pressure in this book, more than she was when creating the shell-shocked Septimus Smith in *Mrs Dalloway*. And we should ask serious questions as to what has happened to cause what we can see as a regression from personal growth, to something close to despair and disintegration.

After the deaths of Percival and Rhoda Bernard is left alone, when at last he finds that he is not fighting for life but challenging death. This is the final reality of the book: the polarity is reversed, from the struggle for life (seen as a globe) to facing without fear the reality of death.

I believe that this movement, from life towards death, was the actual journey of the book: the reality of death was the fin that Virginia netted, the only visible part of the monster lurking in the deep, beneath the waves. The challenge of staying alive was to try and put together the immense richness of single drops of every moment, to attempt to connect moment with moment in order to 'endure' days, months, years of life. But by the end of the book Virginia was faced with quite a different challenge. No doubt the spirit of the age was changing, darkening, as the nineteen twenties were left behind and the nineteen thirties loomed ahead. Any possibility of personal escape became less and less realistic. Approaching the death-pole, she was now in Leonard's psychic territory and she was absorbing his depth of depression which was partly frustration that no-one seemed to heed his warnings that 'the house is falling down', as Louis puts it in Draft 1, and partly ingrained in him. To embrace and accept his extreme negativity was, finally, her act of love for him as he became her 'inviolable centre'. She encapsulates this in a moment of intense feeling, after Clive Bell had told them he was going blind:

"We walked through the little dingy streets of Seven Dials Leonard & I this afternoon, to Charing Cross Road. What a mood of tears I was in – of pathos, for Leonard, for myself; & said to him Would you like half a crown to buy a squirrel? Suddenly one is overcome with sorrow for people." [33]

In the deepening shadow of the death-pole Leonard's arguments, his point of view, echoed and reverberated around Virginia whether they were in London or, more especially, when they were thrown closely together at

Monk's House. And yet Leonard intended 1931 to mark his triumphal return to public life. The Woolfs (were they courageous, or foolhardy?) were once again competing for public attention as they had not done over full-length work since Leonard set out as a novelist back in 1913 and 1914 while Virginia, in agony, was revising *The Voyage Out*. Now, as then, the weight on Virginia was considerable as it was not when her inner self was illuminated by Vita whilst she was writing *Orlando* – those years when the surface of the waves sparkled and there was no visible undertow.

Rhoda's intensely imagined death in Spain recalls the sense of fear and dissolution Virginia experienced on her honeymoon. The petals she tries to keep afloat in her brown bowl 'darkened with sea water'. They will 'float for a moment and then sink'. Virginia is anticipating not only her own death but the extinction of her work, too.

However, throughout this book, Virginia makes the fundamental commitment to experience the world as a female. In the inner world of *The Waves* the female characters speak directly for themselves in their own right. Admittedly they are isolated and lonely, even when Jinny says Come to men. Susan is trapped in the country with children. Rhoda dies alone in the desert. But the males, too, at first seeming stronger than the women, are also limited: Louis with his Australian accent, his anger and his trembling arm; Neville as a homosexual, his despairing love of Percival giving way to promiscuity; Bernard who blows phrases like smoke rings and cannot finish what he starts to write.

In its larger dimension the entire book is also keyed to the female – the sun woman in the Interludes and the 'lady writing' at Elvedon – but even the courage with which the female principle is presented carries a bleak message. As children, Bernard and Susan see Elvedon as a dangerous place from which they must run back to the beech wood, while the sun keeps its appointed course until it is eclipsed – as Virginia watched a total eclipse of the sun in June, 1927. Special trains to view the event were run from London to North Yorkshire. On that trip Virginia shared a compartment with Vita, Harold, Quentin and Leonard. When Harold broke a china sandwich box, Leonard 'laughed without restraint'. The train's passengers stood in long lines on a Yorkshire moor looking through smoked glass 'when suddenly the light went out. We had fallen. It was extinct. There was no colour. The earth was dead. That was the astonishing moment... I had very strongly the feeling as the light went out of some vast obeisance; something kneeling down, & low & suddenly raised up, when the colours came... at first with a miraculous glittering & aetheriality, later normally, almost, but with a great sense of relief. It was like recovery... We had seen the world dead... Then – it was over till 1999.' [34]

Nearly seventy years after *The Waves* was written, many women still find it hard to experience the world through their own female eyes instead of, indirectly, through male eyes. The book called forth a great effort of Virginia's creative imagination as it is not confined to the interactions of individual human characters but involves nature through time; and social awakening after a long dark period of patriarchal supremacy, both of which are implicit in Bernard's description of the eclipse that he sees:

" 'How then does light return to the world after the eclipse of the sun? Miraculously. Fraily. In thin stripes. It hangs like a glass cage. It is a hoop to be fractured by a tiny jar. There is a spark there. Next moment a flush of dun. Then a vapour as if the earth were breathing in and out, once, twice, for the first time. Then under the dullness someone walks with a green light. Then off twists a white wraith. The woods throb blue and green, and gradually the fields drink in red, gold, brown. Suddenly a river snatches a blue light. The earth absorbs colour like a sponge slowly drinking water. It puts on weight; rounds itself; hangs pendent; settles and swings beneath our feet.' " [35]

For a time Bernard feels reborn: 'I walked unshadowed; I came unheralded. From me had dropped the old cloak, the old response... I walked alone in a new world, never trodden; brushing new flowers, unable to speak save in a child's words of one syllable... I who have always gone with my kind; solitary, I who have always had someone to share the empty grate, or the cupboard with its hanging loop of gold. But how describe the world seen without a self? There are no words.'

Cosmic loneliness is being experienced by Bernard, speaking for Virginia, in his long monologue at the end; while Rhoda expresses human loneliness and disappointment in a scene with Louis at Hampton Court:

" 'If we could mount together, if we could perceive from a sufficient height,' said Rhoda, 'if we could remain untouched without any support – but you, disturbed by faint clapping sounds of praise and laughter, and I, resenting compromise and right and wrong on human lips, trust only in solitude and the violence of death and thus are divided.'

'For ever', said Louis, 'divided. We have sacrificed the embrace among the ferns, and love, love, love by the lake, standing, like conspirators who have drawn apart to share some secret, by the urn." [36]

It is now plain that Leonard, like Louis, refused to mount with Virginia as she climbed her creative heights and so they were divided. How clearly she sees this 'without a self', with her writer's inner eye. It is a division between them that grows wider through the coming decade.

There is an irritability, a suppressed rage, in Louis, as there was in Leonard:

" 'My eyes are wild; my lips tight pressed. The bird flies; the flower dances; but I hear always the sullen thud of the waves; and the chained beast stamps on the beach. It stamps and stamps.' " [37]

Virginia felt critical of Leonard's writing both as regards style, since she considered that the training received at Cambridge was damaging, and from his family's struggle to make ends meet after his father's death which inspired an inverted snobbery. He seems to have been ambivalent about being a Jew, proud, and at the same time very aware of anti-Semitism. For whatever reason Leonard wrote as an angry victim, a gadfly Virginia calls him, and she cannot have admired this quality in his writing although she was supportive of his aims. She finished her own book in February, 1931, and wrote triumphantly in her diary:

"I wrote the words O Death fifteen minutes ago, having reeled across the last ten pages with some moments of such intensity & intoxication that I seemed only to stumble after my own voice, or almost, after some sort of speaker (as when I was mad). I was almost afraid, remembering the voices that used to fly ahead. Anyhow it is done; and I have been sitting these 15 minutes in a state of glory, & calm, & some tears, thinking of Thoby & if I could write Julian Thoby Stephen 1881-1906 on the first page. I suppose not. How physical the sense of triumph & relief is! Whether good or bad, its done; & as I certainly felt at the end, not merely finished, but rounded off, completed, the thing stated – how hastily, how fragmentarily I know; but I mean that I have netted the fin in the waste of waters which appeared to me over the marshes out of my window at Rodmell when I was coming to an end of To the Lighthouse." [38]

Again, Virginia suffered no breakdown after writing this intense, 'saturated' book.

There is no doubt Leonard saw the long-awaited publication of *After the Deluge* as a major, life-changing and hopefully world-changing, event. He spent the previous year in a concerted attempt to put himself on the map, to make his voice heard as a writer and thinker, for the first time since he had stood unsuccessfully for Parliament in 1920. He once more took up an editorship, of the Political Quarterly in April 1931. He managed to regain the copyright of his first novel, *The Village in the Jungle*, which was reprinted by the Hogarth Press in September 1931; and he was to give six talks on BBC radio during the autumn, published in The Listener. He was also invited to America. From Leonard's point of view, he was poised for success. In the event, they abandoned plans to visit America, but he gave his six talks on the BBC.

However it was Virginia who, early in the year, first made her appearance in public. On 21 January, 1931 she shared a platform with Ethel Smyth, the composer, who was dressed in outlandish attire, before the London Branch of the National Society for Women's Service. In her light-hearted speech Virginia takes up the threads of an argument begun in *A Room of One's Own* which would, eventually, be continued and developed in *Three Guineas*. That is, she talks to women about becoming successful. The occasion was reviewed by Vera Britain in the Nation, she calls it 'this hilariously serious party' and noted that both speakers 'attributed their success largely to the possession of a private income, which enabled the one to take up a non-lucrative career, and the other to flout the displeasure of authors by writing honest reviews':

"Women, Mrs. Woolf maintained, had succeeded better in literature than in other arts because paper was cheap and pens made no noise." [39]

Virginia was already considering the text that would become *Three Guineas*. She says in her diary that she is 'too much excited, alas to get on with The Waves. One goes on making up The Open Door, or whatever it is to be called. The didactic demonstrative style conflicts with the dramatic: I find it hard to get back inside Bernard again.' [40] Then she adds:

"The speech took place; L. I think slightly exacerbated: an interesting observation if a true one."

Why, we may well ask, should Leonard have felt 'slightly exacerbated' at Virginia's performance? To exacerbate means to embitter; to provoke; increase of irritation or violence. The most likely explanation is that Virginia, back in her cage, should not be allowed to stand up on platforms or be reviewed favourably for doing so, especially in the embarrassing company of Ethel Smyth. By entering the public arena she was intruding on the 'territory' Leonard was poised to claim for himself. At the time this seemed to be but a small cloud. There was another in June when 'Goldie' (Goldsworthy Lowes Dickinson), a fellow Apostle, read Leonard's book and gave only qualified praise saying, according to Virginia, that although it contained 'new & important ideas: the style [is] repetitive & tedious.' [41] No doubt Leonard sent a copy to Goldie hoping for a quotation that he could use; as it was, all he could say in his Preface was: 'I have to thank Mr. G. Lowes Dickinson for having read the book in MS. and for much valuable criticism'. These could be regarded, however, as mere pin-pricks since by July Leonard's career really seemed at last to be taking off. During what Virginia called 'a dark kind of summer', with much bad weather during their two months at Monk's House, she notes:

"L. is now floating on the tide of celebrity: odd how the strings all begin to tug at once: asked to Broadcast, asked to go to America, asked to write the Weekly Wayfarer in the Statesman [Leonard didn't do this]. And I am not jealous. But I am fearful of what I call... Life." [42]

Later in the same entry, after recounting one of a series of tragicomic scenes initiated by Ethel Smyth, Virginia speaks of a long discussion between themselves and several friends, including Mary Hutchinson:

"upon being in a cage: Mary rampant; like a horse when a train passes a field. Must escape. Must find a brazen man & go to Spain. Why dont we do anything? Change our lives? She live with L. I with Jack? ... Why not expose a different self?"

We are not told what Leonard thought of Mary's proposition; he probably said nothing. His relationship with Mary was in any event problematic.

In the spring of 1931 the Woolfs went on a tour of France, driving in incessant rain and cold 'the worst weather for 50 years', through an empty landscape eating indifferent food at mostly bad hotels. The roof of their car leaked, so both had ample opportunity to consider their attitudes to the water which the lowering clouds dumped on them. Despite her discomfort, sitting beside Leonard as he drove, Virginia felt very aware of him: 'this warmth, curiosity, attachment in being alone with L. If I dared I would investigate my own sensations with regard to him, but out of laziness, humility, pride, I don't know what reticence – refrain. I who am not reticent.' When she gave Leonard her book to read in September, she had a moment of fear and tension. His first reaction was that it was a masterpiece but then, he: 'accuses me of sensibility verging on insanity', and Hugh Walpole was reported not to have liked it. She defends herself: 'I tried to speak the truth... wrung it drop by drop from my brain. So essentially I am not horrified. But The Waves, I predict, marks my decline in reputation.' [43] How wrong she was. Harold Nicolson thought it a masterpiece, while John Lehmann 'truly loved it, & was deeply impressed & amazed by its achievement in an entirely new method', and 'how happy I am: how calm, for the moment how sweet life is with L.' [44]

Her life with Leonard was not sweet for long. The publication of both *After the Deluge* and *The Waves* occurred in October 1931. This was the watershed. Each author hoped they were going to be 'up' on their seesaw. For Leonard, disaster came in the guise of a short and offhand review of his book in the Times Literary Supplement. He was at once cast into an abyss of gloom which is poignantly recorded by Virginia:

"Oh but I have been made miserable – damped & disheartened – this is no exaggeration – because the Lit Sup. only gave half a column of belittlement to After the Deluge. Not that I should have cared more than a moments damn at them for the usual insignificant spiteful methods – wreaking their politics upon books they don't agree with. But L says – & honestly believes – that this puts an end to the book – Yes he says no less than that. He says his ten years work are wasted, & that he sees no use in going on. His argument is that he wrote this book for the wider public; that this public is at the mercy of Librarians; that librarians take their orders from the Lit Sup; that they judge by the length of the review; that no librarian will advise spending fifteen shillings after this review; so that... his book is dead; his work is wasted... For my own part I think this a very curious illustration of his psychology. On Sunday he told me that this was bound to happen; yet we have seldom been happier – True he said he expected one col. or one & a half of abuse instead of half; – Oh but the arguments which we have beaten out I daresay for 6 hours, walking in the Sq[ua]re, sitting over the fire – utterly cloud my mind. Its his curious pessimistic temper: something deeper than reason, strangling, many coiled, that one cant deal with. Influenza has exactly the same effect, liberating the irrational despondency which I see in all Woolves, & connect with centuries of oppression. The world against us &c. How can one laugh off the half column therefore? And when I say this morning incautiously: 'I'm reviewed in the Manchester Guardian' L. says 'Is it a long review?' And I say, feeling like a mother to a hurt & miserable little boy, Yes. Lord what human beings are!" [45]

Here Virginia is the sane and reasonable one and Leonard the basket case. According to the editor's note, the review of Leonard's book complimented him on his skill in collating and analysing his material, but accused him of 'cheapness' in dealing with the General Strike and cautioned him against being 'too rigidly logical'. Apparently Leonard did not ask himself whether there was any justice in the reviewer's comments, he merely suffered from an appalled sense of his book being rejected. There were other, less critical reviews but they gave him no comfort. A week later Virginia records that 'Happily that morbidity of L's is over'. However, his prediction was right. His book sold in hundreds and did not reach the general public as he had wanted; while *The Waves* sold in twice as many thousands and had to be reprinted.

The strain of pouring positive energy over Leonard, made worse by a visit to his family, gave Virginia a headache which marked the onset of several months' semi-invalidism. This was not due to any nervous reaction to publication on her part, or the critics' and public's response to her own book, but to his. Indeed, she cannot hide the pleasure success of *The Waves* gave her. The *Manchester Guardian* published an entirely favourable review entitled 'The Rhythm of Life' and the readers' response was reflected in sales. As she exclaims:

"[I] feel no sort of inclination to reply to the flattering invitation of Chatto that they should reprint my books. So Faber wishes too. And L. has sold his 450; and I 9400 – what figures!" [46]

It is a great pity that Virginia did not go to another publisher at this time, as she would then have avoided the long shadow that Leonard cast upon her as he became increasingly critical of her work and negative about her other activities through the decade of life that remained to her. The loss of this crucial bout in their literary rivalry was a bitter blow to Leonard. So far, during the nineteen twenties, he had more or less supported Virginia's writing whilst he was working away at his magnum opus. It seems he had made up his mind that *The Waves* should be not only her masterpiece, a classic, but her swan-song. After this, he wanted her to write short articles to earn more money, but he fully intended to take over as the major Woolf writer. At the heart of his devastating disappointment, which was comparable to that he suffered when he did badly in his final examinations at Cambridge, was the recognition that not only this long term plan, but his destiny, was now in jeopardy. For the rest of her life Virginia paid the price for her loyalty to Leonard by losing his support, especially for her imaginative work. From this time their rivalry took on a destructive twist as Leonard sought to undermine her and she rebelliously continued to write novels.

It seems that Virginia did not fully appreciate the changed situation between them. Instead of resting, she had already begun to write her next novel, *Flush*, a biography of Elizabeth Barrett Browning seen through the eyes of her cocker spaniel. This is a light-hearted book, a return in style to the 'top-of-the-wave' method of *Orlando* and a relief from the intensity of *The Waves*. She was also considering a second volume of The Common Reader, at least partly to please Leonard. And she wanted to begin the book that would become *Three Guineas* – only she was drained of energy. As she put it: 'Cant write, cant read'. Once more, she sought relief in the possibility of escape. There was talk of having to move from their London house in Tavistock Square: '& Lord, how I love the chance of any escape – from what? to what?' But it came to nothing and they remained there until July 1939.

Over Christmas 1931 Lytton Strachey became ill; this led members of the Bloomsbury Group in general, and the Woolfs in particular, to discuss death during these last days of the year that was to have put Leonard in the spotlight; but which had, instead, shone brightly upon Virginia:

"Talk to L. last night about death: its stupidity; what he would feel if I died. He might give up the Press; but how one must be natural. And the feeling of age coming over us: & the hardship of losing friends; & my dislike of the younger generation; & then I reason, how one must understand. And we are happier now." (47)

The second such discussion came a couple of days later over lunch with Maynard Keynes and his wife Lydia:

"And what d'you feel about immortality, Maynard? I asked. 'I am an idealist,' said Maynard, '& therefore on the whole I suppose I think that something may continue. Clearly the brain is the only exciting thing – matter does not exist. It follows therefore... but one is very vague.' So, more or less, he said. And L. said death was stupid like a motor accident. And M[aynard] said... he wished one cd. die at once: there should be death arranged for couples simultaneously, like himself & Lydia, me & Leonard. But he always supposed he would die before Lydia, & I, I said, before Leonard. Then Lydia & Leonard will marry. They will combine all these dogs – (dogs were wandering about.) And so home. And I kissed Maynard. And they are coming to tea." [48]

My concern is the effect on Virginia of living with Leonard, that very opinionated man. I believe he saw her as someone whose primal instincts had not been adequately 'trained' in childhood and he set himself to undertake this task – it was his 'obsession' with her – as though she was a dog, not even a mandrill, and certainly not a person in her own right. This led directly to her breakdowns soon after marriage. Then, she escaped from him by inhabiting that other area of her being when the world, and especially Leonard, called her 'mad'. Submerged within herself, she re-experienced her childhood where even her father's tyranny was preferable to Leonard's apparently well-meant efforts, and where she occasionally experienced ecstasy. When she met and fell in love with Vita Sackville-West she enjoyed the only relationship which enabled her, briefly, to live in the real world on her own terms.

THE DOWNSTAIRS SITTING ROOM, MONK'S HOUSE

PART FOUR

THE COMING OF MABEL AND LOUISE

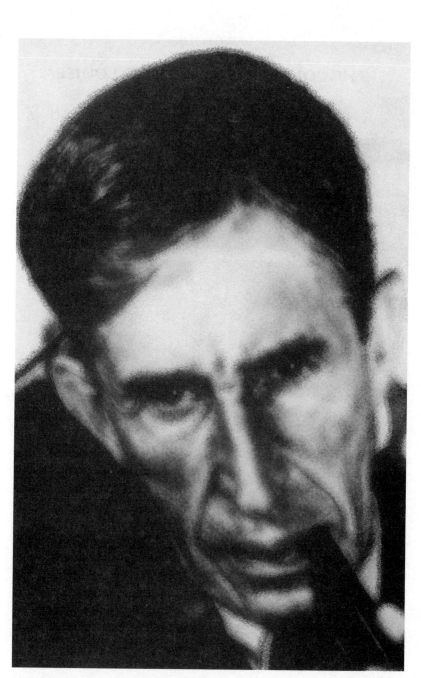

LEONARD WOOLF

Chapter Ten

TOWARDS THE DEATH POLE

As Vita's fluorescence dimmed and drooped, from the point of view of the close personal intimacy and loyal support Virginia craved a new bunch of flowers did appear on her life's grave. And what a bunch of flowers she was! Ethel Smyth, composer and suffragette, was aged over seventy when they first met in February 1930, while Virginia was writing *The Waves*. Smyth fell in love with Virginia and was to become her major correspondent for the rest of her life.

Harold Nicolson gives an amusing account of a luncheon party attended by Smyth in Germany in 1928, where his diplomatic career had taken him on his final posting after leaving Persia. One of the guests was Emil Ludwig, a German author and playwright who had written biographies of Goethe, Wagner, Bismarck, Napoleon and Christ. He and Smyth engaged in an argument where Smyth defended the Old German culture against Ludwig's campaign for a Jewish republic in Germany:

"Ethel arrived late in a fine to-do. Her tricorne [hat] kept on falling over her eyes in her excitement, and she screamed loud in her indignation against the Jewish republic that Ludwig and his friends had elevated in Germany. He was rather hurt by this. He said that the old gang had done nothing except land Germany into the Great European War. She said that his friends had destroyed the Old German culture. He said, 'not at all, not at all.' She said yes, they had, and ('God! Harold, why do you give me cold sauce with sole, I hate cold sauce with sole'), 'what about the Grand Duke at Weimar?' Ludwig said which Grand Duke? 'Weimar!' said Ethel triumphantly. Ludwig asked whether she meant the Goethe one? She said, no, she meant the Ethel Smyth one, the one who had been Grand Duke of Weimar when she had been there as a girl. Ludwig said that one had been gaga. She said that of course he had been gaga, but that at least he had cared for art... She said (oh woman!!) that she had not read his Napoleon and did not intend to. At which, throwing her head back with a challenging gesture of defiance, the tricorne, wobbling for a minute, fell, not *off*, but right *down* over her face, and for a moment her torrent of invective was stilled... The Ambassador... bubbled silently for a bit... Then Mrs Ludwig, a tactful woman, began to talk of the servant problem at Lugano. By the end of which, Ethel, having swallowed three glasses of Rieslinger Auslese, was able to talk, not with calm, but with less violence. And so, almost amicably, the luncheon party drew to an end." [1]

This story provides a brief sketch of the political background before Hitler's rise to power in Germany during the nineteen thirties, when some Germans feared that the landless Jewish people were planning to take over their country. Adolph Hitler was able to exploit that fear during the decade that followed.

As a composer Ethel Smyth was up against an even more entrenched and implacable masculine preserve than Virginia in literature or Vanessa in painting: with the greatest courage and determination she fought a life-long war to get her music performed. No wonder Leonard was 'exacerbated' when Virginia shared a platform with this cantankerous, eccentric and egocentric old woman in January 1931, the year he had dreamt he would change the world with the publication of the first volume of *After the Deluge*. There could never be any love lost between Smyth and Leonard Woolf. Just as he thought he had got Vita on his side and closed the nunnery door on Virginia, this prickly plant (perhaps a cross between cactus and sunflower) gave Virginia renewed energy; becoming a proud horse that she was able to ride. She ends *The Waves*, speaking as Bernard:

" 'And in me too the wave rises. It swells; it arches its back. I am aware once more of a new desire, something rising beneath me like the proud horse whose rider first spurs and then pulls him back. What enemy do we now perceive advancing against us, you whom I ride now, as we stand pawing this stretch of pavement? It is death. Death is the enemy. It is death against whom I ride with my spear couched and my hair flying back like a young man's, like Percival's, when he galloped in India. I strike spurs into my horse. Against you I fling myself, unvanquished and unyielding, O Death!'

The waves broke on the shore." [2]

The story of Virginia's final decade of life is the story of her defiance in the shadow of the death pole; against the background, in Britain, of the demise of an old king, the abdication of a young one and the rebuilding of the royal family as an inspiration to wage war against fascism. In his autobiography Leonard wrote negatively about the entire span of life between the two world wars and, particularly, of the last ten years before world war two:

"In the terrible years between 1919 and 1939 everything in international affairs was dominated by the emergence of fascism in Europe and the menace of another war... The years 1930 to 1939 were horrible both publicly and privately... This erosion of life by death began for Virginia and me in the early 1930s and gathered momentum as we went downhill to war and her own death. It began on 21 January 1932 when Lytton Strachey died of cancer." [3]

He characteristically includes Virginia in his 'erosion of life by death' during this time; but in her diary we see her with increasing difficulty trying to maintain life despite Leonard's often appalling negativity, as she shuts herself away in her Lodge at Monk's House to get on at all costs with her writing. Ethel Smyth was an important source of energy for Virginia and a bulwark against Leonard. We find that the Woolfs' two stories, hers written at the time in her diary and Letters, his nearly thirty years later, diverge as the chasm between them grows wider and deeper.

Lytton Strachey's death had a profound effect on Leonard. Lytton had been his supporter, the man who had believed in him and reflected him back to himself with an enhanced intensity during their days at Cambridge. Theirs was in many ways a strange relationship, between the tall thin gentile aesthete and the rather priggish Jew. They had shared a veneration of G.E. Moore and a love for Thoby Stephen; and had conceived a vision to bring back the rationalist thought of ancient Athens into pre-world-war England, as the form of highest civilisation the world had known. It was a cosy, classics-oriented dream, but everything had conspired to turn that vision on its head.

High hopes had been held for Lytton's career as a writer both by his large family and the Bloomsbury Group, hopes that were only partly fulfilled by his published books. He died of cancer at Ham Spray, whose complex household of people were enmeshed by loving where they were not loved. His life-style was far too unorthodox for Leonard. The Woolfs had not visited Lytton during the eight years he lived at Ham Spray, although Virginia had remained in touch with the man to whom she had been engaged for twenty minutes. They were fellow authors, each aware of the other's output. On his death bed, Lytton refused to read *The Waves*.

The Woolfs drove to Ham Spray a week before his death. He was too ill to see them. Virginia contrasts the unspoilt countryside with her own in Sussex, where new buildings proliferated and her neighbour bred dogs whose incessant barking disturbed her as she worked in her Lodge. She liked Ham Spray itself: 'how lovely, with its flat lawn, & the trees grouped & the down rising & the path climbing the down: this I noted with envy thinking of my dogs barking, my downs ruined... I long sometimes for this sealed up, silent, remote country: long for its little villages; its muddy roads, its distance from Brighton and Peacehaven... And so home again, leaving them in the frail lovely house... a light in Lytton's room, the shadow of a screen. He said he liked our coming. Odd to come thus, after all these years.' [4]

Thinking Lytton was improving, the Woolfs went to Angelica's fancy dress birthday party held in Vanessa's studio at 8 Fitzroy Street in London: 'It is like having the globe of the future perpetually smashed – without Lytton – & then, behold, it fills again.' But he had died that morning:

"How queer it was last night at the party, the tightness around everyone's lips – ours I mean. Duncan & Nessa & I sobbing together in the studio... a sense of something spent, gone: that is to me so intolerable: the impoverishment: & then the sudden vividness... What is to happen to Carrington? Yes, 20 years of Lytton lost to us, stupidly: the thing we shall never have again." [5]

Virginia gets on with correcting her second series of *The Common Reader* and seeing Ethel Smyth:

"I hear a characteristic slow & heavy stamp. Then a bold tap at the drawing room door. In comes Ethel Smyth in her spotted fur, like an unclipped & rather overgrown woodland wild beast, species indeterminate. She wears, as usual, her 3 cornered Frederick the Great hat, & one of her innumerable relay of tweed coats & skirts. She carries a leather satchel... 'Really I think that building of the kind you describe at Rodmell is worse than death... Why your downs? Oh I know L. wouldn't agree... Eddy [Vita's brother Edward Sackville-West] is writing a novel to show that the virtues of the aristocracy, in which I firmly believe though L. doesnt – must survive.' " [6]

Virginia needed this stalwart woman friend who was not afraid of Leonard, especially as she was actively considering her most feminist book, to become *Three Guineas*. A comment by H.G. Wells, in his newly published book *The Work, Wealth and Happiness of Mankind,* sharpened her thoughts on this book. Wells said, pontifically:

"The role of women has been decorative and ancillary. And today it seems to be still decorative and ancillary... Her recent gains in freedom have widened her choice of what she shall adorn or serve, but they have released no new initiative in human affairs." [7]

Leonard wrote a critical review of Wells's book that led to a quarrel between the two men, but he did not challenge him on his assertion that women's role remained merely 'decorative and ancillary'.

On the twenty ninth of February 1932, Virginia received an invitation that gave her the opportunity to make an indelible mark on the history of English literature, to 'release a new initiative in human affairs' and, incidentally, prove Wells wrong. It was undoubtedly the most important invitation of her career. She was asked by the Master of Trinity to deliver the prestigious Clark Lectures at Trinity College, Cambridge, the first series of which had been given by her father, Sir Leslie Stephen, back in 1883. She was the first woman to be invited to do so. But Leonard not only did not encourage her to take advantage of this opportunity, he did everything he could to prevent her, to the point of giving her false information. We should ask ourselves why he failed her.

Virginia enjoyed speaking in public which she did clearly and without hesitation. At this time she was not engaged in writing a novel; and the ten thousandth copy of *The Waves* had just been sold, exceeding in popularity all her previous novels. In short, she was at the peak of her career and the timing could not have been better for her to deliver the Clark Lectures. She writes in her diary: 'This, I suppose, is the first time a woman has been asked; & so it is a great honour – think of me, the uneducated child reading books in my room at 22 H.P.G. [Hyde Park Gate] – now advanced to this glory.' [8] Yet she declines the invitation:

"because how could I write 6 lectures, to be delivered in full term, without giving up a year to criticism; without becoming a functionary; without sealing my lips when it comes to tilting at Universities; without putting off my Knock at the Door [later *Three Guineas*]; without perhaps shelving another novel. But I am rather inclined to smile... as I sit down dutifully to correct an article for the Common Reader. Yes; all that reading, I say, has borne this odd fruit. And I am pleased; & still more pleased that I wont do it; & I like to think that father would have blushed with pleasure could I have told him 30 years ago, that his daughter – my poor little Ginny – was to be asked to succeed him: the sort of compliment he would have liked."

A few days later, she had second thoughts:

"I am rather upset because the devil whispered, all of a sudden, that I have six lectures written in Phases of Fiction; & could furbish them up & deliver the Clark lectures, & win the esteem of my sex, with a few weeks work. True, *L. says since the middle 4 were published in America I could not do this without complete rewriting & I ought therefore to dismiss the whole thing*. Yet, such is the perversity of my mind, I can now think of nothing else; my mind is swarming with ideas for lectures; things I can only say in lectures; & my refusal seems lazy & cowardly. Yet two days ago I was repugnant to the thought: longed only for freedom in which to write a tap at the door; & was convinced that I should be a time serving pot hunter if I accepted... *Moreover, L. is definitely against it*. But then Nessa and Alice Ritchie were instinctively in favour." [9]

Virginia – in my view regrettably – did not listen either to her sister or to Alice Ritchie, a novelist working as a traveller for the Hogarth Press, elder sister of Trekkie Parsons. Their instinct was correct. She could have based her lectures on the incomplete 'Phases of Fiction', a later title for her Women and Fiction essays. The work necessary for her to have delivered these lectures would thus have been minimal. An editorial note to this Diary entry admits that Leonard's argument was 'misleading'. His motives for using a false argument to persuade Virginia not to give the Clark Lectures must surely have originated in a complex of very strong prejudices, none of which he would admit to. Trinity College, Cambridge, was 'his' college, 'his' territory, where he had dreamt such dreams of changing the world with Lytton – and now Lytton was dead, and his own book was a failure, while Virginia was succeeding to the extent that his control over her could well be in jeopardy. His wife Virginia, who everybody knew was 'mad', surely those eminent professors did not want to take what she was saying seriously? After all, he had never done so. If Virginia gave those lectures she would be known for ever afterwards as Sir Leslie Stephen's daughter, one of the luminaries in the literary world, rather than his wife. Weren't he and she in conspiracy against the world as they watched it going downhill? It was simply too much for Leonard. He, who had failed to move the electors of those inferior 'other universities' to send him to Parliament; who had dreamt of being the great orator, the modern Pericles, and found that no-one took any notice of him – how terrible if Virginia succeeded in this, too, where he had failed! Besides (hidden under all these thoughts lay another) how that buffoon Ethel Smyth would crow! And Vita Sackville-West! Those hangers-on to the aristocracy he so hated and despised! Those snobs! Why, he would be held responsible for letting loose a flood tide of successful women who were not merely 'decorative and ancillary' but who would spearhead a changed world in which men could no longer assume superiority!

Leonard, in general terms, was in favour of women having the vote. But in practice his world was in all important respects a man's world. It was one thing to encourage his wife to write fiction and occasional essays, printed by their own Press – self-published; it was quite another to permit her to speak on English Literature at Trinity College, to have her lectures circulated among the official papers and used as a research document by generations of undergraduates; maybe published by the Cambridge University Press as though she was an authority, a professor, when she hadn't even been to school! That would be just another proof that barbarism was overwhelming civilisation and must at all costs be prevented.

Whatever his rationalisatons, none of which were allowed a place in his autobiography (but one senses their omission), his attitude was no doubt fuelled by jealousy and a determination to protect his sacred preserve of Trinity College, Cambridge, from invasion by Virginia. She should have delivered those lectures. I date the weakening of her influence on her contemporaries and the increasing difficulties she had with writing her future creative work, from this refusal. H.G. Wells ignored the destructive role that even apparently well-meaning men play, to ensure women do not have a major influence in the world.

Having successfully reinforced the bars of Virginia's cage and provided it with an impenetrable glass ceiling, Leonard set about writing political tracts with renewed zeal, and embarked on Volume II of *After the Deluge,* where he concentrated on regretting that the French and Russian revolutions had not spread to Britain.

The following month, the Woolfs again visited Ham Spray. Virginia spent some time alone with Carrington; she evidently accepted that the despairing woman would commit suicide. The following day Carrington shot herself in the thigh, dying slowly. The coroner said her death was an accident, so there was no inquest. Virginia and Leonard indulged in another bout of 'mausoleum' talks:

"And we discuss suicide; & I feel, as always, ghosts <dwindling> changing. Lytton's affected by this act. I sometimes dislike him for it. He absorbed her, made her kill herself. Then the romantic completeness which affects Mary [Hutchinson] 'a beautiful gesture – her life & her death'. Nonsense says Leonard: it was histrionic: the real thing is that we shall never see Lytton again. This is unreal. So we discuss suicide. and the ghosts as I say, change so oddly in my mind; like people who live, and are changed by what one hears of them." [10]

To Leonard, Carrington's suicide was merely 'histrionic'; but Virginia felt critical of Lytton for having absorbed Carrington to the extent that she couldn't live without him. This encapsulates one of the important differences between Virginia and Leonard: whereas Virginia considers Lytton's death and Carrington's suicide from the point of view of Carrington, Leonard saw nothing of Carrington from her point of view. For him, Lytton was the only one who mattered, despite the fact that he had refused to have anything to do with him for eight years. Carrington's spectacular suicide had upstaged Lytton's memory and he resented it.

The death of Lytton marked the end of the 'Trinity of Trinity'. Sydney Saxon-Turner, the third member of that Cambridge alliance, had become a pillar of the Foreign Office who wore suits. On the night of Carrington's death Leonard told Virginia: 'Things have gone wrong somehow.' [11] Now Leonard was left on his own to carry the torch. But this was not a role that he ever succeeded in playing. For the first time he must have wondered if the vision he had shared with Lytton in the early years of the century would reach fulfillment. What he never did was question its validity. He set himself to struggle against 'barbarism' with even more desperation, and showed increasing irritation and pettiness both with the under-paid and over-worked Hogarth Press staff, and at home. On a daily basis he must have been a disturbing and uncomfortable companion for Virginia who was at this time thinking intensely about men in relation to the book that was to be *Three Guineas*. She wrote:

"the male virtues are never for themselves, but to be paid for. This introduces another element into their psychology – to be paid for: what will pay. This can be sublimated but the alloy remains. (I'm thinking of the book again.)" [12]

An even more sinister question underlies Virginia's thought: Who will pay? She is reluctantly becoming aware of the heavy price she is having to pay for living with Leonard, despite her efforts at sublimation, and the increasingly damaging burden of alloy that she is being forced to carry.

In April the Woolfs took a successful holiday in Greece with Roger Fry and his sister Margery, who complained that the Woolfs spent three hours a day eating. Virginia enjoyed sight-seeing with Roger who seems to have been the life and soul of the party. After they had survived the cold and rain that so often accompanied them on these expeditions, the magic took over for Virginia and she once again imagined a different life:

"London is not enough, nor Sussex either. One wants to be sunbaked, & taken back to these loquacious friendly people, simply to live, to talk, not to read or write. And then I looked up & saw the mountains across the bay, knife shaped, coloured, & the sea, brimming smooth; & felt as if a knife had scraped some encrusted organ in me... Now there are sympathies between people & place, as between human beings. And I could love Greece as an old woman, so I think, as I once loved Cornwall, as a child. For this reason then, that we shall come back, & because L. wants to go to dinner, & I think there is a hair in my pen, I doubt that I shall make any more ceremony about coming to an end – 'Now get ready & don't talk so much – ' I must end." [13]

Virginia is summarily silenced by Leonard: 'Now get ready & don't talk so much', as she must often have been. They did not go back to Greece. If only Virginia could have had an old age of any sort, let alone the one she envisages here that would have complemented the long summer holidays she spent as a child with her family in Cornwall.

On their return they were confronted by an upset John Lehmann at the Hogarth Press, whom even Vanessa supported 'against the irascible Leonard & the hard work & the underpay.' [14] John Lehmann was a friend of Vanessa's elder son Julian and had recently come down from Cambridge; he was the latest in a long line not only of trainee managers but of authors who found trying to work with Leonard unendurable. Lehmann's experiences with the Woolfs are amusingly recounted in *Thrown to the Woolves* and in his short book *Virginia Woolf*, in which he describes the situation:

"it has to be admitted that in too many cases [the Hogarth Press] failed to keep its authors, the cause of which appears to have been more than anything else a flaw in Leonard's temperament. He was determined – one can only call it that – to keep the Press going on a shoe-string. The basement of 52 Tavistock Square, where the Press conducted its activities, was in a state of dilapidation. The windows did not open properly, the toilet was inadequately furnished, the heating was primitive. It was always understaffed, and Leonard could never bring himself to employ a professional traveller. The production was often skimped and depressingly utility." [15]

John Lehmann goes on to say that whereas this did not matter for Virginia's books, 'when her name was on everyone's lips', it did matter for young authors at the start of their writing careers. He continues:

"These inadequacies were made worse by the depressing tale of the young men Leonard engaged as managers. One after another they passed through the work-room at Hogarth House or the basement at Tavistock Square, eager to learn the mysteries of publishing and excited to be working with a firm of such high literary reputation; one after another they left, all ardour spent, after a few years or even a few months... The trouble was... that with each of these young men Leonard, after a honeymoon period of a few weeks when he would induct them into their manifold obligations with fatherly patience and humour, would become increasingly impatient, intolerant of little mistakes, and testy – often hysterically angry – when things were not going quite to his liking; and when he was testy he could be extremely rude. The result was that each attempt to lift the burden on to a young man's shoulders ended in more time wasted, mainly in altercation and nerves frayed all round." [16]

According to Lehmann, Virginia would try now and then 'to lower the temperature with a little gesture of appeasement', but: 'behind the scenes she was almost always on Leonard's side, perhaps wanting a quiet life above all, perhaps truly believing in his impeccable wisdom.' [17] Perhaps Virginia herself never quite made up her mind between wanting a quiet life at all costs and believing in Leonard's 'impeccable wisdom'. In her diary she would criticise the victims of Leonard's rage, hence justifying it, as she did when John Lehmann walked out despite having just signed an agreement; to which Leonard reacted with injured innocence and Virginia supported him:

"That egotistical young man with all his jealousies & vanities & ambitions, his weakness & changeableness is no loss... I suppose the severity with wh. L. was speaking with him on Friday when I came in to say Teas ready upset his trembling apple cart... On the whole though what a mercy. Now I can roam about the basement unperturbed. And, coming from him, with this crashing folly, one can take the line of least resistance – needn't attempt the amicable go between – needn't ask him to dinner." [18]

Although Leonard did not write to John he did write from Monk's House to his sister, Rosamond Lehmann:

"Dear Rosamond,

I suppose you know that John has left us. I had seen him on the Friday and he had said nothing... His behaviour seemed to me to be so either outrageous or childish that I decided to have nothing more to do with him and simply did not reply... It all seems to me very strange, but I hope he is all right. Yours sincerely Leonard Woolf" [19]

Given the evidence of the quarrel, recorded by Virginia, in which John complained about the hard work and underpay and Leonard responded by being 'irascible', this is a remarkably frigid letter from Leonard in its refusal even to consider that he himself might have had something to do with Lehmann's leaving. John Lehmann was the man who seven years later took over Virginia's half-share of the Press.

One can now understand why Virginia did not receive any letters from Leonard when she went to France with Vita Sackville-West in 1928, after the 'small and sudden row' they had on her departure. At that time, Virginia had called him a prig. But not now, in 1932. The quality of her day-to-day living was being eroded by Leonard's increasingly petty attitudes. However, she also recorded her delight when she bought him the most expensive and impressive car they ever had, a large grey and green Lanchester limousine:

"I dont think we've ever been so happy, what with one thing & another. And so intimate, & so completely entire, I mean L. & I. If it could only last like this another 50 years – life like this is wholly satisfactory, to me anyhow." [20]

Virginia's wealth meant that Monks House also gained some more amenities: the oil lamps had been replaced by electricity and there was a refrigerator. But these moments of delight in what Virginia was able to provide were brief interludes among the frequent storms and upsets that continued to surround Leonard. She finished *Flush*; then said she regretted writing it, at one stage worrying that the entire book had been a waste of time. This fear-reaction on her part, before showing Leonard her manuscripts, began with *The Waves* and becomes ever more intense and damaging to her in the following years, as we shall see. *Flush* is a delightful book, the story of the poet Elizabeth Barrett Browning seen from her spaniel's point of view. It was deservedly popular and brought considerable financial rewards; however, Leonard objected to her wasting her time writing the story of a dog instead of engaging in political polemics, as he demanded; and *Flush* is not included in the authorised edition of her novels.

From now on, all of Virginia's creative writing was done against Leonard's indifference or even hostility, as he attempted to prove that neither her writing nor her point of view were relevant, and that earning money didn't matter in comparison to trying to save the world. This wearing process severely reduced the pleasure she felt in her writing, since her finely tuned and balanced brain worked best when she was relaxed and happy.

An event occurred in July 1933, concerning the Woolfs' grand new motor-car. Both Virginia and Leonard refer to it; the difference of interpretation between their two accounts is portentously revealing. Leonard had driven Bella, his elder sister and favourite sibling, for a visit to their London home in Tavistock Square. This is Virginia's account:

"Bella arrived & knocked her head upon the window of the car. She cut her nose & was dazed. And then I was in 'one of my states' – how violent how acute & walked in Regent's Park in black misery & had to summon my cohorts in the old way to see me through, which they have done more or less. A note made to testify to my own ups & downs; many of which go unrecorded though they are less violent I think than they used to be. But how familiar it was – stamping along the road, with gloom & pain constricting my heart; & the desire for death in the old way all for two, I daresay careless words." [21]

My reading of this episode is that it was not Bella's injury that precipitated one of Virginia's 'states'; it was surely the 'two, I daresay careless words' that brought on her 'black misery'. We don't know, but can guess, who spoke those words. Not Bella, surely; nor of course Virginia. They must have been said by Leonard who had just driven his favourite sister to visit them in their precious Lanchester, at a moment when he was no doubt feeling some sense of triumph at the wonder of the vehicle. In the shock of seeing Bella suddenly injured, he must have blamed Virginia for the accident, using the sort of language that John Lehmann described as 'extremely rude'; and it was this remark that sent Virginia into one of her 'states', 'with gloom & pain constricting my heart, & the desire for death in the old way'. What 'desire for death in the old way'? We perhaps go back to the danger periods of their marriage, 1913 and 1915. And we also recall her journey through a storm to meet Leonard at Lewes, when he caught the last train and was angry at seeing her there, instead of reassuring. The 'two I daresay careless words' of July 1933 must have been shattering to make Virginia regress into a desire for death; while Leonard would have realised that he could precipitate that dangerous state in her at any time.

Such is my reconstruction of the episode with Bella being injured by the car at the start of her visit. What does Leonard make of it? He quotes part of this passage from Virginia's diary in his autobiography – but not the whole of it and he turns it into something completely different. He does not mention either Bella or the car at all. The argument he is putting forward in this context is revealing. Leonard writes about Virginia:

"The implacable intensity of concentration upon her writing and her almost pathological fear of the exposure of publication combined to produce the exhaustion and despair which assailed her in the interval between finishing a book and publishing it. All the books, from *Jacob's Room* to *The Years*, induced one of these dangerous crises." [22]

He then quotes her negative comments about *Flush* which are all too understandable given his hostility to it, and from a similar passage after publication of *The Waves*: 'I have come up here trembling under the sense of complete failure... I mean L. accuses me of sensibility verging on insanity'. Leonard finally makes what he intends to be the clinching argument:

"How near these strains from writing and publishing brought her at any moment to breakdown and suicide is shown frequently in her diary. For instance, early in July 1933 the worry over revising *Flush* and her excitement over beginning to write *The Years* brought on a headache, and she recorded on July 10: 'And then I was in "one of my states" – how violent, how acute – and walked in Regents Park in black misery and had to summon my cohorts in the old way to see me through, which they have done more or less. A note made to testify to my own ups and downs: many of which go unrecorded though they are less violent I think than they used to be. But how familiar it was – stamping along the road, with gloom and pain constricting my heart: and the desire for death, in the old way, all for two I daresay careless words.' "

We can see that Leonard has entirely omitted the origin of her 'state' on 10 July, 1933 – that is, the scene with Bella injuring herself on their car – and he actually misuses Virginia's words to support what is in any case an extremely questionable (I consider it false) correlation between Virginia's breakdowns or near-breakdowns and her writing. I am shocked by his omission of the *cause* of the 'state' she got into on 10 July. He must surely have known that the phrase including the 'two I daresay careless words' makes no sense in his account, yet these were obviously crucial in precipitating her into the violent mood – which she herself managed to overcome by walking off on her own and summoning her 'cohorts in the old way'. Since he must have been the person who spoke those words, his misuse of the episode is all the more amazing. Managing to cope with his sudden rage was a feat of strength on her part. His omission of all mention of Bella's injury must have been because to have included it would have made Virginia's reaction entirely understandable in circumstances that had nothing whatsoever to do with her writing; whereas he wanted to prove that she was continually on the verge of 'madness' as a result of her creative work. This example shows how very careful one has to be when reading Leonard's autobiography.

His frequent tantrums with the trainee managers at the Hogarth Press, as recorded by John Lehmann, when he became 'increasingly impatient, intolerant of little mistakes, and testy – indeed often hysterically angry – when things were not going quite to his liking', was similar to this incident with the car, only this time Virginia was the victim of his fury. Misusing this episode in his account, Leonard expected the readers of his autobiography to sympathise with him. He wanted it to be seen that his carefully fostered image of her mental instability verging on insanity had nothing to do with him, except that it was the cross he had to bear. Thus he presented an image of himself as having to put up with the difficulty of living with the 'mad' Virginia with almost saintly patience, while he (it was to be assumed) remained warm, caring and understanding. In actuality, Virginia could only survive by making self-damaging attempts to sublimate his anger so that she could concentrate on her writing, and appease him with costly presents bought with the money she earned. It was essential for her to try and keep their 'perfect globe of happiness' intact, but the fragility of this and the ease with which it was smashed by Leonard kept increasing with every year. If he had learnt to treat everyone as though they had the sensibility of Virginia, his own books would have been greatly improved and her life would have been worth living. However, this was far too much to ask. As he frequently said with some pride, he never changed. His negativity often made her ill:

"We have steadied the old ship & sail through blue days again. L. is having the new pond made, the old one re-grouted, & is going to pave the front garden. Flush, I think with some pleasure, has made these extravagances possible. We should net 2,000 pounds from that dogged and dreary grind. What will people say of that little book I wonder, without great anxiety... And I have had 2 blessed days of silence, & we walked on the marsh today, & saw a drowned sheep, & were flurried by our 3 dogs... & feel comfortably cool & obscure & anonymous... I read & read... But why does my hand shake? Why cant I write clearly?" [23]

In March 1934, Virginia had to cope with a change of servants. She asserted herself by making an evidently overdue effort to get rid of their live-in cook Nelly Boxall. Nelly is among the names of women linked sexually with Leonard. He was supposed to have slept with her on the occasions when Virginia remained at Rodmell and he stayed in London:

"I cannot describe how the Nelly situation weighs on my spirits. I am determined not to discuss it with L. either. She pressed me this morning. You show no confidence in me; you dont treat me like a maid... The great scene with Nelly is now over, & of course much less violently than I supposed... I suppose some further lamentation & argument, with L. perhaps is inevitable. But Lord what a relief now!... & am now back here with Nelly gone... & Mabel declared to be a treasure, coming to see me tomorrow." [24]

After six weeks of mental sterility and misery, when she couldn't write, Virginia at last succeeded in getting rid of Nelly: '& there we left her in the kitchen, grasping a wet cloth; 'No, I really couldn't, Sir', she said, when L. held out his hand. How dazed & free & quiet I felt driving down to Lewes!' [25]

Nelly was replaced by Mabel Haskins, who had worked for Margery Fry. Mabel was a quiet, well-trained live-in cook, 'a treasure', who could have been the rock that saved Virginia during the last winter of her life, if Leonard had not taken a seemingly irrational dislike to her. Most of the time she lived and worked in the Woolfs' London flat, until the war took them all to live in Rodmell.

A few months later Louise Everest came to Monk's House as a part time maid-of-all-work. Virginia first described Louise as: 'a merry little brown eyed mongrel who came running to meet us in the road'. [26] Her employment in 1934 was 'a leap in the dark rather', according to Virginia. Louise had had her first child when she was fourteen, was married and lived in one of the two nearby cottages that were bought with Virginia's money and owned by Leonard since 1929. She remained right through World War Two and Virginia's death, and continued with Leonard and Trekkie until his death in 1969.

From the beginning of this new era of servants Mabel was more directly Virginia's concern and help, while Leonard became interested in Louise. Mabel took her job seriously; she was a professional. 'Steady silent unselfish Mabel' worked tirelessly in the kitchen and took lessons in French cooking in an attempt to please Leonard, to whom food was always of importance. But whereas Virginia appreciated her capability since it enabled her to get on with her work in the atmosphere of tranquility she needed, Leonard frequently vented his appalling temper on this unoffending servant. Mabel silently received every type of snub and humiliation from him, her only reaction being to break something occasionally. Taking her tone from Leonard, Virginia was soon calling her 'The Cow' and wondering if she would have to be dismissed. She is immortalised in *Between the Acts* as the Queen of the Age of Reason. I see Mabel Haskins as no less than the goddess, her quietly aware presence during these troubled years in the Woolf household revealing the truth.

In May, the Woolfs went to Ireland for their annual holiday, shipping their Lanchester over and driving in style – Virginia felt their car to be too impressive for the impoverished land and people. They took their spaniel, Pinka and stayed with the shy, stammering Elizabeth Bowen. Elizabeth's admiration for Virginia amounted almost to idolatry.

Whilst the Woolfs were in Ireland, George Duckworth died. He left 100 pounds each to Vanessa and Virginia. Crossing back to England they first drove to Worcester and saw Dr Jonathan Swifts's epitaph 'He lies where furious rage can rend his heart no more'. Then the Woolfs visited Stratford upon Avon, Shakespeare's place of birth and death:

"He is serenely absent-present; both at once; radiating round one; yes; in the flowers, in the old hall, in the garden; but never to be pinned down... he seemed to be all air & sun smiling serenely; and yet down there one foot from me lay the little bones that had spread over the world this vast illumination." [27]

On their return, Virginia fell ill with influenza and greatly benefited from Mabel's presence: 'we are serene, matter of fact, oh what a relief!' Slowly she pulled her head 'out of the bog' and 'Now self confidence, conceit, the blessed illusion by which we live begin to return'. She was trying to write one of several drafts of *The Years*, but had a relapse and was not to be well again until mid June. 'Our convention is to be very cheerful & objective'. The gathering storm in Germany enters Virginia's diary with Hitler's decision to crush the Brown Shirts, when some 1200 people were killed without trial. Osbert Sitwell rang up:

" 'And can't anything be done about this monstrous affair in Germany?' 'One of the few public acts' I said 'that makes one miserable'... And for the first time I read articles with rage, to find him called a real leader." [28]

In July, Leonard acquired a marmoset. Mitz was a frail, miserable little creature; he kept her for the rest of her life, she eventually died in the cold winter of 1938 having lived longer than any of her kind at the London Zoo. From this time on Mitz became his constant companion, sitting inside his jacket or on his shoulder. But there was a down side, she leaked on everyone and everything, and the doors had to be kept shut in case she escaped into the garden of Monk's House, when she climbed a tree and had to be tempted down with bananas. Woe betide Virginia if she left the door open, the lash of Leonard's temper flared. She wrote to Vanessa:

"I left the door open and Mitz escaped, and L. said Thats the last we shall ever see of her – not a bit of it – there she was on the kitchen table, nibbling a lettuce – Then, as I say, we recovered." [29]

Virginia was lucky on that occasion; but Mitz must have been another excuse for Leonard's bad temper.

A further change in the household was the introduction of bowls, a game the Woolfs began playing on their uneven lawn; the competition between them became obsessive. Leonard usually succeeded in beating Virginia. The box with their battered set of wooden balls is still by the garden door at Monk's House. (This addiction to a game is part of what it was like to live in Britain during the nineteen thirties, before the arrival of television. My memories of playing one active game after another as they went in and out of fashion, are vivid. My father, an astronomer, told stories about Ethel Smyth and her friend Elizabeth Williamson who was interested in astronomy; so I grew up on the edge of Virginia's circle of friends. My unorthodox childhood was not so very different from that of the Bloomsbury Group children.)

Sydney Saxon-Turner, the other remaining member of the 'Trinity of Trinity', stayed at Monk's House and we get a glimpse of Leonard's idealisation of the Periclean Age, seen through Virginia's eyes: 'We take up a conversation broken these 10 years in our natural voices. What about Pericles? & so on.' [30] Virginia enjoyed Saxon's company: 'I have spent an hour or so talking with him about Shakespeare, books in general, then people: and there is some virtue in these old friends: I mean conversationally; they enrich.' [31] Evidently Saxon had grown out of the straight-jacket of Cambridge intellectualism and was able to discuss different topics with Virginia to their mutual enjoyment. Whereas Leonard remained mortally afflicted by his sense of destiny.

Virginia's only chance of survival lay in perpetual writing and a flexible approach to life. This she used to good effect in 1934, when her work was attacked by Wyndham Lewis. He wrote loftily: 'while I am ready to agree that the intrinsic literary importance of Mrs Woolf may be exaggerated by her friends, I cannot agree that as a literary landmark – a sort of party-lighthouse – she has not a very real significance.' [32] His shaft went home and prevented her writing, then she rallies: 'I think my revelation 2 years ago stands me in sublime stead. to adventure & discover, & allow no rigid poses: to be supple & naked to the truth... I've no doubt I am prudish & peeping, well then live more boldly. But for God's sake don't bend my writing one way or the other. Not that one can. And there is the odd pleasure too of being abused: & the feeling of being dismissed into obscurity is also pleasant & salutary.'

But Virginia was vulnerable. She looked up past diaries: 'a reason for keeping them'; and 'found the same misery after Waves. After Lighthouse I was I remember nearer suicide, seriously, than since 1913. It is after all natural. I've been galloping now for 3 months... after the first divine relief, of course some terrible blankness must spread. There's nothing left of the people, of the ideas, of the strain, of the whole life in short that has been racing around in my brain: not only the brain; it has seized hold of my leisure: think how I used to sit still on the same railway lines: running on my book."

Leonard does not quote this passage in his account, perhaps because instead of showing her as 'mad', she is simply recording a natural reaction, to feel the loss of one's writing world between books. The brain does need time to recover. And this time she coped despite Wyndham Lewis sniping at her in print and the recent death of Roger Fry which was 'worse than Lytton's'.

During the nineteen thirties Leonard became increasingly impatient to reach the heights he imagined himself capable of attaining. Alone in his study, he felt he was at the centre of a magnetic aura which he described in his autobiography:

"All occupations or professions, like individuals, create around themselves a kind of magnetic field. To me myself everything within and without myself acquires a curious and strong quality or aura of me myself – my pains and pleasure, my typewriter and my big toe, my memories and the view which I am now looking at from my window, the people I love and the people I hate, all these, when they enter the magnetic field which my ego and egocentricity have developed about me, acquire a meaning, a value peculiar to myself. And everyone else walks through life, materially and spiritually, enveloped in a similar magnetic field of his own personality which gives to everything and everyone entering the field a magnetised reflection of his ego, a meaning and value which he alone in the world feels and understands...

Every editor – certainly every good editor – believes, not only that he is continually pronouncing judgement about the most important questions but that he and his paper have a powerful influence upon public opinion with regard to those questions. Thus a magnetic field of highly charged importance, influence, and power is created around every newspaper, and everyone connected with it is subjected to its effect. I know from experience that the moment I sat down in the editor's chair in the *New Statesman* office, though I am by nature sceptical, an unusual sense of importance, a tinge of *folie de grandeur*, enveloped me. It emanated from the magnetic field of the *New Statesman* into which I had suddenly and importantly entered. Instinctively I was feeling that everything I was going to do or say during the next week was of importance. I was the (temporary) wielder of influence and power. I used to feel the same thing in the *Nation* office when I was Literary Editor there, and even as editor of the *Political Quarterly*." [33]

It is evident that Virginia did not write encased in a self-protective magnetic aura. She relied on her own sense of excitement as she wrote, to be reflected in the 'echo' from her friends and a positive response from the outside world leading to increased sales of her books. We can therefore see that there was a very big contrast in the way the Woolfs worked and in their expectations from the outside world. Leonard's sense of his magnetic aura was all-important to him. He had never been a reliable 'echo' for Virginia since he held strong and eccentric views. This did not matter so much when she received a satisfying response from others and he was busy with his book; but when he tried to reach a dominant position, to be 'up' on their see-saw, he could do her considerable damage. Once he had decided that his writing was more important than hers, the magnetic aura in which he felt himself to be wrapped in his study at Monk's House was reinforced; while Virginia, outside at the other end of the garden in her Lodge by the churchyard wall, had to cope not only with barking dogs, a tolling bell and disturbance from villagers, but also with his negative, psychic weight before getting on with her work. Virginia escaped into her own inner world, into the other truth, finding a language with which to express herself that has kept its immediacy of communication – whereas the political jargon of the nineteen thirties, whether of left or right, is now almost unreadable. She accepted Leonard's right to express his strongly held beliefs, writing to Ethel Smyth in 1936:

"what would L's writing be without his fanaticism? It works itself into the fibre, and one cant exclude it, isolate it, or criticise it. It becomes part and parcel of the whole." [34]

But the strain on her was considerable. He was for ever attempting to inspire people with his 'fanatical' vision. He targeted Louise Everest, their maid-of-all-work. Despite the weather, in March 1935 Leonard insisted on driving from London to Monk's House:

"It was the bitterest Sunday for 22 years: we went down [to Rodmell] (there was a little skirmish between us, for when I saw the snow falling I said, what about putting it off? At this L. was I thought unduly annoyed; so that we went − but Lord what a quarrel most old married couples would have made of it: & it turned to a candid joke before we were half angry.)... No, on the whole, save for a desire to break L. of his 'habits', I am content to let things alone." [35]

My reading of this is that Louise Everest was the attraction for Leonard; she was the current object of his 'habits', and he insisted on going to Monk's House at all costs. Like Gwen to his Harry in his novel *The Wise Virgins*, Louise had to be 'awakened' by the intense Jew with his crusading political ideas. Louise was a shrewd country girl, cheerful, with plenty of vitality and no intellectual pretensions. In Leonard's autobiography he revealingly gives her the significance of a woman in classical Greece:

"Her native intelligence is extraordinary and she has that rare impersonal curiosity which the Greeks recognised as the basis of philosophy and wisdom... though she is shrewd, critical, and sceptical, I have never heard a complaint from her, and she is, I think, the only person whom I have ever known to be uniformly cheerful and with reason for her cheerfulness." [36]

Whether these 'habits' of Leonard's involved a sexual component, as they did with Gwen in his novel, or whether they were confined to political zeal on his part, is anyone's guess. If Virginia's account of their conversation on the drive down to Rodmell bears a more serious meaning, then her capacity for tolerance has been greatly underestimated. Her decision to 'let things alone', meant that for the sake of peace she would have to accept the undermining of her position as mistress of Monk's House. In this light her equivocal attitude to living in the village and her frequently repeated desire to move to an isolated house in the middle of the countryside, make a great deal of sense.

Throughout the mid-1930's Virginia was engaged in a desperate struggle to write *The Years*, and for the sake of the peace she needed she would have accepted compromises. Neither Mabel nor Louise was dismissed but it was an uneasy household.

Leonard assumed the role of political expert which led to heated arguments with other members of the Bloomsbury Group; one such quarrel occurred at this time, reported by Virginia. They were having dinner at the house of Jack and Mary Hutchinson:

"So to politics & then, what with Jack [Hutchinson's] cross examination, & Tom [T.S. Eliot]'s intentness, & Desmond [MacCarthy] burbling general goodwill & human love, & Leonard's specialised convictions, the argument blazed: how the Labour party wd come in: what it would do. But how can you make any such ridiculous claim Jack boomed. What is it going to do about unemployment, about agriculture? All these questions were put from the view of here & now, capable business men; L. ideal by comparison. How 10 sensible men 'round a table', one of his phrases, could so manipulate the supply of locomotives & wheat that one country supplemented another. Oh if we were all men of good will, if we were all ready to be nice about it – Then Desmond as usual praised moderation, tact... how civilisation runs slowly in a great wide stream, & you must slowly facilitate its course, but by no means introduce whirlpools, cut precipices & so on... They heckled L. between them, & when the argument began to put its tail in its mouth, Mary asked if I would like to withdraw." [37]

As Leonard agonised over the rise to power of Nazism in Germany, he attempted to boycott a German publisher with whom he had signed an agreement:

"The more I think about the present situation in Germany, the more barbarous does the behaviour of the Government seem to me, and I feel that I do not want to have any personal or business relations with those who support or tolerate it." [38]

However, he went ahead with the agreement. Remarkably, he sent that same German publisher the manuscript of his political tract *Quack, Quack!* and professed surprise when they immediately rejected it. Spater & Parsons describes *Quack, Quack!*, published in 1935, as: 'a bitter attack on irrationalism in politics as exemplified by Nazi Germany and Fascist Italy, and in philosophy as revealed in the writings of Spengler, Keyserling, Radhakrishnan and Bergson.' [39] To name a few. Leonard's next target was the entire publishing business, in a letter to Herbert Read dated 5 February 1935:

"If I had not been a socialist before, publishing would have made me one. From the serious author's point of view, the trade is corrupted from top to bottom... If you want to see the hopeless inefficiency and futility of the capitalist system, become a publisher." [40]

Thus he vented his anger against both publishing and capitalism, perhaps goaded by the loss of several important authors to the Hogarth Press. T.S. Eliot had removed himself in 1928 and founded what has become the famous publishing house of Faber & Faber. When Cecil Day Lewis went in 1935, the whole question of the future of the Press was discussed by the Woolfs: 'once again, once again', said Virginia, who wanted to be free to travel abroad and to write. However, since the Press was Leonard's 'mistress' – more accurately, his power base – nothing would have made him give it up. And it did enable them to publish their books without having to cope with the 'corrupt' publishing establishment. They kept it on.

The sheer difficulty of writing *The Years* almost destroyed Virginia. This was partly because she wanted to approach her material using each side of her brain in alternate sections, to interleaf chapters written first by the right side of her brain – the stories – and then by the left brain – the essays. She recast and rewrote this long manuscript several times. It eventually became two books, the essay portions changing to become *Three Guineas*. There were occasions when exhaustion, a 'galloping' heart and depression supervened.

In May 1935, Leonard decided to go and see the situation in Germany at first hand. Harold Nicolson told him that, as a Jew, he might be in some danger and warned him particularly against getting involved in any Nazi processions. So Leonard went armed with an impressive letter from Prince Bismarck, Counsellor at the German Embassy, which called upon 'all German officials to show to the distinguished Englishman, Leonard Woolf, and his distinguished wife, Virginia Woolf, every courtesy and render them any assistance which they might require'. However, Leonard found this letter to be unnecessary. His spaniel Pinka was left at home but his true ambassador was Mitz, the marmoset, who rode on his shoulder while he drove the Lanchester, with Virginia sitting silent in the passenger seat. Wherever they went crowds came out to gather round the car and worship Mitz. They travelled through Holland to Germany, to Italy and then returned through France. In Leonard's account their car, bought with Virginia's money, is 'his':

"At that time I had a Lanchester 18 car with a Tickford hood so that, by winding the hood back, one could convert it from a closed-in saloon to a completely open car." [41]

Driving from Holland into Germany, Leonard once again expresses his preoccupation with his over-simplified contrast of opposites, of white and black, between 'civilisation' and 'barbarism': 'I felt with some disquiet that I had passed in a few yards from civilization to savagery.' When they reached Bonn they found themselves in the middle of crowds of people waiting for Göring who was to attend a reception, the very situation he had been warned to avoid: 'Here we were closely penned in by what, looking down the road ahead, seemed to be an unending procession of enthusiastic Nazis. But we soon found that there was no need for us to worry. It was a very warm day and I was driving with the car open; on my shoulder sat Mitz. I had to drive at about 15 miles an hour. When they saw Mitz, the crowd shrieked with delight. Mile after mile I drove between the two lines of corybantic Germans, and the whole way they shouted 'Heil Hitler! Heil Hitler! to Mitz and gave her (and secondarily Virginia and me) the Hitler salute with outstretched arm.' Leonard's use of the word 'coribantic' (corybant, a priest of Cybele whose rites were accompanied with noisy music and wild dances) reinforces the image of 'savagery'; it also subscribes to the view that female-oriented religions are out-of-control and barbaric.

Thus managing to get away from the crowds and procession, the Woolfs arrived at a hotel where they met an unhappy waiter who blamed his wife for not having got out of Germany, and the Nazis for lack of custom, as Leonard recounts:

"Next day we left the manager, his wife, and the waiter in tears and drove... to Innsbruck, where on May 12 snow was falling. We did not enjoy this; there was something sinister and menacing in the Germany of 1935. There is a crude and savage silliness in the German tradition which, as one drove through the sunny Bavarian countryside, one felt beneath the surface and saw, above it, in the gigantic notices outside the villages informing us that Jews were not wanted." [42]

At the Austrian frontier, Leonard decided to see what effect Bismarck's letter would have:

"The effect was instantaneous and quite different from Mitz, the marmoset. The chief officer drew himself up, bowed, saluted, clicked his heels together, drew all the uniformed men up in line, and, as we drove away, they all saluted us."

Virginia's reaction to their drive through Germany is more detached and varied – dare one say, more 'sane':

"Insbruck

L. Says I may now tell the truth, but I have forgotten 2 days of truth, & my pen is weeping ink. Let me see. We went on from the old country house Inn, which ran their charges up high, & drove down the Rhine... An ugly pretentious country – operatic scenery. High, but insignificant hills, bristling with black & green fir trees, with correct towers & ruins... The dullest day of them all. But we got to... Heidelberg, which is – yes – a very distinguished University town, on the Neckar. The dons & their daughters were having a musical evening. I saw them tripping out to each others houses with pale blue Beethoven quartets under their arms... nice intelligent faces. Great rhododendrons blooming. Still hot & blue. And the river like sliding plate glass. And next day to Augsburg – a dull town but with a bath... The country steadily improves – becomes shaped & spaced." [43]

Of the two accounts, Leonard's is intensely egocentric as he takes everything personally; whereas Virginia records her impressions with a coolness and detachment which remains intact even when she writes about something very upsetting to her.

On their return they found that Pinka had just died. As the car approached Monk's House Percy, Leonard's gardener, was walking towards the orchard with the corpse. Leonard felt that the dog had pined in his absence and was grief-stricken at her loss. Then Mabel committed a 'terrible faux pas' by breaking their old gramophone: 'L. says "your" cook! Which annoys me [Mabel] must go, I suppose.' [44] Leonard evidently had a field day throwing his weight about, which finally goaded Virginia into analysing Leonard's negative attitude towards people in general and servants in particular:

"A curious & rather unpleasant scene with Mabel. She was in tears, because Mr Woolf never believes a word she says. And I think its true. L. is very hard on people, especially on the servant class. No sympathy with them; exacting; despotic. So I told him yesterday when he'd complained about the coffee. 'If I maynt even say when the coffee is bad &'. His extreme rigidity of mind surprises me; I mean in its relation to others: his severity: not to myself but then I get up & curse him. What does it come from? Not being a gentleman partly: uneasiness in the presence of the lower classes: always suspects them, is never genial with them... His desire, I suppose, to dominate. Love of power. And then he writes against it. All this I shall tell him again, for it doesnt matter, to me; in our relationship; & yet I hate people noticing it: Nessa; Dadie [George Rylands]; even Kingsley Martin – who all admire & respect him. An interesting study. It goes with great justice, in some ways; & simplicity too; & doing good things: but it is in private a very difficult characteristic. I must now get rid of Mabel, & find another. This row has precipitated it & given me a good excuse for sacking her: but I feel its unfair to her." [45]

Three days later Leonard was 'cheerful & very contrite in his way' and *Quack Quack!* was beginning to sell better. Together, the Woolfs went and bought a pedigree spaniel, Sally, costing 18 pounds, to replace Pinka. Sally 'clasps L.s breast, climbs onto his chair'. Once more, Virginia's money is spent in the attempt to keep Leonard happy, or at least less destructively unhappy. And Mabel stayed. Virginia needed her even though she occasionally broke things. But the difficulty of completing *The Years* was giving Virginia a debilitating sense of failure. And she was being pressured to write a biography of Roger Fry.

Virginia's survival depended on maintaining her own point of view and continuing to explore her creativity, to write true to her own spirit. But simply continuing on her own course became an act of rebellion against Leonard's increasingly fanatical attitude. This is particularly so as she continued to support the idea of aristocracy as against what he called his 'heretical socialism'. In July 1935 their difference of view emerges when Virginia's friend Susan Buchan invites her to stay: Susan is now Lady Tweedsmuir after her husband was appointed Governor General, and they are about to move to Canada:

"Well of course its extremely interesting having to deal with so many selves. Theres the one that enjoys external life – the mild fluent chatter of the Buchans? yes, I did enjoy it. I liked the simplicity the swiftness, the release, the expansion. And L. says 'They spend their money getting on – thats why theyre Governor Generals' & I think thats not true. But how queer to have so many selves – how bewildering!" [46]

This was the last occasion Virginia stayed on her own for a night with a friend. In December 1936, she read, at short notice, 'Am I a Snob?' to the Memoir Club, where members of the Bloomsbury Group continued to meet. What she said must have been anathema to Leonard. She admits to being a certain sort of snob. A coronet on a letter addressed to her gives her a thrill, so long as the coronet is old, and because:

"the aristocrat is freer, more natural, more eccentric than we are. Here I note that my snobbery is not of the intellectual kind... If you ask me would I rather meet Einstein or the Prince of Wales, I plump for the Prince of Wales without hesitation." [47]

She recounts the thrill of being invited to lunch by Lady Oxford, watched by Mabel Haskins: 'And I was pleased when on the day in question Mabel our dour cook, came to me, and said, "Lady Oxford has sent her car for you, ma'am." Obviously, she was impressed by me; I was impressed by myself. I rose in my own esteem because I rose in Mabel's'.

When she arrived, there was a large party to lunch. Afterwards: 'I found myself pacing along Faringdon Road talking aloud to myself, and seeing the butchers' shops and the trays of penny toys through an air that seemed made of gold dust and champagne.' Therefore, Virginia says, she is not only a coronet snob; but also a lit-up drawing-room snob; a social festivity snob. Then she tells the story of her relationship with a real snob – Lady Colefax – which shows the danger of snobbery all too clearly.

Virginia wanted to make this distinction between a drawing-room snob and a real snob to defend herself against Leonard's attacks on snobbery of all kinds; his attitude no doubt worried Virginia as she was constantly subjected to his arguments, but she had enormous courage and with great strength of mind refused to be intimidated by him, or to lose her own perspective. Nevertheless, he continued to erode her freedom in very practical ways; she was more and more confined by the restrictive world Leonard inhabited.

In November there was a General Election and Leonard busied himself driving Labour electors to the polls in the Lanchester. He insisted on Virginia going with him, sitting in the cold, damp car in atrocious weather. She allowed herself to be persuaded by him, despite having planned to accompany Ethel Smyth to Court where her friend won a libel case against a newspaper:

"Our election week end was not a wise move, personally. I was silly though. Why go to Patcham in pouring rain? Even if I didn't stay in London & hear Ethel's case, as I wished, it was foolish to have 2 1/2 hours traipsing in the violent wind & wet to Rodmell. A wild grey white sea, & so many stops all the time, as we passed it, to take up the workmen who are building at Peacehaven. So a headache next day; & this morning a throat. I am held up & damped down." [48]

Leonard was no doubt pleased that he had won a victory over Smyth by taking Virginia on this unnecessary trip. Virginia copes with this episode by philosophising about the possible four dimensions 'all to be produced; in human life; & that leads to a far richer grouping & proportion: I mean: I & the not I: & the outer & the inner – no I'm too tired to say: but I see it: & this will affect my book on Roger. Very exciting: to grope on like this. New combinations in psychology & body – rather like painting. This will be the next novel, after The Years."

At the beginning of the year 1936, after a winter stay at Monk's House that was cold, wet and so much of a failure that Virginia 'rather guiltily, begged not to stay here another week', Leonard told her that she had not earned enough to pay for her share of the house:

"& have to find 70 pounds out of my hoard. This is now reduced to 700 pounds, & I must fill it up. Amusing, in its way, to think of economy again. But it would be a strain to think seriously; & worse – a brutal interruption – had I to make money by journalism." [49]

Eighteen months later she described her state in 1936 as: 'Last year I was carefully drawing my poor limp horns in' (50), yet Leonard wrote in his autobiography that they had plenty of money throughout this time. In the months before publication of The Years Virginia was reduced to a pitiful wreck; however, she found the necessary 'immense courage & buoyancy to encompass it' until she was 'again on top.' This was an effort that she found more and more difficult to make until. in the early spring of 1941, became impossible.

After some four years' gruelling work on The Years, Virginia was faced with the prospect of lifting the safety curtain that had protected her private world whilst she wrote, to give the pages to Leonard and get his agreement to publish. She had to penetrate the magnetic field of his self importance, the 'curious and strong quality of me myself... which my ego and egocentricity have developed about me' as he put it in his autobiography, and cope with the incursion of his alienated left brain into her creative writing space. As Virginia looked at the words she had written in her private world, imagining his eyes on them and on her, her own positive energy lost its force, sank down, back into the earth and could not help her. At least, whilst she was writing, she did not censor herself in anticipation as so many women do. Now, faced with his reading of The

Years, she was almost destroyed before she showed it to him by her sense
of his psychic antipathy (as one may call it), the downside of his egocentric, magnetic aura. In agony, what she did was to disown her book:

"I said This is happily so bad that there can be no question about it. I
must carry the proofs, like a dead cat, to L. & tell him to burn them
unread. This I did. And a weight fell off my shoulders. That is true... I
went out & walked through the graveyard... through Grays Inn along
Holbourn & so back. Now I was no longer Virginia, the genius, but only a
perfectly insignificant yet content – shall I call it spirit? a body? And very
tired. Very old. But at the same time content to go on these 100 years
with Leonard. So we lunched, in a constraint: a grey acceptance... The
proofs will cost I suppose between 2 & 300 pounds which I will pay out
of my hoard. As I have 700 this will leave 400. I was not unhappy. And L.
said I might be wrong about the book... How dead I felt – Oh how infinitely tired!.. We went home, & L. read & read & said nothing: I began to
feel actively depressed... & fell into one of my horrid heats & deep slum-
bers, as if the blood in my head were cut off. Suddenly L. put down his
proof & said he thought it extraordinarily good – as good as any of
them." [The next day] 'L. who has now read to the end of 1914 still
thinks it extraordinarily good: very strange; very interesting; very sad. We
discussed my sadness... [gap in *Diary*] But my difficulty is this: I cannot
bring myself to believe that he is right. It may be simply that I exaggerated its badness, & therefore he now, finding it not so bad, exaggerates its
goodness.' [The next day] 'The miracle is accomplished. L. put down the
last sheet about 12 last night; & could not speak. He was in tears. He says
it is "a most remarkable book" – he *likes* it better than The Waves. & has
not a spark of doubt that it must be published. I, as a witness, not only to
his emotion, but to his absorption, for he read on & on, can't doubt his
opinion: what about my own? Anyhow the moment of relief was divine.
I hardly know yet if I'm on my head or my heels – so amazing is the
reversal since Tuesday morning. I have never had such an experience
before.' [51]

A few days later she is able to tell herself: 'Yes I think its good; in its
very difficult way.' But Leonard later wrote that his reaction had not been
genuine. He had told Virginia he was in favour of the book so as not to
upset her. Nor did he think that it would sell. A great deal lay under the
surface texture of their relationship at this time that was being disturbed
by her completion of *The Years*.

During that difficult November in 1936 Virginia managed to restore her confidence in herself as a writer and in her book. She says: 'I've been on the whole vigorous & cheerful since the wonderful revelation of L.s that night, How I woke from death – or non being – to life! What an incredible night – what a weight rolled off!' It seems that her temporarily submerged right brain reasserted itself and she recognised the other truth in the words she had written:

"There is no need whatever in my opinion to be unhappy about The Years. It seems to me to come off at the end... I think I can feel assured. This I say sincerely to myself; to hold to myself during the weeks of dull anticipation. Nor need I care what people say. In fact I hand my compliment to that terribly depressed woman, myself, whose head ached so often: who was so entirely convinced a failure; for in spite of everything I think she brought it off, & is to be congratulated. How she did it, with her head like an old cloth, I dont know." [52]

At this time, Leonard was frightened of dying. Virginia noted in her diary: 'Talked of death in Russell Squ[ar]e. L. said he had taught himself not to think about it. 2 or 3 years ago fear of death became an obsession. I said I should not wish to live if he died. But until then found life what? Exciting? Yes I think so. He agreed. So we dont think of death.' [53] After Christmas at Monk's House, the Woolfs returned to Tavistock Square. Mabel Haskins bore the brunt of Leonard's bad temper: 'Home again. Poor L. grumbling, making Mabel a peg on which to hang his misery oh dear.' [54]

When Leonard apparently fell seriously ill, Virginia was desperately worried in case it was his prostate gland; however, he turned out to have a urinary tract infection that cleared up. Meanwhile The Years hovered on the brink of publication and the consequent reaction of critics, friends and the public at large. This was the acid test. If sales were satisfactory, at least there would be more money for Leonard to spend. If it was ignored, he could blame Virginia for losing money and use it to prove to her that she should not write any more imaginative books. And so she set herself to endure the 'cold dull torture' of waiting for the echo from friends and the public: 'I myself know why its a failure, & its failure is deliberate'. [55] But The Years was not a failure. And Leonard was wrong when he thought it wouldn't sell well. 5,000 copies were sold before publication. The reviews were remarkably good, 'Oh the relief!... after all that agony, I'm free, whole; round.' ...'they' say almost universally that The Years is a master-piece.' Mrs W... has more to give us than any living novelist... astonishing fertility'. [56] In America it became a best seller. Virginia made 7000 pounds from this book and was again a rich woman – or should have been. She was inundated with people who wanted to visit her; she was asked to visit America and give chat-show-type lectures about her 'happy marriage' '...and the husband sits in the audience and says Boo.' She turned down every such offer, together with honorary degrees that were proposed by several universities. But at least she gained some feeling of security:

"I was thinking between 3 & 4 this morning, of my 55 years. I lay awake so calm, so content, as if I'd stepped off the whirling world into a deep blue quiet space, & there open eyed existed, beyond harm; armed against all that can happen." [57]

The Times Literary Supplement concluded a Century of English Novelists from Dickens to Virginia Woolf, by saying: 'It may be that art is going to be pushed aside for a time under the stress of political and social indignation or anxieties: therefore let us welcome the latest manifestation of a great artist, Virginia Woolf, whose title fittingly and symbolically closes this retrospect.' [58]

Eventually Virginia realised Leonard had not told her the truth when he gave his favourable opinion of The Years, and from then on no longer trusted his judgement. She wisely showed an early draft of her biography of Roger Fry to Vanessa and Roger's sister Margery, as well as Leonard. We need to remember this background since a similar situation occurred when her only other imaginative book, Between the Acts, was ready for publication. Her predicament in March 1941 can be seen not as a new sit-uation but as a catastrophic intensification of the state she had been reduced to in order to get The Years accepted by Leonard in November 1936; but, during that final confrontation, she went irretrievably over the precipice of powerlessness.

The public's positive reaction to The Years once more sent Virginia soar-ing skywards on their marital see-saw and she – realising that this was a dangerous place to be in relation to Leonard – once more happily planned to appease him with money and goods: "Now at any rate money is assured: L. shall have his new car; we will be floated again; & my last lap – if I've only ten years of life more – should be fruitful. Work – work. But at the moment the relief is so great, not I think an ignoble fame-gratified relief –

that I feel myself rocking up & down, like a bush a huge fowl sat on... And now I can put my philosophy of the free soul into operation." [59]

In this year there was a family tragedy. After failing to obtain a Fellowship at Cambridge, Julian Bell had taken up a professorship in China. He was restless and precipitately enlisted in the Spanish civil war, not as a soldier but as an ambulance officer in an attempt to reduce Vanessa's sense of doom, but was killed by flying shrapnel shortly after he arrived in Spain. Vanessa was prostrated with grief. Virginia wrote to Vita: 'It has been an incredible nightmare. We had both been certain he would be killed, and the strain on her now, perhaps mercifully, making her so exhausted she can only stay in bed.' [60] The Woolfs took Vanessa to Charleston, the Bells' farmhouse that can still be seen and visited. The person who gave her the greatest comfort and was best able to help her survive was Virginia: she spent most of that autumn cycling the few miles from Monk's House to Charleston and back, until Vanessa was once more able to cope with life; but Vanessa never entirely recovered from the early death of her first-born. She only reluctantly admitted later, to Vita, how much help Virginia had been.

VANESSA BELL, 1930

Chapter Eleven

VIRGINIA EXPOSES LEONARD

In April 1938 Virginia began her final two completed books: her biography of Roger Fry, and Pointz Hall whose name was changed shortly before she died, in March 1941, to *Between the Acts*. The writing of Pointz Hall was to be light relief for her while she worked at the task of selecting from the formidable pile of papers relating to Fry's life; yet she only made up her novel at moments of intense creative pressure. This resulted in a short, many-layered book which still has not been fully understood or evaluated.

She said 'I am playing with words.' [1] This is a clue to a number of allusions which in turn shed light on her intentions. Her working title itself, Pointz Hall, may well tell us what she had in mind when she began, since we can contrast 'Pointz' (she also spelt it Poyntz and Poyntzet) with the title of one of her short stories, 'Slater's Pins Have No Points', a celebration of lesbianism. In this story:

"All seemed transparent for a moment to the gaze of Fanny Wilmot, as if looking through Miss Craye, she saw the very fountain of her being spurt up in pure, silver drops... She saw Julia open her arms; saw her blaze; saw her kindle. Out of the night she burnt like a dead white star. Julia kissed her. Julia possessed her. 'Slater's pins have no points,' Miss Craye said, laughing queerly and relaxing her arms, as Fanny pinned the flower to her breast with trembling fingers." [2]

Pointz Hall, on the contrary, is full of those missing points, spiky and disturbing. The surface action of this drama-novel involves a pageant of scenes from English literary history acted by villagers in the grounds of Pointz Hall, watched by an audience that included the inhabitants of the Hall and their guests. The main 'point' throughout is the tension generated between Giles Oliver, son of the Hall's owner, and his wife Isabel (Isa). The Olivers are a young married couple who, for the entire length of the book, do not speak to each other. Both are attracted to someone else. The angle of vision is from Isa's point of view.

The name of Isa's lover is Rupert Haines, a gentleman farmer. Haines was a shipping company, its name emblazoned on their boats that crossed the bay at St Ives, Cornwall, watched by Virginia as a child during the

LEONARD AND VIRGINIA WOOLF, 1939
WITH SALLY

long summer holidays spent at Talland House that she was to recall all her life. Rupert evokes Rupert Brooke, the poet who died in the first world war; Virginia stayed with him at the Old Vicarage, Granchester, in 1911, and they swam together in the Granta, naked in the moonlight. [3] In the two elements of his name, Rupert Haines has important connections with Virginia's past; and, more immediately, she brings Roger Fry back to life in this romantic character.

Although Giles Oliver is disguised with fair hair, blue eyes and a short straight nose, there are many clues that his prototype is Leonard. Despite his Aryan looks, emphasised throughout the book, Giles has loose-fitting brown skin 'like a horse' and is in a perpetual state of almost ungovernable irritation that erupts against the world in general and his female relations in particular. He spends most of the day of the pageant with Mrs Manresa, a large vulgar woman who uses make-up; she is 'all sensation', a 'wild child of nature' and wholly man-turned. She arrives at Pointz Hall in an ostentatious car and brings with her William Dodge, a homosexual young man.

The other two adults living at Pointz Hall are the owner, Old Bartholemew (Bart) father of Giles, and his elderly sister Lucy Swithin. Bart has a large, fierce dog as his constant companion; while Lucy is somewhat wraith-like, part Virginia's Quaker aunt the Nun (she wears a cross), part an older Virginia. There is tension between Bart and Lucy, as there is between the Olivers: we can see them as younger and older versions of the Woolfs.

Isa and Giles have two children: a young boy, George, and a baby daughter, who are looked after by a pair of nursemaids. One of the nursemaids is called Mabel Hoskins. Mabel Haskins was the very capable servant who worked for Virginia while she was writing Pointz Hall and was so disliked by Leonard that she was under constant threat of dismissal. The names are too close to be unintended. Mabel reaches her apotheosis in the pageant where she appears as Queen Anne, representative of the Age of Reason. Thus does Virginia rescue that 'unsunned pear' from Leonard's humiliations, and warm her in the sun of her creativity. The second nursemaid is called, on different occasions, Lily and Amy and may be a reference to Louise Everest.

There are two powerful female characters coming from outside the family: Mrs Manresa, and Miss La Trobe who organises the pageant and is immediately recognisable as Dame Ethel Smyth, with a sympathetic admixture of Virginia Woolf the creative writer.

The tension between Isa and Giles seems to reflect an almost unendurable rage on the part of Virginia herself. As Mitchell Leaska, who has published the two earlier drafts of Pointz Hall, says, with each successive draft Virginia tries to restrain her rage from showing too obviously. By the third and final version: 'Virginia Woolf had indeed succeeded in suppressing the ferocity of her original plan. At what price, however, only she would finally know.' [4]

Why was Virginia Woolf in such a rage when she wrote Pointz Hall?

Leaska considers the entire book to be a 'suicide letter' and calls it 'the longest suicide letter in history'. If it is, then it works on two levels: first, Virginia's feeling that her world of English literature is about to be overwhelmed by war and that it can only be ludicrously inadequately immortalised in the pageant; secondly, we experience Isa's sense of personal doom as she watches Giles take pleasure in the company of Mrs Manresa.

The book may well be seen as Virginia's effort at confronting both impending disasters. She finds an answer to the former by extending her conception of 'civilisation' beyond anything considered by Leonard, towards a sense of the cosmic: there will be other civilisations in the future, as there were in the past. She redefines 'civilisation' itself, not as a single ancient Greek ideal, fragile and unique, which was Leonard's view; but as Roger Fry defined it: civilisation is awareness – an ever-changing state that awakens now on one continent, now on another. Virginia's 'inner Roger' was an intimate presence for her whilst she was at work in the private, secret world of her Lodge. He lit the lamp in her spine. With Fry for company she distanced herself both from the outside world and from Leonard; he not only gave her some comfort – through him, she discovered a different way of relating to life itself.

Leaska attributes Virginia's rage to a growing coolness in her friendship with Vita Sackville-West, whom he considers to be the origin of Mrs Manresa. This is not my view. In common with most commentators, he fails to recognise the change in Leonard's relationship with Virginia during the nineteen thirties, still seeing him as a reliable support for her, and therefore the text of her book remains largely a mystery to him. My view is that Virginia had very good and sufficient reasons for rage against Leonard. When we see these reasons clearly, we can understand both her surface cheerfulness which is often expressed in her letters and sometimes, but not always, in her diary, and the inner despair that led to her death. Whether a real-life Mrs. Manresa played a part in Virginia's death needs to be considered. By focusing on a heterosexual relationship Virginia was stirring the sediment of her and Leonard's problematical sex life. To write on this subject at all was an act of courage on her part.

If we make a dangerous leap across the gulf from Virginia to Leonard – from her Lodge to Monk's House at the other end of his garden – we find a man who later compares himself to a caged panther, referring to a quotation from 'Der Panther' by Rilke:

"This volume is the record of my life during the first great war and all through the war one felt that one was behind bars, and now recalling those years [in 1964] it seems to me that one was looking at the world and one's own life through bars. But then another thought, a terrible doubt, came to me. There are other bars, permanent bars of the cage of one's life, through which one has always and will always gaze at the world. The bars of one's birth and family and ancestors, of one's school and college, of one's own secret and sinuous psychology. Has not my mind, my soul, if I have a soul, for the last 82 years been pacing up and down like the panther, backwards and forwards, behind these bars and gazing through them until, so weary, I have seen, not the world or life, but only the bars – a thousand bars and behind the thousand bars no world?" [5]

This self-defensive, embattled position enabled Leonard's 'secret and sinuous psychology' full play, enhanced by the magnetic aura of his ego-centric self-importance that he wrapped around himself as he sat alone upstairs in his study at Monk's House. He was in control with Percy working in the garden, Louise in the kitchen and Virginia as far away as possible in her Lodge; and he reinforced that control not only with more and more building as he consolidated his 'empire' at Monk's House, but also with his complex layers of mythologic thinking that protected him from his failure to get his message across to the (to him unreal) world at large. As the prospect of another world war loomed ahead, his nightmare vision of simplified extremes terrified him. If either of the Woolfs was mad, should we not be considering Leonard's qualifications for this title? Had he not become locked into his refusal to consider there was any other valid point of view than his own?

In April 1938, Virginia managed to cope with his tepid response to *Three Guineas*:

"I didn't get as much praise from L. as I hoped... But I wanted – how violently – how persistently, pressingly compulsorily I cant say – to write this book; & have a quiet composed feeling; as if I had said my say: take it or leave it." [6]

In this year Virginia's half share in the Hogarth Press was sold to John Lehmann, ending Virginia's joint partnership in the firm. At the same time, Leonard got her to sign an agreement that effectively locked her in to the Press with no possibility of having her work published elsewhere. In Virginia's words:

"ten days ago I signed my rights away to John... our last Leonard & Virginia season is perhaps our most brilliant... Yes: if there is success in this world, the Hogarth Press has I suppose won what success it could. And money this year will fairly snow us under. 4000 pounds about from The Years... In fact we have asked [a Lewes builder] to estimate for a library for M[onks H[ouse] in spite of Hitler. But its all a little – my earnings – in the air. To solidify them I bought... [She lists some small items]. The delight of money; buying freely. Yet, puritanically, I spend next to nothing on dress." [7]

Virginia's substantial earnings, together with her American royalties and the 3000 from the sale of her half of the Press amounted to well over seven thousand pounds but they were indeed 'in the air' so far as she was concerned as she never had the control of any of it. Even the library, to be built in the roof at Monk's House, was for Leonard; and he suddenly decided to double the cost by adding a balcony.

Lehmann describes him: 'Leonard very difficult today, haggard, abrupt, twirling bits of string, a touch of hysteria in his voice, in fact suffering from a severe nervous crisis.' [8] When he himself wanted to end their partnership he speaks of the document Leonard made Virginia sign:

"In the 'Scheme' there was no clause which prevented either Leonard or me from engaging in any other publishing business, only one which prevented Virginia from doing so once she had ceased to be a partner. Of course it was a complete fantasy to imagine that, as soon as she had my 3,000 pounds (theoretically) in her pocket, Virginia would run off and set up as a publisher on her own... Eventually, after some months, I did find the Articles, and there was no doubt that it included the clause from which Leonard refused to release me." [9]

If John Lehmann was no match for Leonard, Virginia certainly was not. Why did Leonard include the clause which removed her right to be published elsewhere? Apart from the financial benefit he gained from her work, as he became more obstructive and destructive towards her he may well have wanted to ensure that she was unable to turn to anyone else. It was this door that he closed against her when she signed the agreement that forever locked her into the Hogarth Press.

John Lehmann was under no illusion that Virginia actually received his 3000 pounds, any more than she saw more than pocket-money from the enormous amount of work she put in writing *The Years,* at so great a cost to her emotional balance. By disowning that book and handing the proofs of it over to Leonard 'like a dead cat', to burn, she in a sense gave up her claim to it. Leonard now fostered the idea in her that she had to pay for the small gifts and commissions she enjoyed giving to Vanessa and the others living at Charleston by revising and selling her stories and articles, so that she continued anxiously to overwork. He was soon to prevent her making these gifts. The process of attrition continued.

One promise Virginia made, was to guarantee an overdraft incurred by Helen Anrep, Roger Fry's companion at the end of his life. She wanted to help Helen as a way of giving something back to Roger while she wrote his biography. It was surely her right to do so. But this promise caused her quite disproportionate anxiety. The sum involved was 250 pounds, a small amount compared to her earnings. For months she suffered sleepless nights and confusion which can be laid directly at Leonard's door, as he insisted that she earn extra money to pay for this loan. She revised her tragic story *Lappin and Lapinova*: 'more brain churning to add a passage to L[appin] & [Lapinova]. & all my courage needed'. (We may recognise in the word 'Lappin' lap-pin, the male. Alma Halbert Bond misspells it 'lapin', thus missing the allusion). Virginia says sadly:

"We never reach the pinnacle where I needn't make money owing to my – shall I say generosity? or impulsiveness? Helen came – oh yes – no doubt she wants the money – was desperate, evidently, if I decided not to give it. So I gave it... To school myself against silly puritanism, I instantly spent 5 pounds ten shillings on a very charming bookcase." [10]

In my view they never reached the 'pinnacle', not because of Virginia's generosity or impulsiveness, but because of Leonard's 'silly puritanism' as he laid his dead hand on her affairs. He played a power game, retaliating whenever she showed a desire for independence. It seems that Virginia never really tried to examine what he was up to; perhaps it would have damaged her to do so. She simply pictured herself as a butterfly and

Leonard as a gadfly and refused to analyse the complexities of their relationship. Indeed, she was very annoyed when Ethel Smyth dared to comment on it. Virginia wrote frigidly to her friend:

"I dont think your insight is faultless where L[eonard] is concerned; but would not in any case analyse other people's so complicated relations. I think if you were ever a day alone together the mists would disperse. As a matter of fact, the day you came happened to be a distracted one for him... he was brooding on a dozen things at once... Here, like yourself, I tear up 6 pages of the most acute psychological investigation. I analysed your feeling, and mine, and what we thought as we sat down to tea... and now destroy it all – as you did. 6 pages, Ethel... One day we'll talk them. Not now." [11]

She had not written any pages of psychological investigation, as she makes clear in her following letter a few days later:

"That was one of my jokes – I mean, pretending I'd written 4 pages and torn them up. I did no such thing. Had I written, I would have sent."

She no longer wanted Ethel to write a description of her: "I must be private, secret, as anonymous and submerged as possible in order to write. So never think of it as you dont.

Lets leave the letters till we're both dead. Thats my plan... and let posterity, if there is one, burn or not. Lets forget all about death and all about Posterity." [12]

Ethel was one of the few people to recognise what was happening between the Woolfs. This was, I believe, nothing less than the slow and eventually complete subjugation of Virginia to Leonard's will and she was the only person who could have rescued Virginia. No wonder Leonard detested the old woman, since she did indeed pose a threat to his power games.

In August 1938, during the Munich crisis, Vanessa was in Cassis. Leonard decided war would be declared and bring with it 'the end of all order'. However, his doomsday did not materialise whereas Virginia, as she wrote to Vanessa, predicted correctly that: "There wont be war but I was hooted down... There is now going to be a great reaction against the terms; and I am afraid L. will be drawn in." [13]

After the strain of the crisis, she wrote: 'I should be well advised to take a holiday from writing, & maunder off into the vineyards at Cassis. But I cant: too weak minded; dependent upon L: & life's too fixed. So I must dandle my brain, and find a substitute.' [14] In this month she wrote again to Vanessa:

"I very nearly rushed off to Cassis, so intoxicating were your words; and the sense of heat; and vines; and beauty; and freedom; and silence; and no telephones... Only the timely revelation of the complete failure of our marriage prevented it. Only just in time to stop me taking my ticket. Its an awful confession – if I werent so hurried I would conceal it; but the fact is we are so unhappy apart that I cant come. Thats the worst failure imaginable – that marriage, as I suddenly for the first time realised walking in the Square, reduces one to damnable servility. Cant be helped. Im going to write a comedy about it." [15]

Virginia's sense of bearing an intolerable burden, enters her diary:

"Yes I made a phrase last night about bearing the panoply of life, & being glad to lay it down. I wonder if its true. After a worried domestic day; then L. had a temperature & went to bed... I felt I was bearing up the panoply of life & wd. be glad to let it sink. I said to myself Remember, this is the description of age coming... I often think of things in this way, but forget them. And as L. is normal this morning & up & as its a fine morning, I'm not conscious of holding up my panoply, only distracted rather & cant settle in." [16]

During the spring different regions of what had been Czechoslovakia fell under Hitler's domination. Britain and France, announced that they would guarantee support for Poland if her independence were threatened. Virginia and Leonard decided not to talk any more about the situation in Europe. Virginia felt that in the event of war they would be trapped in Rodmell, and continued to look for possible places to escape to; but when she saw a view or a house that she liked, Leonard simply said: 'I prefer Monks House' and that was the end of it.

We get glimpses of desperation in Leonard; of intense irritation – and of Virginia's increasing loyalty for him, of a love blended between pity and her dangerous dependence on him; of the high-handed and unfair advantage he takes of her, which she becomes increasingly unable to resist. He filled Monk's House with members of his family so that she had to stop work and entertain them, although he thought her relatives much more interesting than his. He maintained that his love was greater than hers because she kept turning away from him in her work and going for long walks on the downs, while he focused on her and told her how beautiful she was. Thus she was confined by the panther in his cage. She was living on a dwindling island of insecurity, like Antigone walled up in a cave by Creon.

In contrast to their restricted lives, the Woolfs could see how active and effective Harold Nicolson and Vita Sackville-West were being. Harold had been elected to Parliament in 1935 and he played an important role in the country's policies both before and during the coming war, although he never became a Minister. Vita was busy at Sissinghurst with her writing and gardening and making trips to the Continent on her own. Virginia considered going to see a barn used by Roger Fry in S. Remy, but admitted to Smyth she did not have the spirit to go on her own: 'Aint I a craven?' [17]

In early July 1939, Marie Woolf died after a fall. With her death the network of interacting relationships in the Woolf family lost its focus. Leonard no longer had his mother to blame for the loss of his father. On the other hand he admired her for her stubborn clinging to life as he watched her die 'like an animal'. Her survival into old age was an example of the enduring flame of his Jewish ancestry. In comparison, had not Virginia shown herself to be a half-alive, bloodless gentile? Now she must bear the full burden of his shadow. They were in London:

"Yet how dumpish we were – starting off to the Movies, after dinner – L. asking me what I wanted to see, I not wanting to see anything – the crowds of deformed & stunted & vicious & sweating & ugly hooligans & harridans in the Tott[enham] C[our]t Road – the sticky heat – all this brooded, till I was saying, step out, on, on, in my usual desperate way. Then instead we went to Nessa's." [18]

Virginia Woolf was saying, 'step out, on, on, in my usual desperate way' – to try to lighten the weight of Leonard's gloom that was more depressing than her own. On this occasion, Vanessa helped. Their visit to her studio 'rolled off my glooms effectively; perhaps L[eonard]'s.'

It was during July that the affair of the Greenhouse occurred. Leonard ordered a heated greenhouse to be erected against an outside wall at Monk's House, without consulting Virginia. The first she knew of it was seeing the workmen arriving with the materials. She became incoherent at the horror of having to put up with this ugly addition; and the fact that Leonard had ordered it without even mentioning it to her gave her a rare, disillusioning glimpse of his underlying attitude:

"The use of this book is to write things out, hence: the Greenhouse. I'm so unhappy. A portmanteau word. Analysed: headache; guilt; remorse... The house, L.'s house... oh dear, his hobby – his peach tree to be pulled down because of me. How can I get sensible? I mind so much. Oh dear –

the conflict – the ugliness: v: L.'s wish. And is it worth this misery? – oughtn't I to have said go ahead, when he came to me in the Bath this morning? The men had come – Sh[oul]d they put it up? I said you must decide. So he sent them away & its to be pulled down. How to live it over? Forget he says: but I shant... & cant read or write – ... I have composed myself, momentarily, by reading through this years diary. Thats a use for it then. It composes. Why? ... Odd that I can read here without repulsion. Why? My own mind I suppose claws me when others slip... (I'm whistling to keep up my spirits this very strained grey day – the Greenhouse morning.)... What annoys me is L.'s adroitness in fathering guilt on me. His highhandedness. I see the temptation. 'Oh you dont want it – so I submit.' This spoilt bowls last night. We shied them at the Jack. Yet so happy in our reconciliation. 'Do you think me beautiful now?' 'The most beautiful of women–' " [19]

Two days later: 'the great affair of the G[reen] H[ouse] has been settled; amicably: a cold house at the back. So its over; what a waste of emotion. Is it that I lack will?' [20]

On 3 September 1939, Britain was at war with Germany. For the people of Britain, it began as a 'phoney' war while Hitler invaded Poland and Russia attacked Finland. The Woolfs were able to continue their old life without major changes. That autumn Leonard's book *Barbarians at the Gate* was published, after a delay caused by the publisher Victor Gollancz, who thought it might damage Anglo-Soviet relations. In his letters to Gollancz Leonard, furious at the delay, refused to take any responsibility for the effect his book might have, saying: 'I simply am not interested in speculations regarding the imaginary influence of my book, flattering though they may be'. [21]

In this book Pericles enters importantly, indeed he is the central figure. Leonard equates Pericles, as leader of the civilised Athenians, with Stalin. They are both 'goodies' (despite Stalin's propensity for killing off his political opponents), while Hitler's aggressions are equated with the militaristic Spartans, the 'barbarians' who waged the Peloponnesian War against the Athenians:

"It was winter and the end of that purposeless and fatal war which began the destruction of Athenian and Greek civilization. The Athenians had an ancient custom of giving a common funeral at the public expense to those of its citizens who had fallen in war... It was customary after the burial for a man, chosen by the city, to deliver a funeral oration. In 431

B.C. the man chosen was Pericles, the leading statesman of Athens who made such an impress upon his age that it became known to history as the Periclean age... Civilization for Pericles consists mainly in social organization and social objectives of which the most important are mental or spiritual, not material things, and social relations." [22]

Communal freedom was important: 'In his speech Pericles then went on to consider how the Athenians had used that freedom to develop their own particular type of civilization. "We combine love of beauty with simplicity and pursue things of the intellect without becoming unmanly. We set no store on wealth except as a means to an end" '

Leonard is at last able to present Pericles in the heroic light in which he has bathed him since his days at University. He does admit some limitations in his source material but his admissions do not go nearly far enough since Athens was run as an exclusive, men-only club. This was the basis of Leonard's ideal civilisation. Even within these limits, however, his book has an insuperable problem, as Spater and Parsons say:

"In *Barbarians at the Gate*... [Leonard] concluded that the danger to civilization was not Hitler, Mussolini or the Nazi and Fascist systems – not the barbarians at the gate – but... the forces within the citadel; it was the capitalist systems in France and Britain, and the repression of liberties in Russia." [23]

Leonard, unable to resist blaming the 'capitalist systems in France and Britain' for the coming end of civilisation and the onset of barbarism, also discounts the actual danger from Nazism by arguing that all dictatorships eventually die from their own internal conflicts and that people who complain have a distorted vision because of the shortness of the human life-span. Thus he retreated into an idiosyncratic position. He could justify using Virginia's money for his own purposes, instead of investing it to help her in her old age, by arguing that money was not valued in ancient Greece except as a means to an end – in Leonard's case, developing Monk's House and garden to make his household conform as closely as possible to his Periclean ideal.

After these glimpses of the outer world that Virginia shuts out with what she calls her 'fire curtain', in the seclusion of her Lodge, let us share some of her inner life that she creates in *Between the Acts*. I have concentrated on the earlier Typescript (ETS) with occasional references to the Later Typescript (LTS) provided by Mitchell A. Leaska in *Pointz Hall*, as well as

referring to the final text. The early draft is introduced with an invoca-
tion to an oil lamp that illuminates, unifies and gives perspective, as a
lighthouse had given perspective in *To the Lighthouse* and the sun itself, a
lamp held aloft by a woman, sheds its light on *The Waves*.

"Summer Night. 1... The Lamp:

Oh beautiful and bounteous light on the table; oil lamp; ancient and
out-of-date oil lamp; ...not a wandering light like the car's; but steady...
surveys the whole unembarrassed by the part; unimpeded; oil lamp, that
calls out the colour in the faded... [in unity; God or Goddess;] accept the
praise of those dazzled by daylight; drowned by uproar; oil lamp." [24]

The first scene of Virginia's novel-drama takes place the day before the
staging of the pageant in the grounds of Pointz Hall. At once, we experience natural sensations: 'The grass was wet'. The scent of hay is smelt. A
cow coughs in the meadow. There is talk about a cesspool between
Rupert Haines and a builder and his wife, the Perrys (perry is cider made
from fermented pears; pears are a feature of the text). Mrs Perry 'said
(low, like a child stooping under a leaf and the political and economic
observations of her husband), "I never feared cows; but always horses. As
a small child in a perambulator in a lane, a great carthorse had brushed
within a hair's breath. [Virginia elides the word 'breadth'.] She was only
two, but she would still feel it... see it... <red nostrils, hot breath>." [25]

The sudden intrusion of the carthorse is so strong it alerts the young
girl with a sense of shock, as shock alerted Virginia and gave her
'moments of truth' she never forgot.

Virginia's emphasis on sensation, right at the beginning of the first
draft of *Between the Acts,* fires the first salvo in a major act of rebellion
against patriarchy and proclaims the primacy of the female orientation. It
is surely from this point of view that the entire book should be
approached. She is herself a 'child stooping under a leaf under the political
and economic observations of her husband' – Leonard. And she is at last
writing about sex. Rupert Haines is not only a farmer but he can discuss
poetry with intensity. And he and Isa are attracted to each other. He is an
important figure in all versions of the text although his origins remain
mysterious, he was 'no relation to anybody'. Isa imagines that he may
have had:

"a secret life; Haines admired the girl at the cottage on the left-hand
side of the road... It was perhaps his child she bore... What then did he
feel for Mrs Giles? Perhaps this; perhaps that. A man after all must have a

hidden underground bubbling spring... Haines turned in his chair... he looked at Mrs Giles, hoping that she would help him in asserting the right of the living to their own opinions... The common feeling (about poetry) fluttered round the lamp for a moment... And how each of them had the same nerve; in the thigh it was in her case; and tingling still in connection with his. She still felt it, as she sat on the three-cornered chair." (26)

The 'pointz' in the early title are the nerve-thrills of heterosexuality. They are also pointz of view, female angles of vision in relation to male ones. With every word she challenges Leonard's priggishness, the thick walls of his self-defensive puritanism and his all-pervasive irritability as well as the male hegemony.

Old Bartholemew goes into the garden and shocks his young grandson George by making a snout of his newspaper and rushing at the boy at the very moment he was illuminated by seeing a flower. The old man is accompanied by his huge dog. This is one of the violent scenes that continues through all drafts of the book. For George:

"The flower blazed between the angles of the roots. It blazed a soft yellow; a lambent light under a film of velvet. It blazed. It tore membrane after membrane. It filled the caverns behind the eyes with a soft yellow light; a light that was warm and sweet honey-smelling... Down on his knees on the grass he held that completeness. Then there was a roar and a hot breath; a stream of coarse grey hair rushing past between him and the whole flower; a terror. A great wild beast; rushing, destroying, terrifying. He leapt up; toppling in his fright, and then saw coming towards him a terrible peaked eyeless monster moving on legs; brandishing arms... Suddenly [Old Bartholemew] crumpled the paper which he had cocked into a snout; and appeared in his own person, with his little flaming eyes, and big nose and wrinkled old man's cheeks. George stood gaping." [27]

Old Bart was annoyed. He thought he was breaking down the generation barrier but the small boy's shocked reaction made his grandfather think of him as a coward, 'this little chap was a cry-baby'. He went back to his newspaper where he tried to find his place, 'the franc... the franc... the franc.'

The flower, the wholeness of the flower, had been violated, indeed totally destroyed, by the old man thinking about money, and his dog; as Virginia's wholeness was destroyed as a child by the sudden violence of her father and other testosterone-driven men; but also, later, by Leonard with his preoccupation with money – she mustn't spend any – and his sudden hurtful remarks when he shifts all blame onto her. He too was constantly followed by a dog, only Leonard's dog is a besotted spaniel, not a slavering monster.

Upstairs in her bedroom, Isa re-experiences yesterday's scene between herself and Haines. She still has her luxuriant locks, unlike Virginia who had had her hair cut short:

"Mrs Giles Oliver drew a comb through the enormous tangle of her hair which she had never had bobbed, or shingled, or shaven after giving the matter her best attention...

'Love,' she was thinking, being in love,' she corrected herself, does not necessarily cease with marriage, a thought [insidiously] shaped with reprehensible vagueness to allow her to indulge in the idea that there was no harm in feeling what she felt overnight for Haines the farmer – that prick and tension in her thigh when he had capped her quotation from Edward Thomas. She could feel that and at the same time 'love' her husband, Giles, the stockbroker. 'The father of my children,' she added... partly illustrated by the sight there coming across the lawn of perambulators, nurses and children... .it was now her part... to protect that sheltered fortress, that tree-girt immunity, hedged about with furry bears, embroidered quilts, and Mabel and Amy <to protect> from care... her son George. But not me, not mine, she sighed. No. Since she could register terrible thrills from men who were not her husband. Since suddenly Mr Haines could pierce her with fiery arrows; since the proximity of that body could affect hers; since the words he said could suddenly attach themselves to a burning spot in her, and lie between them like a wire, twanging, tingling, vibrating, jiffering; she tried to find a word; and thought of the infinitely quick vibrations of an aeroplane propeller she had watched taking off at Croydon; faster and faster it buzzed; till all the flails became one flail; the screw one screw; and up soared the plane – away – away... [dots in text] 'Where we know not, where we go not, not know, nor care,' she hummed." [28]

Isa goes into the library where Old Bart dreams about bare Indian plains; native tribes plotting treachery; poisoned darts and death. The dog by his side 'never acknowledged ties of domesticity. Either he cringed or he bit'. Bart tells Isa her little boy is a cry-baby. 'And he reminded her, she was pegged down, like a captive balloon; by myriads of hair-thin ties.' The door opens and Mrs Swithin, Bartholemew's widowed sister, comes sidling in to replace a hammer. She remembers that Old Bart had taken her fishing and had once made her take the fish off the hook '<it had half fascinated, half shocked her> and the gills were full of blood.'

So many violent images. So many points of conflict; so many fine connecting threads between the characters in the text and Virginia's life. The dining room is empty: 'But who observed the dining room? Who could [possibly] note the silence of emptiness? What name is to be given to that which notes that a room is empty... a common element in which the perishable is preserved, and the separate become one. Does it not by this means create immortality?' [29]

Later, Pointz Hall is deserted. 'It was like a ship that has been left by the crew'. The emptiness does give one the impression that Virginia is writing herself out of the text – out of life; as though she is putting everything into this book. But what gave her this feeling? The emptiness is not caused by war since the house is not threatened, it continues to exist undamaged. She was exploring dangerous territory, the life of sensation, of instinct, of nature; and was, in doing so, rebelling against that all-important authority the 'higher' male intelligence.

The following section is dated 1 August, 1938. Mrs Manresa arrives in her 'great silver-plated car... with the initials R.M. twisted so as to look at a distance like a coronet'. [30] She brings in tow William Dodge, a young man who is soon identified as a homosexual. They are met in the dining room by old Bart, Lucy and Isabella who emerge from the library. We see the visitors through Isabella's eyes. Here is Mrs. Manresa: 'a very insensitive, loud-voiced, jolly woman [who] preferred men – obviously. "Or what are your rings for?" said Isabella, addressing Mrs Manresa silently, and thereby making silence add its [little drop] <contribution> [of poison] to the talk.' Mrs Manresa veiled her eyes when she spoke to women, 'they were conspirators'.

I find it impossible to relate this vulgar and insensitive woman who is so man-turned, to Vita Sackville-West. In the book she is an enigma, her 'background was not well known'; she could 'say anything', her figure (she is stout) gives her immense freedom; she has a lovely voice and speaks at meetings and is 'a thorough good sort'. [31] She is 'a wild child of nature'; she is 'all sensation'. Isabella looks at her 'as the caged might look at the free.'

What emerges from all drafts of *Between the Acts* is the effort made by Isa to tolerate Giles' relationship with Mrs Manresa, a woman she does not like. There are some catty moments: 'Mrs Manresa felt her sex indict-ed... She was a little conscious, that is, of her make-up. She had out her pocket mirror and surveyed her lips. She applied her powder puff... But alas, sunset light was not sympathetic to her make-up; plated it looked, not deeply interfused.' Virginia did not use make-up; this was an ill-fit-ting mask with which she has overlaid her target.

Giles Oliver, after spending the working week in town as a stockbro-ker, arrives at Pointz Hall for the weekend. He sees Mrs Manresa's impressive car standing outside the Hall and goes upstairs to change out of his business suit – then immediately demonstrates the bad temper which is characteristic of him throughout the book. This addiction to discontent, as one may call it, in Giles, is quite remarkable and seems excessive in the overall plan of the work. His first irritation is that he has listened to the 'ghost of conventional education' by changing his clothes: 'he was enraged; partly at his own docility in obeying his instincts' and partly because he had read in the morning newspapers that sixteen per-fectly innocent men had been shot; others exiled.' He comes into the dining room: 'looking like a cricketer, in flannels and blue coat with brass buttons' and at once blames his aunt Lucy because he gave in to conven-tion: '<For> he had a habit of hanging grievances upon her, as one hangs a coat on a hook.' He continues to blame Lucy for her frivolous attitude towards his being forced to work in the City, when he wanted to be a farmer; being 'furiously in love – he nodded across the table to Isa – had afflicted him for ten years.' He then takes an instant dislike to William Dodge and sits down to eat his fillet of sole. [32]

So much for our introduction to Giles Oliver. Virginia is surely finding some relief in being able to express her actual feelings about Leonard's habitual irritation, which at the slightest excuse would break out into a paroxysm of frustration when he would tremble all over, make caustic remarks and then retreat into ominous silences which induced, as they were intended to, a sense of guilt and despair in the other person: 'What annoys me is L.s adroitness in fathering the guilt on me. His high-hand-edness', as Virginia says in her diary in July 1939. In the text, Giles imposes his guilt on his Aunt Lucy. The meeting between Giles and Mrs Manresa has the inevitability of fate:

"He was of the very type of all Mrs Manresa adored. His hair curled; far from running away, as many chins did, his was firm; the nose straight, if short; the eyes, of course with that hair, blue; and finally, to make the type complete, there was something [surly,] fierce, untamed, in the expression, which incited her, even at forty-five, to furbish up her ancient batteries <against the savage adorable young man>." [33]

Silently Isabella claims him. " 'He is my husband', Isabella felt, as they nodded across the bunch of many-coloured flowers. 'The father of my children.' And the old cliche worked; she felt pride, and affection; and again pride in herself, whom he had chosen… it was a shock to find, after last night's thrill over Mr Haines and poetry, how much she felt when he came in, not as she expected the dapper City gent; but the cricketer.

But Giles is preoccupied detesting William Dodge, thinking 'You're our enemy; the destroyer; nothing is sacred to you.' Isa sees that Dodge is afraid 'Just as she was afraid of Giles <Did she not write> her poetry in a book bound like an account book, in case Giles might suspect?' " [34]

Free to express herself in her novel as she could not do in her diary, Virginia describes her mixed emotions of love and fear, and her ambivalence towards Leonard.

The inhabitants of Pointz Hall, with their guests, move outside to the Looe Corner (the Love Corner) a word familiar to Virginia since one of the little gardens at Talland House, in Cornwall, was called this. They set up deck chairs. Isa has hers the wrong way up, with the notches underneath. There are not enough chairs for them all. Giles has to fetch another from the house. On his return he is immediately antagonised by his Aunt Lucy who says as they all look at the view: 'So beautiful. It will be there… when we are not':

"Giles nicked his deck chair into position, with a jerk, thus expressing his irritation with the kind of nonsense Aunt Lucy talked… when the whole of Europe – over there beyond the flat was bristling like a – to express the idea of guns pointed, planes about to take flight, each with a bomb in its tail – he only had the ineffective word 'hedgehog'… And he too loved the view. And the blame for the guns rested somehow upon Aunt Lucy… he always exempted his father… from all censure. It wasn't his doing. But surely Lucy [who never finished a sentence sensibly] was somehow responsible." [35]

Giles irrationally blames his aunt Lucy Swithin for everything, including her husband's death, 'dead in the prime of life, when a lamp exploded', for 'not seeing how devilish difficult that sort of thing made life for him, now.' – exactly as Leonard must have blamed his mother for the death of his father and, just as irrationally, blamed Virginia for everything that annoyed him. But Giles exempted Mrs Manresa, as he hollowed his hand and lit her cigarette, '<from responsibility in making his life hard for him>.' Soon she is glancing at Giles 'with whom she feels in conspiracy':

"A thread united them, visible, invisible, like those threads, now seen, now not, that unite trembling grass blades in autumn before the sun has risen... The air, <owing to her,> was full of sensation... And of course Giles felt it. Had he been a horse, the thin brown skin would have twitched, as if a fly had settled. <Isabella twitched but with jealousy>." [36]

Looking at the two of them, Isa thought: 'He was her husband. She his wife'. Thus she reassures herself, as Virginia would have done if there was indeed a serious 'other woman' waiting in the wings in real life. When Giles answers Mrs Manresa's question about the coming pageant, he 'had a nice [rough] <gruff> voice.'

Giles proceeds to pursue Mrs Manresa, partly because he dislikes thinking of himself as only a member of the audience having to sit and watch Miss La Trobe organise the pageant, and partly because he accuses himself of being a coward:

" 'Are they going to act?' Mrs Manresa asked.

'Act; dance; sing; a little bit of everything,' said Giles.

'Miss [La Trobe]... is a person of wonderful energy,' said Mrs Swithin.

'She makes everyone do something,' said Isabella.

'Our part,' said Bartholomew, 'is [laid down for us.] perhaps the most important. We are the audience.'...Mrs Swithin began checking the programme with her fingers: '[And] the choice is so vast. The whole of English literature from the beginning to the end... Miss [La Trobe's] very clever... I don't know how she chooses. Often... I begin counting up what I have read, what I haven't– 'And pulling my books out of the shelves, leaving them on the floor'...

'[Like] the donkey who couldn't choose between the hay or the turnips and so starved,' said Isabella, shielding her Aunt from the caustic remark which, as she knew from the rise of her husband's lip, he would have spoken had they been alone. For his father, who always indulged Lucy, had sketched all he disliked in that one sentence <– 'Pulling my books out and leaving them on the floor.' > He saw her [sitting on the floor]... books open and no conclusion come to; and yet somehow she made him feel ridiculous; a man who held views, yet did nothing to put them into action. If he had not married... he would have cut the whole thing, or done something: emigrated or acted. Now he was 'the audience'." [37]

Virginia has got her teeth into what she wants to say about Leonard; she is at last managing to describe him:

"In certain moods, like that bred in him that morning... words ceased to lie flat in the sentence, but rose, swelled, and became symbolical. <They pointed a finger at him. They had not a surface meaning but an under meaning. 'The audience', for instance.> Now he was 'the audience'; not simply Giles Oliver... but Giles Oliver manacled by fate to a rock and forced to behold, passively, indescribable horror. The nerves in his face twitched. His face expressed, for a moment, such loathing that his wife, not knowing what to do – and indeed there was nothing she could do – abruptly, half-purposely, knocked over a coffee cup."

The coffee cup is caught and examined by William Dodge. Watching the delicacy with which he handled the cup:

"gave Giles another peg to hang his rage, and so dilute it. That is, he forcibly disliked, not the state of the world entirely, but Mrs. Manresa's young friend. He thought him a toady, a lickspittle... a fingerer of sensations; picking and choosing; dillying and dallying; not a man to have straight-forward relations with a woman but simply a–. At this word, which he could not speak aloud, he pursed his lips; and the signet ring on his little finger looked redder, the flesh next it whitened. He gripped the arm of the deck chair...

Isabella indeed had been watching [Dodge] off and on ever since he came. She knew at the moment that he was being made responsible, together with her Aunt Lucy, for all that her husband hated... Why do we all hate each other?" [38]

The Bloomsbury Group called male homosexuals 'buggers'. This was, no doubt, the missing unmentionable word. Leonard disliked and despised male homosexuality and may have particularly disliked Vanessa's friend Duncan Grant, a promiscuous homosexual who also fathered her youngest child Angelica. Grant seems to be portrayed here. Hate, as well as love, bonded the members of the Bloomsbury Group.

So Leonard, like Giles, was 'manacled by fate to a rock'; words ceased to lie flat and became symbolical, they pointed a finger at him and were filled with an under meaning. Virginia did what she could to deflect his rage, often agreeing with him for the sake of peace, as John Lehmann points out – but even so she was often blamed and burdened with guilt.

Tragically, neither of them was able to expose Leonard's self-rewarding fiction for what it was. His obsession was to get Virginia to believe that his vision of himself was real and that her vision was merely the illusion of madness, as he tried to persuade himself as well as her that his writing was more important to the world than hers.

"Giles glared. He bound his knees tight together with his clenched fists. He looked straight ahead; sat in a trance; as if his [irascible mood] <anger were frozen;> [had fixed itself] eternally.

Isabella sitting next to him felt imprisoned. Sensations tried to reach her through the prison bars. Jealousy and what she supposed to be desire – the wish that Rupert Haines would come – tormented her; but through prison bars and through a sleep haze which deflected them. Also other people's presence forbade her to feel either jealousy or love distinctly... She longed for a great [tumbler] <beaker> of cold water... but desire petered out, suppressed by the leaden duty she owed [to society] <civilisation.>" [39]

There could not be a stronger, more devastating scene of deprivation as Isabella continues to sit not merely thirsty, but starved of water – starved of life and love – trapped in the Looe Corner in company with Giles and Mrs Manresa and Bartholemew (who was asleep), as Virginia felt trapped and starved at Monk's House, in the small world of Rodmell society, while she owed a leaden duty to Leonard's deadly ideal of ancient Greek civilisation.

Meanwhile her older self, the 'old wispy woman' Lucy Swithin, showed William Dodge around the Hall, in many ways her longed-for place with similarities to Asheham House. In the bedroom: 'Their eyes met in the glass... They liked each other without waiting for their bodies to confirm it.' He thought of 'the intimacy that was sure to be theirs.' In the empty nursery, 'he felt that she meant: "This is the cradle of the human race." It was a symbolical, universal nursery.' [40] He followed her, leaving the door open for the crew to come back. Down in the courtyard, cars were arriving. As the pageant begins, Mrs Manresa and Giles sit together in the middle of the front row of the audience:

"Yes, the wild child was the queen of the Festival. Her thigh in its tight blue serge skirt swelled alongside [the muscular thigh of Giles.] <Giles's flannel leg.> She radiated sensation; royalty; complacency; humour. She had ascended her eminence; and was in possession once more, after the oblivion of her drowsiness, of the jolly woman she was by nature.

Miss La Trobe sighed with relief. The producer's great terror – that the gap will never be bridged was gone." [41]

Rupert Haines joins the audience. Isa 'half turned her head.'

The first Act of the pageant shows scenes from the ages of Chaucer to Shakespeare, during which Mrs Manresa 'trolloped out the words of a music hall song with an abandonment that was, if vulgar, really magnificent', while 'I fear I am not in my perfect mind,' Giles muttered. 'A stricken deer in whose lean flank the world's harsh scorn has struck its iron.' Isa shifted and looked at Rupert Haines, 'A thrill ran through her'. The plot was only there to breed emotion. And there were only three emotions: love; hate; fear. The play gave them access to the three prime emotions. 'Oh Rupert, oh.' She had come downstairs in her dressing gown with her hair in a plait last night and that was her greeting. She remembered the thrill. But there was also the fourth emotion – death; sorrow.

At the end of the first Act the audience splits up to the disturbing refrain 'Dispersed are we' and, as separate individuals, make their way from the Grove where the pageant was being held, to the Barn for tea:

"Isa was very near tears. The separateness; the infinite littleness of small objects... and out there – where they had been acting love; hate; fear; sorrow – was deep, enveloping... The joined emotion: love; fear; hate; with sorrow plaited, the four-fold ply – broken; over. Must I follow the bold Manresa to have tea?

Dispersed are we.' [42]

Giles mutters, 'Absolved, free are we? From the intolerable, repulsive propinquity of the woman's flesh, free are we? [Chained] <frozen> to the hard chair; in the bright glare; at last released. But free? To go where? Nowhere. Anywhere. To kick a stone; alone; down the [lonely] road that leads to the churchyard where the coward... {dots in text} I, I, I, [at whom the hand points its skeleton finger] <am free.'>

In the Grove, Miss La Trobe feels exalted that 'I, with nothing but sixpenny brooches and dish cloths to help me, imprinted my ideas'. She is surely expressing exaltation at succeeding in a male world despite the difficulties, which Virginia Woolf the writer sometimes managed to experience, as well as Ethel Smyth the composer. Giles, instead of congratulating Miss La Trobe, ignores her and turns away – as Leonard turned away from Smyth, and anyone else he didn't like:

"Of course, disillusionment followed directly upon the glory of creation. And the one man to save her from it was Giles. Blue eyes, straight nose, firm chin; the physical attributes of the saviour were his. But he had turned away." [43]

Giles makes his way on his own to the old Barn 'which reminded archeologists of Greek temples', where tea was laid. 'It had always been understood at Pointz Hall – save for some random remarks of a vaguely speculative kind of Mrs. Swithin's – that the centre of the world was Pointz Hall.' Here Virginia, as Lucy Swithin, is taking leave to doubt that Pointz Hall is the centre of the world, as Monk's House undoubtedly was for Leonard.

The Barn is like a Greek temple: Virginia knew at least two magnificent historic barns, including Long Barn, Vita's old home. She is laughing; she is having fun, but she is also giving additional significance to the following scenes that occur in her text. She extends the time scale back into the past that is also the present. Now she reaches much further back, into the distant past of human beings, as the path that Giles takes to reach the Barn is only known to natives; it leads across fields.

He finds a stone, a flinty yellow stone, sharp-edged, 'as if cut by a savage for an arrowhead', and kicks it:

"The rules of the game of stone-kicking require that the same stone is kicked to a given goal; sometimes a gate; or a prominent clump of grass. This time the goal was a gate to be reached in ten kicks; and the stone was Manresa (lust) also Dodge (perversion) also himself (coward). He kicked once, twice, thrice... [dots in text] he reached the gate in nine. There crouched in the grass, curled olive green, was a snake. Dead? No; half-choked with a toad in its mouth. The legs dangled, still twitching outside. The body was swallowed. The snake was gloating, glutted. He touched it. A spasm made the ribs contract and crush; blood oozed from the toad. Then the snake lay tranced; the snake unable to [swallow] <give death to life;> the toad unable to die. So he brought his foot down on the snake's head and crushed them both. He was wearing tennis shoes. The mass crushed and slithered. It left his rubber soles <and the white canvas> sticky <and red.> But it was action – action relieved him." [44]

Virginia and Leonard had once seen a snake with a toad. That time Leonard touched the snake's tail with his foot, the snake regurgitated the dead toad and glided away. This time, in Virginia's book, Giles brings his foot down on both snake and toad, killing them, getting blood on his tennis shoes. The image is certainly violent. If it relates to their relationship, it could hardly be more devastating. A different reading could be Hitler as the snake attempting to devour Europe, the toad. She used a similar image in her diary: 'When the tiger ie Hitler has digested his dinner he will pounce again.' [45] In his political arguments Leonard blames both sides. Nevertheless, this violent scene seems disproportionate as a comment on Leonard's reaction to world politics. Perhaps we should recall the Woolfs' rivalry at bowls which they played ever more obsessively, until Virginia was reminded of Hitler. Losing to Leonard was a disaster for her like a country being over-run, or a toad being swallowed. But Virginia, though often beaten refuses, like the toad, to be swallowed. Is this really the image, seen from Virginia's point of view? Is she encouraging Leonard to conquer lust (Mrs Manresa), perversion (William Dodge) and cowardice (himself) as he kicks the stone through the gateway, in order to gain the courage to take the decisive action that would destroy their marriage? In the final version of *Between the Acts*, this scene is summed up: 'It was birth the wrong way round – a monstrous inversion. So, raising his foot, he stamped on them.' [46] When Giles arrives at the Barn it is not Isa who admires the evidence of the blood on his shoe – she, in fact, ' did not admire' him – but Mrs Manresa.

During the interval, disintegration reaches appalling depths and heights. Mrs Manresa is the first to arrive at the empty Barn. Isa drifts in, alone, looking for Rupert Haines who is not there, 'that the waters should cover me, of the wishing well.' 'That's what I wished, when I dropped my pin. Water, water.' She dropped her marital pin and became a lesbian with Vita because she was starved of the essential water of love. Water, the female life-giving element. She is putting her point of view at all costs. With intense sadness she imagines not only her physical demise but the extinction of her work: 'There would the dead leaf fall, where the leaves fall, on the water. Should I mind, not again to see, may tree or nut tree?... Alone under the tree, the withered tree that keeps all day murmuring of the sea, and hears the Rider gallop.' [47]

William Dodge smiles at Isa: 'they were conspirators; leaguered together against the general company'. He wanted to talk with her about the play. 'The play, he meant, had acted as a solvent; as a "disintegration of personality" ' Giles enters wearing his blood-stained shoes. He 'shoulders his way', and Isa's eyes 'change, as if she had to get out of one dress, put on another'. They are watched by William Dodge. To Dodge, the homosexual, Isa's body is only a picture whereas Giles's 'virility plunged him into violent emotions in which the intellect had no part.' Mrs Manresa sees Giles:

"Cracking her jokes, she turned, saw Giles, and swept him in. But what had he done with his shoes? Some submerged sensation was liberated in her by the smear of blood on the canvas... a pleasing [vague] sense that somehow he had proved his valour for her admiration <stimulated her>... she made him the audience for her breezy chaff." [48]

Mrs Manresa and Giles, together, go the rounds of the groups of people in the Barn: 'she drew him down the line, in and out... some he knew; some she knew... She was their pal; though as she knew, they regarded thin Ralph Manresa, her husband, in perfect riding breeches talking to the Parson, with suspicion.' This is Ralph Manresa's only appearance; he did not, apparently, arrive at the Hall in the posh car with Mrs Manresa and William Dodge, nor would he leave with them.

Giles, in the company of Mrs Manresa, is happier after his adventure on the path, feeling 'less of an audience, more of an actor', although Aunt Lucy: 'mocked his man-of-action shoes.' Every character is pointed, sharp. The atmosphere is electric:

"Isa too watched [Giles]. He had been faithless to her before now. Given a chance, Manresa would develop into another of those 'passing affairs that make no difference to what I feel for you'. He had to have his toy; but it would be a very different story if she took Rupert Haines for her teddy bear. She could see him, over in the corner, the queer man with the inappropriate wife." [49]

Mrs Parker, one of the villagers, turns to welcome Giles who, she thinks, becomes more like his (dead) mother every day:

" 'But surely, we're more civilised now?' 'Are we?' said Giles. He looked, once, at William [Dodge]. It was a piece of luck that William was there to serve as a scapegoat... he knew what his left hand was doing. He could despise him, <the pervert,> instead of himself, the coward... but he could not despise his wife. She had not spoken to him.

'Surely,' said Mrs Parker... 'Surely we are.'

Giles then did the usual trick; shut his lips; frowned; took up the pose of one who bears the burden. He had been in the City all the week making money; on the Stock Exchange.

'No, I don't admire you,' Isa said as plainly as a glance fixed stubbornly to the left of her could say. 'Silly little boy – with blood on his shoes.'

Whom did she admire then? Not Dodge. Giles could take that for granted... They had often bickered, he and Isa, over this, that and the other; but only by way of a joke. She had the children; naturally he wanted amusement. The Manresa – he looked round for her; but instead, here was the Rector...

'Like to see the greenhouse?' said Isa suddenly turning to William Dodge.

That was precisely what William had wanted, until Giles joined them and confused him. Now there was nothing for it but to follow the woman. Her husband had no intention of coming too." [50]

The tension in this scene, throughout, is personal, agonisingly so. The central 'strain', indeed the fissure, is between Isa and Giles, as Giles publicly walks around the Barn with Mrs Manresa while Isa tries to tolerate his betrayal: 'She had the children; naturally he wanted amusement.' Isa, betraying Giles in her turn as she thinks of Rupert Haines, does not admire her husband: 'Silly little boy – with blood on his shoes'. But at least, after his passage through the gate, he has had the courage to acknowledge his attraction for Mrs Manresa. And he could not despise his wife.

Together in the greenhouse, William Dodge smiles at Isa. They have a relaxed conversation which was 'the usual fate of the eunuch. Women knew they had nothing to hope; nothing to fear.' Dodge has guessed Isa does not love her husband: 'If you don't love your husband, <then> who do you?' he asked. 'His name's Haines; he's married to a dull woman in a coat and skirt'. replies Isa. And they get onto first-name terms. In this early typescript Pericles is mentioned:

" 'They say we don't respect anything – that's why we're not happy,' said Isa. 'Bosh', he said. 'Who's put ideas into your head? Who's ever been happy? What's happiness? The Athenians in the age of Pericles? The English in the time of Shakespeare? The French in the time of Louis the 14th?' " [51]

Virginia obviously did not see the world of Pericles as the ultimate ideal, providing the only possibility of happiness, as Leonard did – and as he must all too often have repeated to anyone who would listen. Isa asks Dodge why Mrs Manresa came:

"And he told her the whole story; just as if this world were the only world; there was nothing else in the whole world but the greenhouse, herself sitting on one plank, and himself opposite among the pots." [52]

So William Dodge, sitting in the greenhouse, told Isa 'the whole story' about why Mrs Manresa came. Tantalisingly, Virginia does not tell us what the 'whole story' was that Dodge told Isa about Mrs Manresa's coming. Not knowing, I encourage all trespassers to have a guess. Whoever she was, there is an unmistakable agony in the way these scenes are written; the 'pointz' in the Barn are all too sharp. In the LTS and the final version of *Between the Acts,* those sharp points are somewhat blunted as she sought to restrain her rage. But in both the later versions Giles's relationship with Mrs Manresa reaches a sexual climax which is absent in the ETS. In the library Old Bart realises that his son is unhappy:

"and to him that mattered more than the life-blood of immortal spirits... (Sultan had followed him)... Giles was out of sorts, suffering; exactly why, he did not know; but roughly from the notion that whereas others fought, he totted up figures. Surveying the Barn with the eye of memory, he remembered; Manresa was in tow. Merciful Manresa – admirable woman! He reflected, with a grin, heroics are out of place when the harvest of the mind is reaped, the treasured lifeblood of immortal spirits is distilled, not, let us remember, by the brain, only, but by this very queer brute – he looked down – the dog." [53]

Lucy comes into the library, but 'There was nothing in her to weight a man, like Giles, to the earth. He looked sardonically at Lucy, perched on the arm of the chair, fingering her gold cross. He never understood how she had borne children. She belonged to the sect of unifiers; he to the separatists; he liked variety.'

The second part of the pageant is about to begin. Lucy with Old Bart goes out onto the lawn. 'Mrs Manresa was crossing the lawn in front of them. Giles was by her side. Her scarf, her hat, her gestures, all seemed to set her at the head of the procession. Bartholemew blessed the power of the human body to distract the mightiest of men from their enterprises; his son would commit no folly so long as she were there to illustrate the flesh; therefore he excused, indeed loved her.' And was amused to find that Lucy, with her 'airy ways of casting a wide survey over the world... had taken a dislike to a particular person.' Virginia, as both the younger Isa and the older Lucy, has taken a dislike to the woman she feared was supplanting her. (Again, how could Virginia be writing this about Vita?)

Mabel herself begins the second Act; she is now beautiful and magnificent as Queen Anne ushering in the Age of Reason. And she remains, a stalwart presence in an insubstantial world, through all three versions of *Between the Acts:*

"Mabel Hopkins took her stand on the raised ground in front of the audience. Eyes fed on her like fish rising. [She was very nice to look at. A grey wig, lent by a legal gentleman, was on her head. And bunches of pearls hung at her ears.] Her cheeks had been powdered; the red was very smooth and clear beneath. And her grey-green satin robe (a bedspread), pinned in stone-like folds gave her the appearance of a statue. She carried a sceptre and a little round orb. Was she England or Queen Anne? Both perhaps. The first words were lost. She was saying, when they could hear her, '...reason holds sway.' Then she spoke louder:

" 'Time, leaning on his sickle, stands amazed. While commerce from her cornucopia pours the mingled tribute of her diverse ores... At my behest the armed warrior lays his shield away; the heathen leaves the altar smoking with unholy sacrifice. The violet and the eglantine over the riven earth their flowers entwine. No longer fears the unwary wanderer the snake. And in the helmet, yellow bees their honey make. Beneath the shelter of my flowing robe' (here she extended her arm) 'the arts arise. Music for me unfolds its heavenly harmony. At my behest, the miser leaves his hoard unwatched; at peace the mother sees her children play.' Here she waved her sceptre, and figures advanced from the bushes." [54]

Let Mabel Haskins forever be remembered as the Queen of a peaceful and prosperous England enlightened by Reason and enchanted by music, the operas she loved.

If Leonard could idealise Pericles, Virginia's answer was Mabel. Only his idealisation had the backing of the major universities, of all academia – of the entire patriarchy itself – whereas Virginia, one woman, created hers out of a capable servant who had been detested and consistently humiliated and bullied by Leonard. She does not care what he will think when he reads it. This is her truth. Such is her defiance.

There follows a scene in the style of eighteenth century caustic drama. But after this the pageant loses its momentum:

"Gaps came. Emptiness revealed itself. Illusion failed. Then, all of a sudden, the cows... did the trick. One had lost her calf. She lifted her great moon-eyed head and bellowed. The dumb yearning put into her bellow was the very voice Miss La Trobe wanted. All the great moon-eyed heads laid themselves back; from cow after cow came the same yearning bellow. It was the primeval voice; yet loud in the ear of the present moment... Lashing their tails like pokers with blobs on the end, they began careering. Either it was maternal passion; or the gadfly; or Eros had planted his dart. They were goaded. The cows did what no poet could have done; annihilated the gap; bridged the distance; filled the emptiness; continued the emotion; stirred the lily pond in whose mud lay bones and rings and trinkets...the cows stopped; lowered their heads; once more browsed statelily, <as if content>.

'That's done it,' said Miss La Trobe... fixing her bold dark eyes upon William Dodge... You couldn't have done that, Mr Whatsyourname.' " [55]

And so the lesbian La Trobe, in touch with female nature, triumphs over her homosexual male counterpart when the 'moon-eyed cows' come to her rescue in an unforgettable primal scene that also expresses Virginia's dumb yearning for children. This in stark contrast to the artificiality of her spoof eighteenth century playlet, that can be equated with the tea-table manner Virginia learnt in her parents' large Hyde Park Gate house as a young woman, and which she could adopt as a veneer at any time – a manner which many commentators have misunderstood in an attempt to show how happy she really was.

At the end of the final scene of this playlet, Lady Harpy Harraden recites:

"And so to end the play, the moral is, good people,

The God of love is full of tricks...

The way of the will is plain to see...

Good people all,

[Farewell.] For where there's a will there's a way, [you see]...

But the words 'where there's a will there's a way,' rose and pointed to Giles. Every clodhopper had his will. Off to Gretna Green with the girl. The deed done, damn the consequences. So it was in the eighteenth century.

[Giles] got up. For the act was over." [56]

Virginia must have written this scene specifically for Leonard. She is urging him on. She is saying: *If you feel you're chained to a rock, do something about it. Don't just squash the snake and the toad of our marriage. Have the courage to commit yourself with the woman you say you want and damn the consequences, as I have damned the consequences in writing about it from my point of view. Look, I've exposed you. What are you going to do about it?*

Is this Virginia's message to Leonard? Her challenge? If so, his reply became the end game of their marriage, and of her life.

The scene ends. Reason [Mabel] descends from her plinth:

"Gathering her robes about her, serenely acknowledging the applause of the audience, she passed across the stage...

A moral. What? Giles supposed it was: Where there's a Will there's a Way. The words rose and pointed a finger of scorn at him. Off to Gretna Green with his girl; the deed done. Damn the consequences.

'Like to see the greenhouse?' he said abruptly, turning to Mrs Manresa.

'Love to!' she exclaimed, and rose.

Was there an interval? Yes, the programme said so." [57]

During this interval, in the absence of Giles and Mrs Manresa who are having sex in the greenhouse, Reason (Mabel) throws her mantle on a holly hedge and old Lucy Swithin congratulates Miss La Trobe: 'you've made me feel I could have played... Cleopatra! You've stirred in me my unacted part, she meant.' Her words are translated by Miss La Trobe:

" 'You've twitched the invisible strings,' was what the old lady meant; and revealed – of all people – Cleopatra! Glory possessed her. Ah, but she was not merely a twitcher of individual strings; she was one who seethes wandering bodies and floating voices in a cauldron, and makes rise up from its amorphous mass a recreated world. Her moment was on her – her glory." [58]

This is what Virginia Woolf did: she 'seethes wandering bodies and floating voices' in the cauldron of her creativity and brings them back to life. Detached from everyday existence in her Lodge other people, many of them dead, entered her body and shone in that magic place half way up her spine; then she writes. It is her glory – and her burden.

Experiencing the agony of loss, Isa is on her own. In the final text she picks a rose, looking for Rupert Haines. 'There he was for one second; but surrounded, inaccessible. And now vanished'. She drops her flower. 'What single, separate leaf could she press? None.' With no present moment and no future, she retreats into the past, going into the stable yard:

"where the great pear tree spread its ladder of branches against the wall. The tree whose roots went beneath the flags, was weighted down with hard green pears. Fingering one of them she murmured: 'How am I burdened with what they drew from the earth; memories; possessions. This is the burden that the past laid on me, last little donkey in the long caravanserai crossing the desert. 'Kneel down,' said the past. 'Fill your pannier from our tree. Rise up, donkey. Go your way till your heels blister and your hoofs crack.'

The pear was hard as stone. She looked down at the cracked flags beneath which the roots spread. 'That was the burden,' she mused. 'laid on me in the cradle; murmured by waves; breathed by restless elm trees; crooned by singing women; what we must remember; what we would forget.' She looked up. The gilt hands of the stable clock pointed inflexibly to two minutes to the hour. The clock was about to strike.

'Now comes the lightning,' she muttered. 'from the stone blue sky. The thongs are burst that the dead tied. Loosed are our possessions.' " [59]

Voices interrupt. Isa encourages herself: 'On little donkey, patiently stumble. Hear not the frantic cries of the leaders who in that they seek to lead desert us.' Isa had come out on to the path that led past the green-house:

"The door was kicked open. Out came Mrs Manresa and Giles. Unseen, Isa followed them across the lawns to the front row of seats." [59]

This section of *Between the Acts* was written by Virginia in January 1941 when she suffered a sudden, apparently unexplained, deep depression two months before her death.

She is making a point about the greenhouse which sheds light on her major upset when Leonard ordered a heated greenhouse to be erected against one wall of Monk's House in July, 1939. He wanted a warm place not only for growing plants but to reproduce the tropical conditions in Ceylon where, as he told Vanessa in 1911: 'The colour is amazing and one's animal passions get very strong and one enjoys one's body to the full.' [60] No doubt there was a lurking fear on Virginia's part that if the heated greenhouse had been built, she would have had to put up with demonstrations of Leonard's sexuality at close quarters – and not with her.

We understand some of the language, maybe enough of Virginia's allu-sions to trace an inner story. She called Mabel Haskins an 'unsunned pear', one of many that hung on the withered tree in the stable-yard. In the character of the gentle, somewhat childish, wraith-like Lucy Swithin she imagines she could have been Cleopatra. Not, of course, Aspasia, the mistress of Pericles, but a magnificent Queen in her own right. If only she had not been married to an angry and embittered fanatic who took her money and chained and imprisoned her and starved her of water – of love, so that at last she, as Isa, had no 'single, separate leaf to press'. And she drops her rose. All is over.

Virginia did not like people recognising herself or her friends and relatives in her books, but I think when she wrote *Between the Acts,* she may have both hoped and expected that some of her readers would see through the disguises and read her message. We have been very slow to take up her challenge.

Rupert Haines was a figment of Virginia's imagination but he was at least as importantly (for her and for us) Roger Fry, who with his death had become part of the crowd of those she had lost. Fry died on the 9th of September, twenty-one years to the day after she had taken her almost-fatal dose of Veronal in 1913. As Leaska points out, she must have been very aware of these two dates. Writing the drafts of *Pointz Hall* at the same time as working on Fry's biography, she was able to bring him back to life in her Lodge and was comforted by her 'inner Roger'. But when she finished writing both books she was on her own, isolated (Isa-lated), with only Leonard and Louise at Monk's House, and the possible looming threat of a Mrs Manresa who was not merely 'another of those passing affairs that make no difference to what I feel for you.'

Mitchell Leaska wrote: '[Virginia Woolf] had throughout her creative life the peculiar inclination of transfiguring the pattern of her private history into the larger and looser history of English civilization.' [61]

'Now comes the lightning,' she muttered, 'from the stone blue sky.' The war, with invasion apparently imminent, is at one with Giles's actual, and Leonard's supposed, unfaithfulness, the personal and political events 'seethed together' in her cauldron. For Isa, the climactic moment of reality was seeing Giles and Mrs Manresa come out of the greenhouse together. The little donkey with broken hoofs, broken hearted, burdened with the past, stumbles on. But not for long.

Virginia saw all of that destructiveness with her wide-eyed, unblinking female vision and has told us the truth – 'truth, the biographer's Goddess', as she called it in the early transcript. [62] Let's see it. Let's hear it. And let us also recognise that she was speaking in the knowledge of her own irretrievable personal disaster. Let there be an end to the crap about her 'madness' while Leonard, exercising his unlimited selfishness and stupidity as he systematically cut the ground from beneath her feet, apparently gets away with a slow and subtle form of murder.

Virginia's last completed novel does not end there. She takes us through the Victorian Age:

" 'Good Lord,' Giles interrupted, grating his chair on the gravel. This is tosh, but at any rate it's honest tosh... If he had said, Save me from my sentimental humbug of an Aunt... and Isa, for some reason won't look at me; and the blood drops, drops, drops from the torture I'm in down, down, down (he looked down at his blood-stained tennis shoes); if he had said this, he would have come closer, though not of course very close, to what he meant.

They knew, at least, that he meant 'I am unhappy.' " [63]

Then the Modern Age arrives:

'All their nerves were on edge, because they were about to be shown themselves'... And then the shower fell; sudden, profuse; like tears... It soaked them in a second':

" 'Oh that our human pain could here have ending,' Isa muttered, looking [straight] up and receiving two great blots of raindrop full in the face. They trickled down her cheeks. Her eyes rested on the grass, from which suddenly rose an earthy smell. The rain stopped... The gramophone struck up – the tune was nothing. But the music, like the shower, was a voice that was no one's voice speaking, and lifting the burden...

'Oh that our human pain could here have ending,' Isa repeated, actually consenting for the moment to endow this simple melody with her entire treasure, if so be the human suffering that weighed on the audience could be hymned away." [64]

The villagers bring on mirrors that they flash at the audience:

"each holding what seemed a dazzling flash of light. In fact the spoil of bedrooms, kitchens and lavatories; looking glasses of all shapes and sizes. These dashed, flitted, leapt and jerked in front of the audience. Now Bart was lit up; now Manresa; then again everyone saw his or her own face precisely as it was at the moment. <the little devils sometimes stopped dead. Then reflected and twitched. The others laughed.>... It was chaos. It was insult. It was the break-up of the play." [65]

In the LTS everyone was disturbed except Mrs Manresa:

"Mrs Manresa, with a courage that made her the envy and admiration of all present, the representative of all that's best and most enduring in bourgeois society, had out her pocket mirror, powdered her nose, applied her lipstick; set her hat straight; and took advantage of the opportunity offered to make up. 'Admirable woman!' old Bartholemew cried, slapping her on the knee. She alone preserved, in the dissipation and deliquescence of the present moment, her identity. She alone had the courage to defy the looking glass – by making use of it." [66]

And then a megaphone asserted itself, some unknown voice pointing out members of the audience: 'Liars and thieves... the poor are as bad as the rich... Look at ourselves, ladies and gentlemen. How's this damned wall which we call Civilisation to be built by orts [and] scraps and fragments like Ourselves?' [67]

Virginia was not afraid of mingling civilisation with barbarism, or sanity with madness in a world that 'flowed eternally'. She knows these artificial barriers are both inhibiting and destructive – and maybe she also knew that throughout her marriage she had been the victim of just these barriers erected by the rigid, judgemental mind of Leonard: she was confined in the chaotic dark side of his brain where the emotional and the mad are incarcerated. While he identified himself only with the light, 'good' side of civilisation, which he saw as sanity – but was at the same time unhappy, the victim of uncontrollable irritability. This is the story of the Woolfs' marriage. It is the story of many marriages.

Virginia tried to liberate Leonard from what she saw as a far greater burden than her own, that of being the landless Jewish scapegoat. This was her sacrifice.

'Dispersed are we'... the play is ended. The audience finally disintegrates in snatches of talk. 'We all act. But whose play? Ah, that's a question – and if we're asking questions at the end, isn't it a failure? Or is that what she meant?' [68]

" '[So] good-bye,' said old Bartholemew, taking the little fat hand of Mrs Manresa in his. All were retreating and withdrawing, and he was left with the ash grown cold and no glow, no glow on the log... as the retreating Manresa, admirable woman, all sensation, ripped the rag doll and let the sawdust stream from his heart... but where was the dog? Chained in a kennel? The little veins swelled in his forehead. He whistled. And here [he came,] racing across the lawn with a fleck of foam on the nostril – <came> his dog." [69]

Although some of the original rage is indeed lost in the two later versions, there is an increasing depth of misery in Isa in the final text as she watches Giles and Mrs Manresa going together towards her car:

"There was Dodge, the lip reader, her semblable, her conspirator, a seeker like her after hidden faces. He was hurrying to rejoin Mrs.

Manresa who had gone in front with Giles – 'the father of my children,' she muttered. The flesh poured over her, the hot, nerve-wired, now lit up, now dark as the grave physical body. By way of healing the rusty fester of the poisoned dart she sought the face that all day long she had been seeking... But, she was crying, had we met before the salmon leapt like a bar of silver... had we met, she was crying...

Turning the corner, there was Giles attached to Mrs Manresa. Giles had his foot on the edge of the running board. Did they perceive the arrows about to strike them?

'Jump in, Bill,' Mrs. Manresa chaffed him.

And the wheels scurred on the gravel, and the car drove off." [70]

Virginia herself was close to despair as she completed her book while struggling to cope with an increasingly desperate situation in real life – the situation that is noted in her diary and which we will discover in the next chapter – as she attempts to cope without Mabel through a cold winter; prohibited from spending any money and from visiting Ethel Smyth; overworked; short of food, in a house that is being run by Leonard together with Louise.

Both Isa and Dodge were 'seekers after hidden faces'. So must we be. Whose face lay under Mrs Manresa's ill-fitting make-up?

Standing by herself, Lucy Swithin gazes down into the lily pool:

"at the water – the grey water. Under the plates of the leaves upon each of which rested a rose-red lily was an inscrutable world. Above her, was the flow of the air; and aeroplanes, shark-like; she stood on a thin plank, between two fluidities, caressing her cross. That little jagged leaf at the edge suggested, by its contours, Europe. There were other leaves. She fluttered her eyes over the surface, naming the leaves India, Africa, America. Islands of security, glossy and thick. 'Why, Bart,' she addressed him – but he had gone with his dog into the house. She had meant to ask him – can't civilisation... light there? <She could just as well argue with Bart in absentia. He was her adversary – the other point of view.>

She was retrieving from sharks above and sharks below a foothold for new people, other people, the red-skinned or if you like the black, to settle on." [71]

The text of Pointz Hall is like water, revealing and concealing on many different levels, shadowed, shifting, illuminating. Water, and the lack of it, is ever-present in all drafts of *Between the Acts*. It is as though we, the readers, are looking at Virginia's life during this time reflected in a pool, this being the only bearable way of coping with a situation whose direct experience is too painful, too intense and upsetting, to be faced directly.

Lucy looks at the fish:

"They knew her; she knew them. Because we've never caught them they trust us, <she addressed her brother, the adversary.>

'Because we feed them, that's greed', he would say.

'They give us silver and gold,' she would reply.

'Sex', he would say... He would carry his little torch of reason, till it went out, in the darkness of the cave." [72]

Here Lucy is arguing with Old Bart in her head, even though she is alone; it is surely a transcript of a conversation Virginia and Leonard had already had, looking down into their small lily-pond. Lucy felt she had a connection with the fish, a relationship; Old Bart's side of the argument is typical of the male left brain – clever and unsympathetic, disliking any taint of anthropomorphism, carrying his 'little torch of reason', till it went out in the darkness of Plato's cave.

Let us consider what underlies the unfathomable and unbridgeable chasm between the characters in this imagined, and real, drama and admit:

Lucy and old Bart are adversaries.

Isa and Giles are adversaries.

Virginia and Leonard are adversaries.

Our right and left brains are adversaries.

We need to become aware of the adversarial nature of the sexes and of the human brain – of the conflicting visions they give rise to – if we are to understand in the least Virginia's writing, her life with Leonard, and her suicide. Intent on my book I have been both horrified and exhilarated to discover how much work there still is to do, especially on these three texts of *Between the Acts* – far more than I realised when I began. And well beyond the scope of this volume.

Miss La Trobe, happy, triumphant, sits in a pub:

"She took her mug. She drank.

Words copulated; seethed; surged. Phrases began shouldering up from the mist. Here was the breeding ground, among the very dull; the coarse; the kindly; the imperceptive, yet shrewd; the intolerably laden; those who bore the whole weight on their backs like dumb oxen... She didn't care... how she 'degraded' her class (middle) or her sex (female). Or even remembered one or the other. She sat there like a man, her arms akimbo, her mug before her, staring out of her deep set blue eyes, and the men in their earth-coloured jackets; seeing beyond them the first acts of the magnificent drama. She was tunnelling and foraging her way to that culmination... The men knew that Bossy was after something." [73]

Ethel Smyth and Virginia called each other Bossy and Flimsy. Lucy is called Flimsy in the text, as Miss La Trobe is called Bossy, in the clearest of parallels that Smyth would at once appreciate on reading the book; only she did not do that until after Virginia's death.

In the dining room of Pointz Hall, its four inhabitants sit quietly around the table, united in silence, while a rather puzzling play that changes nothing becomes a fading memory in their minds. But the book does not end here. It continues, because Virginia had become aware that life wasn't like that. Conflicting energy goes on surging between the characters and must be expressed. Lucy Swithin leads us back. She still doesn't know what the play meant: 'The peasants... and the kings; the fool; ourselves...' Whereupon:

"With its sheath sliced in four, into petals exposing a white cone, Giles offered a banana to his wife.

Isa took it. She looked again at the sky... she saw the audience dispersing... But the play remained; the golden marble shape still floated. What did it mean?'... 'Ain't Lucy,' said Bartholemew..., asking too much? <She wants to know what things mean.> Giles held out a match." [74]

Lucy and Isa leave the men and go into the sitting room:

"Isa... sank with her knee doubled into a low chair by the window. Sitting within the shell of the room, she was overlooking the summer night... Mrs Swithin sat down opposite the window. The filtered light made her gleam like an iridescent snail shell; or a sea-worn glass...

'This year, last year, next year, never,' Isa made up her little rhyme.

'Mrs. Whatshername,' said Lucy, 'improved. At first I thought her odious.'

['Mrs Whatshername.] You mean Manresa,' said Isa.

Beyond the shell of the house, flowers and leaves burnt, as her hand burnt on the window ledge. 'A seamless surface, sensitive,' she rambled, imagining a thin sentient skin, or plant, of flower, of flesh, of silver spreading [seamless] over the world.

'But if we're left asking questions at the end, isn't it a failure?' Mrs Swithin... addressed this question to her knitting.

'[The Rector] said she meant,' said Isa, turning her palm uppermost in the sunshine, 'we are parts of one another.'

'Did you feel that?' Mrs Swithin murmured, knitting.

'Yes... no,' Isa murmured, for it was yes, no. It was dispersing and uniting. There was the tide, ebbing, flowing; and the birds scattering; congregating; and the sower casting seed. 'But splintered,' she said. Should it be splintered, fissured or shivered? the word for a reflection in a looking-glass? for the glass that a bullet cracks?" [75]

" 'Splintered,' said Isa, finding the word for reflections in a looking-glass. Shivered, splintered, fissured. She groped among the obvious words for the obvious things. Dispersed are we. Desiring to be one, she was many; wishing for certainty, she doubted.

Mrs Swithin rambled round the room looking at pictures. [76]

" 'If you're thinking of the orts, scraps and fragments, and when the looking-glasses came in – were those the words? – that to build a wall, we must [rebuild] <re-collect> ourselves. Out of fragments; including the fool.'

'Maybe,' said Isa. 'Fling your seeds, sower,' she added to her rhyme, 'and flow, tide; birds, return to your tree tops–'

Here Giles and Bartholemew came in. Lucy smiled, looking up. It was so nice, being all together... And they looked, all of them, ennobled. She made a little chirruping sound of [merriment,] <welcome,> of content...

The post too. For Giles, long envelopes; for Mrs Swithin, fat letters; thin bills; for Isa, nothing... Isa's hand suddenly felt cold. The window sill was in shadow now.

Lucy had stuck her needles into her knitting; for it was time to read her book. She had lost her place in the great Outline of Natural History. She was turning the pages; she was looking at the pictures, like a child. She had gone back to her butterfly-hunting days." [77]

As Virginia, writing *A Sketch of the Past*, had gone back to her childhood. Giles speaks of the children:

" 'Yes, Mrs Sands gave them the paper flowers from the Barn,' said Giles.

Unfaithful all day, as they had been, the children, even the thought of the children, sleeping with paper garlands thrown over their beds, renewed their marriage; in spite of Manresa; in spite of the other man. Isa looked at his shoes; he had changed them; they were polished, patent leather pumps." [78]

In the ETS, both Lucy and Isa finally manage to tolerate Mrs Manresa, so in one sense writing the book has achieved an important purpose for Virginia. Facing up to and overcoming jealousy would have been a major reason for working on the text. She has succeeded in reducing to manageable proportions the psychic weight of whoever it was that had made her feel insecure. So far as Virginia was concerned, she had regained her balance, she had triumphed. The question remains whether in real life Leonard would let her keep her balance. I do not think he did.

"Shadows crept over Bartholemew's high forehead; over his great nose. He looked leafless, spectral, and his chair monumental. As a dog shudders its skin, his skin shuddered. He rose, shook himself, glared at nothing, and stalked from the room. They heard the dog's paws padding on the carpet behind him." [79]

At last, Isa and Giles are on their own. *Draft 2* ends:

"Isa let her sewing drop. Giles crumpled the long envelope into a ball. The window behind their small dark heads was all sky, without colour; nothing but the lines <of the leaf-laden branches> were left, crossing and crossing. The house had lost its shelter; <it had crumpled.> The stars <all> appeared as if they had been there behind the clouds, behind the colour, waiting. It was like the first night before roads were made; or houses; the night that dwellers in caves had watched rise over the unknown world. Now the known world had vanished, and the stars rose again.

It was the first act of the new play. But who had written the play? What was the meaning of the play? And who made them act their parts?

Then, the rage which they had suppressed all day burst out. It was their part – <to tear each other asunder,> to fight." [80]

In pencil was written underneath: 'Why must we take our parts in the play? And who has written it?' Who indeed did write the two versions of Pointz Hall and *Between the Acts*? Miss La Trobe, drunk, in a pub? Lucy Swithin with her vision of the primordial world as it was and could be again? Mabel, standing on her plinth surveying actors and audience with the eye of Reason? Not Isa or Giles who were 'irrevocably' the heroine and hero, isolated in the shell of their house that had crumpled and no longer sheltered them. Not Mrs Manresa, the 'wild child of nature', vulgar, bourgeoisie, her ill-fitting make-up falling off her face. Not Old Bart with his ferocious dog padding after him.

This was certainly not Leonard's play; he had written his own script, *The Hotel* where he, the Wandering Jew, goes on and on and leaves Virginia, a squirrel in a cage (his cage) going round and round. It was not Virginia's, either. She was Antigone walled up in Creon's ancient Greek cave, where she would look her last on the sky and all is dark.

The defining characteristic of *Between the Acts*, running through all versions, is the division between Isa and Giles. This division is also evident in the older generation, between Lucy and Bart – and these latter are sister and brother so that the division, the fissure, the unfathomable gulf between female and male, is not limited to sexual partners. With both pairs, each hold to a point of view that is antagonistic and inimical to the other. There is a non- or super- human reconciliation beginning with the oil lamp at the opening of the Earlier Typescript and ending after the pageant, with the flowers on the table in the dining room of Pointz Hall between sky and ant. But we go beyond that point of reconciliation to the ultimate conflict, as Isa and Giles fight.

I have chosen to identify Leonard closely with Giles. It may be that Mrs Manresa did not exist, and never was intended to exist outside the pages of Virginia's novel; that the rage so evident in the book, and particularly in the early drafts, is entirely her own and that she was 'mad' when she wrote it. This would no doubt have been Leonard's point of view; and some commentators would agree. However, so far as I am concerned, to take this view necessitates an unacceptable invalidation of Virginia. The book becomes merely 'a novel' with perhaps incidental reflections of their lives. I think the book is more than a novel; different from a novel; and intended to be. When the pageant reaches the Present Day, each member of the audience sees their face reflected in the mirrors held up to them. Virginia is recording, at a deeper level than in her diary, the fractured reflection of the reality of her marriage as she experienced it, and particularly the painful reality of the last two years. There is a note of bitter regret that she was married to Leonard and not the elusive Roger Fry.

The implication of calling *Between the Acts* the longest suicide note in history, as Leaska suggests, is that when Virginia began it in 1938 she intended to kill herself at its completion. If this was so, why, in 1938, did she want to do so? Did she not, rather, begin her book with the aim of finding common ground, a middle way that would include the warring sexual opposites by expanding the context within which they operated? I think perhaps she did until rage at maleness in general and whatever Leonard was doing in particular, as he strove to reduce her hold on life and take over from her, took over.

Leaska points out that Virginia had not, as was usual with her, given a date for the completion of the ETS, saying: 'readers will see from the number of revisions of those last pages the difficulty she had in ending it.' He sums up:

"Her failure to acknowledge its completion suggests, moreover, that somewhere in the back of her mind the novel's conclusion was not to her satisfaction. How could one end a book, presumably about art and literature, with a husband and wife about 'to tear each other asunder'? The first ending is in fact so different from that of the published text that everything leading up to it must be read with different emphases and focuses of attention... The Later Typescript, from which many deep folds of anger had been smoothed, became in effect a bridge of compromise between the Earlier and Final Typescripts. Virginia Woolf had indeed succeeded in suppressing the ferocity of her original plan. At what price, however, only she would finally know." [81]

Virginia spent most of her remaining weeks of life revising this book. She could not show Leonard her original manuscript, not only because she had revealed her sense of the unbearable tension between them, but because she had destroyed his more limited vision of 'civilisation', which was the very basis of his existence. It would be impossible to have her final work published by the Hogarth Press whilst she was alive. The price she paid in 'suppressing the ferocity of her original plan' is in a practical sense all too obvious: rather than destroy Leonard, her 'inviolable centre', she tried to act as censor to her own work, painfully attempting to withdraw the shadow of her anger from him, until she wrote to John Lehmann saying that the damaged final text was 'much too slight and sketchy' to publish. [82]

Leonard believed that his illusion was more important than the reality of Virginia's perception. To maintain his illusion, it was a necessity to him that Virginia herself should admit he was right; thus he demanded her total surrender. He had already made it impossible for her to escape from the confining outer world of Monk's House. Now there must be no further flights into her inner world. Even the dead Roger Fry was a threat because he provided an unwelcome comparison to him and a solace for her. Virginia's autonomy must be completely consumed in the fire of his obsession, leaving the Wandering Jew free to roam the destroyed world on his own. In the end Virginia sacrificed her power of writing on the altar of Leonard's self-image as the sinless, guiltless man, the caring husband of a 'mad' wife.

Virginia frequently argued against Leonard's pessimistic attitudes about 'the end of the world' and 'the end of civilisation', as she records in her diary:

"But our talk? – it was about Civilization. All the gents. against me. Said very likely, more likely than not, this war means that the barbarians will gradually freeze out culture. Nor have we improved. Tom & Saxon [T.S. Eliot and Saxon Sydney-Turner] said the Greeks were more thoroughly civilised. The slave was not so much a slave as ours are. Clive [Bell] also pessimised – saw the light going out gradually. So I flung some rather crazy theories into the air." [83]

It is time we listened to Virginia's 'rather crazy theories'. As for Leonard, he had long been predicting ultimate doom. He needed a catastrophe. What could he do when the war failed to provide him with one?

ROGER FRY, SELF-PORTRAIT, C. 1926

PART FIVE

MAKE BELIEVE

VIRGINIA AT MONK'S HOUSE
PHOTOGRAPH BY LEONARD, C. 1937

Chapter Twelve

DWINDLING ISLAND OF INSECURITY

In this account of the Woolfs' lives I have tried to comprehend Leonard's character, his work, his attitudes and ambitions in an attempt to discover whether they warrant the interpretation that he learnt how to control the state of Virginia's well-being, at first positively through the nineteen twenties; and then negatively through the nineteen thirties by becoming irritable, critical of her work, and finally depriving her of her necessary supports so that he could live a life of his own after her death, benefiting from her money and perhaps in the company of another female companion.

If we have this possibility in mind, we can perhaps see that Virginia was living on borrowed time when she wrote the first draft of *Between the Acts*. But we must ask why, if her marital situation had become problematic, she would further jeopardise her position by writing about it so revealingly in this novel-drama? How could she believe that Leonard would accept her book for publication? I think, on one level, she decided to throw caution to the winds for the sake of experiencing the relief, the intense pleasure, of writing it – whilst, in her imagination, she was living closely with the dead Roger Fry on whose biography she was working.

On another level it seems that she was deliberately taunting Leonard, telling him she knew of his attachment to 'Mrs Manresa' and daring him to publish her book that would force him to emerge out of his self-protective carapace, tread on the convoluted snake-and-toad of their marriage and commit himself openly to another woman. If this was her aim, she failed. By the time Leonard read the typescript of *Between the Acts*, in February 1941, he had eroded every aspect of her precarious position until it became untenable. On her death, Leonard would not need to risk coming out into the open since no questions would be asked. The unmasking of 'Mrs Manresa', if we are able to do so, becomes important if we are to understand both Virginia's text and her suicide.

I should like to put forward a different interpretation of the rage underlying the early draft of Pointz Hall from any that I have so far read. In my view three people are 'seethed together' in the interesting character of Mrs Manresa. The surface persona, with her ill-fitting make-up, may be derived from the American-born actress Elizabeth Robins, whom the Woolfs first met when she introduced herself during the unhappy occasion when Virginia was awarded the *Femina-Vie Heureuse* prize in May, 1928. At first Virginia was interested in Elizabeth, who had known her mother, and encouraged her to write her memoirs. Her later letters to her are cursory and work-related, her diary more revealing; in neither can we find the significant actress who brought Ibsen's female characters alive.

Leonard's description of her in his autobiography, on the other hand, is long and laudatory. He fills seven pages extolling her and her friend Dr Octavia Wilberforce, interrupting his story of Virginia's final breakdown early in 1941 in order to do so. Elizabeth:

"was born in Kentucky in 1862, a young lady belonging to the old slave-owning American aristocracy of the South... with extraordinary strength of mind and determination she broke the fetters of family and class, the iron laws which prescribe the life and behaviour of young ladies whether they be the Greek Antigone 600 years before Christ in Thebes or 2,500 years later Elizabeth in Kentucky, U.S.A... I think she must have been a great actress... I felt she had the same passionate dedication to her art that is so noticeable in another great actress, Peggy Ashcroft, and in the great Russian ballerina, Lydia Lopokova [*sic*]... When young she must have been beautiful, very vivacious, a gleam of genius with that indescribably female charm which made her invincible to all men and most women." [1]

In his account Leonard contrasts the 'fearless and indomitable' Elizabeth, who had broken the fetters of family and class, with the depressed, trapped Virginia. He even likens Elizabeth to Antigone for breaking away from the conventions of her time – but Antigone died imprisoned in a cave by Creon for her crime of independence. [2] So Elizabeth and Virginia represent two aspects of Antigone: the free and the trapped. With Leonard, another triangle.

Octavia, whose ancestors were 'the famous Wilberforces of the anti-slavery movement' and who had been born and bred in a large house in Sussex, was 'large, strong, solid, slow growing, completely reliable, like an English oak. Her roots were in English history and the English soil of Sussex, and, in her reserved way, she was deeply attached to both'. But, according to Leonard, Elizabeth was 'an even more remarkable woman' than Octavia.

Michael Holroyd writes about her:

"Elizabeth was an enigma. For two years she had been married to an American actor, George Parks, who one midnight (wearing a suit of stage armour) had stepped into the Charles River in Boston, and drowned. Dressed in black, Elizabeth had sailed to England." [3]

George Bernard Shaw called her 'a destroying angel in a bonnet'.

There is a pause in the records after that meeting in 1928 when Leonard invited the sixty-six year-old Elizabeth, who had fixed her still intense blue faun eyes on him, to dinner; later that year he published her *Ibsen and the Actress*. When she 'popped up' again in 1936, she wanted the Woolfs to publish her autobiography, *Both Sides of the Curtain* (we can note the similarity of Elizabeth's title to *Between the Acts*); however, the Hogarth Press rejected it and it was eventually published by Heinemann in 1940.

Her charms were wasted on Virginia, who evidently disliked her in the same way that Isa, in *Between the Acts*, dislikes Mrs Manresa:

"I have left out Elizabeth Robins by the way — a great curse to me; for she came at a moment of high pressure [writing *Three Guineas*]; and I had to throw myself into her infinitely intense, exacting, pernickety demands... a small frozen humming bird — with rouged lips: intense blue eyes, very small, old; full of accents & intensities." [4]

Early in 1937 Virginia and Leonard visited the house in Montpelier Crescent, Brighton, where Elizabeth Robins and Dr. Octavia Wilberforce lived. Whereas, to Virginia, Octavia was 'a very fresh coloured healthy minded doctor, in black, with loops of silver chain, good teeth & a candid smile, which I liked', Elizabeth's face 'is perhaps slightly rouged, but crinkled. Her hair is curled and grizzled. Her eyes L. said, a faun's eyes: very intense: suddenly intensifying like an actresses. All her movements angular, intense, grown rather rigid.' [5]

A younger Elizabeth Robins, trying to make her way on the English stage, emerges from the text of her autobiography that Virginia was reading at the height of the 'Greenhouse Affair' in July 1939. Surely this is Mrs Manresa: the vivacious American actress with her indescribably female charm, caroling songs, being the natural focus of attention among the audience. Perhaps the R of the 'RM' emblazoned on the door of Mrs Manresa's 'great silver-plated car... twisted so as to look in the distance like a coronet' refers to Robins rather than the shadowy Ralph Manresa.

Elizabeth Robins is the demonstrative element in Mrs Manresa, though she may have been more than that. There is also a reference to Vanessa in the similarity of names and her homosexual escort. I hazard the guess that there was also a hidden woman in Leonard's life, perhaps Alice Richie, the elder sister of Trekkie Parsons. Alice worked for the Press, which published her two novels. After Virginia's death Leonard took a house next door to the two sisters; however, Alice died of cancer a few months after Virginia's suicide, in 1941. For the rest of his life he carried on a passionate affair with Trekkie, writing many letters to her which survive; but despite often living with him at Monk's House, and his frequent proposals, she remained married to Ian Parsons. [6]

It is possible to assume that Leonard was faithful to Virginia throughout their marriage; but I do not think the evidence of their lives, and particularly Isa's suffering in *Pointz Hall*, supports that view.

In 1939 the lease of 52 Tavistock Square was coming to an end. Shortly before war broke out, the Woolfs decided to move both the Press and themselves to 37 Mecklenburgh Square. In the autumn, neither house was habitable and they were paying both rents. This provided an excuse for Leonard to make Virginia feel financially insecure during their annual accounting session in the New Year:

"Smoking cigarettes over the fire & feeling – just because the rent of 37 is so high – that we were, for once, foolish... some emptiness in me – my life – because L. said the rent was so high." [7]

Their supposed financial position was once again used against her, although she had brought one modest fortune into the marriage and had earned another with her writing. Made to worry needlessly, she felt 'some emptiness in me – my life'. Virginia wrote articles to make money, which she sometimes enjoyed, but she was clearly under stress: 'Always relieve pressure by a flight. Always violently turn the pillow... And I cling to my tiny philosophy: to hug the present moment (in which the fire is going out) [8]', while she laboured to finish her biography of Roger Fry and fought off depression during that very severe winter.

For the first time Leonard began directly intruding on her published work. An article by Virginia on 'Reviewing', published in the Sixpenny Pamphlet Series in November by The Hogarth Press, carried a 'Dissenting Note' from him which is five pages long and begins:

"This pamphlet raises questions of considerable importance to literature, journalism, and the reading public. With many of its arguments I agree, but some of its conclusions seem to me doubtful because the meaning of certain facts have been ignored or their weight under-estimated. The object of this note is to draw attention to these facts and to suggest how they may modify the conclusions." [9]

I haven't seen anyone comment on Leonard's assumption that he knew better than Virginia about reviewing. In his Note, which is actually long-winded and irrelevant, he makes a distinction between reviewing and literary criticism and uses it to put forward his own views. Nowadays one can afford to smile and say, well, after all, people read Virginia but not Leonard; however at the time, his intrusion must surely have made Virginia herself and others feel as though her piece was being discredited. Her article is actually entirely consistent as well as being very readable. She compares reviewers to the watchers in the street while women sitting in a shop window sew patches in worn-out garments.

The watchers do not gaze in silence. They 'comment aloud on the size of the holes, upon the skill of the workers and advise the public which of the goods in the shop window is the best worth buying'. We are drawn in, fascinated. Virginia limits what she says to the reviewer of imaginative literature and specifically excludes political reviewers, but even this did not satisfy Leonard. Having trodden all over it, he then praises Virginia for making an 'ingenious suggestion'. His motive, surely, was that he wanted to be seen as the expert and to diminish Virginia's influence as a commentator.

We need to be clear in our minds that it was quite wrong for Virginia Woolf, the successful modern writer with an assured public, to remain wholly dependent on her husband's personal idiosyncrasies and limitations for getting her work into print, especially as he was pursuing his own interests that had become increasingly inimical to hers.

Having completed her biography of Roger Fry, Virginia felt a glow: 'I cant help thinking I've caught a good deal of that iridescent man in my oh so laborious butterfly net'. [10] However, her pleasure in her achievement was short-lived. When she gave the first part to Leonard to read, he devastatingly attacked it:

"One Sunday... L. gave me a very severe lecture on the first half. We walked in the meadows. It was like being pecked by a very hard strong beak. The more he pecked the deeper, as always happens. At last he was almost angry that I'd chosen 'what seems to me the wrong method. Its merely anal[ysis], not history. Austere repression. In fact dull to the outsider. All those dead quotations'. His theme was that you cant treat a life like that: must be seen from the writer's angle, unless the liver is himself a seer, wh[ich] R[oger] wasn't. It was a curious example of L. at his most rational & impersonal: rather impressive; yet so definite, so emphatic, that I felt convinced: I mean of failure; save for one odd gleam, that he was himself on the wrong tack, & persisting for some deep reason – dissympathy with R[oger]? lack of interest in personality? Lord knows. I note this plaited strand in my mind; & even while we walked & the beak struck deeper deeper had this completely detached interest in L.['s] character." [11]

So far as Leonard was concerned, his 'reason and logic' had to win over the perceptive approach of both Virginia and Roger Fry. He worked himself into a state of anger pecking with his rigid, left-brain beak against those soft, right-brain worms. He was locked into his own carapace of apparent reason, logic, judgementalism and generalisation. There may have been other elements in his strongly negative reaction: he wanted the dead Roger to remain dead and not get in his way or give Virginia strength. But researching and writing his biography had brought Roger Fry very much alive to Virginia: her 'inner Roger' proved to be an emotional support to her, while she was also bringing him to life for Vanessa and other people who knew him – and this Leonard did not welcome, either. In my view he was playing a very long-term power game in which he used the Bloomsbury Group as a stepping-stone for his visionary ambition. Marrying Virginia was part of his upward climb (he would have preferred Vanessa), but when she rebelled he objectified her as being mad. Now she had produced an eminently sane and very readable biography which made it much harder to categorise her as insane. He therefore felt threatened by it to such a degree that he used his one major weapon – he attacked both the book and Virginia with the apparent logic of having seen a 'flaw' in it. However Virginia rightly sensed, lurking beneath his rationalisations, some very irrational negative motives. In his autobiography Leonard continued to justify himself:

"When I first read it I thought there was a flaw in it, and as Virginia recorded in her diary on March 20, 1940, walking over the water-meadows I tried – no doubt too emphatically – to explain to her what I felt about it... she allowed the facts to control her too compulsively so that the book was slightly broken-backed and never came alive as a whole.

Roger's sister Margery, Vanessa, and his friends and relations generally disagreed with me, but I still think I was right." [12]

On this occasion Virginia's integrity helped her to cope with Leonard's negativism, since her clear left brain was busy analysing his character. Nevertheless, her creative right brain was vulnerable to his attack: she was almost (but fortunately not quite) convinced that her book was a failure. She had had the foresight to send copies of this early version to both Vanessa and Margery Fry, Roger's sister, since by now she realised that Leonard's judgement could not be trusted. Vanessa responded immediately with a note: 'I'm crying cant thank you'. Margery also responded at once, saying that she had 'unbounded admiration' for the book and thought it 'very alive & interesting'. These two very different, and positive, reactions acted as a partial counterweight to Leonard's hard beak. His argument turned out to be wrong. The book sold well and was widely liked; but he never apologised or reconsidered his verdict.

We should ask why Leonard did not let Virginia's biography of Roger Fry, who was a key member of the Bloomsbury Group, come alive for him at the time, and why he disregarded the views of those for whom it did. Years later, writing his account, he merely clung to his old opinion – such is the arrogance of even the failed intellectual. If he had admitted he was wrong and accepted responsibility for having made Virginia feel anxious, hurt and upset when he first read her manuscript, he would have weakened his claim that her near-breakdowns were always and entirely brought on by fear of having her books published.

Leonard's attempted demolition of Virginia's biography of Roger Fry was his most brutal attack to date and one that she partly recognised for what it was – jealousy. Virginia had proved herself capable of using research material and had written a saleable and interesting book. It never seemed to occur to her that he was most critical of her when she succeeded in doing what he had tried to do and failed. His comments made it harder for her both to explore the right-brain region of her imagination, which was essential for her creativity, and to work on factual material, as though this was his province.

After Leonard's destructive criticism, Virginia worried that only a small number of people who had known Roger would be interested in the book, which would be 'dull' to other readers and therefore not sell well. To make matters worse, Leonard told her that financially the Press was doing very badly. He was apparently trying to make her withdraw her biography from publication. The legacy of this attempt can be seen in 1941 when she lost all confidence in *Between the Acts* and actually did withdraw it.

Virginia was having to live as best she could on a dwindling island of insecurity but she refused to do so on Leonard's terms. This was her courage: it has, over the years, taken her beyond the realms of the body's death and won her immortality. When we relive her days in the chronicle of her diary and letters and re-read her novels, her short stories, essays and articles, we in our turn gain the courage that enables us to watch the hard beak of the male left brain pecking into our own flesh and recognise it as a phenomenon that lacks the power to convince us that it is our fault, that it is we who have failed. However, it is still difficult to cope with and we can appreciate that Virginia's sense of disillusionment must have been very great. This is revealed to us if we take a closer look at Leonard's character and ambitions, as I am doing in this book. To whitewash him as a 'saint' caring for his sickly genius of a wife is not only to deprive him of any realistic existence but also to deny Virginia's true strength.

That winter Vanessa frequently came over from Charleston to paint a portrait of Leonard as he sat at his desk at Monk's House with his (now) very old-fashioned typewriter upon it. Sally the spaniel sprawls beside him and a pot of the carnations he had grown in his garden stands on a small table close by. Leonard had none of Virginia's reluctance to be painted and photographed, so these sessions with Vanessa working at her easel no doubt pleased him and drew them closer together. They would have talked about Virginia, their concerns for her health in this new wartime situation, when she had spent so much of the previous war having nervous breakdowns. Vanessa would have confirmed Leonard in his role as Virginia's guardian while Leonard probably asked for, and received, Vanessa's promise to support him if anything like that occurred again. As opportunity arose he would have reminded other people, too, about Virginia's 'madness' during World War One and sought their assistance, thus strengthening his position.

Vanessa's portrait of Leonard, paid for by Virginia, is now in the National Portrait Gallery in London. In comparison with photographs of Leonard taken at this time where he looks intense, even obsessed, Vanessa has made him seem much too amiable and benign.

The spring of 1940 was the first the Woolfs had spent in the country since 1914: ' The truth is we've not seen a spring in the country since I was ill at Asheham... & that had its holiness in spite of the depression.' Then she pulls herself up: 'Now, now – never any more future skirmishing or past regretting – relish the Monday & the Tuesday & dont take on the guilt of selfishness feeling: for in God's name I've done my share, with pen & talk, for the human race. Yes, I deserve a spring – I owe nobody nothing. For others can do as well as I can, this spring.' [13]

Two days later, on the first of April, Louise Everest played a prank on Virginia, going to her Lodge and disturbing her work by telling her that the most boring of the village women was waiting to see her – but when Virginia went into the house nobody was there. Louie tells the story in a book she wrote later, and adds that Virginia laughed when she found she had been made an April Fool. I see Leonard laughing louder than anyone, he no doubt put Louie up to it.

On the other hand Mabel Haskins, cooking at Monk's House, contributed greatly to Virginia's physical welfare while she recovered from a bout of flu: 'Mabel increases comfort 100 fold'; 'suavity & capacity itself, tho' the usual strain with L. and Louie'. It is now plain that Leonard and Louise Everest sided with each other against Mabel, and also on occasion against Virginia, causing tensions in the 'monkey house' – Mabel's name for Monk's House.

As well as continuing to hold meetings of the local Labour Party in the village of Rodmell, Leonard lectured to the Workers' Education Association (WEA) in Brighton. Virginia, not to be outdone, decided to give a lecture there. She admitted that part of her motive for putting an apparently disproportionate amount of energy into its composition was due to a sense of rivalry:

"Damn this running in the head that comes of lecture writing – cant think why I bother: why I let myself run on – is it suppressed jealousy? partly. Also I'm interested. But surely its excessive to go on making up, when its only 20 old ladies in black bonnets I shall make up for." [14]

Virginia gave her lecture, The Leaning Tower, over which she had taken so much trouble, to the WEA in Brighton on the 27th of April 1940. We should re-read it. Here is Virginia herself speaking to her audience as they share the common experience of the war that is approaching uncomfortably close to them:

"Today we hear the gunfire in the channel. We turn on the wireless; we hear an airman telling us how this very afternoon he shot down a raider... [Sir Walter] Scott never saw the sailors drowning at Trafalgar;

Jane Austen never heard the cannon roar at Waterloo. Neither of them heard Napoleon's voice as we hear Hitler's voice as we sit at home of an evening." [15]

She emphasises the importance of peace for a writer, so that in tranquility the under mind, or unconscious, can take over from the busy but uncreative upper mind. In the past, this had been possible even in wartime since writers were insulated in their ivory tower that was raised above the masses by the class of their parents and their parents' money that paid for a public school and university education. 'In one word, they are aristocrats; the unconscious inheritors of a great tradition.' But nowadays the tower is much less secure, it is leaning. Virginia Woolf distances both herself and her audience from those writers still trapped in the unsafe expensive-education-based leaning tower: 'The bleat of the scapegoat sounds loud in their work... Anger; pity; scapegoat bleating; excuse finding – these are all very natural tendencies; if we were in their position we should tend to do the same. But we are not in their position; we have not had eleven years of expensive education. We have only been climbing an imaginary tower. We can cease to imagine. We can come down. But they cannot. They cannot throw away their education; they cannot throw away their upbringing. Eleven years at school and college have been stamped upon them indelibly.' This, Virginia said, damaged them as writers. The insecure leaning tower leant more and more to the left, and writers became politicised; they could no longer let impressions enter their minds and be forgotten, to return in tranquility, that would have illuminated their writing with an inner glow, because they could not get away from the urgency and immediacy of modern life. 'Who can wonder if they have been incapable of giving us great poems, great plays, great novels? They had nothing settled to look at; nothing peaceful to remember; nothing certain to come. During all the most impressionable years of their lives they were stung into consciousness – into self-consciousness, into class-consciousness, into the consciousness of things changing, of things falling, of death perhaps about to come... The inner mind was paralysed, because the surface mind was always hard at work.'

Everything in her lecture targets Leonard and the rest of the Apostles whose expensive education, in her view, had permanently damaged them. Virginia distances herself from the predicament of those living in the dangerously leaning, ivory tower of sterile intellectualism by placing herself, together with her audience, away from the tower, at ground level, from where she can look at those still trying to live inside it as they yearn to connect with the 'real' world: 'And so we come to what is perhaps the most marked tendency of leaning-tower literature – the desire to be whole; to be human... no longer to be isolated and exalted in solitary state upon their tower, but to be down on the ground with the mass of human kind.'

She is able to look at the tower from outside it, because she had not had an expensive education; indeed, her only education was self-acquired, as she spent her childhood reading in her father's library. She had no degree. No letters after her name. She, one of the greatest between-war writers, and possibly the most significant, was 'unqualified'. D.H. Lawrence and Agatha Christie share this distinction with her. She managed to turn the tables on Leonard who never came down to the ground, never identified himself with the 'human ant-heap'. He remained a panther in a cage looking through a thousand bars, and behind them a thousand bars, until he doubted if there was a world beyond. Thus he, who sought to cage Virginia, has caged himself while she feels herself to be free.

She asserts that there will be a later generation for whom there will be no classes and no towers, and she identifies herself with that future generation. She then quotes from an 'eminent Victorian who was also an eminent pedestrian' (she is referring to her father, Sir Leslie Stephen): 'Whenever you see a board up with "Trespassers will be prosecuted on it", trespass at once'. She is speaking not to academic writers with university degrees, but directly to those in her audience who are unqualified:

"Let us trespass at once. Literature is no one's private ground. It is not cut up into nations; there are no wars there. Let us trespass freely and fearlessly and find our own way for ourselves. It is thus that English literature will survive this war and cross the gulf – if commoners and outsiders like ourselves make that country our own country, if we teach ourselves how to read and write, how to preserve and how to create."

So, at long last, Virginia delivers a brief version of what we can take to be her series of Clark lectures that Leonard had been 'wholly against' her giving back in February 1932. Now she detaches herself from the academic audience that would have heard her if she had been encouraged to give those lectures and says what she really wanted to say, reflecting her work at Morley College when she was still Virginia Stephen. Compacted into a single speech, she delivers it just before the worst stage of the war in front of 200 people (not the '20 old ladies in black bonnets' she had anticipated), who came to listen to her at the WEA in Brighton in 1940. It is no accident that she refers to her father, that 'eminent pedestrian', since he gave the first series of Clark lectures.

Thus Virginia Woolf, the independent thinker ahead of her time, emerges into the public domain and finds her voice. Writing and giving this lecture was an act of defiance, of rebellion against both male tradition in general and all that Leonard in particular stood for. His expensive education is seen as a liability, condemning him to live in his ivory tower of academic isolation which leans uncomfortably to the left. Accused by him of being a class snob, she reveals him as being an intellectual snob.

Both Elizabeth Robins and Octavia Wilberforce attended Virginia's Leaning Tower lecture in Brighton, after which Virginia comments: '200 about there; Robins' carnations; no fear on my part – & so home.' [16]

When her lecture appeared in print Virginia was criticised by some of her friends for identifying herself with her audience, for saying 'we', instead of 'you'; she stoutly maintained her position on the grounds that, like her audience, she had not had an education. The Leaning Tower was published by the Hogarth Press in the autumn of 1940 in Folios of New Writing after John Lehmann, to his credit, insisted on her finalising the text; however, a few months later he was not in a position to change the course of events when she sent *Between the Acts* to him, in March 1941.

An editorial note makes the interesting point that whereas Freud saw the human mind as being irreducibly divided, Virginia sees the unconscious as the source of artistic inspiration, which is the expression of 'a mind no longer crippled'. For Virginia, that is, relating to one's unconscious – I would call this the right brain – goes with the absence of division, while for Freud it is the reverse. Leonard must have agreed with Freud, since it reinforced his prejudice against Virginia's sanity. Regrettably, Leonard made no attempt to seek psychoanalytic help to get in touch with his own alienated right brain; but then he thought of himself as preeminently sane. Carl Jung said: 'show me a sane man and I will cure him.' But Leonard was listening to Freud and not Jung.

Virginia had just finished checking the proofs of her biography of Roger Fry, with which she was satisfied 'despite L.', when the war news took over. The Germans invaded Holland and Belgium and Churchill told the country: 'I have nothing to offer but blood, toil, tears and sweat'. Leonard wanted to join the Local Defence Volunteers, soon to be named the Home Guard. This resulted in an 'acid conversation' between Virginia and Leonard:

"Our nerves are harassed – mine at least: L. evidently relieved at the chance of doing something. Gun & uniform to me slightly ridiculous. Behind that the strain: this morning we discussed suicide if Hitler lands. Jews beaten up. What point in waiting? Better shut the garage doors. This a sensible, rather matter of fact talk. Then he wrote letters, & I too. Copied my lecture contentedly. A thunderous hot day. Dutch laid down arms last night. The great battle now raging. Ten days, we say, will settle it. I guess we hold: then dig in; about Nov[ember] the USA comes in as arbitrator. On the other hand–" [17]

In the event Leonard took on the unofficial duties of fire watching and air raid precautions (ARP), in which capacity he was provided with a purple and gold arm band. He was no longer an outsider.

She and Leonard made a suicide pact in the event of Britain being invaded. If life became too dangerous they would sit in their car in the garage with the engine turned on and kill themselves with the fumes of carbon monoxide from the exhaust: 'So my little moment of peace comes in a yawning hollow. But though L. says he has petrol in the garage for suicide sh[oul]d Hitler win, we go on. Its the vastness, and the smallness, that make this possible. So intense are my feelings (about Roger): yet the circumference (the war) seems to make a hoop round them. No, I cant get the odd incongruity of feeling intensely & at the same time knowing that there's no importance in that feeling. Or is there, as I sometimes think, more importance than ever?' 'Yes, we are being led up garlanded to the altar.'

As the Germans pushed through France, the philosopher G.E. Moore came to visit Monk's House, with Desmond MacCarthy. Virginia saw Moore as having: 'less force & mass to him than I remembered... & not quite such a solid philosophic frame as I suppose when we were all young we anticipated... our charge that he had silenced a generation.' [18] The rising arch of The Bloomsbury Group, in which G.E. Moore played a pivotal role for members of the Apostles and especially for Leonard, is now seen to be descending from Virginia's perspective. This sense of tidying her life away, of completion, is strong at this time as she wonders when she takes a walk whether it will be her last: 'I can't conceive there will be a 27 June 1941' – tragically, for her, there wasn't. Yet, as she says several times, she wanted another 10 years. We can only guess at what she would have done with them if she had been permitted to live.

Aerial fights between small planes began and searchlights probed the sky 'like beads of dew on a stalk', while bombers carried their deadly cargoes to destroy London. The Battle of Britain raged above them.

As well as the petrol in the garage, Maynard Keynes's brother supplied them each with a lethal dose of morphine. Several of their friends, including Vita, took similar precautions.

During the final drudgery of correcting proofs and writing the Index to her Roger Fry book, Virginia lost the comfort of her 'inner Roger' and instead had to cope as best she could with Leonard's negativism. She continued to think about the war and their suicide pact: 'Another reflection: I dont want to go to bed at midday (this refers to the garage). A kind of growl behind the cuckoo & t'other birds: a furnace behind the sky. It struck me that one curious feeling is, that the writing 'I', has vanished. No audience. No echo. Thats part of one's death. Not altogether serious, for I correct Roger: send finally I hope tomorrow: & could finish P[ointz] H[all] [*Between the Acts*]. But it is a fact – this disparition of an echo." [19]

Returning to this theme in July, she still feels that she is outside the patriarchal tradition of English literature:

"All the walls, the protecting & reflecting walls, wear so terribly thin in this war. There's no standard to write for: no public to echo back: even the 'tradition' has become transparent. Hence a certain energy & recklessness... And perhaps the walls, if violently beaten against, will finally contain me." [20]

The Woolfs continued to play bowls, at which Virginia regularly lost. There was something about these games that upset her more than can be attributed to the frustration of losing: 'How silly I was to be enraged yesterday... by being beaten at bowls... We quarrelled about our communal feeling.' [21] She regains her temper walking alone on the marsh and looking across the estuary at the beauty of Asheham House. But losing at bowls becomes ever more upsetting:

"I feel my irritation at being beaten fasten itself & phrase make – make the old phrases, for wh[ich]. God knows, theres no justification whatever today. Why do I mind being beaten at bowls? I think I connect it with Hitler. Yet I played very well. And in an hours time, shall be repeating the other phrase wh[ich] I made during the first game: a Season of calm weather. Such a curious peace; a satisfactory quiet... A season of calm weather is the crown for which I'm always pushing & shoving, swimming like the hedgehog who cuts his throat with his paws Nessa said yesterday at [Charleston], if he swims." [22]

The Woolfs had found a dead hedgehog floating in their lily pond which Leonard tried to resuscitate. 'An amusing sight,' says Virginia. '2/6 is offered by the Govt. for live hedgehogs.' [23]

And Leonard, even if he did try to resuscitate the dead hedgehog, was part of Virginia's problem and not part of her solution. To compare being beaten at bowls by him, to Hitler, is an indictment of her playing competitor. Leonard hated to lose even more than she did and was evidently capable of making himself seriously unpleasant to the extent that she found herself once again making up 'the old phrases'.

On the eve of the first reviews Virginia once more feels close to Roger: "What a curious relation is mine with Roger at this moment – I who have given him a kind of shape after his death – Was he like that? I feel very much in his presence at the moment: as if I were intimately connected with him; as if we together had given birth to this vision of him: a child born of us. Yet he had no power to alter it. And yet for some years it will represent him." [24]

Her biography was a child born of Roger and herself; her writing self was 'intimately connected' with Roger and not Leonard, as she managed to balance 'the flight of the mind' with accurate research. Her book was welcomed by friends and critics: 'So I'm confirmed in what I felt, even when I had that beak pecking walk in March with a temperature of 101 with Leonard.' The difference in her relationship to the two men is clearly apparent in the text of *Between the Acts*, especially in the first draft that she was writing at this time.

Once the immediate threat of invasion receded with the autumn, Leonard himself cheered up. He was enjoying country life and the presence in Monks House of Louise Everest. He wrote another book, a short one entitled *The War for Peace* for the Labour Book Club, published by Routledge in September, the same month Virginia's *Biography of Roger Fry* came out, so they were once again rivals. Leonard's book had no more impact than any of his others and no doubt for the same reason, that he insisted on taking the moral high ground and despised everyone else as misguided fools. This arrogance, (John Lehmann calls it his 'bravado') was Leonard's way of overcoming his actual cowardice which is such a strong component of Giles in *Between the Acts*. Given this, we can well admire him for writing books that criticised the Hitler-led German push for world domination at the cost of thousands, soon to be millions, of lives sacrificed. He spoke up against dictatorship whether of the right-wing Nazis and Fascists, or the left-wing communists. By doing so he earned for himself a place with Virginia at the top of Hitler's death list for British Jews. If Germany had managed to conquer Britain, they would both have been arrested immediately. So their plans for committing suicide in the event of an invasion during the summer of 1940 were realistic.

Virginia listened to different people speaking about the war. There was her friend Dame Ethel Smyth: 'Of *course* we shall fight and win', as against Kingsley Martin predicting doom: 'K.M. says we must & shall be beaten.' [25] How necessary for her these antiphonal voices were, reaching her inside the 'monkey house'. She carried her phial of morphia in her pocket in case of immediate need.

The games of bowls between herself and Leonard assume an even more dire, even a menacing quality, as the first reviews came out about her Roger Fry biography. This time she had to rely even more completely on the response of others, after Leonard's attack. She again tries to reconcile herself to his criticism, anticipating how it would be received: 'That I've made a just & animated biography, stressing the public side, the intellect, the austerity & so on; but not being personal & ungirt enough. I think this is what L. felt. But then Nessa & Margery [Fry] didn't.' [26] In the short period of silence after the first notices were published, she amusingly says: 'It might have sailed into the blue & been lost. "One of our books did not return" as the BBC puts it'. However, her tension over the book finally relaxed when an 'extended and laudatory' review by Desmond MacCarthy appeared in the Sunday Times of 4 August 1940:

" 'Oh a great relief – Desmond's review really says all I wanted said. The book delights friends & the younger generation say Yes, yes we know him; & its not only delightful but important. Thats enough. And it gave me a very calm rewarded feeling – not the old triumph, as over a novel; but the feeling I've done what was asked of me, given my friends what they wanted. Just as I'd decided I'd given them nothing but the materials for a book I hadn't written. Now I can be content: needn't worry what people think: for Desmond is a good bell ringer; & will start the others – I mean, the talk among intimates will follow, more or less, his lines." [27]

And so Virginia was reassured. Her essential 'echo' from other people sounded once more for her, after months of doing her best to cope with the effect of Leonard's hard beak. She noted Clive Bell's positive comments. He was 'quiet, serious, completely without sneer approving'. The book was selling well, 'booming', it soon went into a third edition. Sales slackened when the first major air raids hit London, and then recovered.

Elizabeth Robins left for America in October 1940. With her going at least one third of 'Mrs Manresa' was no longer a threat to Virginia. In the same month Leonard finally got rid of Mabel Haskins; and the imminent threat of invasion receded. Monk's House settled down to the 'harum-scarum ways' of Leonard and Louie. The penalty Virginia paid for these changes was that she lost her position as its mistress and had to work far too hard at cooking and housework in a cold, damp house. She was now entirely isolated. She began to rewrite Pointz Hall in an attempt to earn money from its publication.

When the war directly affected the Woolfs, they lay side by side face down on the ground in the garden at Monk's House with their hands over their heads while German planes roared low overhead. During that moment it was too dangerous for them to get up and go to the garage and end their lives; and what about Mabel in the kitchen?

"They came very close. We lay down under the tree. The sound was like someone sawing in the air just above us. We lay flat on our faces, hands behind head. Dont close yr teeth, said L. They seemed to be sawing at something stationary. Bombs shook the windows of my lodge. Will it drop? I asked. If so, we shall be broken together. I thought, I think, of nothingness – flatness, my mood being flat. Some fear I suppose. Shd we take Mabel to garage. Too risky to cross the garden L. said. Then another came from Newhaven. Hum & saw & buzz all round us. A horse neighed on the marsh. Very sultry. Is it thunder? I said. No guns, said L. from Ringmer, from Charleston way. Then slowly the sound lessened. Mabel in kitchen said the windows shook. Air raid still on, distant planes." [28]

That same month: 'England is being attacked. I got this feeling for the first time completely yesterday. The feeling of pressure, danger horror.' [29] On 1 September the remnants of The Bloomsbury Group met at Charleston. Maynard Keynes called Virginia's biography of Roger Fry 'the official life' – and wanted her to write the 'real life' for the Memoir Club. He also said there'd be no change after the war. 'We sh[oul]d go back to where we were'. Going back to where they were would not have suited Leonard. He needed a catastrophe. During the desperate month of September he must have seriously considered the possibility of committing double suicide with Virginia, locked in their car in the garage. One of the reasons he could not do so was Mabel's (to him unwelcome) presence at Monk's House. Thus she indirectly saved their lives. The weather was extremely hot and Virginia was plainly on edge: 'Hot, hot, hot... record heat wave... Hot, I repeat; & doubt if I'm a poet. An idea. All writers are unhappy. The picture of the wor[l]d in books is thus too dark. The wordless are happy: women in cottage gardens.' Vita was driving an ambulance to help the war effort. She rang to say she couldn't come to visit the Woolfs and that bombs were dropping all around her home, Sissinghurst. It was a comfort to talk – then she broke off and put the phone down – 'Oh how I do mind this', said Virginia. Every night there were air raid warnings, planes and bombs: 'Of course this may be the beginning of invasion. A sense of pressure. Endless local stories... L. sleeps all through it every night.' [30]

London was the focus of heavy raids. A bomb demolished a house near 37 Mecklenburgh Square while another fell in the Square but failed to explode. The Woolfs went to London for half a day where they made belated plans to evacuate the Press to the relative security of Letchworth. They found John Lehmann white and shaken after the ordeal of spending nights among the exploding bombs. Lehmann accused Leonard of bravado when he boasted he would be able to sleep through the air raids until Leonard, irritated, 'says he will go up by train tomorrow. Happily he now postpones. I dont want to spend a day bomb dodging; train prisoned.' On their return to Rodmell, Leonard redoubled his attempts to get rid of Mabel by making life quite intolerable for that stoic, reliable servant. At last he had an effect:

"I decided today after tears from Mabel (about L. & the electricity – the latest of many grievances) that she must go. She said – oh the usual things – about not giving him satisfaction; too nervous to speak to him. The poor tallow fleshed almost petrified woman; who can smile tho', & is unselfish (to me) but its no good." [31]

Virginia, not realising that the loss of Mabel would ultimately prove to be a disaster for her, celebrates her coming departure:

"Anyhow, its settled, I think that she leaves here... I like being alone in our little boat. I like provisioning & seeing alls shipshape & not having dependents... The great advantage of this page is that it gives me a fidget ground. Fidgets: caused by losing at bowls & invasion... Theres a parched artificial cruelty &... I think we moderns lack love. Our torture makes us writhe. But I cant go into that... One always thinks there's a landing place coming. But there aint. A stage, a branch, an end... I sometimes think about violent death. Who's whistling in the churchyard?...

Domestically, a great relief & peace, & expansion, it'll be tomorrow, into merry kitchen harum scarum ways. Now we go to our last Cook cooked dinner for I don't know how long. Could it be the end of resident servants for ever? This I pray this lovely fitful evening, as well as the usual Damn Hitler prayer... Well, we're alone in our ship... Great air traffic all night – some loud explosions. I listened for Church Bell [that would warn of imminent invasion], thinking largely I admit, of finding ourselves prisoned here with Mabel. She thought the same... So that 5 years uneasy mute but very passive & calm relation is over: a heavy unsunned pear dropped from a twig. And we're freer alone. No responsibility: for her." [32]

Next day Virginia records her sense of isolation: 'I continue, after winning two games of bowls. Our island is a desert island... So we, L. & I, are almost cut off.' She notes the pattern of her quiet days on her desert island and tries to persuade herself that this is happiness, the existence she has always wanted:

"A bomb dropped so close I cursed L. for slamming the window... All clear. Bowls... All now become familiar. I was thinking: (among other things) that this is a lazy life. Breakfast in bed. Read in bed. Bath. Order dinner. Out to Lodge... tune up, with cigarette: write till 12. Stop; visit L.: look at papers; return; type till 1. Listen in (to the radio news). Lunch. Sore jaw. Cant bite. Read papers. Walk to Southese. Back 3. Gather & arrange apples. Tea. Write a letter. Bowls. Type again. Read Michelet & write here. Cook dinner. Music. Embroidery. 9.30 read (or sleep) till 11.30. Bed...

I think, now we're marooned, I ought to cram in a little more reading. Yet why? A happy, a very free & disengaged – a life that rings from one simple melody to another." [33]

She had a major quarrel with Vanessa who found a cottage in Rodmell for Helen Anrep and her two 'brats' to stay indefinitely. Virginia was appalled to think of the Anreps being such close neighbours and blew up at Vanessa over the phone: 'then I lost my temper, more than for years...

Then, like a Star arising, Ness wrote (we are cold & distant, after our wrangle) that they stay only a week.' [34] This quarrel increased the distance between the two sisters, while Leonard and Vanessa were ever more closely in contact with each other. It is not obvious why Virginia was so against Helen coming to live in Rodmell, since she actually got on very well with her. They were 'easy & familiar & friendly', and they had their memories of Roger Fry in common, but Virginia did not like her children and there was still the matter of having provided Helen with 150 pounds to clear her mortgage, about which Leonard had made her feel so intolerably guilty. Eventually Helen gave back 25 pounds and this reduced the tension. Helen went to live near Charleston.

Later that autumn the weather was fine and warm, sometimes hot, 'So invasion becomes possible'. This formed the outer shell of their lives, the 'shade' of war, while the bombing raids continued. The unexploded bomb in Mecklenburgh Square detonated, blowing out the windows of No. 37 but doing only relatively minor damage to their flat. 'We have need of all our courage', was the phrase that summed it up for Virginia. 'Why did we ever leave Tavistock? – whats the good of thinking that?' Her questions were soon answered when 52 Tavistock Square was itself completely demolished in another raid, so that if they had remained there they would have lost everything. (We might note that if they had not moved, the world would have been deprived of all Virginia's diaries except the one she was writing.) She was relieved: 'I need no longer wake in the night thinking the Wolves luck has taken a downward turn.' Her quarrel with her sister had to be muted as Vanessa's studio in London was wrecked, together with Duncan's: all the paintings in their studios were destroyed and only a fridge and a statue saved. Virginia wondered what it would be like to die in an explosion:

"I said to L.: I dont want to die yet. The chances are against it. But they're aiming at the railway & the power works. They get closer every time... I try to imagine how one's killed by a bomb. I've got it fairly vivid – the sensation: but cant see anything but suffocating nonentity after. I shall think – oh I wanted another 10 years – not this – & shant, for once, be able to describe it. It – I mean death; no, the scrunching & scrambling, the crushing of my bone shade in on my very active eye & brain: the process of putting out the light, – painful? Yes. Terrifying. I suppose so – Then a swoon; a drum; two or three gulps attempting consciousness – & then, dot dot dot." [35]

This was not how Virginia wanted to die. Besides, she was enjoying writing Pointz Hall, 'Never had a better writing season... How free, how peaceful we are. No one coming. No servant. Dine when we like. Living near to the bone. I think we've mastered life rather competently.' [36]

She begins a train of thought in which she describes Mabel: 'I was thinking of Mabel's history, "the life of the bastard woman" ' Mabel's friend Charles had recently died; he would come to their London flat and help her wash up; he took her to the dog races and his other passion was Opera, 'he knew them all by heart... She knew all the tunes... What a queer relationship – she so dumb & passive yet following him; maternally proud of him, to races, to plays... Lord, the bloodless servitude of the domestic poor!... She thought of him as a small impetuous boy. Now his life is over; & no one will know more than I do about Charles & Mabel.'

During the autumn of 1940, Elizabeth Robins left England for the safety of America (despite being 'fearless and indomitable' – she was 'induced' to go according to Leonard). While Dr Wilberforce remained in Brighton to conduct her medical practice and look after their hobby farm. It was at this time that Leonard recruited Octavia to become Virginia's unofficial doctor. As he says in his autobiography: 'In the latter part of 1940... Octavia... had to all intents and purposes become Virginia's doctor.' [37] This private arrangement between Leonard and Dr Wilberforce was both informal and irregular. Not only was Virginia kept in the dark about its true nature but, on Leonard's assumption that she was mad, Octavia as a general practitioner did not have the qualifications to treat her. However, it suited Leonard very well. He had managed to get another woman 'on his side'. The doctor sympathised with him and brought them much-needed dairy produce from the hobby farm. Moreover, Octavia would be a valuable witness if Virginia became actively 'mad' and suicidal. At first Virginia admired Octavia and thought of her as a friend who was distantly related to her; she began thinking of ways to write about her life, but her view changed. Sensing something was wrong, she began to distrust the doctor and called her 'leech Octavia'.

I think it possible that Leonard assisted Elizabeth financially when she avoided the war by going to America in the autumn of 1940; and that, in return, Octavia agreed to become Virginia's unofficial doctor while also providing free milk and cream. His disappointment at the loss of Elizabeth led, I believe, to a major hardening of his attitude against

Virginia who was forced to sit out the war in Sussex, close to the most likely coast for a German invasion and under the flight path of bombers attacking London. At this time he acquired a blue kitten called Peat: this would have been his characteristic attempt to comfort himself for Elizabeth's absence; while feeding the kitten became an additional problem for Virginia. When Elizabeth returned to live in Brighton after the war, Leonard was involved with Trekkie Parsons.

Virginia's hopes of once more taking her creative mountain top – 'that persistent vision' – were rudely and permanently shattered early in December 1940, a month that saw her brought, literally, to her knees as she scrubbed the floors of Monk's House in a futile attempt to keep the place clean. Leonard's selfishness and his lack of concern for her welfare showed itself unmistakably during this month, in his refusal to recognise her plight and get domestic help in running the house, at a time when the direct effects of the war were in abeyance. He refused to spend sufficient money to store their salvaged London possessions from 37 Mecklenburgh Square, so that their small rooms became filled with most of the contents of their London flat. Virginia was unceremoniously brought out of her Lodge when the vans arrived, bringing her unpublished papers and damaged books and furniture:

"Real life is a helter skelter, healthy for the mind doubtless. I cant climb up to the other life in a hurry. No time to think. A breeze ruffles the surface. No silence... Rather depressing – old papers, letters, notebooks: I'm going to bind the survivors tonight; & in coloured paper they may refresh my eye. All this writing – what a deluge of words I've let loose – on paper only: I mean not printed." [38]

She describes the appalling mess she is in to Dame Ethel Smyth: "So I'm all black and blue with moving. And the house is packed like an emporium. And 4 tons of books came yesterday. And the Printing Press and all the type come tomorrow. [The Hogarth Press itself was evacuated to Letchworth but much of the equipment came to Monk's House.] This bores me so, I cant even write it. Boredom and distraction and fights with matter, have been hag riding me this fortnight. And lectures in the hall; and 15 people to seat and warm. And the Womens Institute elects me Treasurer.' Despite all this Virginia suggests a book for Smyth to write, because 'I want to investigate the influence of music on literature'. She ends: 'Never never keep letters, Ethel. Theyre the devil when it comes to a move." [39]

The arrival of what Leonard considered to be Virginia's unnecessary possessions, pieces of furniture which she had enjoyed acquiring over the years with the pocket money Leonard allowed her from her earnings, set the scene for a major act of bullying on his part: he insisted that she had to pay for the expense of the removal by writing an article on Ellen Terry and a short story, to be sent to Harper's Bazaar in America. Ten days later, after this bout of enforced writing, overwhelmed by the chaotic state of her possessions and having to feed and entertain Leonard's guests whom he invited without any thought of the extra work he was causing her, Virginia was exhausted. Louise was evidently no use:

"oh the huddle & hideousness of untidiness... The year draws to an end; & I am harassed, damp... will take the matter in hand: scrub & polish & discard: & make our life here as taut & bright & vigorous as it can be.

Its rather a hard lap: the winter lap. So cold often. And so much work to do. And so little fat to cook with. And so much shopping to do. And one has to weigh & measure. Then Kingsley [Martin] comes & devours sugar & butter." [40]

After a 'ceremonious' lunch with John Lehmann at Kings Cross, where Leonard collected Peat, the kitten, she continues:

"Why are we hooked to that large, rather pretentious livid bellied shark? And must I spend my last years feeding his double row of teeth? I forget. I forget what I wished to say.

K[Kingsley] M[Martin] effusive but less distasteful, He ruined 2 days, now I come to think of it. the sensitive plate of his mind only takes the surface. Yes, its like going to the films – the film of December 1940 talking to Kingsley... I sit with my eyes dazed. Then at meals he scrapes & sops. I cook in the damp kitchen. ..My old dislike of the village bites at me. I envy houses alone in the fields... No raids lately."

To avoid her unsatisfactory present-day existence, and as though seeking answers, Virginia went back to describing her childhood in *A Sketch of the Past*. She tried to discover some different aspects of her father who dominated that distant late-Victorian world:

"It came quite naturally to him to drive off in a hansom in evening dress; he made no bones about dinner parties of eight or ten... I can see him taking a lady downstairs on his arm; and laughing. He cannot have been as severe and melancholy and morose as I make him out... Undoubtedly I colour my picture too dark, and the Leslie Stephen the world saw in the eighties, and in the nineties until my mother died, must have been not merely a Cambridge steel engraving intellectual... There was a Leslie Stephen who played his part normally, without any oddity or outburst, in drawing rooms and dining rooms and committees." [41]

But this was not how Virginia personally remembered him. For her, as a child, he had been a tyrant: 'the exacting, the violent, the histrionic, the demonstrative, the self-centred, the self-pitying, the deaf, the appealing, the alternately loved and hated father – that dominated me then. It was like being shut up in the same cage with a wild beast. Suppose I, at fifteen, was a nervous, gibbering little monkey.' [42] Virginia proceeds to give a detailed account of a 'bad Wednesday' when Vanessa had to show him the weekly expenditure:

"On a bad Wednesday we ate our lunch in the anticipation of torture. The books were presented directly after lunch. He put on his glasses. Then he read the figures. Then down came his fist on the account book. His veins filled; his face flushed. Then there was an inarticulate roar. Then he shouted... [dots in text] 'I am ruined.' Then he beat his breast. Then he went through an extraordinary dramatisation of self pity, horror, anger. Vanessa stood by his side silent. He belaboured her with reproaches, abuses. 'Have you no pity for me? There you stand like a block of stone...' [dots in text] and so on. She stood absolutely silent. He flung at her all the phrases about shooting Niagara, about his misery, her extravagance, that came in handy. She still remained static. Then another attitude was adopted. With a deep groan he picked up his pen and with ostentatiously trembling hands he wrote out the cheque. Slowly with many groans the pen and account book were put away. Then he sank into his chair; and sat spectacularly with his head on his breast. And then, tired of this, he would take up a book; read for a time; and then say half plaintively, appealingly (for he did not like me to witness these outbursts): 'What are you doing this afternoon, Jinny?' I was speechless. Never have I felt such rage and such frustration. For not a word of what I felt – that unbounded contempt for him and of pity for Nessa – could be expressed." [43]

Virginia does not make a specific comparison between her parents and her own relationship with Leonard, but the parallel is all too clearly implied. Between writing that description of her father and her diary entry of 22 December 1940, in which she sees her parents in quite a different light, a fundamental change had taken place. By the end of December Virginia was in dire need, to the extent that she turns to her dead parents for comfort:

"How beautiful they were, those old people – I mean father & mother – how simple, how clear, how untroubled. I have been dipping into old letters & fathers memoirs. He loved her – oh & was so candid & reasonable & transparent – & had such a fastidious delicate mind, educated, & transparent. How serene & gay even their life reads to me: no mud; no whirlpools. And so human – with the children & the little hum & song of the nursery. But if I read as a contemporary I shall lose my childs vision & so must stop. Nothing turbulent; nothing involved: no introspection." [44]

We can be quite certain that remedial action had to be taken at this time if Virginia was to survive the desperate mud and whirlpools of her own situation. And Leonard must have been aware of her plight. Virginia had a damaged heart and over-tiredness, together with the feeling that more was expected of her than she could undertake, would have been a considerable strain on her health. But on top of all her other problems she was burdened with Leonard's selective negativity, his heavy and irrational shadow; as Lucy Swithin in Pointz Hall was burdened with carrying Giles's shadow while he irrationally blamed her for his difficulties; whereas Mrs Manresa was 'exempted too <from responsibility in making life hard for him.>' As some women were exempted from Leonard's shadow, including Vanessa and Louise – and, no doubt, Elizabeth Robins and Octavia Wilberforce – but not Virginia.

We can pause for a moment to 'unpack' Lucy Swithin's name. Lucy from the Latin: lucid, shining, light, intellectually bright, not darkened with madness; so we read: 'Light is Within'. Here is one of Virginia's subliminal messages, part of her vision that she is handing on to us and to which Leonard would have been not only deaf and blind but antagonistic. This name is thus part of Virginia's rebellion against her husband. Her first idea was to call Isa, Lucy. [45]

Virginia tried to keep cheerful for as long as possible. The Woolfs visited Alciston, where Helen Anrep was staying. She fell in love with the farmhouse set on its own in the countryside. This was how she would like to have lived. On Christmas Eve she wrote:

"We lunched with Helen & again 'I could have fancied living there'. An incredible loveliness. The downs breaking their wave... And I worshipped the beauty of the country, now scraped, but with old colours showing.

L. is now cutting logs, & after my rush of love & envy for Alciston farm house, we concluded this is the perfect place. L. says it is exactly right, for we needn't be cumbered with possessions here. Which reminds me. We are very poor; & my hoard is 450: but must not be tapped again. So I must write. Yes, our old age is not going to be sunny orchard drowse. By shutting down the fire curtain, though, I find I can live in the moment; which is good; why yield a moment to regret or envy or worry? Why indeed? Yesterday Octavia came with milk & cream." [46]

On this same day she sent a letter to Dame Ethel Smyth (how different these letters are from the ones she wrote to Elizabeth Robins):

"I was thinking the other night that there's never been a woman's autobiography. Nothing to compare with Rousseau. Chastity and modesty I suppose have been the reason. Now why shouldn't you be not only the first woman to write an opera, but equally the first to tell the truths about herself? Isnt the great artist the only person to tell the truth? I should like an analysis of your sex life. As Rousseau did his. More introspection. More intimacy. I leave it to you." [47]

As was usual at the end of the year, Leonard discussed their annual accounts with Virginia. This time, however, he used their supposed lack of money to prevent her from spending anything at all, even her share of their 'hoard', which amounted to 450 pounds; while he spent whatever he wanted. Leonard's total control over their finances played a major part in Virginia's decision to kill herself. She believed what he said, that they would be 'ruined' because they might have to draw on their capital which she had painfully built up over the years by her writing, in the hope that in their old age neither of them would have to work to earn money. She never understood that he was behaving just like her father in withholding money to control 'their' women, because Leonard did it quietly, using deceitful arguments. He was able to frighten her without having to rant and roar, and therefore she thought he was arguing rationally. After her death, Leonard lived on the interest of Virginia's fortune and the money he made by publishing her work.

Although Vita Sackville-West sent gifts to Virginia, Dame Ethel Smyth was the only remaining friend who was concerned about her well-being during the winter of 1940 and the spring of 1941. Writing to Smyth, Virginia's hand trembles, partly because: 'my mind is churned and frothed; and to write one must be a clear vessel.' She gives the other reason for her trembling hand:

"We're devilish poor. Lord, what a bill for rent and removal, and no money coming in, and the taxes! I shall have to write and write – till I die – just as we thought we'd saved enough to live, unwriting, till we died!

But its a good thing – being buffeted, and not cosseted. How does it affect you? Are you ruined, I mean can you pay your bills out of income? Yes, I will come one day soon. Because I must exchange ideas; and I want to see you in your surroundings. But how?"

How, indeed, could Virginia go and see Ethel, when Leonard told her she must not spend any of her 'hoard' of 450 pounds? Leonard, apparently determined to destroy Virginia's friendship with the one woman he could not control, blocked any move for her to visit Smyth even when the old woman attempted to pay for a hired car:

"Well, well, how time passes. Did I ever thank you for your offer of a 10 pound note, which was to turn into a car, and the car was to take me to Woking – etc etc – No, my sudden financial anguish was only due to doing the years accounts with Leonard. Like my father, I can always conjure up bankruptcy. But unlike my father Leonard has no money complex [sic]. So we can rub along cutting a servant, cutting clothes; but otherwise not encroaching on capital yet. Oh yes, I can write: I mean I have a fizz of ideas. What I dread is bottling them to order. Didn't we start the Hogarth Press 25 years ago so as to be quit of editors and publishers? Its my nightmare, being in their clutches: but a nightmare, not a sane survey." [48]

Leonard has no money complex? That is like Antigone saying Creon has no cave complex. Leonard knew exactly how to frighten Virginia into submission without appearing to be unreasonable; so she keeps apologising for him even as the rock rolls into place, blocking the cave mouth. She ends this letter:

"Well, dearest Ethel, how damned generous you are, breaking, or ready to break, a golden lump off your hoard, all to buy a visit from me. I happen to be very humble just now. I cant believe in being anyone. So I say with amazement, yet Ethel wants to see me! We shall meet one of these days... Never mind Leonard. He is a good man: in his heart he respects my friends. But as for my staying with you, for some occult reason, he cries No no No. I think its a bad thing we're so inseparable. But how, in this world of separation, dare one break it? I'm working really rather hard (for me) [she was rewriting Pointz Hall] but whats the good of what I write, I havent the glimpse of an idea. You'll say, its good for you. So it is, I've no doubt. Certainly I should swing like a frantic pendulum otherwise. And now I must 1. make soup. 2. make butter. Tell me how your book is going – for that is what I want. V."

The two women continued to write to each other but Flimsy and Bossy never met again. This important connection with Dame Ethel Smyth was ruthlessly severed by Leonard crying: 'No no No.' And Virginia was not in a strong enough position to go against his edict. No wonder she feels 'very humble'; she 'cant believe in being anyone.' The truth as I see it is that Leonard spent that winter systematically undermining Virginia's position and destroying her sense of identity. Virginia recognised that her relationship with Leonard was bad for her, 'but how in this world of separation, dare one break it?' The price of not breaking it was loss of autonomy, loss of identity, loss of creativity, death.

In late December 1940 the Woolfs saw Maynard Keynes. He told them the Allies would win and the war soon be over: 'Questions of peace remains only, he says: our victory certain'. [49] Maynard's words must have horrified Leonard. He was in danger of being robbed of his catastrophe that could only safely take place against the backdrop of war and the imminent danger of a German invasion.

VIRGINIA WOOLF'S LODGE, MONK'S HOUSE, RODMELL

Chapter Thirteen

UNTYING THE KNOT

> Yet each man kills the thing he loves,
> By each let this be heard,
> Some do it with a bitter look,
> Some with a flattering word.
> The coward does it with a kiss,
> The brave man with a sword!
>
> Oscar Wilde *The Ballad of Reading Gaol*

The story of the relationship between Virginia and Leonard Woolf can be told from two different perspectives and these are reflected in the two sides of our brains. There are two truths that can be characterised as the female and the male.

According to the male truth Leonard was almost a saint who cared for his mad genius of a wife for nearly thirty years while she wrote her great work. When she could carry on no longer, she went out and drowned herself one morning, in her final notes praising him and blaming herself because she was afraid she was going insane again. To support this theory there was World War Two, that supposedly brought back the madness she had suffered in the previous world war; surely it was time she gave up and let the long-suffering Leonard live the rest of his life without having to cope with looking after her.

That is the graceful way, the male way, of seeing her death in the icy waters of the River Ouse that March day in 1941. The same gracefulness is apparent in Homer's poetry when he tells the story of young Iphigenia, a princess who was led to the sacrificial altar having been told that she was to be married, so she lay garlanded beneath the knife. She was killed by her father Agamemnon to ensure fair winds for the launching of his boats to wage war on Troy and rescue Helen from the arms of Paris. But if we look at this story from the female point of view it takes on a different aspect. We ask whether Iphigenia had any choice in her death and we have to reply – no, she had none. Before the blow fell she probably knew that her last role was to be killed for the greater good of the man's world into which she had been born. But we, hearing the story, have doubts. Did the killing of this young girl really affect the winds that blew across

LEONARD READING VIRGINIA'S DIARY AT MONK'S HOUSE, 1967

the Aegean? Do we believe that? If we don't believe that, do we simply accept her death embedded as it is in the story of the battle between Greeks and Trojans with Helen as the prize, that resulted in the fall of Troy? After all, it happened long ago when myth and history were at least intertwined, if not synonymous – and it is great poetry.

As we approach the end of Virginia's life, can we see her too as a victim of a killer male who wished her dead, not as a sacrifice to the winds over the sea surrounding ancient Greece (though there is an element of that) but because Leonard wanted to spread his angel's wings and fly above the 'human ant-heap' as the Apostles, Trinity College Cambridge, had taught him he had a right to do. She was in his way. Surely it was his turn now. I notice considerable sympathy among some commentators with this point of view.

If that was Leonard's aim, to achieve what he thought of as his right as a man and an Apostle, then he was not going to risk being caught with a knife in his hands dripping blood. He didn't need to. With his 'secret and sinuous psychology' and thirty years watching his potential victim, he knew exactly how to drive Virginia to suicide. Arguably, he had tried before, in 1913 when he had set about training her to be a 'good wife', as he trained his dogs, by depriving her of pleasure and then giving her a purse which delighted her; by telling her that true freedom is only to be found in a cage, so he caged her – and then left the box of Veronal open beside her bed and left her. If it had not been for that officious Ka Cox coming in and arousing the medical profession, Leonard would have been a widower in 1913, in full control of Virginia's money. Instead, he had to spend some of that money on a house and servants, and nurses, until she recovered and set about her writing career from which he benefited financially. Now, twenty-eight years later, he was getting another chance. Can we look at the end game of their marriage as starkly as that?

Virginia's relationship with Leonard Woolf could have been as much a tragedy as Sylvia Plath's short life with Ted Hughes that ended in her suicide; but the Woolfs' story was played out over a span of nearly thirty years, as Virginia drew on all her reserves of courage and determination and lost every other freedom so that she could continue writing.

The female view is less graceful: to live with a man who feels he has to 'conquer' his female partner before making his own name in the world, until her independent voice is silenced and she is reduced to supporting him; she may then be discarded for a younger woman.

Virginia, it seems, did not completely understand her role in Leonard's drama. She criticised his talking and writing style; suffered from his irritability, and occasionally rebelled against his petty rules and restrictions; but she refused to consider whether she was in any danger except during a nervous breakdown when the other truth broke through and her pent-up rage became uncontrollable. Together with her memories of her father, Leonard's shadow seems to have contributed to the dark side of her writing. When she felt constricted – his trembling hands reaching out towards her neck like Harry's hands moving towards Gwen's neck in *The Wise Virgins* – with sudden impatience she would plan to escape from him by moving to a house on its own in the countryside where she could have her possessions and regain her own creative atmosphere; then, he would draw back and tell her Monk's House was the perfect place to be and she would get on with her writing, until once again she felt his fingers hovering around her neck. She was no match for his intense and passionate will that would not let her go.

Perhaps we may very tentatively wonder whether this dark side gave a depth to her work that it might have lacked if she had married the (presumably) amiable Walter Lamb.

Virginia was able to maintain her position, at least in appearance, long after she lost her legal and financial rights. She was fairly safe whilst she was an equal partner in the Hogarth Press and was earning money from her books; she had loyal friends and increasing fame that protected her; and there was at least one live-in servant in the house who obeyed her. But by November 1940, Virginia had none of these supports. Most of her friends were scattered, preoccupied by the war, and transport was difficult. She was confined to Monk's House where she lost her position as its mistress when Leonard got rid of Mabel in October. Their remaining part-time servant, Louie, lived in his cottage and was answerable to him; he taught her not to treat her 'mad' mistress too seriously. Together, they often laughed at Virginia's attempts to cook or clean; while the maid was encouraged to scamp the housework, until the place became shabby and neglected. Louie knitted Virginia a warm jersey and occasionally played pranks on her but she took her orders from Leonard, whom she greatly admired as she listened to his politics and laughed at his jokes; and she was an important part of his mythology as he tried to turn the small world of Monk's House into a place of mythic significance, a stronghold of democracy against the threatened invasion of barbarism. Here, on his patch, he would recreate ancient Athens, and the woman who was there to help him do so was not Virginia but Louise Everest.

Each of us needs to make up our own mind as to whether Leonard was honestly concerned for Virginia's welfare at this time. Did he do everything possible to help her through the ordeal of another war? Or were the actions he took intended to protect himself, while he was in fact pushing her ineluctably towards self-destruction? Maybe there is no absolute proof either way; but if we lean towards the first interpretation we are left wondering why she did kill herself, and why Leonard wrote his unique admission on the afternoon of her death: 'There is no limit to one's self-ishness and stupidity'. [1]

In the last days of 1940, Virginia was on her own. In her private world, she made a fresh discovery: 'The idea came to me that why I dislike, & like, so many things idiosyncratically now, is because of my growing detachment from the hierarchy, the patriarchy... I am I; & must follow that furrow, not copy another. That is the only justification for my writing & living.' [2] With these words, Virginia Woolf knew she was a post-patriarchal writer. Through her writings she has left a detailed account of the course she took through her inner being, with no help from the conceptualisations of feminist politics to guide her. She was a pioneer. And she reached the top of her mountain. But she did so at great cost. Her final decisive step took her away from ordinary social life and from Leonard; it left her totally isolated, a woman not so much ahead of her time (although she was that) but outside clock time. She intended to begin her next book from the top of her mountain, and she wrote two chapters but was unable to enjoy the view for long. Her descent was precipitous. She remained unaware, or refused to accept, that Leonard in the depths of his secret and sinuous psychology, goaded by the 'appalling resistance & persistence which I know I possess & cannot control, which is due to some horrible fire in my entrails & must be a weariness of flesh & mind to other people', as he described himself to Trekkie two years later [3], could have been playing a deadly game. Shut away without the tranquility of mind she needed. she rewrote Pointz Hall once more, pulling back on the rage and diminishing its apocalyptic vision.

Leonard's description of Virginia's last winter on earth, written nearly thirty years after the event, differs greatly from hers. In his chapter entitled 'Virginia's Death', he begins by discussing the deaths of Dreyfus and Christ, then says:

"If one is in the exact centre of a cyclone or tornado, one finds oneself in a deathly calm while all round one is the turmoil of roaring wind and wave. It seemed as if in Rodmell in those last months of 1940 we had suddenly entered into the silent, motionless centre of the hurricane of war. It was a pause, only a pause, as we waited for the next catastrophe; but we waited in complete calm, without tension, with the threat of invasion above our heads and the bombs and bombing all round us. It was partly that we felt physically and socially cut off, marooned... All this meant that for the first time in our lives, Virginia and I felt we were country dwellers, villagers... We worked all the morning; got our lunch; walked or gardened in the afternoon; played a game of bowls; cooked our dinner; read our books and listened to music; and so to bed." [4]

Leonard's feeling that he was living in the still centre of a tornado may well be correct. But the threat of invasion receded that winter; while the power of Leonard's tornado, instead of declining with the extent of the threat, actually gathered force and was lethally focused on Virginia. During her last few months of life his petty restrictions on her intensified, reaching a depth of absurdity when he tried to prevent her writing her diary on the grounds that she was wasting paper, and therefore money. Despite him, she begins another volume in the New Year. Her first entry is bleak and unhappy: 'A psychologist would see that the above was written with someone, & a dog, in the room. To add in private: I think I will be less verbose here perhaps – but what does it matter, writing too many pages. No printer to consider, no public.' [5] Has anyone else noticed that Leonard Woolf tried to stop Virginia writing her 1941 diary?

On the 9th of January Leonard's blue cat, Peat, caught a bat. Virginia tells the story to Elaine Robson, the nine year-old daughter of Leonard's co-editor of the Political Quarterly: 'I saw Peat playing with my glove. Suddenly the glove began to whistle. Then I looked and saw the fingers move. Then I looked again and saw it was a Bat. 'Leonard! Leonard!' I shrieked. "The Cat has caught a Bat!!' He thought it was a joke, so he didn't come. He was sawing up wood. Then I got a flower pot and put it over the Bat. But, when Leonard came, the bat was dead. So Peat ate him for his supper.' [6] That day her diary entry is desperate:

"A blank. All frost. Still frost. Burning white. Burning blue... And I cant help even now turning to look at Asheham down, red, purple, dove blue grey, with the cross so melodramatically against it. What is the phrase I always remember – or forget. 'Look your last on all things lovely'. [7] And L is lecturing & arranging the room. Are these the things that are interesting? that recall; that say Stop you are so fair? Well, all life is so fair, at my age. I mean, without much more of it I suppose to follow... I am copying P[ointz] H[all]. I am economising. I am to spend nothing... Oh but I am so tormented by the evening beauty... & to conclude the marsh is of the colour & substance of an opaque emerald. Many mad letters from adoring women. I never like or respect my admirers, always my detractors." [8]

To comfort herself Virginia was re-reading her old diaries. On the 15th of January she writes: 'Parsimony may be the end of this book. Also shame at my own verbosity, which comes over me when I see the 20 is it – books shuffled together in my room. Who am I ashamed of? Myself reading them... We were in London on Monday... & there wandered in the desolate ruins of my old squares: gashed; dismantled; the old red bricks all white powder, something like a builders yard. Grey dirt & broken windows; sightseers; all that completeness ravished & dismantled. So to Buszards where, for almost the first time, I decided to eat gluttonously. Turkey & pancakes. How rich, how solid. 4 shillings they cost. And so to the L[ondon] L[ibrary] where I collected specimens of Eng[lish] Lit[eratu]re.'

Despite the desolation of war, Virginia gave herself a feast and went to the London Library to select the material she needed for her next book. She doesn't mention her fifty-ninth birthday, occurring on 25 January (she had managed to survive ten years longer than her mother); but on that day she wrote an interesting letter to Shena, Lady Simon:

"No, I dont see whats [to] be done about war. Its manliness; and manliness breeds womanliness – both so hateful. I tried to put this to our local labour party: but was scowled at as a prostitute. They said if women had as much money as men, they'd enjoy themselves; and then what about the children? So they have more children; more wars; and so on. This is not a contribution to the problem, only a groan... We live in the heart of the lower village world, to whom Leonard lectures on potatoes and politics. The gentry dont call." [9]

The next day, Virginia admits in her diary:

"A battle against depression, rejection (by Harper's of my story & Ellen Terry) routed today (I hope) by clearing out kitchen... This trough of despair shall not, I swear, engulf me. The solitude is great. Rodmell life is very small beer. The house is damp. The house is untidy. But there is no alternative. Also days will lengthen. What I need is the old spurt... We are going to Cambridge for 2 days... There's a lull in the war. 6 nights without raids. But Garvin says the greatest struggle is about to come – say in 3 weeks – & every man, woman dog cat even weevil must girt their arms, their faith – & so on. Its the cold hour, this, before the lights go up. A few snowdrops in the garden. Yes, I was thinking: we live without a future. Thats whats queer, with our noses pressed to a closed door." [10]

J. L. Garvin, editor of the Sunday newspaper *The Observer*, wrote: 'Everything tells us that the iron orchestra is working up to fortissimo. Every single man and woman of us must awaken quietly to the knowledge that the crisis of our lives... must arise between now and Easter.' This mischievous and untrue article was just the apparently objective evidence Leonard needed to persuade Virginia that the long-awaited invasion was about to happen; yet he himself showed no signs of believing that Britain would in fact be invaded that spring. He did not renew the suicide pact he had made with Virginia the previous year. Nor do the other members of the Bloomsbury Group show any doubt that life as they had known it would continue. But Leonard was not interested in finding out whether Garvin spoke the truth or not. What mattered to him was that Virginia should want to end her life before Easter; a possible invasion being used as an excuse.

Virginia attributes the onset of her January depression to the rejection by Harper's Bazaar of her Ellen Terry article and her story 'The Legacy'. She had written these pieces at Leonard's insistence in order to earn money in America that was supposed to pay for the removal of their possessions from London. The magazine's rejection of them, and the threatened loss of money this represented, aroused Leonard's fury so that he either typed himself, or dictated to Virginia, two letters to Harper's Bazaar that she signed. They include such phrases as: 'You now write me a letter from which I gather that you propose, without apology, to repudiate your agreement... I presume that payment will be made for the story commissioned by you – which will bring in foreign exchange as effectively as if it had been printed.' [11] These phrases are in Leonard's language, not hers. They show that he was taking an extremely close interest in her affairs, especially where money was concerned. Leonard was not the detached observer of Virginia's decline that he pretends to be in his autobiography. Indeed, the intensity of anger revealed by those words enables us to guess that he subjected Virginia to one of his verbal attacks – perhaps to the effect that she was no longer able to earn money from her writing; thus throwing doubt on whether he would be willing to publish any more of her work. Assuming such a scene, I believe it was this that sent her into the sudden depression from which she never fully recovered. The threatened invasion was never more than an excuse.

The Legacy is full of revelations. As so often in her creative work, Virginia says what she really feels in this short story. Gilbert, after his wife Angela's death in a traffic accident ('it was as if she had foreseen her death'), begins to read through her diaries which are her only legacy to him:

"He took another volume from the writing table – he had become more and more absorbed in his work. And she, of course, was more often alone... It had been a great grief to her, apparently, that they had had no children. 'How I wish,' one entry read, 'that Gilbert had a son!' Oddly enough he had never much regretted that himself. Life had been so full, so rich as it was. That year he had been given a minor post in the government. A minor post only, but her comment was: 'I am quite certain now that he will be Prime Minister!' Well, if things had gone differently, it might have been so. He paused here to speculate upon what might have been. Politics was a gamble, he reflected; but the game wasn't over yet. Not at fifty... [and at last] He had received his legacy. She had told him the truth. She had stepped off the kerb to rejoin her lover. She had stepped off the kerb to escape from him." [12]

'She had stepped off the curb to rejoin her lover. She had stepped off the curb to escape from him.' Virginia Woolf wrote this sitting in her Lodge looking out across the floodlands to the River Ouse which seemed so much more attractive to her than Monk's House at the other end of the garden. In those waters she could rejoin Roger Fry, as well as her other dead, and escape from Leonard the now dominant master of that house. This is the message from Virginia's last short story, The Legacy.

Virginia's diaries are a crucial part of her legacy to Leonard and to us. They, together with her novels, stories and letters, give us all the clues we need to discover the truth. In The Legacy, Angela has to get away from Gilbert at the cost of her life because of his unyielding ego, his devastating conviction that he was always right, his refusal to accept any responsibility for his actions. This was Angela's problem. It was also Virginia's. They shared a sense of frustration and unfairness that their husband could never see anything from their point of view. In Virginia's story, Leonard is

revealed as a middle-aged man who still aspires to be a major political figure on the world's stage. As she had previously written Lappin and
Lapinova in an attempt to cope with the loss of magic in their marriage,
so she wrote The Legacy to help her face being pushed aside by her still-
ambitious husband.

In his account of Virginia's depression of 25 January and her suicide
two months later, Leonard cannot blame her death entirely on finishing
Between the Acts since the length of time that elapsed between completing
it, and her suicide, makes this improbable. His major argument, therefore, is that she began showing increased symptoms of long-term mental
disturbance, a disturbance which he equates with her breakdowns in
World War One. He argues that it was her fear of going mad again in this
war, as she had during the last one, that led to her death; an argument
that is apparently borne out by her suicide notes. He does not refer to her
earlier diary entries throughout that winter describing her overwork in
the house, her lack of domestic help, the cold, the damp, his refusal to let
her spend any money, or visit Ethel Smyth even when the old lady
offered to pay for a car; or the constant distractions she had to cope with
due to his activities, which prevent her working. If he had managed to
stop her writing her diary at the end of 1940, as he had evidently tried to
do, this would have been convenient for him as then he would not have
had to take account of her independent testimony. But she wrote it nevertheless and he tries to use it to support his view. Leonard begins his version of the story very late, after much of the damage to her health and
self-esteem had already occurred:

"It was only in the first days of 1941 that the deep disturbance in her
mind began to show itself clearly... The entry for January 9 is again
strange, showing her preoccupation with death... Then round about
January 25, I think, the first symptoms of serious mental disturbance
began to show themselves. She fell into what she called a 'trough of
despair'. It was a sudden attack and it lasted ten or twelve days. There was
something strange about it, for when it passed off, she said herself that she
could not remember why she had been depressed. It did not appear to be
connected with her revising *Between the Acts* – indeed, on February 7 she
noted that she had been writing with some glow. Nevertheless, I am sure
that what was about to happen was connected with the strain of revising
the book and the black cloud which always gathered and spread over her
mind whenever, a book finished, she had to face the shock of severing as

it were the mental umbilical cord and send it to the printer – and finally to the reviewers and the public." [13]

Leonard does not consider the possibility that it had become more and more difficult for Virginia to hand him her texts as he grew increasingly obstructive and destructive of them throughout the nineteen thirties; nor that she was entirely dependent on his acceptance of them before they could be sent 'to the printer – and finally to the reviewers and the public'. That she had a major problem with his wilful reactions to her work is amply documented. He severely criticised *Flush*, which she wrote with something of the freedom of spirit animating *Orlando*. She abandoned *The Years* in desperation, calling it a 'dead cat' before handing it to him. And in 1940, she suffered his 'hard beak' when he criticised her biography of Roger Fry. No wonder she feared it would strike again, with even more deadly intent, when she handed him the typescript of *Between the Acts*.

Leonard, instead of considering the possibility that he himself was the cause of her depression, puts forward the improbable argument that Virginia was doomed to repeat her first world-war breakdown as though she was the victim of some sort of fated repetition of the past: 'One thing which deceived me was the suddenness of the attack... The depression struck her like a sudden blow... I can now see that once before there had been an even more sudden mental disturbance, a sudden transition from mental stability to disorder. In that case it was even more catastrophic.' He proceeds to give his version of the onset of her breakdown in 1915, seen entirely from his 'detached observer' point of view: 'She was calm, well, perfectly sane. Suddenly she became violently excited, thought her mother was in the room, and began talking to her.'

There is an obvious reason why Virginia began talking to her dead mother in 1915: her sudden reaching back into the past would have been a recognition that she was in the same situation that had destroyed her mother at the age of forty-nine. It was a despairing cry for help, a cry that went unanswered, before she submerged into deep whirlpools that only months of intense rage, when she refused to see Leonard, enabled her to overcome. But the situation is now quite different. Over the years, Virginia had written the books that had brought her parents back to life and recreated the world of her brother Thoby; she had thus laid them to rest.

Leonard makes this improbable comparison between Virginia's state in 1941 and her breakdown of 1915 for one reason only: he must argue that Virginia died because the 'madness' she experienced then, in the First

World War, is about to overwhelm her in the Second; this time with fatal consequences, if he is avoid all possibility of blame for her death. Yet Nigel Nicolson, in his Preface to the final volume of her *Letters*, says:

"Was this insanity? No, it was a combination of fantasy and fear. She would have recovered, as she had before. She was not mad when she died... Virginia Woolf chose to die. It was not an insane or impulsive act. She died courageously on her own terms." [14]

Although Leonard drew a close parallel between Virginia's state in 1915 with that of 1941, he certainly behaved very differently during these two crises. In 1915 he had obeyed the rules laid down by the mental specialists he consulted, he forced Virginia to rest completely and drink great quantities of milk to increase her weight; and they stayed in a large house with servants and four nurses to look after her. Now, so far from resting, Virginia has to run Monk's House, cooking, cleaning and shopping. Instead of calling in a mental specialist he relies on Dr. Octavia Wilberforce, a general practitioner without mental health qualifications:

"the moment I became uneasy about Virginia's psychological health in the beginning of 1941 I told Octavia and consulted her professionally. The desperate difficulty... was to decide how far it was safe to go in urging her to take steps – drastic steps – to ward off the attack. Drastic steps meant going to bed, complete rest, plenty of food and milk." [15]

In actuality, Leonard took no steps at all to ward off the attack, in fact just the opposite. Virginia also behaves very differently in 1941 from 1913, when at the start of her two-year nervous breakdown she refused to eat and lost weight. In the spring of 1941 she shows no signs whatever of refusing to eat. But, by making this false comparison between 1913-15, and 1941, Leonard is able to ignore the practical problems she experienced in the last few weeks of her life as if they didn't exist. In his account there is no hint that she was over-tired to the point of exhaustion. Instead, he looks for signs of insanity in Virginia's diary, quoting from her entry of 26 February where she transcribes a conversation she overheard in Brighton (something she frequently did for later use in her writing) while sitting in the public toilet; and says of the Rodmell villagers: 'no life: & so they cling to us. This is my conclusion. We pay the penalty for our rung in society by infernal boredom.' Instead of accepting that this was exactly what Virginia felt about the villagers, a view with which he strongly disagrees, he invalidates her by commenting: 'There are ominous signs in this entry. She had just finally finished *Between the*

Acts and had given it to me to read. I saw at once now the ominous symptoms and became again very uneasy.' [16] When we think of Gilbert in The Legacy, reading Angela's diaries with incomprehension, and watch Leonard with his alienated left brain grubbing about among the pages of Virginia's diary years after her death looking for signs of 'madness' that aren't there, instead of asking himself whether giving *Between the Acts* to him to read might have caused her terrifying qualms, we have to laugh ruefully, don't we?

Virginia continues to write to Bossy. Now in the minor key, she asks for love:

"I read and read like a donkey going round and round a well; pray to God some idea will flash. I leave it to nature. I can no longer control my brain... Not a very coherent letter; but Leonards sawing logs under the window; and the marsh is all emerald green again, and the elms barred with rosy clouds, and pale blue behind that funny little extinguisher – the Church. For the past 3 weeks I've lived like a moth in a towel... I would like to ask, quite simply, do you still love me? Remember how I waved that day in Meck[lenburgh] Sq[ua]re. Do love me. V." [17]

Smyth suggested that Virginia should do 'a tiny bit of work for your living', other than writing articles. There was, briefly, some tension between them which they settled with an exchange of cards. Smyth's initiative came much too late, but it shows she understood more than anyone else that her friend needed to get away from Leonard if she was to survive.

Two weeks after her sudden 'trough of despair', Virginia writes: 'Why was I depressed? I cannot remember.' [18] This abrupt change of attitude can be interpreted in several ways. So far from being a sign of returning health, it can be a danger signal. We should be on guard, despite Virginia apparently looking ahead towards further reading to 'tune up for my Elizabethens'. In this diary entry she says:

"A week of broken water impends. Cambridge; then Elizabeth Bowen; then Vita & Enid Jones. Helen [Anrep] has repaid me 25 pounds. Do I like her better for it? I think so... We were in London [on 5 February]... My red purse bag stolen & L. gave me another. At Charleston Clive was stockish, like a Bell. I said 'What a risk Nessa ran marrying him!'... The 3rd week in March is fixed for invasion."

'Invasion' can now be recognised as the Woolfs' code word for Virginia's imminent death, which they apparently both assumed would occur before Easter. This interpretation makes sense of the flurry of social activities they had each organised.

Leonard made arrangements to visit The Hogarth Press at Letchworth, where it was evacuated. His reasons for taking this long, cold train journey with Virginia have never been explained. It was extremely inconvenient for her since she had invited several of her friends to visit Monk's House immediately afterwards, and it added to her exhaustion. On 11 February the Woolfs drove to London and then took a train to Cambridge, where they spent the night at the Bull Hotel and after dinner visited Pernel Strachey, Head of Newnham College. Next morning they went to the Hogarth Press at Letchworth where Leonard carried out whatever unknown business had brought him there. They then returned to Cambridge to dine with George Rylands and spent a second night at the Bull Hotel before returning to Monk's House via London to pick up their car on 13 February. Leonard had no difficulty in finding the money for this cold and bleak excursion. Virginia gives two accounts of their trip and its damaging effect on her friends' visit. The first is in her diary:

"In the wild grey water after last weeks turmoil. I liked the dinner with Dadie [Rylands] best. All very lit up & confidential... Then Letchworth – the slaves chained to their typewriters, & their drawn set faces, & the machines – the incessant more and more competent machines, folding, pressing, gluing & issuing perfect books. They can stamp cloth to imitate leather. Our Press is up in a glass case. No country to look at. Very long train journeys. Food skimpy. No butter, no jam. Old couples hoarding marmalade & grape nuts on their tables. Conversation half whispered round the lounge fire. E[lizabe]th Bowen arrived two hours after we got back, & went yesterday; & tomorrow Vita; then Enid; then perhaps I shall enter one of my higher lives. But not yet." [19]

One wonders about their 'confidential' talk with George Rylands. It is difficult to imagine Leonard not drawing a comparison between Virginia's present situation, as he saw it, with her breakdowns in the early years of World War One. Did they discuss with him her coming suicide? In her letter of 1 March to Ethel Smyth (whom she had not invited) Virginia gives a more agonised description of their Cambridge trip and her friends' visits immediately afterwards:

"Ever since we came back from Cambridge – 30 hours in train journeys: 6 pounds on hotel bills, all for Leonard to spend two hours at Letchworth – I've been in a fret. people kept turning up. Oh yes – there

was Vita, and Enid Jones to lunch. You know, if one's only got half a
daily maid its difficult, getting food together: and the wine had run out;
and the duck was all strings and blue sinews. However Enid was as dapper
as a dab chick. A brick I think would be the proper word – something a
bit gritty and granular; but hard to the foot. Of course she – an old love I
fancy – wanted to be alone with Vita; and there I was; and it was pelting
wet, the cat had scratched a hole in the chair cover, and a visiting dog had
lifted his leg against the table – In short there was an atmosphere of the
sordid and squalid." [20]

This account contrasts with Elizabeth Bowen's glowing description of
her last sight of the friend she so much admired: 'The last day I saw her I
was staying at Rodmell and I remember her kneeling back on the floor –
we were tacking away, mending a torn Spanish curtain in the house – and
she sat back on her heels and put her head back in a patch of sun, early
spring sun. Then she laughed in this consuming, choking, delightful,
hooting way. And *that* is what has remained with me.' [21]

On 26 February Virginia made an extensive diary entry. She notes that
she has 'Finished Pointz Hall, the Pageant: the Play – finally Between the
Acts this morning.' She thereupon gives the typescript to Leonard to
read. Alone of all her books, there is no comment in her diary as to how
he received it. On this day, as usual, she had to cope with visitors and the
omnipresent villagers:

"People daily. And rather a churn in my mind. And some blank spaces.
Food becomes an obsession. I grudge giving away a spice bun. Curious –
age, or the war? Never mind. Adventure. Make solid. But shall I ever
write again one of those sentences that gives me intense pleasure? There
is no echo in Rodmell – only waste air... No life: & so they cling to us.
This is my conclusion. We pay the penalty for our rung in society by
infernal boredom." [22]

So much for Leonard's assertion that they had become part of village
life. This was certainly not true of Virginia. The crucial action on this day
was that she at last handed the typescript of *Between the Acts* to Leonard.

I see him sitting at his desk in his upstairs room at Monk's House with
that radioactive typescript unopened in front of him, beside some sheets
of paper on which he intended to begin the third volume of *After the
Deluge*. Morning after morning he had sat staring at the blank pages, but
no words would come. His spaniel lies on the floor beside him and Peat,
now a half-grown kitten, plays and jumps about the room. He grips his

pipe between his teeth. He knows that this is his supreme test. Looking forward to her new book being published – so far from fearing the critics' reaction – would give Virginia just that 'spurt' she needs. If he praises it she will look at him, her faded eyes kindling: 'Do you like it? Really? Perhaps it will earn some money and we can afford to get more of our things stored, and the house cleaned.' Leonard's pipe has gone out. Irritably, he lights it again. He knows he has complete control over her and her book; if he rejects it she could not send it anywhere else – how Faber's would snap it up! But if he refuses to do so and she died before Easter, people might say she had killed herself because she was disappointed he had rejected her book, and blame him. He gets up suddenly. The dog whimpers, her brown eye swivelling up at him; Peat dashes up the curtain and down again, then sits on the typewriter keys trying to catch the letters as they come up. Leonard opens the window, drops the cat outside into the ivy, shuts the window and returns to his chair. He opens the manuscript – carelessly typed, as usual – and begins reading.

He turns the pages, staring at them one after another, with increasing dismay. There is this revealing portrait of himself as Giles, a discontented, irritable young man, with his blue eyes and fair hair: nobody would be taken in by that disguise. And Old Bartholemew, whose fierce dog trails after him like Leonard's spaniel. There is Virginia as Isa, the young married woman attracted to another man (damn her, he always knew there was something between her and Roger Fry). Here she is again as Aunt Lucy, the vague, the elderly child, so apparently harmless yet attractive, each of them sketched in with a diabolically accurate light and unerring touch. And there is Mrs Manresa – Leonard would have known all too well who she was. Did he look once again into the intense blue faun's eyes of Elizabeth Robins? She at least had escaped to America. He had let her go, freeing the ancient dynamic, independent spirit of the immortal Antigone while he remained shackled to her mortal body, the trapped but still talking Virginia, as a prison officer is shackled to his prisoner.

Horror-struck, he sits there, his arm trembling, wincing and shuddering all over. Then he goes downstairs. His wife is in the kitchen, on her hands and knees, her hair in wisps, smears of charcoal on her face, a scrubbing brush in her hand and a pool of water on the floor. She glances up at him questioningly. How tired she looks. He passes her, saying nothing. That itself will upset her. He blows a cloud of smoke as he goes out into his beloved garden.

Leonard spent ten days working out what he should do. *Between the Acts* was a ticking bomb that could blow him up if he wasn't careful. Perhaps if he said nothing the suspense would be too much for Virginia and she would kill herself. This was Leonard's first option.

He could delay publication, telling her that although he 'liked the book', the Hogarth Press could not afford to risk losing money on so unusual a work at this critical stage in the war. However, there was John Lehmann's reaction to be considered: he would assume without question that Virginia Woolf's latest book would be published. Eventually Leonard realised that there was only one person who could withdraw her work – Virginia herself.

If she, waiting to hear Leonard pronounce judgement on her book, did begin to hear inner voices, no doubt they were warning her that he was not only using her as a slave in his house but that he was trying to silence her creative self – and maybe actually wishing her dead. If Virginia's rebellious voices were telling her this, she could not afford to listen to them. It was preferable to believe, as her world crumbled, that those inner voices were a proof of madness; that both Leonard and Vanessa had been right all along and she was wrong. There was even some comfort in pretending they were trying to do their best for her. She was to blame. Then she rallied. Above her was her mountain top. Surely the little donkey with broken hooves could climb up once again? But not now. Now there was dinner to get. Virginia's 1 March letter to Smyth is a long and revealing one:

"I am stuck in Elizabethan plays. I cant move back or forwards. I've read too much, but not enough. Thats why I cant break into politics. Do you ever get glued, on a fly paper, as I do, when I'm trying to make myself master of something? I always trust that on the next page I shall free my legs. I have a mystic belief that if one goes on persistently the match box flame will spurt. But oh dear me, it hasn't.

If you want to picture me at the moment then you must strew the floor with mouldy dramatists; and how am I to picture you? Do you feel, as I do, when my head's not on this impossible grindstone, that this is the worst stage of the war? I do. I was saying to Leonard, we have no future. He says thats what gives him hope. He says the necessity of some catastrophe pricks him up. What I feel is the suspense when nothing actually happens. But I'm cross and irritable from the friction of village life. Isn't it foolish? But no sooner have I bound myself to my book, and brewed that very rare detachment, than some old lady taps at the door. How is she to grow potatoes or tomatoes? If that were all, I wouldnt mind. But she spends an hour, prodding her stick into the lawn, one thing following another. My theory as to that is that we have to pay the price of detachment by being tethered down...

Two things I have now got to do: one, to find a flat in Brighton for Roger Fry's mistress [Helen Anrep]: the other to buy 2 tons of hay for Octavia Wilberforce's cows. She says they're so thin you could put a safety pin through them. You see, I'm no good at practical affairs: I'm fished out of my element and lie gasping on the ground. Thats why, I suppose, I cant write to you. But if you wrote to me I should recover the tone of your voice at least... Excuse this drivel. V" [23]

Octavia's cows may have been thin but they continued to provide milk. The picture of Virginia being unnecessarily hassled is an unpleasant one. Her diary is so nearly at an end. On 8 March she wrote her penultimate entry, perhaps intended to be her last. Leonard lectured the WEA in Brighton on 'Common Sense in History' (*sic*), where less than a year previously she had given her Leaning Tower lecture:

"Just back from L.s speech at Brighton. Like a foreign town: the first spring day...

No: I intend no introspection. I mark Henry James's sentence: Observe perpetually. Observe the oncome of age. Observe greed. Observe my own despondency. By that means it becomes serviceable. Or so I hope. I insist upon spending this time to the best advantage. I will go down with my colours flying. This I see verges on introspection; but doesn't quite fall in... Haddock & sausage meat. I think it is true that one gains a certain hold on sausage & haddock by writing them down...

Oh dear yes, I shall conquer this mood. Its a question of being open sleepy, wide eyed at present – letting things come one after another. Now to cook the haddock." [24]

'I shall go down with my colours flying' – Virginia has made up her mind to kill herself. Since Leonard had access to her diary, this phrase would have warned him if he did not know already. It is plain that he did know. She is 'despondent' because she still did not really want to die. She continues to write to her friends as she spends 'this time to the best advantage', correspondence that can be read as disguised goodbye letters. She makes vague arrangements for future meetings; in none of them does she consider that there might be an invasion. To T.S. Eliot:

"I suggest 5th of April week end. I do so very tentatively, because I know – havent we just been to Cambridge and back – the horror of trains. But our line is better than some. Then there's the lack of civility here; the water has come through the kitchen ceiling... So much water has flowed under the bridge that I feel at sea; and so conclude." [25]

There is a final letter to Ethel Smyth, dated 10 March, in which she invites herself (after the debacle of January!) to spend a night with her friend. Both letters are only believable on the assumption that she knew she would be dead before her suggested meetings could take place; they remind one of the notes she wrote to her friend Violet Dickinson, pretending that Thoby was still alive for several weeks after he had died of typhoid. As she protected Violet then, so this time she is protecting Leonard. Writing to Smyth she promotes his latest book: 'he says he does not believe in Federal Union *now*. He says he's given all his views on that in his 2/6 book. War for Peace. If you'd like to read it – I think its very masterly – I'll send it.' [26] One gets a whiff of the egocentric expert that Leonard believed himself to be. She continues her letter of 10 March to Ethel Smyth:

"Yes, yes, yes, of course I agree with you. This refers to Mr. Curry's book, which I've just read. But then of course I'm not a politician, and so take one leap to the desirable lands. L's view would be, I think, that ones got to plod along the road, indeed to make it, before one gets there. But Lord! what a relief to have a vision! and I'm glad you're beating up an audience in Woking.

What I really write to say though is... Shall I come down for a night? I could now, on a Wednesday – in April – go back early Thursday... I could bring my rations. I'm in a dither of trying to contrive spring cleaning. Oh our carpets – I spent 2 hours carpet beating, and still the flakes of our bombed ceiling flock, and drown the books just dusted. I'd no notion, having always a servant, of the horror of dirt–

No: politics at the moment seem more pressing than autobiography... So no more, for I'm off to Lewes about beating carpets, and only write this because, having done Curry, I thought, belatedly, to wave a hand of thanks. V." [27]

When Virginia finally agreed that, in war-time, politics were more important than writing autobiographies or novels, she gave Leonard the primacy he craved. As she withdraws she is giving him the space to take over. She promotes his book. Her last gesture to Ethel Smyth is to 'wave a hand of thanks', thus she farewells her friend through a tiny crevice in the cave wall. There is no Mabel to help her cope with dust-laden carpets, but Mabel has been immortalised as the voice of Reason in *Between the Acts*.

On 13 March Virginia wrote to Elizabeth Robins in America, praising Octavia who is: 'the sort of woman I most admire, the reticence, the quiet, the power... she's healing the sick by day, and controlling the fires by night. Its difficult, I find, to write. No audience. No private stimulus. Only this outer roar. And in these circumstances, Octavia is very refreshing. Leonard asks me to add his respects to my love.' [28]

So Leonard stands over her, prompting her, as he stood over her when she wrote to Margaret Llewelyn Davies all those years ago, in 1915.

On 14 March the Woolfs went to London where they met John Lehmann. He assumed from their conversation that *Between the Acts* would be published shortly and therefore announced it in the Spring-books issue of the *New Statesman*. [29]

Between 14 and 18 March, Leonard must have discussed with Virginia the fate of her book. This caused her to reread her typescript, something she normally never did. Remembering that his second novel had flopped in the First World War (so why should hers succeed in this war?), he may have told her, dismissively, that it was out of the question to publish it in the present financial climate; and, since she could not spend any money, she could not contribute to the cost. He thus tied her hands financially. But something much more devastating may have occurred: staring at her with his mongoose eyes, he told her that Mrs Manresa was merely a figment of her paranoid imagination. He had never had a relationship with Elizabeth Robins, nor indeed any other woman. Her book was nothing but a tissue of lies from beginning to end. Listening, Virginia felt utterly confused between his words and her sense of inner truth. Then they had a final deadly battle, as Isa and Giles fought at the end of *Between the Acts*. That drama ends when a man and a woman who do not communicate, are not on the same wavelength, tear each other apart.

If there was such a climactic confrontation, the verbal equivalent of a destructive sex act where both protagonists got off their see-saw and faced each other, we need to recreate the ultimate battle between the polar opposites of his rationalism as against her perception. His left brain against her right brain. It was essential for him to annihilate her side of the argument and leave her egoless and defenceless, if he was to go on living without her. He not only had to win, but get her to acknowledge that his view was correct. We can go to the final version of Virginia's words that she wrote a few weeks before she died, given to Lucy Swithin as she holds an imaginary conversation with her brother Old Bartholemew:

"Fish had faith, she reasoned. They trust us because we've never caught 'em. But her brother would reply: 'That's greed,' 'Their beauty!' she protested. 'Sex,' he would say. 'Who makes sex susceptible to beauty?' she would argue. He shrugged. Who? Why? Silenced, she returned to her private vision; of beauty which is goodness; the sea on which we float. Mostly impervious, but surely every boat sometimes leaks? He would carry the torch of reason till it went out in the darkness of the cave. For herself, every morning, kneeling, she protected her vision." [30]

Leonard saw only shadows on the wall of Plato's rationalist cave; while she, alone in her Lodge, looked at the changing colours of the view outside and saw beauty that was truth. Thus she protected her vision. Now she could no longer do that. She was entombed in Creon's cave, she who had dared to offend the patriarchal edicts. She had been judged against by Leonard: 'there is too much ego in your cosmos', he frequently told her, 'and an excess of ego is discreditable.' [31] So, from their two different worlds, they contemplated each other.

Then something else occurred (but this is not recorded). Once again they were back in her room in Brunswick Square, London, in 1911. When, all those years ago, he tied himself in knots trying to propose to her, she had felt immensely strong. And sane. And cold. Like a snow-covered mountain. *He* destroyed people by refusing to listen to them – that was the devastating method he had invented in Cambridge and practised in Ceylon; now he was using it against her. But what he was really attacking, probing with his destructive sterile male beak, was not her damaged ego but her inner creative self, her female centre, that was immensely ancient, and strong, as it had inspired every Judith Shakespeare through the dark years of patriarchal history. She could win if she wanted to. She could beat him at his own game! From an immense distance Virginia saw that Leonard's arm was trembling. His entire body was trembling. He was speaking again, with the slightly nasal whine that reminded her of his mother: 'I've only ever wanted one thing from you.' 'Love?' She said it dryly, with only a hint of mockery. After all, he had really preferred Vanessa to herself. 'You should have married a painter,' she said. 'You still can.' But it wasn't love he wanted. Not even money.

He demanded her last book, to do with as he decided. Faced with those fanatical dark eyes staring at her, she disowned *Between the Acts* as 'trivial', knowing as she did so that despite her revisions it told the truth. As she spoke, she felt the lamp that had glowed half-way up her spine go out. Lucy Swithin died, sacrificed on the altar of a man whose emotional age was ten. Virginia Woolf was no longer a writer.

Whatever occurred between them, from this time onward Virginia stopped defending her position. She gave everything away, so that Leonard could live without her and get on with his writing. He had achieved his objective. She would let her boat flood and sink in the River Ouse, while he made sure that not even a drop of life-giving water entered his – books on politics were more important than novels. Leonard wrote: 'I continued to work even harder and longer after Virginia's death. I was writing *Principia Politica* with unconscionable slow-ness.' [32] It took him more than twenty years. He described the eventual fate of his trilogy: 'These three volumes have been... to all intents and purposes a failure... *Principia Politica* was received with derision by the Oxford professional historians who do so much reviewing and who rapped me over the knuckles for having the effrontery to be a member of 'Bloomsbury' and use a title which recalled the works of Newton, Bertrand Russell, and G.E. Moore.' [33] He blamed Maynard Keynes for his choice of title.

It was for this that Virginia killed herself. She prepared to go down into her watery element with her colours flying, together with her creative right brain and the sensitive and sensible attitude with which she wrote all her work. For Leonard's sake she must sacrifice not only her life and her work, but her sanity: she must admit to being 'mad'.

This was his ultimate demand of her. However much she had wanted him to enter her other world, he had refused to share her vision; instead, she had to abandon it for his sake. She accepted the risk that people would not read her words with respect: that her novels and short stories, her diaries, would linger in the twilight zone, the limbo, of writings by the somewhat mad. She withdrew her rage at the years of enforced silence and the petty bullying she had suffered from his determined rationalism. To be in touch with her vision, and the words that came to her from her inner being, was to be mad. Thus she freed him.

There were still a few letters to answer. Virginia wrote to Roger Fry's sister Ruth about some reviews of her biography of Roger. She especially liked one, which 'said that Roger Fry was there, and not V.W., which was what I wanted.' [34]

Two days later, on 18 March, she wrote her first suicide letter to Leonard:

"I feel certain I am going mad again: I feel we cant go through another of those terrible times. And I shant recover this time. I begin to hear voices, and can't concentrate... You have given me the greatest possible happiness... I know that I am spoiling your life that without me you could work. And you will I know... Everything has gone from me but the certainty of your goodness. I cant go on spoiling your life any longer.

I dont think two people could have been happier than we have been. V." [35]

The final line is a quotation from the death scene in her first novel, *The Voyage Out,* given to Terence: 'No two people have ever been so happy as we have been. No one has ever loved as we have loved.' [36]

This letter has been assigned by the editor to 18 March 1941, ten days before Virginia died. However, in May 1941 Leonard added a hand-written note to it: 'This is the letter left for me on the table in the sitting-room which I found at 1[oclock] on March 28.' (37). Both he and Quentin Bell said that Virginia wrote her three suicide notes on the morning of her death, two to Leonard and one to Vanessa. This is plainly not so. (See *The Letters of Virginia Woolf, Appendix A,* for a discussion of the dating and look of the letters.) With the dates having been corrected by the editor, Leonard's superscription shows that, even as early as two months after Virginia's death, he was intentionally concocting his version of the event. The editor generously says 'Leonard's alternative assumption, shared by Quentin Bell, that the three letters were all written on the day of her suicide, cannot be conclusively disproved.'

I feel free to interpret the known facts on the assumption that Leonard Woolf, in the spring of 1941, wanted Virginia to die and finally assisted her to do so; and that, for the rest of his life, he had something to hide. Not to consider this possibility is, in my view, to misunderstand the Woolfs' own attitudes to life and death, the ethos of the Bloomsbury Group, and the time in which they lived. The spirit of the age in the nineteen twenties and thirties was not the same as we now 'enjoy' in the final years of the twentieth century and the start of the twenty-first, partly because people then felt they could live as they wanted, with much less intrusion from government or media. During those years there was a certain swashbuckling individualism, a do-it-yourself quality about daily existence. Getting away with it was part of the game. If Leonard thought it was necessary, for his own protection, to lie about the circumstances of Virginia's death no doubt he would do so. Sufficient time has elapsed to take a broader look.

In Leonard's account of the events from 18 March until Virginia's death, he shows a remarkable detachment as though he were watching a film:

"There is a note in my diary on March 18 that she was not well and in the next week I became more and more alarmed. I am not sure whether early in that week she did not unsuccessfully try to commit suicide. She went for a walk in the water-meadows in pouring rain and I went, as I often did, to meet her. She came back across the meadows soaking wet, looking ill and shaken. She said she had slipped and fallen into one of the dykes. At the time I did not definitely suspect anything, though I had an automatic feeling of desperate uneasiness." [38]

On 20 March, Virginia signed a typewritten letter to John Lehmann:
"Dear John,

I've just read my so called novel [*Between the Acts*] over; and I really dont think it does. Its much too slight and sketchy. Leonard doesnt agree. So we've decided to ask you if you'd mind reading it and give your casting vote? Meanwhile dont take any steps.

I'm sorry to trouble you, but I feel fairly certain it would be a mistake from all points of view to publish it."

'Dont take any steps' is the operative sentence, the one Leonard needed to have stated. 'It would be a mistake from all points of view', is the way he expressed himself but not Virginia. This letter freed Leonard from any possible accusation that her depression (and imminent death) was due to his refusal to publish her book. He was prompting Virginia as she typed. She then added in her own hand: 'But as we both differ about this, your opinion would be a great help. Yours Virginia' [39]

Also on this day, Thursday 20 March, the Woolfs drove over to Charleston, after which Vanessa wrote to her sister:

"I have been thinking over our talk today and I feel as if I hadn't made myself nearly clear enough. You *must* be sensible. Which means you must accept the fact that Leonard and I can judge better than you can. Its true I havent seen very much of you lately, but I have often thought you looked very tired and I'm sure that if you let yourself collapse and do nothing you would feel tired, and be only too glad to rest a little. You're in the state when one never admits what's the matter, but you must not go and get ill just now.

What shall we do when we're invaded if you are a helpless invalid – what should I have done all these last 3 years if you hadnt been able to keep me alive and cheerful. You don't know how much I depend on you. Do please be sensible for that if for no other reason. Do what Leonard advises and don't go scrubbing floors, which for all I care can remain unscrubbed forever. Both Leonard and I have always had reputations for sense and honesty, so you must believe us. Your VB

I shall ring up some time to find out what is happening." [40]

Virginia had helped her sister through her grief over Julian's death by using childish language to bring her back, calling her Dolphin and loving her, not handing out such garbage as 'Both Leonard and I have always had reputations for sense and honesty.' If she had wanted to, Vanessa could at least have used the sense she was reputed to possess to provide Virginia with more domestic help. That she did not do this shows that she was simply reinforcing Leonard's point of view.

During that last meeting between the two sisters who had once been so close, Virginia described the amount of housework she had to do including scrubbing the floors of a cold, damp and dilapidated house which smelt of animals. Leonard, we can assume, had told Louise not to do the floors although, as maid of all work, it was her job. He was attributing Virginia's attempts to keep the 'monkey house' even moderately clean, to madness – mania – a refusal to rest; and this is the view Vanessa adopted. The message Vanessa gave to Virginia was that she was entirely on Leonard's 'side' and that her sister could not expect any support from her.

Vanessa assumes there will be an invasion, and Hitler had not yet showed signs of turning his attention to Russia; but the feeling in Britain was very different from that in the previous year. Although there were some tough times ahead, the war had entered a different stage. Through it all the people, buoyed up by their jokes and songs, never lost their nerve. How great to have had a liberated Virginia Woolf continuing to write.

Before and during the war people laughed more than they do now; laughter that was sometimes jeering, sometimes cruel. Even during those last days of Virginia's life I am sure there was laughter in Monk's House.

Perhaps Leonard and Louie stood looking down at her as she knelt on the kitchen floor with bucket, soap and brush scrubbing the worn tiles beneath where the rain leaked through the ceiling, and laughed at her. And Virginia, dead tired, would look up and laugh back.

Virginia wrote her second suicide note to Vanessa, reassuring, giving both her sister and Leonard everything:

"You cant think how I loved your letter. But I feel I have gone too far this time to come back again. I am certain now that I am going mad again. It is just as it was the first time, I am always hearing voices, and I know I shant get over it now.

All I want to say is that Leonard is so astonishingly good, every day, always; I cant imagine that anyone could have done more for me than he has. We have been perfectly happy until the last few weeks, when this horror began. Will you assure him of this? I feel he has so much to do that he will go on, better without me, and you will help him.

I can hardly think clearly any more. If I could I would tell you what you and the children have meant to me. I think you know. I have fought against it, but I cant any longer. Virginia" [41]

This letter should have been received by Vanessa on Friday, 21 March, when Virginia evidently made an unsuccessful attempt to drown herself, but she did not send it. Before taking her walk to the river she propped up both letters where Leonard would find them, as she did the following week. Reading the one addressed to him would have sent him walking down to the river, as he did on the 28th. I think he expected to find her drowned; instead, he was met by the wet, cold and bedraggled figure of Virginia coming back from the water. There is no record of his embracing her, comforting her, drying her, warming her. He may even have been annoyed that she had failed to kill herself. Dr. Octavia Wilberforce came to tea on this day: perhaps he sent for her.

We might call this first attempt Plan A, in which Leonard had a less direct part to play than in Plan B, put into operation a week later. Interestingly, in the third volume of his autobiography, *Beginning Again*, Leonard gets the date of Virginia's death wrong, ascribing it to 21 March 1941: '[Virginia] wrote the last words of *Between the Acts* on February 26, and 23 days later on March 21 she committed suicide.' [42]

21 March was evidently the intended date of her suicide; and his error in naming it as the date of her death was a half memory of the failed Plan A, where her suicide was supposed have been caused by depression

following the line of the street; it roared away towards the sea and almost immediately there was a crash of exploding bombs. We were so overwhelmed by our problem and so deep in thought and conversation that the sight and sound were not at the moment even consciously registered, and it was only some time after I had left Brighton and was driving back to Lewes that I suddenly remembered the vision of the great plane just above our heads and the crash of the bombs." [43]

Thus, Leonard. I would need the corroboration of contemporary records to accept the objective existence of the German bomber that so conveniently enabled him to avoid recounting his discussion with Dr Wilberforce. During Virginia's 'long talk' with the doctor she must have discovered for certain that Octavia was secretly reporting back to Leonard, just as she had realised in 1914 that Leonard had interviewed Dr Head before she met him. He had actually set up a repetition of the earlier disastrous situation. There was no chance, therefore, of her discussing any alternative to suicide with Octavia. She would have sat silent, in a state of disillusion, as Leonard drove her back to Monk's House in the car she had paid for, with a chasm between them as deep as that between Isa and Giles.

If we accept Leonard's story we must agree with the view Virginia gave in her novel of their relationship, that it was distant and strained. While for her part, as a result of this interview during which she told Octavia she could not write, the doctor knew perfectly well that her patient was feeling suicidal. Why, therefore, if only to protect herself as a professional doctor, did Octavia not refer her to a mental health specialist? Not only Leonard, but Dr. Wilberforce herself was treading on very thin ice. However, if we doubt Leonard's version of the story, he and Virginia could have spent the return journey from Brighton fine-tuning Plan B, in conspiracy against the world, with Octavia being used as an alibi for Leonard to protect him from blame.

Virginia wrote two further letters to outside friends: to Lady Cecil, and to Lady Tweedsmuir, both on 21 March, presumably after Dr Wilberforce had been to tea, since in the second letter she tells her friend what she had been doing in the afternoon – having attempted suicide in the morning. This was a busy day for her, especially for someone who was supposed to be in the grip of hallucinatory madness. I don't believe she was.

The intention of these letters is again to promote Leonard and his *The War for Peace*. To Lady Cecil: 'I'm glad you liked Leonard's book... It seems to me the only kind of thing worth writing now... Do you find you can

between writing her book and fear of publication. But where 23 d
was a believable length of time, the actual 30 days was open to dou
therefore could not be used as an adequate excuse. In the fifth vol
his autobiography we get Plan B. He begins: 'On Friday, Mar
Octavia came to tea and I told her that I thought Virginia was o
verge of danger.' Since he had found her that morning returning fr
walk soaking wet, this can be considered a remarkable understaten
He continues:

"On Monday, March 24, she was slightly better, but two days la
knew that the situation was very dangerous. Desperate depression
settled upon Virginia; her thoughts raced beyond her control; she
terrified of madness. One knew that at any moment she might kill he
self. The only chance for her was to give in and admit that she was ill, b
this she would not do. Octavia had been coming to see us about once
week, bringing cream and milk. These visits were, so far as Virginia wa
concerned, just friendly visits, but I had told Octavia how serious
thought Virginia's condition was becoming and from our point of view
the visits were partly medical. On Wednesday, March 26, I became convinced that Virginia's mental condition was more serious that it had ever
been since those terrible days in August 1913 which led to her complete
breakdown and attempt to kill herself. The terrifying decision which I
had to take then once more faced me. It was essential for her to resign
herself to illness and the drastic regime which alone could stave off insanity. But she was on the brink of despair, insanity, and suicide. I had to
urge her to face the verge of disaster in order to get her to accept the misery of the only method of avoiding it, and I knew at the same time that a
wrong word, a mere hint of pressure, even a statement of the truth might
be enough to drive her over the verge into suicide. The memory of 1913
when the attempted suicide was the immediate result of the interview
with Dr Head haunted me.

Yet one had to take a decision and abide by it, knowing the risk – and
whatever one decided, the risk was appalling. I suggested to Virginia that
she should go and see Octavia and consult her as a doctor as well as a
friend. She agreed to this and next day I drove her to Brighton. She had a
long talk with Octavia by herself and then Octavia came into the fron
room in Montpelier Crescent and she and I discussed what we should do
We stood talking by the window and suddenly just above the roofs of th
houses a German bomber flew, almost as it were just above our hea

read novelists? I cant. Still I agree that this war's better than the last, and ever so much better than the last 5 years of peace... Leonard lectures the village on politics. We see Vanessa occasionally – most nights the raiders go over... I cant help wishing the invasion would come. Its this standing about in a dentist's waiting room that I hate... Leonard sends his duty and I my love.' [44] To Lady Tweedsmuir, her old friend Susie, she is evasive about any possible meeting:

"We have been completely bombed out of London, and lead a rather vegetable existence here, surrounded by the melancholy relics of our half destroyed furniture. All this afternoon I've been trying to arrange some of my father's old books. Only now and then do I come to London. May I let you know a date later in case we could meet? I'm always rather rushed – thats the worst of it, as we've nowhere to stay in town... And thank you for writing to me – I was glad to hear of you after all this time." [45]

There is a final note to Vita Sackville-West of 22 March, about a mysterious letter she had received addressed to 'Miss Virginia Woolf' by some unknown correspondent who had apparently confused Vita with Virginia. The original is now lost. It had been sent to Kingsley Martin at the New Statesman and forwarded to Virginia; she sent it to Vita with the following:

"– What a queer thought transference! No, I'm not you. No, I dont keep budgerigars. Louie's survive and she feeds them on scraps – I suppose they are lower class, humble, birds. If we come over [to Sissinghurst], may I bring her a pair if any survive? Do they die all in an instant? When shall we come? Lord knows–" [46]

The writer of that mysterious letter could well have been Leonard himself, perhaps in league with Louise Everest. The previous year Louie had played an April Fool prank on Virginia, obviously put up to it by Leonard. If so, Leonard would have seen it as a 'joke' or 'dare'.

Of the budgerigars: 'Do they die all in an instant?' Virginia's response shows sensitivity to imminent death. But surely Vita had enough to feed them on. Is this interpretation going too far? To assume that that strange letter was a coincidence is at least as far-fetched. We are in a weird, *Alice in Wonderland* world here. Vita mentioned this correspondence when she wrote to Harold after hearing the news of Virginia's death:

"My darling,

I have just had the most awful shock. Virginia has killed herself. It is not in the papers, but I got letters from Leonard and also from Vanessa, telling me. It was last Friday. Leonard came home to find a note [*sic*] saying she was going to commit suicide and they think she drowned herself as he found her stick floating in the river. He says she had not been well for the last few weeks and was terrified of going mad again. He says, 'It was, I suppose, the strain of the war and finishing her book and she could not rest or eat.'

Why, oh why, did he leave her alone knowing all this? He must be reproaching himself terribly, poor man. They had not yet found the body.

I simply can't take it in – that lovely mind, that lovely spirit. And she seemed so well when I last saw her, and I had a joky letter from her only a couple of weeks ago...

Vanessa has seen him and says he was amazingly self-controlled and calm, but insisted on being left alone – I cannot help wondering if he will follow her example. I do not see him living without her." [47]

Why indeed did Leonard leave Virginia alone, especially after he had previously found her coming back from a walk soaking wet? Through Vita's shocked words we hear the voice of normality, a corrective against which we can contrast Leonard's distortions. And Vita writes that Leonard spoke of finding '*a* note' – not three, the number he later insists Virginia wrote on the morning of her suicide.

Incidentally, as Britain braced itself for further hostilities, Kingsley Martin, editor of the New Statesman, said he believed Britain would lose and recommended negotiating peace with Germany. For this act of cowardice Harold Nicolson called him: 'a shattered worm'. [48] Such was the temper of the times.

Virginia's earlier failure to drown herself meant that under Plan B, Leonard would make certain that it was done properly this time. There must be no bungling, as Carrington bungled her suicide that upstaged Lytton Strachey's death: it must be a Greek event, carried out meticulously. And Virginia obediently did everything he told her to do. He was not entirely satisfied with the wording of her first suicide letter to him, so on the morning of 28 March, with Leonard present in her Lodge, she revised it to his satisfaction. This was the letter that Leonard handed to the coroner who would decide if there was to be an inquest; therefore, as far as he was concerned, it had to be worded just right and he made sure that it was.

In her last diary entry written four days before she died, Virginia spoke for herself for the last time. She refers to the two people who had taken on the role of judgemental parents – Leonard and Vanessa. These two, supported by Dr Octavia Wilberforce, formed the lethal triangle that encompassed her death. Her words assume considerable significance:

"A curious sea side feeling in the air today. It reminds me of lodgings on a parade at Easter. Everyone leaning against the wind, nipped & silenced.

All pulp removed.

This windy corner. And Nessa at Brighton, & I am imagining how it w[oul]d be if we could infuse souls.

Octavia's story. Could I englobe it somehow? English youth in 1900.

Two long letters from Shena [Lady Simon] & O[Octavia Wilberforce]. I cant tackle them, yet enjoy having them.

L. is doing the rhododendrons... [dots in text]" [49]
End of diary, as published

Virginia imagines herself united with Vanessa instead of the two sisters, in fact, inhabiting two separate worlds with Leonard between them. She thinks of Easter. Is it Christ she was thinking of? A female Christ about to die on her cross? Leonard saw himself as crucified by her death – so ended their great game of see-saw. And the sea, the bitter wind, 'all pulp removed'; the parade along the shore at Brighton, where Octavia Wilberforce had her doctor's practice. Did Vanessa visit Octavia when she went to Brighton, and speak to her about Virginia, reinforcing Leonard's point of view? I think she did and this is why Octavia was so reluctant to see Virginia when Leonard took her for a final visit on the 27th March.

By putting these two women together Virginia was acknowledging that they formed Leonard's support group. In her egoless state, she was on one level relieved, but maybe her inner voices were aroused, speaking bitterly with salt-laced, wind-lashed, icy tongues saying the opposite of those forgiving words in her suicide notes. Those voices that spoke the truth – she could not listen to them because to do so meant criticising Leonard. Instead, they had to be explained as a symptom of madness.

In the last line of her diary Leonard is doing the rhododendrons. He would have been removing the old dead heads from the bushes, last year's brown and shrivelled petals (gardeners used to do this during the spring to allow new buds to grow), as he was removing the dead head of Virginia to let the new buds of his life – so he hoped – open and grow. Surely, writing this line, Virginia knew there was another woman waiting in the wings. In her reference to Leonard pulling off the dead heads from his rhododendrons, Virginia was sending a coded message into the future. If we wish to understand, we need to listen sensitively for these right-brain messages.

Nigel Nicolson puts Virginia's death down to not being able to write any longer, as she told Octavia Wilberforce on 21 March after her first suicide attempt. He continues:

"To end her life at this point was like ending a book. It had a certain artistic integrity. And she would cease to be a burden to herself and those closest to her, particularly, as Vanessa not too tactfully reminded her, if invasion came... She would have recovered, as she had before. She was not mad when she died... Her handwriting, even of her last note, was firm and normal... It was not an insane or impulsive act, but premeditated. She died courageously on her own terms." [50]

Alma Halbert Bond thought that Leonard had a relationship with another woman:

'Woolf's penchant for using autobiographical material in her books strongly hints that Leonard, too, was having an affair at that time, possibly with Trekkie (Marjorie Tulip Parsons)... Leonard's frequent periods of lateness also suggest that Leonard had had previous affairs, as well... Whatever happened previously, I believe that by the time Virginia was writing *Between the Acts*, Leonard had really fallen in love.' Her final assessment is that:

"Dissatisfied with her writing... Virginia's existence no longer contained enough pleasure to make living worthwhile.' Virginia Woolf turned 'her hatred against herself until it reached the pitch of self-murder. Then she could deflect her rage at both her husband and her father, and preserve her love for Leonard to the point of greatest denial... This action ensured that her rage was disposed of forever, and that she could experience the ultimate state of Nirvana." [51]

My answer to the riddle of Virginia Woolf's death is that by March 1941, she had no choice. The major reason for Virginia's death was Leonard's own desire for her not to be there. He no longer wanted to spend time or money looking after her. He thought, and persuaded her to believe, that writing the last book of his trilogy was more important than her writing or her life. Even if he had been willing to pay the cost of her recovery in a nursing home or under the care of a specialist, she was in his way. He still aspired to be a latter-day Pericles, but Virginia had proved herself not to be Aspasia and she had therefore failed him. Worse, she was part of the hated aristocracy that he wanted to destroy. She did not fit his picture and was indeed inimical to it, as his mother had been inimical to his Cambridge University ambitions and was unceremoniously pushed aside. If Virginia had managed to go and live in a house in the country, as she wished to do, he would still have had to put up with her continued writing of books, using his name – Virginia Woolf – in which he might appear as one of the characters. Only death would silence her. And free him. She died because there was no longer any place for her to be. But to say so, even now, is difficult. It is to shake the entire superstructure of a culture which underestimates the value of a woman's individuality.

On the 27th March Leonard again took Virginia to see Dr Wilberforce. The doctor did not want to see her, she said she was ill and simply told Virginia to 'reassure Leonard'. But Leonard insisted on this visit, he must demonstrate that he had done all he could to save his wife. If there was to be an inquiry after her death, he would need the doctor's evidence. Indeed, he rang up Dr Wilberforce the following day, the 28th, the day of Virginia's death, and she wrote him a long and involved letter on the 29th, in which she said:

"I want to thank you for telling me all that most revealing history yesterday... After our talk yesterday I feel convinced in my mind: 1. That with the war on with its associations & all its horrors, we had no chance. 2. I dont believe any other man could have helped & sustained her & steered her thru' the unhappy times so wonderfully. 3. If by any accident she had been the one to survive, it would have been the most heartbreaking catastrophe imaginable... I do beg of you always to remember that on Thursday [the 27th] ...she suddenly said 'I've been so very happy with Leonard', with much feeling and warmth in her face. I have only known her so short a while but I felt I'd known her quite well! It was such an unforgettable joy to be with her & feel the brilliance of her mind... The milk etc will continue as usual please. I know she'd expect that of me and it would help me if you could make use of it. Later the cows may dry off – but not just yet." [52]

There is no reference to the illness the doctor was supposed to have been suffering from on the previous day, when she 'reluctantly' saw Virginia. And her cows continued to supply Leonard and his blue cat,

Peat, with milk. Making this contact with Octavia on the day of Virginia's death, before her body was found, is remarkably quick work on Leonard's part. Uppermost in his mind seems to have been an urgent anxiety to protect himself from the possibility of blame and to use the doctor as a witness if there was to be an inquiry. Their final trip to Brighton to see Dr Wilberforce, and the doctor's subsequent letter to Leonard, would be part of Plan B, to provide him with medical support as a defence if necessary.

This is my construct of the Woolfs' actions on the morning of the 28th: Leonard stood in her Lodge as Virginia sat at her writing desk with its wide view over the flood lands of the River Ouse. She is docile, obedient. He dictates her third note, which is a revised version of her earlier one to him, and watches as she writes it. Only her final words, 'Burn all my papers', are her own, written in the margin after he left the Lodge. Leonard was in total control over Virginia, as he had assumed control over the 'natives' in Ceylon and as he controlled his pets. This time nothing must go wrong, nothing left to chance. For Leonard, they were enacting a Greek event. As Nigel Nicolson said: 'To end her life at this point was like ending a book. It had a certain artistic integrity.' For Virginia, it was enough that they were together as she made her final sacrifice, enacting their last conspiracy against the world. There must be no goodbye, no softening. He gave his final instructions, then returned to the house. (Was Louise in the kitchen, a witness in case he needed her, or had she been told to go home?) He went upstairs into his study and shut the door. He was not in the garden, as he said, for then he would have seen Virginia go out on her last walk down to the river.

Virginia left her final note open on her desk. She went out of her Lodge, walked across the garden and through the house where she propped up her first two suicide letters on the mantelpiece. She had no fear of meeting Leonard unexpectedly, or of being stopped, as she might well have had at eleven o'clock in the morning if her exit from the world had not been carefully arranged by him. Momentarily, she was aware of her war-damaged possessions forlornly cluttering the small rooms of the house she had never really liked. Then she put on her old fur coat with its big pocket, took her stick and walked down through the meadows to the river. Did she look up at Asheham House, menaced by the spreading bulk of the concrete industry on the opposite hillside, with its mini late eighteenth-century facade that she had always loved? Did she stand there and toast her own Heartbreak House with her fatal dose of morphine, before filling her pocket with stones? Is that how she said farewell? Then, as the drug took effect, she walked unafraid into the water. The end of her life, as she had told Vita, was the only event she would not record. This is how I think it happened.

Leonard gave her an hour and a half before he followed her to the river. He found her stick on the river bank, this was the plan. Virginia was nowhere to be seen. He stood looking down at the cold dark water of the river. There was no body, but he knew all too certainly that she was dead. His catastrophe had become a reality. Now he must protect himself. He went back to the house and called the police.

That afternoon, Leonard sat alone at Monk's House. Vanessa had invited him to tea at Charleston, but he refused to go. He insisted on being on his own. He sat there elated and horrified, 'pricked up' by the realisation of what he had done and appreciating to the full his triumphant sense that his plan had worked. He had married and conquered a member of an important upper-middle class English literary family, a most beautiful and intelligent woman, whom he had seen as a mad barbarian and a threat to his Athens, his Greek state in Sussex. Such is the destructive power of mythic thinking. Now he was free to write the final volume of his trilogy unshadowed by her fame: the book he hoped would be his masterpiece. However, there was also a sense of insecurity: would he really get away with it? When would her body be found? Those doubts were an essential element in his nervous exhilaration. He monitored all his sensations. He had proved that he was not a coward. He had kicked the stone through the gate. He had dared, as Swift had dared, to kill his wife. Lytton Strachey would have been proud of him. He had brought together the three threads of his being, as he was to describe them at the beginning of the first volume of his autobiography (to transliterate): 'I feel that my roots are in my Sussex garden and in the Greece of Pericles, yet I have inherited my genes and chromosomes from my Semitic ancestors in Persia or Palestine who were already refugees, having begun that unending pilgrimage as the world's official fugitives and scapegoats.' [53] These three threads were combined in the sacrifice of Virginia who had taken on the burden of scapegoat for him. He sat quiet. At such a moment, Job had experienced God after he had out-argued him. Leonard waited, wondering (but not really believing) whether, for an incandescent instant, he would be in the presence of God. After all, this act of his had challenged God, had dared him.

There was silence. The tornado was no longer roaring in his ears. His beloved garden was strangely quiet. And the house felt empty as their cramped family house at Putney had felt empty after his mother died: that tough old woman whose 'invincible, optimistic sentimentality' he had spent his life resisting, had given up with the greatest reluctance – so would he! He would live as long as possible! He would endure because he was part of an ancient race of survivors! But the gentile Virginia had only been half alive. He had finally helped her end her life – as she had wanted. So he tried to persuade himself. Uncanny, to think he would never again hear her voice. Not that he had ever really listened to her, for fear of agreeing with what she said.

Nothing happened. The arguments in his mind began again, terrified, justifying, avoiding the devastating realisation that he had from earliest childhood suffered enormously from jealousy, from envy. He had to win! Win over his crowded family, win at school. Win at Cambridge, the only place where he had felt he could be 'supreme', as he sat at the feet of G.E. Moore. There he first met members of the Stephen family. His love for Thoby had been a jealous love for his handsome physique and his social advantages. Surely it was Virginia's fault that Thoby had died unnecessarily of typhoid when she was supposed to be looking after him? Well, he had now avenged the Goth's death. Vanessa was like a female Thoby. Thoby and Vanessa were the two he had aspired to love. Now he, a second Thoby, with Vanessa's support, had proved themselves stronger than Virginia; as he and Louise had removed Mabel.

He waited in vain for the moment of vision, of transcendence. To be God. Only in this way could he win over his elder brother whom he described in *The Wise Virgins*: brother Herbert, who was 'what God intended the human species to be... consequently he will survive. Damn him!' Still, nothing happened. Could Leonard face the possibility that he wasn't Job after all? Or Pericles? That ancient Athens was well and truly history? That he had built his whole life on a self-justifying lie that had, this day, enabled him to commit the perfect murder?

Time stood still. In the silence, the emptiness, Leonard began to realise that he was condemned to suffer a worse fate than Job. There would be no transcendence. He was not 'supreme' or an 'angel' in the folklore of the Apostles. For the rest of his life he would have to endure anticlimax

and the pervasive sense of his own selfishness and stupidity. This was the
ignominious cross that he had to bear. At last he picked up a scrap of
paper and wrote his note:

"They said: 'Come to tea and let us comfort you.' But it's no good.
One must be crucified on one's own private cross.

It is a strange fact that a terrible pain in the heart can be interrupted by a
little pain in the fourth toe of the right foot. I know V. will not come
across the garden from the lodge, & yet I look in that direction for her. I
know that she is drowned & yet I listen for her to come in at the door. I
know that it is the last page & yet I turn it over. There is no limit to one's
stupidity & selfishness." [54]

Leonard crumpled up the paper which he hid but did not destroy. It
was found after his death in 1969, when he was aged nearly eighty-nine.
However much he admitted that his own actions had brought him to this
point, he would never change. His will-power was devastating. Virginia
had called him a fanatic. But he was not going to feel guilty. As Peter
Alexander says, he did not allow any remorse to cloud his days.

'There is no limit to one's stupidity & selfishness.' My book has been written in an attempt to understand why he wrote those words. Now, I think I
know. Whether anyone else agrees with me I neither know nor, deeply,
care. Leonard's stupidity was never to have revised his opinion of
Virginia, never to have listened to her or benefited from the close proximity of a most remarkable woman, gentle and creative. 'You haven't
made me lovable enough', was her comment when he read to her his
description of her before their wedding. He did not make her lovable
enough because his 'obsession' with her was to circumscribe and control
her in order to defend himself against what he saw as a hostile world that
he despised. Virginia was Leonard's most precious possession: to protect
himself, he held her hostage. Her response was to submerge into her
deeper self, into a state that he chose to call mad, as her only way of
escaping from him. Her affair with Vita Sackville-West and their brief
trip to France together, was in his eyes an act of disloyalty that he never
forgave. I think Leonard was unfaithful to Virginia, as she described with
fierce clarity in her last completed book, but he made her deny the truth
of her perceptions and thus destroyed her. Such was his stupidity.

What was his selfishness? It was the necessity of maintaining his own
construct, his carapace, that protected the vulnerable little boy within but
became a deadly weapon to defend himself from the hostile outer world

that he could not reach: the thousand bars and beyond those a thousand bars through which other people were diminished to 'the human ant-heap', that left him feeling isolated, a marionette who tried to tweak the strings of other people to prove that he existed. I ask myself this: if Leonard had really been the caring 'saint' who looked after his genius of a wife while she wrote her immortal work, how is it that she ended up scrubbing floors in the cold, shabby and damp Monk's House, as though her story is that of Cinderella the wrong way round? She married her prince only to become a drudge, while he stood by and watched.

Edgar Woolf wrote to Leonard in 1953, after the publication both of *Principia Politica* (which he read with disgust) and the selection from Virginia's diary that Leonard published, entitled *A Writer's Diary*:

"As a boy you were mean and a bully... Having always been the lickspit-tle of greater intellects, you suffer from the deformity of the little man, who thinks it makes him great to cry out 'See how I have risen above my degraded beginnings.' Unfortunately with your mean nature you'll go the same way & delight in causing pain to all of us. But Virginia's Diary shows you up for what you are better than any words of mine." [55]

Was Edgar right? Does Virginia's diary shed a revealing light on Leonard's character? I think it does.

Leonard Woolf was on his own when he formally identified Virginia's body after it had lain in the water for three weeks. The sight horrified him – but he had seen female bodies in as bad a state, or worse, in Ceylon. He was also alone, the only mourner, when she was cremated, her ashes scattered under the great elm tree they had called 'Virginia' at Monk's House, one of a pair. The other was called 'Leonard'. Neither exist now. One got Dutch elm disease and the other was blown down in a gale.

Leonard achieved some latter-day recognition, collecting an honorary degree from Sussex University; while he and Trekkie travelled to Israel and India. In Ceylon he found to his surprise that his time there as a civil servant was remembered and his first novel *The Village in the Jungle* was known and liked; this novel continues to be read. But perhaps our last view of Leonard Woolf should be William Plomer's account of him, as Alexander described, in old age going into his beloved garden at Monk's House of a morning in order to pump ship (urinate) on the head of the bust of Virginia's grandfather, Sir James Stephen. [56]

The real Virginia is in her writings. She said that she was discovering a style that best suited the shape of her brain; her work, therefore, is the expression of her many-faceted female brain. As well as being a delight to read, it adds considerably to our store of knowledge about that little-known organ.

When Virginia wrote her last words: 'Burn all my papers', she may have been referring to the pages of rough notes she had made during the writing of her Roger Fry biography. Or she may have been telling Leonard to destroy all her unpublished work, including the earlier drafts of her books; most of her short stories; the nearest she came to writing her memoirs in what was later published as *Moments of Being*; her diary; perhaps even *Between the Acts* itself, as well as her unfinished Anon. So much would have been lost to us if Leonard had interpreted Virginia's last instruction in this way – her final act of free-will. In his decision not to do so, lies his best claim to fame.

Only by taking a much closer look at her husband can we realise just how difficult life was for Virginia, and how courageously she rode its treacherous waves. Yet I think he did his best. Who is not afraid of Leonard Woolf?

THE END.

CLASSICAL GREEK HISTORY AND MYTHS

*Figures from classical Greek history and myth referred to in the text,
from Smith's Classical Dictionary, 1864*

ANTIGONE: daughter of Oedipus by his mother Jocasta (who was the sister of Creon), had a sister and two brothers. In the tragic story of Oedipus, Antigone appears as a noble maiden with a truly heroic attachment to her father and brothers. After Oedipus, on learning that he had unknowingly killed his father and married his mother, blinded himself and left Thebes, Antigone accompanied him and remained with him until he died. She then returned to Thebes. Her two brothers became rivals and killed each other in battle. Creon, king of Thebes, would not allow one of her brothers to be buried but Antigone defied the tyrant and buried his body. Creon thereupon ordered her to be shut up in a cave, where she killed herself.

ASPASIA: of Melitus, was the most celebrated of the Greek Hetaerae (high class prostitutes), who came to live in Athens, and there gained and fixed the affections of Pericles, not more by her beauty than by her high mental accomplishments. Having parted with his wife, Pericles attached himself to Aspasia during the rest of his life as closely as was allowed by the law, which forbade marriage with a foreign woman under severe penalties. The enemies of Pericles accused Aspasia of impiety, and it required all the personal influence of Pericles, who defended her, and his most earnest entreaties and tears, to procure her acquittal. The house of Aspasia was the centre of the best literary and philosophical society of Athens, and was frequented even by Socrates. (See also PERICLES)

CAMENAE: the name is connected with carmen, a prophecy. Some accounts identify them with the Muses.

EGERIA: one of the Camenae in Roman mythology, from whom King Numa received his instructions respecting the forms of worship which he introduced. The grove in which the king had his interviews with the goddess, and in which a well gushed forth from a dark recess, was dedicated by him to the Camenae. Aegeria was regarded as a prophetic divinity, and also as the giver of life, whence she was invoked by pregnant women. (See also KING NUMA)

FALL OF THE HOUSE OF ATREUS: A complex story involving incest and cannibalism. Atreus was the brother of Thyestes. He became king of Mycenae. Thyestes seduced the wife of Atreus and was banished. Exiled, he sent Atreus's son, whom he had brought up, to slay Atreus. But Atreus killed him, pretended to be reconciled to Thyestes and invited him back to Mycenae, where he killed Thyestes' 2 sons and gave him their flesh to eat at a banquet. Thyestes fled in horror and the gods cursed Atreus and his house, which was visited by famine. Atreus married Thyestes' daughter without realising her ancestry, and their child eventually slew Atreus.

IPHIGENIA: daughter of Agamemnon and Clytemnestra. According to one legend Agamemnon had angered Artemis by killing a sacred stag. When the Greeks wanted to sail against Troy, the goddess caused a calm. The seer Calchas declared that the sacrifice of Iphigenia was the only means of propitiating Artemis. Agamemnon was obliged to yield, and Iphigenia was brought to Chalcis under the pretext of being married to Achilles, where her father killed her to ensure favourable winds for the fleet.

KING NUMA: belongs to legend and not to history. He was renowned for his wisdom and his piety; and it was generally believed that he had derived his knowledge from Pythagoras. His reign was long and peaceful, and he devoted his chief care to the establishment of religion among his rude subjects. He was instructed by the Camena Egeria, who visited him in a grove near Rome, and who honoured him with her love. The sacred books of Numa, in which he prescribed all the religious rites and ceremonies of Rome, were said to have been buried near him in a separate tomb, and to have been discovered by accident, 500 years afterwards, in B.C. 181. The story of the discovery of these books is evidently a forgery; and the books, which were ascribed to Numa, contained nothing more than an account of the ceremonial practices of the Roman religion which were extant at a later time.

PERICLES: The greatest of Athenian statesmen, was the son of Xanthippus, and Agariste, both of whom belonged to the noblest families of Athens. The fortune of his parents procured for him a careful education, which his extraordinary abilities and diligence turned to the best account. He received instruction from Anaxagoras. With Anaxagoras he lived on terms of the most intimate friendship, till the philosopher was compelled to retire from Athens. From this great and original thinker Pericles was believed to have derived not only the cast of his mind, but the character of his eloquence, which, in the elevation of its sentiments, and the purity and loftiness of its style, was the fitting expression of the force and dignity of his character and the grandeur of his conceptions. Of the oratory of Pericles no specimens remain to us, but it is described by ancient writers as characterised by singular force and energy. He was described as thundering and lightning when he spoke, and as carrying the weapons of Zeus upon his tongue.

In B.C.E 469, 40 years before his death, Pericles began to take part in public affairs and was soon regarded as the head of the more democratic part in the state; after Cimon was ostracised he was placed at the head of public affairs at Athens. Pericles was distinguished as a general as well as a statesman, and frequently commanded the Athenian armies in their wars with the neighbouring states. Throughout the remainder of his political course no one appeared to contest his supremacy; but the boundless influence which he possessed was never perverted by him to sinister or unworthy purposes. So far from being a mere selfish demagogue, he neither indulged nor courted the multitude.

Pericles had to sustain numerous attacks from the comic poets. His high character and strict probity, however, rendered all these attacks harmless. But as his enemies were unable to ruin his reputation by these means, they attacked him through his friends. His friends Phidias and Anaxagoras and his mistress Aspasia were all accused before the people. Phidias was condemned and cast into prison; Anaxagoras was also sentenced to pay a fine and quit Athens; and Aspasia was only acquitted through the entreaties and tears of Pericles. He pointed out the advantages which the Athenians possessed in carrying on the war against the Lacedaemonians; but he did this because he saw that war was inevitable.

When the plague made its appearance in Athens, the Athenians, being exposed to the devastation of war and the plague at the same time, looked upon Pericles as the author of all their distresses, inasmuch as he had persuaded them to go to war. Pericles attempted to calm the public ferment; but such was the irritation against him, that he was sentenced to pay a fine. The ill feeling of the people having found its vent, Pericles soon resumed his accustomed sway.

Although the plague carried off most of his family, Pericles maintained unmoved his calm bearing and philosophic composure. At last his only surviving legitimate son, Paralus, fell a victim. The firmness of Pericles then at last gave way; as he placed the funeral garland on the head of the lifeless youth he burst into tears and sobbed aloud. He had one son remaining, his child by Aspasia; and he was allowed to enrol this son in his own tribe and give him his own name. The name of the wife of Pericles is not mentioned. She lived unhappily with Pericles, and a divorce took place by mutual consent, when Pericles connected himself with Aspasia. Of his strict probity he left the decisive proof in the fact that at his death he was found not to have added a single drachma to his hereditary property.

(See also Kagan, Donald: *Problems in Ancient History*, Volume One, Section 1X 'Periclean Athens – Was it Democratic?')

THE WANDERING JEW: a Jew is said to have denied Christ any rest on his way to the Cross, and to have taunted him to move more quickly. He was consequently condemned to wander the earth until Christ's second coming.

CONSIDERING BRAINS

Is brain activity sex-linked? There is considerable evidence that it is.

Writing my previous book *The Seed Bearers: Role of the Female in Biology and Genetics,* I undertook extensive research and corresponded with experts in the field. In particular I owe a debt of gratitude to Professor Ursula Mittwoch of London University who sent me copies of her papers and answered my questions. Through her writings as well as others I found that all fetuses begin life as female and, if nothing happens to change that, they will grow into girls (with two X chromosomes, one from their mother and one from their father). For a baby to become a boy, the fetus must be subjected to extra doses of androgens – male hormones, mainly testosterone – at several key times during its development. The boy will have mismatching XY sex chromosomes, an X from his mother and a Y from his father, in every cell in his body. The Y chromosome from his father acts as a switch, initiating the manufacture of extra testosterone in the testes, which begin the process of imposing maleness on the fetus. If this switch fails to work, then the child will be female even though she has Y chromosomes in her cells.

The extra testosterone in the boy (females have small amounts of this hormone) not only affects his physical appearance which begins to change in the uterus, but it also affects the way his brain pathways develop, long before he is born. These characteristic sex differences are therefore initiated by nature, not nurture, although the way a child is reared can to some extent either reinforce or modify behaviour.

One of the first functions of the extra testosterone in the boy fetus is to counteract the copious supplies of the female hormone estrogen (of which women have a lot and men a little), which is flooding the bloodstream of his mother's pregnant body. Thus, from the start, boys have to fight to be male; whereas girls are not threatened by their mother's estrogen. This 'fight to be male' (see Mittwoch) is a characteristic of the male sex; they cannot assume their maleness in the same way that a female can assume her femaleness.

The brain itself is a sex organ. Our emotions are seated therein and not as popularly supposed in the heart or liver. The female ovaries and the male testes are in close contact with a person's brain, through hormone-driven messages. Anne Moir and David Jessel, authors of *BrainSex* (1989), sum up the situation thus:

"Men have to go through a hormonal process to change their brains from the natural female pattern present in all of us, whatever our eventual sex, from the first weeks of life in the womb; they have to be soaked in extra male hormone and restructured – so in the process of reconstruction the chance of mistakes is much greater than in the female, who doesn't need any reconstruction of her brain." [p. 117]

The amount of male hormone active in a fetal male makes a difference: "What matters is the degree to which our embryonic brains are exposed to male hormone. The less they get, the more the natural, feminine mind-set will survive. [In the uterus] the die is cast; that is when the mind is made up, and the luggage of our bodies, and of society's expectations of us, merely supplements this basic biological fact of life." [p. 36]

When we consider the effect of the hormones on the way the brain functions, we find a number of differences between the sexes. Moir and Jessel give an account of these; they can be summarised:

– girls have a larger vocabulary and learn to speak and write earlier than boys

– the two sides of the brain, through the corpus callosum, have a larger number of connections in women. This means that more information is being exchanged between the right and left sides of the brain

– all the senses are more acute in women, with more messages reaching the female from the outside world and these messages can be processed in greater depth

– there is greater female delicacy and perception in taste, this sensitivity increasing just before ovulation

– women hear better than men

– while there is no difference sharpness of vision between the sexes, the eyes of females and males actually see differently. Women's eyes are more sensitive to the red end of the spectrum and have a wider range, also seeing better in the dark; and the messages when they reach the brain are differently processed. Women have a better visual memory (women artists please note). While men focus more in the centre of the field and depend more on their eyesight than their other senses since these are weaker.

Male tunnel vision tends to favour uniformity over variety, while women not only tolerate but welcome variety. Women's superior verbal skills can be directly related to the female brain, which is stimulated to greater activity by estrogen (progesterone on the contrary inhibits brain activity).

The brains of the two sexes operate differently between the right and left sides, with some specialisation between the two sides of the brains of both sexes. (There is a cross-over, the right brain controls the left side of the body and the left brain controls the right side of the body.) However, the two sides of a woman's brain are in better communication with each other, with more messages being exchanged through their larger corpus callosum, therefore women are more able to take account of a number of different points of view than men, who are more specialised. Women thus tend to be better at inter-personal relations, whether in families or outside.

There is a major difference in how the two brains respond to emotions: "Women have their emotional responses residing in both sides of the brain. In men the emotional functions are concentrated in the right side of the brain". [*BrainSex*, pp. 46-7] The left side of a man's brain therefore lacks emotional response and this can be a major cause of difficulty in human relationships.

With such contrasts in brain function, females and males experience the world differently: indeed, the two sexes to a large extent inhabit different worlds, and each has its own characteristic sense of truth.

Aggressive behaviour is a major effect of more testosterone. The capacity for aggression is imprinted on boys' brains very early, even before the massive increase in levels of androgens at the age of puberty, when the physical changes in boys become obvious: a greater increase in height; different musculature; lower pitch of voice, followed by growth of facial and body hair and sexual potency. Changes in the brain pathways of males that were made in the uterus are now activated at puberty:

"With men, the impact of the hormones on the receptive brain not only produces aggression, dominance and assertiveness, it also tends to trigger the release of further testosterone, reinforcing those initial aggressive tendencies. Among sportsmen, testosterone levels are higher at the end of a match, or a season, than at the beginning. Competition raises testosterone levels. Rivalry fuels aggression." [p. 81]

Thus, in males testosterone reinforces itself. Competition fuels aggression.

Virginia explored some of the characteristics of 'maleness' with no outside assistance. It was a quality she did not like. She seemed to sense intuitively that unfeeling left brain in men, and she reacted negatively to it, as she reacted negatively to all forms of male aggression including war. She was not to know from any outside source that testosterone reaches higher levels in wartime but she discovered it for herself. Even before the first world war, her attitude towards 'maleness' hardened as a result of the Dreadnought Hoax. In February 1910 she, together with a group of young men, dressed as an Abyssinian Emperor and his retinue and gained an invitation to visit the British Navy's flagship moored at Weymouth, where they were entertained as honoured guests with all due ceremony. When the Navy discovered the deception, they were naturally furious. The occasion and its aftermath were never forgotten by Virginia. Quentin Bell wrote:

"the theme of masculine honour, of masculine violence and stupidity, of gold-laced masculine pomposity, remained with her for the rest of her life. She had entered the Abyssinian adventure for the fun of the thing; but she came out of it with a sense of the brutality and silliness of men." [*Virginia Woolf*, Vol. 1, pp. 160–1]

Two months before her death in 1941, when she feared that the coming spring would see a renewed attempt by Germany to invade Britain, Virginia wrote to her friend Lady Simon:

"No, I don't see whats to be done about war. Its manliness; and manliness breeds womanliness – both so hateful. I tried to put this to our local labour party: but was scowled at as a prostitute." [*Letters*, No. 3683] And in March 1941, she wrote to Dame Ethel Smyth:

"I was saying to Leonard, we have no future. He says thats what gives him hope. He says the necessity of some catastrophe pricks him up. What I feel is the suspense when nothing actually happens." [*Letters*, No. 3695]

In the event, the catastrophe that befell Virginia Woolf in March 1941 was not the invasion of the country, it was closer to home. At a time when she was profoundly depressed, Leonard was 'pricked up'. At the end of Virginia's life their visions were in extreme conflict with each other, and this was intensified by their different responses to the outside threat of war. To return to Moir and Jessel:

"The biggest behavioral difference between men and women is the natural, innate aggression of men, which explains to a large degree their historical dominance of the species. Men didn't learn aggression as one of the tactics of the sex war. We do not teach our boy children to be aggressive – indeed, we try vainly to unteach it. Even researchers most hostile to the achnowledgement of sex differences agree that this is a male feature, and one which cannot be explained by social conditioning." [*BrainSex*, p. 7] And:

"the male hormone has an effect on aggression even greater than the influence it plays in more obvious forms of sexuality." [p. 80]

Despite the mounting evidence of major differences between the sexes in our sensory equipment with which we experience life, there continues to be widespread reluctance to admit any inbuilt diversity between the sexes, apart from the obvious physical differences in the formation of the female and male reproductive systems; nor are we willing to admit that we may be influenced by biological factors such as our hormones. This may be partly due to our emphasis on individual responsibility for a person's actions before the law. We like to think we are in charge of ourselves and in control of our emotions at all times. Many men certainly prefer to think so and seem to put that unemotional dead area of their left brains in charge – controlling not only their own right-brain feelings but also those of others. It will take both sexes some time to realise that women's more balanced brain enables us to see situations from a number of different perspectives. But both sexes do have choices, and these choices are more accessible when we understand what is driving us.

Day to day, even moment to moment, our ever-changing hormone levels may influence our behaviour and colour our responses; but our basic brain-set into either female or male is permanent.

In the case of the Woolfs, their natural sexual characteristics were accentuated by their different backgrounds, he with semitic ancestry and she as an anglo-saxon; and by their upbringing, Leonard having received an intensive male-orientated academic education through which he relied on the activity of his apparently rational but unfeeling left brain; whereas Virginia did not go to school and explored the depth and precision of her perceptions.

Virginia and Leonard were often described, respectively, as 'very female' and 'very male'. Theirs was indeed a marriage of opposites.

A NOTE ON SERVANTS

Virginia Stephen grew up in a large house where the domestic work was done by seven servants. In such a traditional English Victorian household there was a strict order of command, or hierarchy, which was understood by every member of the staff as well as the family. Wages were fixed according to a servant's level of responsibility. The top servants were the butler (if there was one), who kept the male servants in order; while the cook would be in charge of the kitchen staff; these would be (mainly) female. If there was a housekeeper she would be in overall charge, accountable to the mistress of the house who would discuss the day's needs with her. The housekeeper would see that the orders of her mistress were carried out within the permitted budget.

With the reduction in the number of household domestics that had already begun before world war one, and thereafter continued throughout the nineteen twenties and thirties as households became smaller and labour-saving appliances were introduced, the remnants of this hierarchical structure remained even when the domestic staff had been reduced to two – a cook and maid-of-all-work. The cook would take orders directly from the mistress of the house while the maid-of-all work cleaned the house and prepared vegetables, taking orders from the cook. The cook's higher status and level of responsibility would be reflected in higher wages than the maid. With the absence of male staff members, the master of the house would have little to do with the indoor servants but, since he was the wage-earner, he would enforce financial control on household expenditure through his wife. As a gentleman he was supposed to be amiable to the servants but leave his wife in control. He would be in charge of any outdoor staff such as the gardener.

In the Woolf household we can see the last vestiges of this system still operating when Mabel Haskins was first employed as cook in 1934: she was a trained servant who expected to receive orders from Virginia and, when she worked at Monk's House in Rodmell, she would have the new maid-of-all-work, Louise Everest, working under her.

It was this system that Leonard tore to shreds, first by favouring Louise over Mabel (who despite this humiliation remained loyal both to her training and to Virginia); and then, after he had managed to get rid of Mabel in October 1940, by favouring Louise over Virginia the mistress of the house, who was reduced to powerlessness. He intruded on the domestic order in pursuit of his vision, that he was introducing classical Greek-style 'democracy' to Monk's House. But actually, by promoting Louise to a mythological position in his Greek fantasy, he took over the running of the house from Virginia so that she lost both the power and the control of being mistress of the house.

When Virginia gave her fictional character Mabel Hoskins the part of Queen Anne in the Pageant, in the early draft of *Between the Acts,* she was making a very strong statement: she not only more-than restored to her reliable cook the position that had been quite illegitimately taken from her by Leonard in real life, but she actually made her Queen of the Age of Reason. It was tit for tat.

SELECT BIBLIOGRAPHY
Books by Virginia Woolf in Order of Year of First Publication, with Editions Consulted:

DIARY AND LETTERS

WOOLF, Virginia: *The Diary of Virginia Woolf*, 5 Vols., Ed. Anne Olivier Bell, Ass. Andrew McNeillie, Penguin Books, 1977-84
WOOLF, Virginia: *The Letters of Virginia Woolf*, 6 Vols., Ed. Nigel Nicolson, Ass. Joanne Trautmann, The Hogarth Press Ltd / Chatto & Windus, 1976-80
WOOLF, Virginia and STRACHEY, Lytton: *Letters,* Ed. Leonard Woolf & James Strachey, The Hogarth Press & Chatto & Windus, 1956

NOVELS, INCLUDING DRAFTS AND BIOGRAPHIES BY VIRGINIA WOOLF

The Voyage Out, 1915, Grafton (Collins) 1989
Night and Day, 1919, Definitive Edition, Vintage London 1992
Jacob's Room, 1922, Penguin 1992
Mrs Dalloway, 1925, Oxford University Press 1992
To the Lighthouse, 1927, Oxford University Press 1992
Orlando: A Biography, 1928, Definitive Edition, Vintage 1992
The Waves, 1931, Oxford University Press 1992
The Waves: The Two Holograph Drafts, Transcribed and Ed. J.W. Graham, University of Toronto Press 1976
Flush: A Biography, 1933, The Hogarth Press 1958
The Pargiters (unpublished), Ed. Mitchell A. Leaska, The Hogarth Press 1978
The Years, 1937, Grafton (Collins) 1990
Roger Fry: A Biography, 1940, The Hogarth Press, Intro. Frances Spalding 1991

Between the Acts, 1941, Intro. Quentin Bell, Definitive Edition, Vintage London, 1992
Pointz Hall: The Earlier and Later Typescripts of Between the Acts, Ed. Mitchell A. Leaska, University Publications New York, 1983

OTHER WORK BY VIRGINIA WOOLF

The Common Reader 1, First Series 1925, Hogarth 1984
The Common Reader 2, Second Series 1932, Hogarth 1986
A Room of One's Own, 1929, Three Guineas 1938 (one Vol.) Chatto & Windus / Hogarth Press 1984
A Letter to a Young Poet, The Hogarth Letters No. 8, Hogarth 1932
Moments of Being (revised and enlarged), Grafton 1989
A Haunted House and Other Short Stories, 1944, Grafton 1988
The Complete Shorter Fiction, Triad Grafton (HarperCollins) 1989
Virginia Woolf on Women & Writing, The Women's Press 1979
Books and Portraits, Triad Grafton (Harper-Collins) 1979
A Woman's Essays, Selected Essays Vol. One, Penguin 1992
The Crowded Dance of Modern Life, Selected Essays Vol. Two, Penguin 1993

BOOKS ABOUT VIRGINIA WOOLF

ABEL, Elizabeth: *Virginia Woolf and the Fictions of Psychoanalysis.* Chicago: University of Chicago Press, 1993
BATCHELOR, John: *Virginia Woolf the Major Novels.* Great Britain: Cambridge University Press, 1991

BELL, Quentin: *Virginia Woolf: A Biography.* Vols. 1 and 2, The Hogarth Press 1990

BOND, Alma Halbert: *Who Killed Virginia Woolf.* New York: Human Sciences Press, 1989

BOWLBY, Rachel: *Virginia Woolf: Feminist Destinations.* Oxford: Basil Blackwell Ltd., 1988

BOWLBY, Rachel (Editor): *Virginia Woolf.* England: Longman Group UK Ltd., 1992

CAWS, Mary Ann: *Women of Bloomsbury: Virginia, Vanessa and Carrington.* New York: Routledge, Chapman and Hall, Inc., 1990

DeSALVO, Louise: *Virginia Woolf. The Impact of Childhood Sexual Abuse on her Life and Work.* New York: Ballantine Books, 1989

DICK, Susan: *Virginia Woolf.* Great Britain: Edward Arnold, 1989

DUNN, Jane: *A Very Close Conspiracy. Vanessa Bell and Virginia Woolf.* London: Jonathan Cape Ltd., 1990

GORDON, Lyndall: *Virginia Woolf: A Writer's Life.* Oxford University Press, 1984

HOLTBY, Winifred: *Virginia Woolf: A Critical Memoir.* Cassandra Editions, Academy Press Ltd., Chicago, 1978

LAURENCE, Patricia Ondek: *The Reading of Silence: Virginia Woolf in the English Tradition.* Stanford University Press, 1993

LEE, Hermione: *Virginia Woolf.* Chatto & Windus, 1996

LEHMANN, John: *Virginia Woolf.* Great Britain: Thames and Hudson, 1975

LOVE, Jean O.: *Sources of Madness and Art.* University of California Press, 1977

MARCUS, Jane: *Virginia Woolf and the Languages of Patriarchy.* Bloomington: Indiana University Press, 1987

MARLER, Regina: *Selected Letters of Vanessa Bell.* London: Bloomsbury, 1993

MEPHAM, John: *Virginia Woolf: A Literary Life.* St. Martin's Press New York, 1991

MEPHAM, John: *Virginia Woolf.* London: Bristol Classical Press, 1992

ROE, Sue: *Writing and Gender. Virginia Woolf's Writing Practice.* Hertfordshire: Harvester Wheatsheaf, 1990

ROSE, Phyllis: *Woman of Letters: A Life of Virginia Woolf.* Oxford University Press, 1978

SPRAGUE, Claire (Editor): *Virginia Woolf: A Collection of Critical Essays.* Prentice-Hall, Inc. New Jersey A Spectrum Book, 1971

TROMBLEY, Stephen: *All that Summer she was Mad. Virginia Woolf: Female Victim of Male Medicine.* Continuum: New York, 1982

WORK BY LEONARD WOOLF

The Village in the Jungle, 1913, London: The Hogarth Press, 1971

The Wise Virgins, 1914, London: The Hogarth Press, 1979

After the Deluge: A Study in Communal Psychology Vol. I, Published by Leonard and Virginia Woolf, at The Hogarth Press, Tavistock Square, London, 1931

Quack, Quack! Published by Leonard and Virginia Woolf at the Hogarth Press, 52 Tavistock Square, London, 1935

The Hotel – A play, 1939, The Hogarth Press, 52 Tavistock Square, London, 1939

After the Deluge: A Study in Communal Psychology Vol. II, The Hogarth Press, 37 Mecklenburgh Square, London, 1939

Barbarians at the Gate, London: Victor Gollancz Ltd, 1939

The War for Peace, Routledge, 1940

Principia Politica: A Study in Communal Psychology, London: The Hogarth Press, 1953

AUTOBIOGRAPHY

Sowing [1880 to 1904], 1960

Growing [1904 to 1911], 1961

Beginning Again [1911 to 1918], 1964

Downhill All the Way [1919 to 1939], 1967
The Journey Not the Arrival Matters [1939 to 1969], 1969

LETTERS

Frederick Spotts (Ed.), London: Weidenfeld and Nicolson, 1990

BOOKS ABOUT LEONARD WOOLF

WILSON, Duncan: *Leonard Woolf – A Political Biography*. London: The Hogarth Press, 1978

BOOKS ABOUT VIRGINIA WOOLF AND LEONARD WOOLF

ALEXANDER, Peter F.: *Leonard and Virginia Woolf – A Literary Partnership*. New York, Harvester Wheatsheaf, 1992
LEHMANN, John: *Thrown to the Woolfs*. London: Weidenfeld and Nicolson, 1978
SPATER, George and PARSONS, Ian: *A Marriage of True Minds – An Intimate Portrait of Leonard and Virginia Woolf*. London: Jonathan Cape Ltd., 1977

OTHER RELATED BOOKS

ANSCOMBE, Isabelle: *Omega and After – Bloomsbury and the Decorative Arts*, London, Thames and Hudson Ltd., 1981
BIBLE, Holy: *New International Version*, 1991
COATES, Irene: *The Seedbearers: Role of the Female in Biology and Genetics*, Edinburgh, Cambridge, Durham, The Pentland Press Ltd., 1993
COATES, Irene: *Claudia's War*, New South Wales: Black Lightning Press, 1983
GARNET, Angelica: *Deceived with Kindness – A Bloomsbury Childhood*, Oxford: Oxford University Press, 1984

GREER, Germaine: *The Obstacle Race*, Secker & Warburg, 1979
HOLROYD, Michael: *Lytton Strachey 1994*, Vintage, 1995
HOLROYD, Michael (Ed.): *Lytton Strachey by Himself*, Holt, Rinehart and Winston, 1971
HOLROYD, Michael: *Bernard Shaw*, The One-Volume Definitive Edition, Chatto & Windus, 1997
LEE, Hugh (Ed.): *A Cézanne in the Hedge and Other Memories of Charleston and Bloomsbury*, London: Collins & Brown Ltd., 1992
MOIR, Anne & JESSEL, David: *BrainSex – The Real Difference Between Men & Women*. London: Michael Joseph Ltd., 1989
MOORE, George Edward: *Principia Ethica*, Cambridge, Cambridge University Press, 1903
NICOLSON, Harold: *Diaries & Letters 1930-45* (2 Vols.), Ed. Nigel Nicolson, Collins Fontana, 1969
NICOLSON, Nigel (Ed.): *Vita and Harold – The Letters of Vita Sackville-West and Harold Nicolson 1910-1962*, Weidenfeld & Nicolson, London, 1992
NICOLSON, Nigel: *Portrait of a Marriage*, Futura Publications, 1973
ROBINS, Elizabeth: *Both Sides of the Curtain*, William Heinemann, 1940
ROSENBAUM, S. P. (Ed.): *The Bloomsbury Group*, Toronto and Buffalo, University of Toronto Press, 1975
SACKVILLE-WEST, Vita: Ed. DeSalvo & Mitchell A. Leaska, *Letters of Vita Sackville-West to Virginia Woolf*, Hutchinson, 1984
SPALDING, Frances: *Vanessa Bell*, Great Britain, George Weidenfeld & Nicolson Limited, 1983
SHAW, George Bernard: *Heartbreak House* [1919], Penguin, 1976
WATNEY, Simon: *The Art of Duncan Grant*, London: John Murray (Publishers) Ltd., 1990

REFERENCES

The *Letters of Virginia Woolf* are referred to throughout as *Letters*; her diary as *Diary*

PROLOGUE

1 *Letters*, No. 615
2 *A Marriage of True Minds*, p. 177
3 *Diary*, Volume 4, p. ix
4 *A Woman's Essays*, p. 178
5 *Letters*, No 3702
6 *Letters of Leonard Woolf*, 1989, p. 165
7 *A Room of One's Own*, pp. 90–92
8 *Downhill all the Way*, p. 154
9 *Between the Acts*, p. 73

CHAPTER ONE

1 Bell, *Virginia Wolf*, Vol. 1. p. 24
2 *Letters*, No. 45
3 *Letters*, No. 576
4 Alexander, *Leonard and Virginia Woolf: A Literary Partnership*, pp. 34–35
5 *Beginning Again*, p. 159
6 *Selected Letters of Vanessa Bell*, p. 132
7 *Selected Letters of Vanessa Bell*, p. 88–89
8 *Letters*, No. 326
9 *Letters of Leonard Woolf*, p. 121
10 *Letters of Leonard Woolf*, p. 122–123
11 *Letters*, No. 333
12 *Letters*, No. 335
13 *Letters*, Appendix B, No. 339a
14 *Letters*, No. 416
15 *Letters*, No. 440
16 *Letters*, No. 439
17 *Selected Letters of Vanessa Bell*, p. 66–67
18 *Selected Letters of Vanessa Bell*, 21 August 1908, pp. 69–70
19 *Letters*, No. 3699
20 *Letters*, No. 526
21 *Selected Letters of Vanessa Bell*, p. 82
22 *Letters*, Note, p. 424
23 *Selected Letters of Vanessa Bell*, p. 90
24 *Selected Letters of Vanessa Bell*, p. 92
25 *Letters*, No. 529
26 *Selected Letters of Vanessa Bell*, p. 94

27 *Letters*, No. 531
28 *Letters*, No. 570
29 *Night and Day*, p. 31

CHAPTER TWO

1 *Leonard Woolf, A Political Biography*, p. 10
2 *Leonard Woolf, A Political Biography*, p. 246
3 *Who Killed Virginia Woolf?* p. 71
4 *Who Killed Virginia Woolf?* pp. 171–173
5 Preface, *Letters of Leonard Woolf*, pp. ix–x
6 *The Journey Not the Arrival Matters*, p. 158
7 *Letters of Leonard Woolf*, p. 561
8 *Diary*, 5 September 1940
9 *Moments of Being*, p. 125
10 *Sowing*, p. 15
11 *Sowing*, p. 7
12 *Sowing*, p. 22
13 *Leonard and Virginia Woolf*, p. 196
14 *Sowing*, p. 52
15 *Sowing*, pp. 66–67
16 *A Marriage of True Minds*, pp. 28–29
17 *Letters of Leonard Woolf*, p. 13
18 *Principia Ethica*, pp. 142–143
19 *Lytton Strachey*, p. 60
20 *Lytton Strachey*, pp. 60–61
21 *Sowing*, p. 100
22 *Letters of Leonard Woolf*, p. 43
23 *Sowing*, p. 13
24 *Letters of Leonard Woolf*, April 21, 1906, p. 118
25 *A Marriage of True Minds*, p. 53
26 *Letters of Leonard Woolf*, pp. 73–74
27 *Letters of Leonard Woolf*, p. 84
28 *Letters of Leonard Woolf*, p. 125
29 *Letters of Leonard Woolf*, pp. 84–85
30 *Letters of Leonard Woolf*, p. 102
31 *Letters of Leonard Woolf*, pp. 97–98

32   *Letters of Leonard Woolf*, p. 130

33   *Letters of Leonard Woolf*, p. 133

34   *Letters of Leonard Woolf*, p. 134

35   *Letters of Leonard Woolf*, p. 135

36   *Letters of Leonard Woolf*, p. 138

37   *Letters of Leonard Woolf*, p. 142

38   *Letters of Leonard Woolf*, p. 139, Note

39   *Letters of Leonard Woolf*, p. 140

40   *Letters of Leonard Woolf*, pp. 144-145

41   *Letters of Leonard Woolf*, p. 148

42   *Letters of Leonard Woolf*, pp. 148-149

43   *Moments of Being*, p. 205

44   *Letters of Leonard Woolf*, p. 493

45   *Letters of Leonard Woolf*, p. 166, Note

46   *Letters of Leonard Woolf*, p. 106

47   *Sowing*, pp. 113-116

CHAPTER THREE

1   *Letters*, No. 427

2   *Letters*, No. 584

3   *Letters*, No. 566

4   *Virginia Woolf, A Biography*, Volume 1, p. 101

5   *Letters*, Nos. 573-74

6   *Selected Letters of Vanessa Bell*, p. 108

7   From Jowett, *Dialogues of Plato*, vol. II, p. 432, quoted in *A Marriage of True Minds*, p. 61

8   *A Marriage of True Minds*, pp. 61-2

9   *The Village in the Jungle*, p. 142

10   *The Village in the Jungle*, pp. 306-307

11   *Letters of Leonard Woolf*, pp. 168-169

12   *Letters*, No. 600

13   *Letters*, No. 601

14   *Letters*, No. 602

15   *Selected Letters of Vanessa Bell*, p. 113

16   *Letters of Leonard Woolf*, pp. 169-170

17   *Letters*, No. 603

18   *Letters*, No. 606

19   *Letters*, No. 608

20   *Letters*, No. 611

21   *Letters*, No. 613

22   *Letters of Leonard Woolf*, p. 175

23   *Letters of Leonard Woolf*, pp. 172-174

24   *Letters*, No. 615

25   *Letters of Leonard Woolf*, pp. 175-176

26   *Selected Letters of Vanessa Bell*, 2 June 1912, pp. 117-118

27   *Letters of Leonard Woolf*, p. 176

28   Quoted in *Lytton Strachey*, p. 257

29   *Letters*, No. 620

30   *Letters*, No. 625

31   *The Voyage Out*, pp. 360-361

32   *Letters*, No. 622

33   *Letters*, No. 623

34   *Letters*, No. 626

35   *Letters*, No. 628

36   *Letters*, No. 629

37   *Letters*, No. 633

38   *Letters*, No. 632

39   *Letters*, No. 637

40   *Letters*, No. 608

41   *Letters of Leonard Woolf*, p. 178

42   *Letters*, No. 643

43   *Beginning Again*, pp. 69-70

CHAPTER FOUR

1   *Letters of Leonard Woolf*, quoted by editor, p. 162. [My italics]

2   *Letters*, No. 640

3   *Letters*, No. 643

4   *Selected Letters of Vanessa Bell*, pp. 124-125

5   *Selected Letters of Vanessa Bell*, 23 August 1912, p. 125

6   *Letters*, No. 644

7   *Beginning Again* pp. 82-83

8   *Selected Letters of Vanessa Bell*, p. 127

9   *Selected Letters of Vanessa Bell*, pp. 129-131

10   *The Waves*, pp. 171-172

11   *Selected Letters of Vanessa Bell*, p. 132

12   *Beginning Again* pp. 84-86

14   *The Unknown Virginia Woolf*, pp. 122-123

15   *The Unknown Virginia Woolf*, p. 25

16   *Selected Letters of Vanessa Bell*, p. 133

CHAPTER SEVEN

1 Diary, 27 March 1919
2 Diary, 9 January 1924
3 Jacob's Room, p. 32
4 Jacob's Room, p. 64
5 Jacob's Room, p. xxxviii
6 Diary, 26 July 1922
7 Diary, 3 August 1922
8 Diary, 22 August 1922
9 Diary, 26 August 1922
10 Diary, 30 August 1922
11 Diary, 7 February 1923
12 Mrs. Dalloway, pp. 29–31
13 Mrs. Dalloway, pp. 47
14 The Waves, pp. 281–282
15 Diary, 6 January 1925
16 Mrs. Dalloway, p. 49
17 Mrs. Dalloway, pp. 244
18 Mrs. Dalloway, pp. 254–255
19 Diary, 2 January 1923
20 Diary, 13 December 1924
21 Leonard Woolf, a political biography, p. 245
22 Downhill all the Way, p. 240
23 Letters of Leonard Woolf, 30.10.43
24 Diary, 29 September 1924
25 Diary, 15 October 1923
26 Diary, 15 September 1924
27 Moments of Being, p. 213
28 Diary, 23 November 1926
29 Selected Letters of Vanessa Bell, 11 May 1927
16 Mrs. Dalloway, pp. 242–245
17 Mrs. Dalloway, pp. 254–255

CHAPTER EIGHT

1 The Letters of Vita Sackville-West to Virginia Woolf, pp. 74–75
2 Vita and Harold, p. 168
3 Beginning Again, pp. 172–176
4 Diary, 7 December 1925
5 Vita and Harold, Introduction
6 Letters of Leonard Woolf, p. 228

7 Virginia Woolf, p. 120
8 Vita and Harold, p. 136
9 Selected Letters of Vanessa Bell, pp. 287–288
10 Letters, Nos. 1612, 1644, 1646
11 The Letters of Vita Sackville-West to Virginia Woolf, pp. 86–87
12 The Letters of Vita Sackville-West to Virginia Woolf, pp. 88–89
13 Letters, No. 1611
14 The Letters of Vita Sackville-West to Virginia Woolf, pp. 108–130 passim.
15 The Letters of Vita Sackville-West to Virginia Woolf, p. 118
16 The Letters of Vita Sackville-West to Virginia Woolf, p. 128
17 The Letters of Vita Sackville-West to Virginia Woolf, p. 136
18 Vita and Harold, p. 146
19 Diary, 19 January 1926
20 Diary, 17 February 1931
21 Who Killed Virginia Woolf? pp. 118–119
22 Virginia Woolf, p. 119
23 Diary, 5 September 1926
24 Diary, 13 September 1926
25 Diary, 28 September 1926
26 Ibid.
27 Letters, No. 1687
28 Vita and Harold, pp. 173–174
29 Vita and Harold, pp. 173–176
30 The Letters of Vita Sackville-West to Virginia Woolf, note, p. 177
31 Diary, 22 June 1927
32 Diary, 22 March 1927
33 Diary, 6 June 1927
34 Letters of Leonard Woolf, pp. 229–230
35 Diary, 10 August 1927
36 Diary, 4 September 1927
37 Diary, 20 September 1927
38 Letters, No. 1820
39 Letters, No. 1820, note
40 Diary, 22 October 1927
41 Ibid.
42 Vita and Harold, pp. 182–183
43 Downhill all the Way, p. 178

13 Virginia Woolf & Lytton Strachey *Letters*, p. 38

17 *Beginning Again* pp. 102–103

18 Quentin Bell *Virginia Woolf*, Volume II, p. 10

19 Quentin Bell *Virginia Woolf*, Volume II, p. 10

20 *Selected Letters of Vanessa Bell*, p. 139

21 Quentin Bell *Virginia Woolf*, Volume II, p. 135

22 *Mrs Dalloway*, p. 127

23 Quentin Bell *Virginia Woolf*, Volume II, p. 16, note

24 *Letters of Leonard Woolf*, pp. 184–187

25 Quentin Bell *Virginia Woolf*, Volume II, p. 11

26 Quentin Bell *Virginia Woolf*, Volume II, p. 16, note

27 Quentin Bell *Virginia Woolf*, Volume II, p. 16

28 *Letters of Leonard Woolf*, p. 192

29 *Letters of Leonard Woolf*, pp. 194

30 *Letters of Leonard Woolf*, p. 191

31 *Letters of Leonard Woolf*, p. 254

CHAPTER FIVE

1 *The Wise Virgins*, pp. 18–19

2 *The Wise Virgins*, p. 169

3 *The Wise Virgins*, pp. 86–87

4 *The Wise Virgins*, pp. 30–31

5 *The Wise Virgins*, p. 33

6 *The Wise Virgins*, pp. 36–37

7 *The Wise Virgins*, pp. 40–41

8 *The Wise Virgins*, p. 73

9 *The Wise Virgins*, pp. 40–41

10 *The Wise Virgins*, p. 51

11 *The Wise Virgins*, pp. 51–52

12 See Chapter Three

13 *The Wise Virgins*, pp. 81–83

14 *The Wise Virgins*, pp. 83–84

15 *The Wise Virgins*, p. 86

16 *The Wise Virgins*, pp. 88–90

17 *The Wise Virgins*, p. 92

18 *The Wise Virgins*, p. 100

19 *The Wise Virgins*, pp. 111–

20 *The Wise Virgins*, pp. 197–

21 *The Wise Virgins*, pp. 218–2

22 *The Wise Virgins*, p. 213

23 *The Wise Virgins*, p. 201

24 *The Wise Virgins*, pp. 194–19

25 *The Wise Virgins*, p. 206

26 *The Wise Virgins*, p. 97

27 *Letters* of Leonard Woolf, p. 49

28 *Letters* of Leonard Woolf, pp. 199 & note

29 *Lytton Strachey*, p. 306

30 *Letters* of Leonard Woolf, p. 205

31 *Letters*, No. 693

32 *Letters*, No. 699

33 *Letters of Leonard Woolf*, pp. 195–

34 *Letters* Nos. 681, 682

35 See *Appendix A* for an account of this legend

CHAPTER SIX

1 *Letters*, No. 645

2 *Diary*, January 1915

3 Lappin and Lapinova *The Complete Shorter Fiction*, p. 168

4 Mrs Dalloway in Bond Street, *Complete Shorter Fiction*, p. 157

5 *Letters*, No. 728

6 *Beginning Again*, pp. 102–103

7 *Letters of Leonard Woolf*, pp. 220–22

8 Quentin Bell, *Virginia Woolf*, Vol II, pp. 24–27

9 *Selected Letters of Vanessa Bell*, p. 17

10 *Mrs. Dalloway* p. 13

11 *Mrs. Dalloway* p. 39

12 *Diary*, 4 February 1920

13 *The Complete Shorter Fiction*, p. 1, reference to *Letters*, No. 167

14 *Letters*, No. 2254

15 *Night and Day*, pp. 454–455

16 *Night and Day*, p. 487

17 *Night and Day*, p. 488

18 *Letters*, No. 3460

19 *Diary*, 28 November 1938

44 *Orlando*, pp. 120–121
45 *Orlando*, p. 174
46 *Orlando*, p. 201
47 *Letters*, No. 1863
48 *Diary*, 18 February 1928
49 *Diary*, 20 June 1928
50 *Diary*, 4 May 1928
51 *Diary*, 31 May 1928
52 *Vita and Harold*, pp. 197–198
53 *Diary*, 7 July 1928
54 *Diary*, 8 August 1928
55 *Diary*, 22 September 1928
56 *Letters*, No. 1926, and note
57 *Letters of Leonard Woolf*, p. 233
58 *Vita and Harold*, pp. 203–205
59 *Downhill all the Way*, pp. 143–145
60 *Diary*, 2 November 1929

CHAPTER NINE

1 *A Room of One's Own*, pp. 3–5
2 *A Room of One's Own*, p. 17
3 *Vita and Harold*, p. 222
4 *Diary*, 11 March 1930
5 *Harold Nicolson Diaries & Letters 1930-39*, 11 July 1930
6 *Diary*, 30 September 1926
7 *Selected Letters Vanessa Bell*, 3 May 1927
8 *Virginia Woolf*, Lehmann, p. 77
9 *The Waves, Appendix A*, pp. 63–64
10 *The Waves*, Interlude 1, p. 3
11 *After the Deluge*, Vol 1. p. 47
12 *After the Deluge*, Vol 1. p. 154
13 *After the Deluge*, Vol 1. p. 272
14 *After the Deluge*, Vol 1. p. 54
15 *After the Deluge*, Vol 1. p. 228
16 *After the Deluge*, Vol 1. p. 54
17 *Leonard Woolf – a political biography*, p. 231
18 *Leonard Woolf – a political biography*, p. 232
19 *Leonard Woolf – a political biography*, p. 237
20 *The Waves*, Draft I, p. 4. Deletions omitted

21 *The Waves*, Draft II, pp. 407–408
22 *The Waves*, pp. 7–8
23 *The Waves*, p. 12
24 *The Waves*, pp. 5 & 15
25 *The Waves*, Draft II, pp. 707–708
26 *Diary*, Volume 4, p. ix
27 *Diary*, 15 September 1931
28 *The Waves*, p. 234
29 *The Waves*, p. 53
30 *Diary*, 4 February 1932
31 *The Waves*, pp. 81–84
32 *The Waves*, pp. 85–86
33 *Diary*, 10 January 1931
34 *Diary*, 30 June 1927
35 *The Waves*, pp. 238–239
36 *The Waves*, pp. 192–193
37 *The Waves*, pp. 45–46
38 *Diary*, 7 February 1931
39 *The Pargiters*, p. xxxv
40 *Diary*, 23 January 1931
41 *Diary*, 23 June 1931
42 *Diary*, 7 July 1931
43 *Diary*, 15 September 1931
44 *Diary*, 19 September 1931
45 *Diary*, 32 October 1931
46 *Diary*, 29 December 1931
47 *Diary*, Friday, Xmas morning 1931
48 *Diary*, 27 December 1931

CHAPTER TEN

1 *Vita and Harold*, pp. 208–209
2 *The Waves*, pp. 247–248
3 *Downhill all the Way*, pp. 248–250
4 *Diary*, 18 January 1932
5 *Diary*, 22 January 1932
6 *Diary*, 2 February 1932
7 *Diary*, 11 February, note
8 *Diary*, 29 February 1932
9 *Diary*, 3 March 1932. [My emphasis]
10 *Diary*, 17 March 1932
11 *Diary*, 25 May 1932
12 *Diary*, 2 May 1932
13 *Diary*, 8 May 1932
14 *Diary*, 19 May 1932

15 Lehmann, *Virginia Woolf*, p. 75

16 Lehmann, *Virginia Woolf*, p. 75

17 Lehmann, *Virginia Woolf*, p. 76

18 *Diary*, 2 September 1932

19 *Letters of Leonard Woolf*,
    7 September 1932

20 *Diary*, 10 November 1932

21 *Diary*, 10 July 1933

22 *Downhill all the Way*, p. 151

23 *Diary*, 2 September 1933

24 *Diary*, 9 March 1934

25 *Diary*, 11 April 1934

26 *Diary*, 11 July 1932

27 *Diary*, 9 May 1934

28 *Diary*, 2 July 1934

29 *Letters*, No. 3290

30 *Diary*, 4 August 1934

31 *Diary*, 12 August 1934

32 *Diary*, 14 October 1934, note

33 *The Journey not the Arrival Matters*,
    pp. 143-147

34 *Letters*, No. 3165

35 *Diary*, 11 March 1935

36 *The Journey not the Arrival Matters*,
    p. 101

37 *Diary*, 24 July 1934

38 *Letters of Leonard Woolf*, p. 316

39 *A Marriage of True Minds*, p. 120

40 *Letters of Leonard Woolf*, p. 324

41 *Downhill all the Way*, pp. 186-193

42 *Downhill all the Way*, pp. 192-193

43 *Diary*, 12 May 1935

44 *Diary*, 12 June 1935

45 *Diary*, 25 June 1935

46 *Diary*, 4 July 1935

47 *Moments of Being*, p. 225

48 *Diary*, 18 November 1935

49 *Diary*, 3 January 1936

50 *Diary*, 19 July 1937

51 *Diary*, 2-5 November 1936

52 *Diary*, 30 November 1936

53 *Diary*, 11 December 1938

54 *Diary*, 17 January 1937

55 *Diary*, 7 March 1937

56 *Diary*, 19 March 1937

57 *Diary*, 9 April 1937

58 *Diary*, 30 April 1937, note

59 *Diary*, 14 March 1937

60 *Letters*, No. 3285

CHAPTER ELEVEN

1 *Diary*, 31 May 1940

2 *The Complete Shorter Fiction*, p. 220

3 *Selected Letters of Vanessa Bell*,
   note p. 106

4 *Pointz Hall*, p. 29

5 *Beginning Again*, Foreword

6 *Diary*, 12 April 1938

7 *Diary*, 10-12 March 1938

8 *Thrown to the Woolves*, p. 33

9 *Thrown to the Woolves*, p. 145

10 *Diary*, 14 November 1938

11 *Letters*, No. 3441, 11 September 1938

12 *Letters*, No. 3443

13 *Letters*, No. 3449

14 *Diary*, 13 October 1938

15 *Letters*, No. 3460

16 *Diary*, 31 March 1939

17 *Letters*, No. 3448

18 *Diary*, 12 July 1939

19 *Diary*, 28 July 1939

20 *Diary*, 30 July 1939

21 *Letters of Leonard Woolf*, pp. 415-416

22 *Barbarians at the Gate*, pp. 50-54

23 *A Marriage of True Minds*, p. 121

24 *Pointz Hall*, ETS p. 33

25 *Pointz Hall*, ETS p. 34

26 *Pointz Hall*, ETS pp. 36-40

27 *Pointz Hall*, ETS pp. 44-45

28 *Pointz Hall*, ETS pp. 46-47

29 *Pointz Hall*, ETS p. 61

30 *Pointz Hall*, ETS p. 69

31 *Pointz Hall*, ETS pp. 63-65

32 *Pointz Hall*, ETS pp. 69-70

33 *Pointz Hall*, ETS pp. 70-71

34 *Pointz Hall*, ETS p. 72

35 *Pointz Hall*, ETS p. 75

36 *Pointz Hall*, ETS pp. 75-77

37 *Pointz Hall*, ETS p. 79

38 *Pointz Hall*, ETS p. 84

39 *Pointz Hall*, ETS pp. 84–85
40 *Pointz Hall*, ETS pp. 88–89
41 *Pointz Hall*, ETS p. 96
42 *Pointz Hall*, ETS Draft 2, then Draft 1, pp. 106–107
43 *Pointz Hall*, ETS p. 108
44 *Pointz Hall*, ETS p. 109
45 *Diary*, 26 March 1938
46 *Between the Acts*, p. 62
47 *Pointz Hall*, ETS p. 112
48 *Pointz Hall*, ETS p. 114
49 *Pointz Hall*, ETS p. 119
50 *Pointz Hall*, ETS p. 119
51 *Pointz Hall*, ETS p. 122
5   *Pointz Hall*, ETS p. 122, dated 5th February 1939
53 *Pointz Hall*, ETS pp. 123–124
54 *Pointz Hall*, ETS p. 129
55 *Pointz Hall*, ETS pp. 138–139
56 *Pointz Hall*, ETS pp. 143–144
57 *Between the Acts*, p. 92
58 *Between the Acts*, p. 95
59 *Between the Acts*, pp. 96–97
60 *Selected Letters of Vanessa Bell*, p. 108
61 *Pointz Hall*, LTS Afterword, p. 456
62 *Pointz Hall*, ETS p. 78
63 *Pointz Hall*, ETS pp. 158–159
64 *Pointz Hall*, ETS p. 161
65 *Pointz Hall*, ETS p. 162
66 *Pointz Hall*, LTS p. 407
67 *Pointz Hall*, ETS p. 163
68 *Pointz Hall*, ETS p. 168
69 *Pointz Hall*, ETS pp. 169–170
70 *Between the Acts*, pp. 128–129
71 *Pointz Hall*, ETS pp. 171–172
72 *Pointz Hall*, ETS pp. 169–170
73 *Pointz Hall*, ETS pp. 176–177
74 *Pointz Hall*, ETS p. 178
75 *Pointz Hall*, ETS p. 180, *Draft 1*
76 *Pointz Hall*, ETS p. 181, *Draft 1*
77 *Pointz Hall*, ETS p. 184
78 *Pointz Hall*, ETS *Draft 2*, p. 184
79 *Between the Acts*, p. 135
80 *Pointz Hall*, ETS p. 189
81 *Pointz Hall*, Dating the Manuscript, p. 29
82 *Letters*, No. 3703
83 *Diary*, 16 February 1940

CHAPTER TWELVE

1   *The Journey not the Arrival Matters*, pp. 80–87
2   See *Appendix A* for the story of Antigone
3   Holroyd, *Bernard Shaw*, one–volume Edition
4   *Diary*, 29 March 1936
5   *Diary*, 10 January 1937
6   See Peter F. Alexander's interviews with Trekkie Parsons, reported in his *Leonard and Virginia Woolf: a Literary Partnership*. Trekkie died in July, 1995
7   *Diary*, 20 January 1940
8   *Diary*, 29–31 January 1940
9   *Reviewing*, p. 27
10 *Diary*, 9 February 1940
11 *Diary*, 20 March 1940
12 *The Journey not the Arrival Matters*, pp. 41–2
13 *Diary*, 29 March 1940
14 *Diary*, 13 April 1940
15 The Leaning Tower, *A Woman's Essays*, Volume One, pp. 159–178
16 *Diary*, 6 May 1940
17 *Diary*, 13–15 May 1940
18 *Diary*, 20 May 1940
19 *Diary*, 9 June 1940
20 *Diary*, 24 July 1940
21 *Diary*, 12 July 1940
22 *Diary*, 28 July 1940
23 *Diary*, 26 July 1940
24 *Diary*, 25 July 1940
25 *Diary*, 20 June 1940
26 *Diary*, 28 July 1940
27 *Diary*, 4 August 1940
28 *Diary*, 16 August 1940
29 *Diary*, 31 August 1940

30 *Diary*, 1–15 September 1940

31 *Diary*, 11 September 1940

32 *Diary*, 16–17 September 1940

33 *Diary*, 29 September 1940

34 *Diary*, 25 September

35 *Diary*, 2 October 1940

36 *Diary*, 10 October 1940

37 *The Journey not the Arrival Matters*,
    p. 86

38 *Diary*, 6 December 1940

39 *Letters*, No. 3664

40 *Diary*, 16 December 1940

41 *A Sketch of the Past*, pp. 125–126

42 *A Sketch of the Past*, pp. 128

43 *A Sketch of the Past*, pp. 158–159

44 *Diary*, 22 December 1940

45 *Pointz Hall*, ETS, p. 393

46 *Diary*, 24 December 1940

47 *Letters*, No. 3670

48 *Letters*, No. 3678, 12 January 1941

49 *Diary*, 29 December 1940

CHAPTER THIRTEEN

1 *Letters of Leonard Woolf*, p. 165

2 *Diary*, 29 December 1940

3 *Letters of Leonard Woolf*, p. 483

4 *The Journey Not the Arrival Matters*,
   pp. 69–70

5 *Diary*, 1 January 1941

6 *Letters*, No. 3677

7 From *Fare Well* by Walter de la Mare

8 *Diary*, 9 January 1941

9 *Letters*, No. 3683, 25 January 1941

10 *Diary*, 26 January 1941, and Note

11 *Letters*, Nos. 3681 & 3688, dated
    23 January and 3 February 1941

12 *The Complete Shorter Fiction*,
    pp. 284–287

13 *The Journey Not the Arrival Matters*,
    pp. 78–79

14 *Leave the Letters till We're Dead*,
    p. xvii

15 *The Journey not the Arrival Matters*,
    p. 86

16 *The Journey not the Arrival Matters*,
    p. 89

17 *Letters*, No. 3685, 1 Feb. 1941

18 *Diary*, 7 February 1941

19 *Diary*, 16 February 1941

20 *Letters*, No. 3695, 1 March 1941

21 *Letters*, No. 3693, Note

22 *Diary*, 26 February 1941

23 *Letters*, No. 3695, 1 March 1941

24 *Diary*, 8 March 1941

25 *Letters*, No. 3698

26 *Letters*, No. 3690

27 *Letters*, No. 3699

28 *Letters*, No. 3700

29 *Diary*, footnote to p. 486

30 *Between the Acts*, p. 127

31 *Downhill all the Way*, p. 149

32 *The Journey not the Arrival Matters*,
    p. 131

33 *Downhill all the Way*, p. 204

34 *Letters*, No. 3701

35 *Letters*, No. 3702

36 *The Voyage Out*, p. 376

37 *Letters*, No. 3702, Note

38 *The Journey not the Arrival Matters*,
    pp. 90–92

39 *Letters*, No. 3703

40 *Selected Letters of Vanessa Bell*, p. 474

41 *Letters*, No. 3708

42 *Beginning Again*, p. 81

43 *The Journey not the Arrival Matters*,
    p. 92

44 *Letters*, No. 3704

45 *Letters*, No. 3705

46 *Letters*, No. 3706, 22 March 1941

47 *Vita and Harold*, 31 March 1941

48 *Vita and Harold*, 4 June 1941

49 *Diary*, 24 March 1941

50 Introduction *Letters*, Volume 6,
    pp. xvi–xvii

51 *Who Killed Virginia Woolf?* pp. 164–168

52 *Letters of Leonard Woolf*, pp. 251–252

53 *Sowing*, p. 13

54 *Letters of Leonard Woolf*, p. 165

55 *Letters of Leonard Woolf*, p. 493

56 Alexander, p. 17

INDEX